Philosophical Foundations
of Historical Knowledge

Philosophical Foundations of Historical Knowledge

Murray G. Murphey

STATE UNIVERSITY OF NEW YORK PRESS

D
16.8
.M882
1994
aug.1995

Published by
State University of New York Press, Albany

© 1994   State University of New York

For information, address State University of New York Press,
State University Plaza, Albany, N.Y., 12246

Production by Marilyn P. Semerad
Marketing by Dana E. Yanulavich

Library of Congress Cataloging-in-Publication Data

Murphey, Murray G.
    Philosophical foundations of historical knowledge / Murray G.
Murphey.
        p.   cm.
    Includes bibliographical references (p.   ) and index.
    ISBN 0–7914–1919–3 (acid-free paper). — ISBN 0–7914–1920–7 (pbk.
:   acid-free paper)
    1. History—Philosophy. I. Title.
D16.8.M882   1994
901—dc20   93–5321
                                                               CIP

10 9 8 7 6 5 4 3 2 1

for
Kathleen, Christopher, and Jessica
who made it all worthwhile

Contents

Introduction

The philosophy of history is not a new subject. In one form or another, it has occupied thinkers since antiquity. It continues to do so. There is today frequent publication in this field, and even journals that specialize in it. In one sense, this is not surprising. Philosophic issues are rarely settled permanently; how long have people been debating ethics or metaphysics or epistemology? But it would be a mistake to think that no progress has been made in the philosophy of history. Earlier works in this field were usually attempts at grand historical syntheses—overviews of the rise and fall of civilizations[1] or of how God's providence is illustrated by the course of human affairs[2] or dirges sounding the knell of culture.[3] However impressive these works were—and one cannot read them today without being awed by the erudition and immense labor that produced them—the attempt to create such vast synthetic works has now been pretty well abandoned. In more recent decades, the philosophy of history has come to center on more technical philosophic issues: How can we know the past? What is a historical explanation? What is the meaning of a historical sentence? Are historical accounts necessarily narratives? and so on. If studies of these issues lack the sweep and majesty of the earlier grand synthetic studies, nevertheless they represent a genuine gain in precision and clarity.

This latter sort of work in the philosophy of history has not been motivated solely by a fascination with the subject of history. Philosophers of various persuasions have often seen in history a proving ground for their philosophic theories. History is generally agreed to be a type of factual knowledge. But since history deals with things and events that no longer exist, it has not been easy to fit history into the mould of classical empiricism. Idealists have therefore seen in history an example of factual knowledge for which empiricist theories could not account,[4] and empiricists have responded by trying to force historical knowledge to fit the model of physics.[5] Neither attempt has been particularly successful. More recently, some philosophers have endorsed essentially literary claims, arguing that history is a narrative art which is—somehow—nevertheless true. Anti-realists claim that many historical statements are devoid of truth value[6] while realists deny such claims.[7] The field has thus become a battleground over which a variety of dubious armies have skirmished. In short, it is fair to say that the philosophy of history is currently something of a mess.

In such a situation, one is well advised to go back to the premises underlying the study of history. If one asks, what are the basic premises underlying our current common sense notion of human history, it seems to me that at least the following theses are essential:

(1) There is a real world of which true knowledge is possible.

(2) There are other persons who have minds.

(3) It is possible for one person to know what another person thinks.

(4) A language spoken by one person can be correctly interpreted by someone from outside that linguistic community, and a text in one language can be translated into an approximately equivalent text in another language of comparable resources.

(5) There exists a past in which human beings lived and acted.

(6) We can have some accurate knowledge of the past.

(7) Members of one culture can understand members of other cultures, including members of antecedent states of their own culture.

(8) Human action is causally explainable.

The common sense view of history surely assumes the existence of a real world of which true knowledge is possible, and that this world includes the past as well as the present. Historical accounts do purport to "tell it like it was"—that is, to give accurate descriptions of what went on in the past. When one reads a history of the French Revolution or the American Civil War, one certainly has the impression that the account one is reading claims to be a true account. If it does not make such a claim, it may be read as a "historical novel" but certainly not as a history. Furthermore, historical works treat of historical persons as thinking, feeling human beings to whose thoughts and feelings we can have access, and this is so whatever the language spoken by the subjects discussed. An account in English of Napoleon or Augustus or Jesus assumes that we can understand what they said in French or Latin or Aramaic and can translate their statements into approximately equivalent statements in English. It also assumes that, creatures of our own cultures though we may be, we can understand the culture of the historical person described. Finally, historical works do seek to tell us not only what happened, but why; that is, they seek to explain in some causal sense why people did what they did and why events turned out the way they did. A historical work that fails to provide such explanations is a failure as a history; a work that does not attempt to provide such explanations is not a history at all.

If it is granted that these eight premises do represent basic premises of our common sense understanding of history, then it is important to examine in some detail the grounds upon which we accept these premises. It might seem that such an inquiry is pointless, for one might think that no sane person could deny such statements. But on the hopeful assumption that philosophers and historians are sane, this turns out to be false—every one of these premises has been questioned, and some of them are presently under attack by influential writers. If we are to investigate the philosophic underpinnings of history, we must examine these attacks and assess the degree to which the proposed premises are warranted.

It is clear that most of the premises have applications that go considerably beyond history. That, after all, is what one would expect. History is or claims to be knowledge; general issues respecting knowledge therefore apply to history. History claims to explain; questions of the nature of explanation are therefore involved. Historical accounts claim to be true; questions of truth are thus raised. Indeed, all of the premises apply far beyond the field of human history (for example, (5) to evolutionary biology, (6) to cosmology, etc.), and the challenges to them accordingly come from different fields. But this is only to state the obvious fact that the world was not made to correspond to our academic disciplines and research specialties. There is no question that one might want to ask about the nature and functioning of a contemporary society that one would not also want to ask about a past society, and the converse is also true. All of the social sciences make the same assumptions about human beings, human cultures, and the possibilities of truth and explanation that history makes.

The book that follows is an attempt to investigate the grounds for accepting these eight premises. Quite clearly, questions of language, interpretation, and translation involve the problems of reference and meaning; these are the subject of Chapter 1. The problems of other minds and intersubjective knowledge are the focus of Chapter 2. In Chapter 3, we begin investigating the issue of explanation—the subject that has vexed the philosophy of history more than any other for the last fifty years. As I hope to show in Chapter 3, the seemingly intractable dispute that has pitted "covering law" theories against simple "causal statement" theories admits of a quite satisfactory resolution. In Chapter 4, we will consider particularly the explanation of action; I shall defend the position that human action is explicable in terms of theories that are consistent with the basic notions of what has frequently been stigmatized as "folk psychology." Chapter 5 concludes the investigation of explanation by examining the role of rules and plans in providing explanations for actions. Chapter 6 will undertake a modest examination of the validity of premise (1) and so will deal with issues of truth and reality. Chapter 7 will be particularly concerned with premises (5) and (6)—the nature of our knowledge of the past and the bases for claiming our knowledge warranted. The concluding chapter will deal with anti-realism and relativism. Readers will not have to be told that this whole program is ambitious, nor be surprised to find that the treatment is often more selective than they would like. But if indeed these eight premises do underly our common sense view of history, no examination of the basis of that view can do less, though doubtless more talented scholars could do more.

The reader will note that at many points my arguments are addressed particularly to doctrines advanced by W. V. Quine. This has proven to be unavoidable because the most powerful challenges to some of the theses I defend have been mounted by Quine—particularly his twin doctrines of the Underdetermination of Scientific Theories and the Indeterminacy of Translation. Yet at the same time, a good deal of what follows is based on other writings of Quine. As this suggests, I do not think that Quine's work, taken as a whole, is entirely consistent. That is a statement calling for some explanation.

That Quine is an important philosopher is not in question; certainly he has been a dominant figure in American philosophy during the last forty years. But Quine's work seems to involve a tension between two incompatible traditions, to both of which he is heir. One is the tradition of pragmatic naturalism, which began at Harvard with Peirce and James, which Lewis significantly enriched, and to which Dewey was a major contributor. It is this tradition that I believe speaks in Quine's writings such as "Two Dogmas of Empiricism"[8] and "Epistemology Naturalized."[9] The relations of "Two Dogmas" to Lewis's *Mind and The World Order*[10] and of "Epistemology Naturalized" to Dewey's theory of inquiry seem to me quite clear. Quine has not only placed himself in the tradition of Dewey[11] but in "Two Dogmas" he described his own position as a kind of pragmatism.[12] Yet Quine is also the heir of Logical Empiricism, as his relation to Carnap makes clear.[13] It is, I believe, this tradition that speaks in *Word and Object*[14] and "Ontological Relativity."[15] These two traditions, in my view, are not consistent with each other, and in what follows I shall be drawing upon the Quine of the former tradition to argue against the Quine of the latter.

I believe that Quine's view of epistemology is right—that it is an empirical discipline located within science, rather than an *a priori* discipline prior to science. If problems of meaning and reference and of interpretation and translation are treated from that perspective, then I shall try to show that Quine's thesis of the Indeterminacy of Translation fails. I shall also argue that if one looks at science as a process of inquiry—a view defended by Peirce, James, and Dewey—then the Underdetermination Thesis also fails. If these arguments are correct, then two of the most formidable barriers to history, and to social science, are thereby removed, and we may get on with the job of finding out how in fact human knowledge of human beings is created.

Finally, I would like to emphasize that the aim of this work is not prescriptive. I have made no attempt to say what scholars ought to do. Nor do I seek to justify our knowledge by creating some sort of "first philosophy." I can imagine no justification of scientific knowledge beyond what science itself provides. My purpose here is to clarify, by examining how we know what we know, what explanations of human behavior and action we use, what "truth" and "reality" mean as applied to our investigation of nature and society, and how it is that we have theories about the past which can be true and explanatory. This is a large undertaking, and doubtless this work has its shortcomings. It would contain many more if it were not for the kind advice of several friends. The penetrating critiques of Robert Schwartz and Bruce Kuklick have been enormously helpful. Elizabeth Flower and Abraham Edel have given me many useful suggestions, and Kimberly Cassidy's expert advice on the first two chapters was invaluable.

Notes

1. Arnold J. Toynbee, *A Study of History* (New York: Oxford University Press, 1934–1961), 12 vols.

2. Georg Wilhelm Hegel, *The Philosophy of History* (New York: Colonial Press, 1900).

3. Oswald Spengler, *The Decline of the West* (London: G. Allen, 1922), 2 vols.

4. R. G. Collingwood, *The Idea of History* (New York: Oxford University Press, 1956).

5. Carl G. Hempel, "The Function of General Laws in History," *Journal of Philosophy* 39:35–48 (1942).

6. Michael Dummett, "The Reality of the Past" in *Truth and Other Enigmas* (Cambridge, Mass.: Harvard University Press, 1978), 358–374.

7. C. Behan McCullagh, *Justifying Historical Descriptions* (New York: Cambridge University Press, 1984).

8. Willard Van Orman Quine, "Two Dogmas of Empiricism" in *From a Logical Point of View* (Cambridge, Mass.: Harvard University Press, 1953), 20–46.

9. W. V. Quine, "Epistemology Naturalized" in *Ontological Relativity and Other Essays* (New York: Columbia University Press, 1969), 69–90.

10. C. I. Lewis, *Mind and the World Order* (New York: Dover Publishers, 1929). See Murray G. Murphey, "Kant's Children: The Cambridge Pragmatists" in *Proceedings of the Charles S. Peirce Society* 4:3–33 (1968).

11. Quine, "Ontological Relativity," in *Ontological Relativity*, 26–27.

12. Quine, "Two Dogmas," 46.

13. W. V. Quine, "Homage to Rudolf Carnap" in *The Ways of Paradox and Other Essays* (Cambridge, Mass.: Harvard University Press, 1976), 40–43.

14. W. V. Quine, *Word and Object* (Cambridge, Mass.: MIT Press, 1960).

15. Quine, "Ontological Relativity."

Chapter 1

Meaning and Reference

Any field of study that takes as its subject human action must be concerned with people's thoughts and feelings and with how they communicate these to one another. If indeed "it is possible for one person to know what another person thinks" (Premise 3), what people think must be expressible in language, and it must be the case that "a language spoken by one person can be correctly interpreted by someone from outside that linguistic community, and a text in one language can be translated into an approximately equivalent text in another language of comparable resources" (Premise 4), even if the languages involved are ideolects of the same tongue. Questions of meaning and reference are therefore critical for the historical enterprise. In this chapter, we shall be concerned with such issues.

We will consider first the relation of thought to language, and argue that although thought is usually expressed in language, it is a mistake to identify the two. Thought is prior to and richer than language; people may make conceptual distinctions that do not find linguistic expression and indeed may have concepts that are not linguistically expressed. Second, we will examine the nature of concepts, which I take to be mental states. Third, we will consider the theory of meaning, and I shall defend the position that meanings are conceptual "cores"—the central theoretical matrices of concepts. Fourth, we will deal with the theory of reference, including issues of naming and ostensive definition. Fifth, since the determinacy of reference has been a matter of considerable recent debate, we will examine two arguments for the relativity of reference. The first is Quine's doctrine of ontological relativity, which will be discussed in some detail. As I hope to show, Quine's doctrine rests on a mistaken analogy between languages and theories—an analogy that underestimates the referential determinacy of natural languages. The second is the famous "hermeneutical circle." Although the discussion here will only be a preliminary one, I will argue that the same instruments that anchor natural languages in the world of experience serve to break the circularity of interpretation. Finally, I will briefly discuss the status of perceptual judgments. The theories advanced here will serve as the basis for the discussion of the following chapters.

Thought and Language

In 1969, Quine published an article entitled "Epistemology Naturalized" in which he argued that the traditional concept of epistemology as a "first philosophy" that justifies our knowledge should be abandoned and replaced by a concept of epistemology as an empirical science that seeks to explain how it is that we have the knowledge we do. As such, Quine held, "epistemology merges with psychology, as well as with linguistics."[1] Although Quine's proposal has not been greeted with universal acclaim,[2] it is hardly a new one; certainly this was William James's view, and James never claimed that it was original with him.[3] Nevertheless, Quine's proposal has had considerable influence in philosophy and in a number of fields beyond.

This development is partly owing to the fact that by 1969 psychology was already resuming the long abandoned task which Locke and the Scottish Realists had undertaken of seeking to account for human knowledge. Linguists, under the influence of Chomsky, were wrestling with the problem of how language is learned, and a variety of other fields were converging on the issue of the nature of cognition. In computer science, the attempt to simulate human thought with machines led to the development of the study of artificial intelligence. In neuroanatomy, advances in the understanding of the electrochemical nature of the brain promised new breakthroughs in our knowledge of how the brain functions. In primatology, work with higher primates was rapidly forcing extensive revisions of our notions of the capacities of our simian cousins. And in philosophy itself, new ideas—particularly those stemming from the work of Wittgenstein—were forcing revisions in long-established views of language, concepts, meaning, and understanding.

This convergence led to the emergence of what is currently called "cognitive science," which lies at the intersection of all of these fields, and to important advances in our understanding of cognition. Clearly, something very like a naturalized epistemology is in the process of development. It is therefore particularly ironic that this development has taken a course very different from that which Quine sought (and seeks) to promote.

Throughout his long career, Quine has been a staunch empiricist, an unrelenting advocate of behaviorism, an enemy of mentalism, and a foe of innatism. In this, he stands in a long and honorable tradition. Ever since Locke declared the mind of the neonate a *tabula rasa*, it has been an article of faith among empiricists that there can be no such things as innate ideas and that all knowledge must be the product of experience, aided by such content-free abilities as the capacity to learn. But the concept of innate ideas is ambiguous. One could mean, as advocates of the Platonic theory of recollection evidently do, that the neonate comes into this world already stocked with certain ideas. But one could also mean that the neonate is so structured that upon the presentation of certain stimuli, he will form certain concepts. If the latter view is taken, it articulates with studies of such phenomena as imprinting among birds; and on evolutionary grounds it is not obvious why human beings could not be so endowed. The question of what neonates know, and when and how they know it, is for a naturalized epistemology an empirical question to be settled by research. One cannot begin with *a priori* assumptions about the nature of cognition if the nature of cognition is to be determined by scientific investigation. Philosophical dogmas have no place here. The innatist hypothesis is not logically self-contradictory, and cannot be dismissed on *a priori* grounds.

The assumption that it is unscientific to talk of mental entities rests similarly on purely dogmatic grounds. Some empiricists, influenced by positivism and by Ryle's ghost stories, have apparently concluded that only an unremitting behaviorism is permissible. Quine's own position here is less clear than one might think from his attacks on mentalism, for although he endorses a form of behavioral dispositionalism, it is one that contains reference to internal neural states about which at present we know nothing at all.[4] Most cognitive scientists, however, reject behaviorism outright and have no hesitancy in speaking of mental states or internal representations. But I know of no cognitive scientist who does not believe that such states are purely physical: Spiritualists and Idealists have not found cognitive science a congenial field. Nevertheless, the issue is a purely scientific one. Certainly it is legitimate to postulate internal states if a better theory of cognition is thereby achieved, and pointless to postulate them unless a better theory is thereby achieved. Here again, dogma has no place and hypotheses should be considered on their merits only.

Quine's anti-mentalism has led him to argue that traditional terms for mental entities, such as "idea" and "concept," should be abandoned and that we should talk only of words; that is, that thought should be identified with language, or, more exactly, with dispositions to verbal behavior. Thus Quine:

> We want to know how men can achieve the conjectures and abstractions that go into scientific theory. How can we pursue such an inquiry while talking of external things to the exclusion of ideas and concepts? There is a way: we can talk of language. We can talk of concrete men and their concrete noises. Ideas are as may be, but the words are out where we can see and hear them. And scientific theories, however speculative and however abstract, are in words. One and the same theory can be expressed in different words, so people say, but all can perhaps agree that there are no theories apart from words. Or, if there are, there is little to be lost in passing over them.[5]

This view is I believe erroneous, and because the consequences of this view are so serious, it is important to point out that recent work in cognitive science is incompatible with it on at least five different scores.

First, and most obvious, is the extensive work done over the past several decades on animal cognition. Many animals, including even pigeons, are able to group objects into categories by similarity,[6] and chimpanzees and rhesus monkeys even by prototypes.[7] The existence of cognitive maps—allocentric representations of physical space—has been demonstrated in dogs, cats, and chimpanzees.[8] Premack has shown the ability of chimpanzees without language training to categorize by matching to sample and even to recognize similarities of proportions. With language training the apes were able to accomplish considerably more, largely because teaching them the words "same" and "different" helped them to focus attention on similarities and differences. These apes were able to compare proportions of different substances—e.g., one fourth of an apple, a bottle one fourth full, etc. In other words, they could attend to similarities of relations, not just of objects.[9] However, this does not show that the *concepts* of similarity and difference were introduced to the apes by language training. As Premack remarks, "There is no evidence that concepts previously unknown to the animal were introduced by language."[10] These and other findings on cognition in animals without language (or only the minimal language that apes can acquire) demonstrate the existence of concepts and conceptual relations that are independent of language.

A second source of evidence is provided by the rapidly growing corpus of work on brain-damaged patients. For example, patients suffering from prosopagnosia[11] can be shown to be implicitly processing information concerning familiar faces although the patient is unaware of the fact and the processing is dissociated from verbal operations.[12] Similarly, studies of patients with various types of disorders—amnesia, blindsight, dyslexia, Broca's and Wernicke's aphasias, and hemineglect—also show implicit knowledge in conditions where explicit knowledge is either absent or poor. This situation does not appear to be explicable in terms of impairment of the language production mechanisms nor their dissociation from other systems. Not only is implicit knowledge sometimes verbally expressed but the phenomenology of those neuropsychological syndromes in which impairment of the language production mechanisms is crucial is different from those cited above.[13] As Kertesz puts it, "the relative preservation of nonverbal performance in the severely affected aphasics . . . argues for a dissociable process of language and high-level thought."[14] Particularly striking are the data reported by Bisiach concerning hemineglect:

> If you ask these patients to describe their mental image of a complex object from a definite vantage point, you may find evidence of an impaired representation of the side contralateral to the lesion. Thus, when describing the appearance of a familiar place, our left-hemineglect patients omitted salient particulars located on the left side of the imaginary line of sight. Most important, these particulars were afterward reported when the patients had to describe the same place from the opposite point of view. Conversely, details which the patient had reported a few instants earlier from the right side of their image were neglected in the description of the reverse perspective, into the left half of which they were to fit. . . . Now, the occurrence of space-related pathological constraints affecting mental representations of the analogue type after focal impairment of neural space may arouse no wonder; on the contrary, it is proof of the actual existence of this kind of representation. Less obvious is the fact that verbal representation alone could not fill the imaginal gap. This suggests that language *per se* cannot be considered an autonomous form of representation, in the sense that it has no independent data-base of its own: all representation (originally) missing in the analogue mode is (derivatively) missing in the verbal mode as well.[15]

Thus there is substantial evidence for the existence of mental representations of a non-verbal sort and for thought processes that do not involve language.

A third source of evidence comes from cross-linguistic studies. As Clark has pointed out,[16] English words for putting on clothes do not distinguish the part of the body being clad. In Japanese, there are four different words used, depending on what part of the body is being covered; one term is used for covering the head, a second for covering the upper body, a third for covering the lower body, and a fourth for accessories (e.g., rings, gloves, etc.). Yet no one would seriously doubt that English speakers make a conceptual distinction between putting on one's hat and putting on one's pants. The point of course is that languages do not always contain distinct words for each concept; the speakers make the conceptual distinctions, but the language does not. There is not therefore a one-to-one correspondence of words to concepts; there are more concepts than words.

In the example above, one can use phrases to do what single words cannot. But Clark uses a second example to show that this need not be the case. English has about eleven basic color terms: black, grey, white, blue, green, brown, yellow, orange, red, purple, and pink. But in Dani, there are only two color terms: *mili* (black) and *mola* (white). However, Clark notes, "Dani speakers appear to organize colors in memory and use colors in matching tasks in just the same way as English speakers: the concepts appear to be much the same, even though the terms available for talking about them differ in the two languages."[17] In this case, the Dani language lacks the resources to articulate its speakers's color concepts. It is not therefore correct to say, as Quine does, that we can dispense with concepts and deal only with words. Words do not fully express the conceptual system of the speakers.

A fourth source of evidence comes from the work on neonate cognition. Recent research in this field demonstrates that if subjected to appropriate stimuli, the newborn child develops a rather remarkable range of concepts at a very early age. Thus there is very strong evidence that by the fourth month the child is able to perceive the world in terms of a three dimensional space.[18] Indeed, neuroanatomists have apparently identified the specific neurological structures that produce this cognition, although exactly how those structures produce that result is yet to be determined.[19] Similarly, the human eye is sensitive to the electro-magnetic spectrum from about 400 to 700 nanometers. Of course, the variation in wavelength over this interval is continuous, but humans perceive the spectrum categorically in terms of focal colors (red, yellow, green, blue). The perception of focal colors is universal, although just where the boundaries are drawn between colors, and the number of hues which receive distinct names, varies from culture to culture.[20] As Anderson somewhere remarks, no one has ever claimed that we learn to see colors. A third example of particular importance occurs in sound perception. Although acoustic stimuli vary continuously, the neonate perceives sounds categorically. Moreover, the neonate is able to form equivalence classes of stimuli which are very different acoustically, and these equivalence classes correspond to phonetic categories. Thus the word "bat" presents acoustically very different stimuli when uttered by a male voice and a female voice, yet the neonate of four months perceives these stimuli as equivalent.[21]

One of the most hotly debated issues concerning neonate cognition is the formation of the concept of a physical object. Until fairly recently, the work of Piaget dominated this subject, and in Piaget's theory the concept of a physical object as an enduring entity in space and time is the product of what he calls Stage IV—the sensory-motor stage—at approximately the end of the first year. Piaget found that, when younger children had observed an object at point A, and then saw the same object covered up at point B, they would still commence the search for the object at point A. Piaget interpreted this to mean that the child had not yet conceptualized the object as enduring in time and space, so that once out of sight it was out of mind, and that the child did not conceptualize the object as an enduring entity until he could make the transition to searching first at point B. This transition comes during the late sensory-motor stage. The formation of the concept is thus held to result from experiences of the physical manipulation of objects, and is prelinguistic—that is, language is not learned until after the object concept is formed.[22] More recent work suggests that Piaget drew the wrong conclusion when he took search behavior to be an indicator of the presence of the object concept. Diamond has shown that the AB pattern—searching at A rather than at B when the object was hidden at B—is probably related to the maturation of the frontal cortex, and that the AB search pattern of young children is virtually identical to that of monkeys with ablation of the prefrontal cortex.[23] If this is so, the AB search pattern may have nothing to do with the development of the object concept but may relate to the development of capacities of action.[24]

During the last decade, Spelke, Baillargeon, and their co-workers have done a series of experiments that have radically advanced our knowledge of neonate cognition. They have shown that by four months a child is able to perceive objects by the principle of common movement. Of course a child of that age cannot use language, so non-linguistic indicators must be used. The one most commonly employed to indicate recognition of a difference on the children's part is the length of time the children look at the object (the longer they look, the greater the difference recognized). The indicator has been shown to be reliable. If an object is partly occluded by a screen (as for example in Figure 1), the child does not recognize it as a distinct single object. But if both non-occluded portions of the object move together behind the screen, either latterly or in depth, the child perceives a single object moving behind the screen. If the screen is removed to show two separate objects which are not joined together behind the screen, the child looks considerably longer. Baillargeon et al. developed a second experiment in which a block was shown to the child, together with a screen larger than the block which was capable of rotation through 180 degrees. The child is seated facing the screen (see Figure 2), so that the rotation of the screen was toward or away from the child. When the child saw the block placed behind the screen and the screen was rotated until its motion was interrupted by the block, the child showed no special interest. But when the screen was rotated through the space occupied by the block (removed without the child's knowledge), the child looked much longer. Thus it seems clear that the child not only expected the object to persist when occluded, but also believed that two objects could not simultaneously occupy the same space.

Figure 1

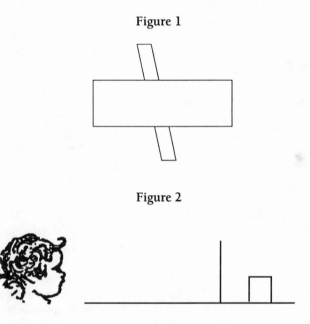

Figure 2

In a third experiment, a toy car was placed on a track which passed behind a screen. The child's gazing time was not affected when the car passed behind the screen and emerged on the other side. Neither did it change when the car which emerged from behind the screen differed in color or shape from the car that had passed behind the screen. Evidently the child's object concept at this early age does not include color or shape invariance. Then the experimental design was altered by lowering the screen so that the child could see the experimenter place a solid block either behind the track in one case or on the track in the other, and the screen was again raised to occlude the track and the block. When the block was placed behind the track, the child showed no change in gazing time when the car passed behind the screen and emerged on the other side. But when the block was placed *on* the track, and the car again passed behind the screen and reemerged on the other side, the child looked considerably longer. These experiments support the hypothesis that the child regards objects as solids and believes that one of them cannot pass through the space occupied by another. They also support the hypothesis that the child has a concept of object identity which is defined in terms of spatio-temporal continuity.[25]

These and similar results have led Spelke to the following conclusions about the object concept in infants.

Objects are apprehended by a relatively central mechanism that takes as input the layout as it is perceived, whatever the sensory mode by which it is perceived, and that organizes events in ways that extend beyond the immediately perceivable world in space and time. This mechanism organizes the layout into bodies with at least four properties: *cohesion, boundaries, substance,* and *spatio-temporal continuity*. Infants are able to find such bodies, because these properties limit where surfaces stand and how they move with respect to one another. The surfaces of a cohesive body must be connected and they must remain connected over the body's free motions; the surfaces of a bounded body must be distinct from the surfaces around them and they must move independently of their surroundings; the surfaces of a substantial body must move through unoccupied space; and the surfaces of a spatio-temporally continuous body must move on connected paths. Infants apprehend objects by analysizing the arrangements and the motions of surfaces, I suggest, because they conceive the physical world as populated with bodies whose properties constrain surface arrangements and motions.[26]

Moreover, Spelke believes that the infant's "mechanism for apprehending objects" is a theory of the physical world "whose four principles jointly define an initial *object concept.*[27] This theory remains basic to the adult view of the physical world; indeed, the adult view is built upon this initial theory by a process of "enrichment" in which further notions are added to "an innately structured domain." But the initial theory always remains as the core of our concept of the physical object. It is important to note that this theory contains within it a theory of object identity, in the form of the spatio-temporal continuity of the object. And this theory is present in infants only four months old.

A final source of evidence comes from the fact that people can and do think without words. Testimonial evidence from people afflicted with extreme dyslexia is compelling on this point, but no less a figure than Einstein has testified that his scientific thinking was not done in words.[28] The mathematician, Jansons, who suffers from an extreme form of dyslexia, has testified to his use of visual and kinesthetic representations rather than verbal ones.[29] Roe's study of distinguished scientists showed a remarkable range of kinds of representations used in thought, including visual, verbal, and kinesthetic.[30] And Goodman has provided a well-known study of the types of symbolic systems that function in the arts, many of them clearly non-verbal (e.g., music).[31]

It seems clear, therefore, on the basis of a wide range of evidence, that there are internal states that constitute concepts and relations among concepts, that these are not linguistic representations, that the linguistic system is not necessarily isomorphic with the conceptual system, and that the study of linguistic representations alone does not succeed in revealing our conceptual structure. Moreover, it should be clear that conceptual structures exist by at least the fourth month of life in a far more complex form than has previously been thought. It is therefore essential to gain further clarity on the nature of concepts, and the relation of thought to language.

Concepts

In recent years, there has been a lively debate over the nature of concepts. The "classical" view—that all instances of a concept share properties both necessary and sufficient for membership in the category it defines, and that the conjunction of these properties defines the concept—has been shown to be inadequate to deal with many of the phenomena discovered by experiments on categorization during the last fifteen years. For many concepts, it has proven impossible to specify what the necessary and sufficient properties are—as Wittgenstein's famous example of games made clear.[32] There are disjunctive concepts—e.g., Scandinavian—that do not fit the conjunctive model.

More crucial is the demonstration by Rosch and others that categorization is often done by prototype.[33] Thus, for example, subjects rate robins the most "typical" of birds, but consider chickens, ostriches, and penguins much less typical. The prototype is taken to be in some sense the central tendency of the various properties of the instances. The prototype, so defined, is not an actual instance, but a conceptual model constructed from the associated properties—a stereotype, in Putnam's terminology.[34] Similarity to the prototype then provides the basis for categorization; because robins are seen as more similar to the prototype than other birds, they are rated the most typical. This view admits of multiple formulations. The "properties" may be taken as purely qualitative or as dimensions in a metric space, and various algorithms have been proposed for combining features, whether qualitative or quantitative, with varying degrees of success.

Prototype theory does avoid some of the problems of the classical theory, and there is substantial experimental evidence to show that people do categorize by something that looks like prototypes. Nevertheless, there are serious problems with this theory. First, it offers no explanation of what particular set of properties should be combined to form the prototype, nor of how those properties are related. Second, it provides no bounds on the variation in dimensions, nor on what properties can be used. Third, which features of a given instance are important clearly depends upon context, but the theory has not provided a way of dealing with context effects.[35] Fourth, no adequate solution has been found to the problem of how the prototype of a conjunctive concept can be generated from the prototypes of the conjuncts. Thus, given a prototypical mouse, and a prototypical large thing, how does one generate a prototypical large mouse?

A variant of this view is the feature-bundle theory, according to which the concept of an object—say, a bird—consists of a bundle of conjoined features. Judgments of typicality have been shown to depend upon the distribution of features; that is, a number of characteristics are associated with membership in the category, and the more of these characteristics a given instance has, the more typical it is judged to be. No one set of properties is true of all instances; hence there are no properties that can be said to be necessary and sufficient for membership. Thus, flying is a feature strongly associated with birds. But the absence of this feature alone does not eliminate a creature from birdhood if enough of the other features in the bundle are present.

An important critique of these views has been written by Armstrong, Gleitman, and Gleitman.[36] Prototype theory, they argue, implies that typicality ratings will be obtained for instances of concepts where there is no classical definition of the concept—i.e., no necessary and sufficient defining properties. But where such necessary and sufficient properties exist and are known to the subjects, all instances of the concept should be equally typical. To test this, they used two sorts of concepts—those for which Rosch's work indicated that a prototype structure should exist (fruits, vegetables, sports, vehicles) and those for which well-known classical definitions exist (even number, odd number, plane geometrical figure[37]). Subjects produced typicality ratings for both sorts of concept instances. Subjects were then asked whether they thought some even numbers were more even than others (and similarly for odd numbers and geometric figures), to which they replied that they did not. But when again asked to rank instances of these concepts by typicality, they did so.

As Armstrong, Gleitman and Gleitman point out, these responses were not contradictory: "Subjects responded differently because they were asked to judge two different matters: exemplariness of exemplars of concepts in the one case, and membership of exemplars in a concept in the other."[38] As Kelley and Krueger have also done,[39] they point out that typically rankings do not imply degrees of membership: a pekinese may be an atypical dog, but it is one hundred percent dog for all that. Armstrong, Gleitman, and Gleitman note that an identification function that enables one to pick out instances for the concept may well yield the typicality rankings quite apart from the core of the concept itself. But their general conclusion is pessimistic: "We are back at square one in discovering the structure of everyday categories *experimentally*."[40]

One particular point made by Armstrong, Gleitman, and Gleitman requires special discussion. Both the prototype and the classical theories of concepts make use of the notion of a "property." But what is a property? If a property is itself a concept, there seems to be an obvious circularity involved in the theory. What theorists have in mind by "properties" are clearly perceptual characteristics such as color, shape, etc.; but while we do perceive colors and shapes, it is also true that the term "property" as used above must represent a concept of which the perceived aspects of things are instances. Is it possible to speak of perceptual characteristics of experiences that are not also conceptual without being at once accused of reintroducing the late lamented "given"?

It will, I trust, be granted that in perception there is *some* aspect of the experience that is not purely conceptual—otherwise, one would be forced into a type of conceptual idealism. But it does not follow that such aspects are not to some degree influenced by conceptual factors. Anyone who looks at his own hand will observe something that has a particular color. Possibly the actual experience of the color is influenced by his color concepts, but we know enough about color vision to know that the principal component is not conceptual. The important point is that we experience objects as having certain aspects—shapes, hues, etc. Normally, we do not have words for just those aspects—it would require a language with an infinite vocabulary to provide such a description—but we can recognize a given aspect and attend to it, thereby prescinding it from the rest of the object. Such aspects are compared and contrasted, and are grouped into equivalence classes on the basis of similarity.

That this presupposes both innate ability to note similarities and differences, and some inborn similarity space, is true, but this much innate endowment is generally admitted by all.[41] Color aspects, for example, are known to be categorized on the basis of similarity to focal colors, and the perception of such focal colors appears to be universal, whether a given language has names for them or not. This is clearly a case of categorization by prototype. Such similarity relations among aspects constitute a property or feature; the similarity relation "as blue as" is not distinct from the property "blue." Such matching relations are reflexive and symmetrical, but not necessarily transitive; color matching, for example, is not transitive, since one can move along the color continuum by steps each of which is less than a just noticeable difference, yet widely separated points on the continuum are clearly discriminable.[42]

The words "property" and "feature" as used in the theories of concepts discussed above are ambiguous because they sometimes refer to such things as the color of an object and sometimes to what I have called an aspect of an object. Both involve conceptualization, but to different degrees. To use Quine's metaphor of the continuum between the conceptual and the observational, "aspects" are at the observational extreme of the continuum while full fledged "concepts" (e.g., bird) are at the conceptual extreme. But in prototype and feature-bundle theories of concepts, it is assumed that the constituents of the concept are further toward the observational end of the continuum than the concept being analyzed. The question is not therefore one of circularity but of more or less.

In the case of logical or mathematical concepts, such as even number, there are no observational components. One can of course distinguish between primitive and defined terms, and one could regard defined terms as in some sense more "complex" than their defining terms, although it is not obvious what would be accomplished by doing so, given that the choice of what terms are to be taken as primitive is purely arbitrary. There is in any case no possibility of reducing "complex" logical or mathematical terms to some combination of "simple" terms in any meaningful sense of "simple" and "complex."

It should not, however, be thought that properties as they occur in these theories are always qualitative. Among the characteristics of an object is the configuration of its aspects—i.e., the relational pattern in which its aspects stand. That configuration is itself an aspect that can be prescinded and in terms of which objects can be compared for similarities and differences. Thus a given bird has many aspects—its colors, its shape, its motions, etc.—but a bird is not an unordered bundle of aspects; rather there is a characteristic configuration of these aspects. That configuration may be far more important in judging likenesses and differences among birds than any individual aspect taken separately.

As these remarks suggest, any n-tuple of objects or aspects has itself an aspect by which it can be compared to other *n*-tuples as like or different. With Peirce and James, I believe that some relations are directly perceived. But what can that mean except that certain aspects of aggregates—in the simplest case, of pairs—are perceived, just as aspects of single objects are perceived? Thus suppose we have a number of pairs (a,b), (c,d), . . . , each of which has a particular aspect, and that these aspects are similar. To fix ideas, let a child have been introduced to the complexes apple-on-the-table and doll-in-the-box. If he has prescinded the aspect of the apple being *on* the table, he should find block-on-the-shelf more similar to the apple-on-the-table than to the doll-in-the-box. Of course, the prescinded aspect must include the order of the pair—that is, it is apple-on-the-table and not table-under-the-apple; otherwise the relations *on* and *under* could never be distinguished. Relations then are abstracted from the aspects of n-tuples.

This way of defining relations will seem bizarre to some, since a relation is usually defined as a set of ordered pairs. For purely extensional purposes, that definition is unexceptional, but it does little to help us with ordinary experience. What after all is the relation defined by <4, 2>, <love, golf>, <Ronald Reagan, Checkers>, <my garbage pail, the moon>, <Joe Montana, Helen of Troy>? To claim there is one is to prefer extensionalism to common sense. It is equally obvious that when we induce a relation from the pairs <Kareem Jabbar, Richard Nixon>, <the Empire State Building, my house>, <Pike's Peak, Cheyenne Mountain>, <Wilt Chamberlain, Margaret Thatcher>, we do so in terms of a particular similarity among aspects of these pairs.

There is, however, some important new work on concept development which suggests a somewhat different view. Keil's research on the development of concepts in young children has yielded some significant new insights into this process. Keil contrasted the development of concepts of natural kinds, such as biological species, with that of nominal or artificial kinds, such as artifacts. Rather than a progression through global stages of sophistication, in the manner suggested by most stage theories of development, he found that transformations tended to be domain specific, occurring first with respect to natural biological kinds, then with other physical natural kinds (e.g., minerals), and last with nominal kinds.[43] Furthermore, it is clear from his experiments that concepts are not just bundles of characteristic features; rather, they involve causal relations that account for the clustering of and relations among features. This integration of characteristics into a causal structure does not include all features associated with the concept, but it includes an increasing number of them as development takes place.

In one particularly interesting set of experiments, Keil used photographs to determine whether kindergarten, second grade, and fourth grade children thought one kind could change into another. Three sorts of transformations were tested: natural kind to natural kind within biological categories (one kind of animal into another, one kind of plant into another, etc.); nominal kind into nominal kind (one type of artifact into another); and cross-ontological changes (animal to artifact, animal to plant, machine to animal, etc.) The children were shown two pictures chosen to maximize common features (e.g., a horse and a zebra, a toy bird and a real bird, etc.), and were told that one represented the creature before a scientist operated on it, the other the creature after the operation. The children were then asked if the object shown in the first picture had been changed into that shown in the second (e.g., "Did he change it into a zebra, or is it still a horse?").[44] At all ages the children were least resistant to accepting the change of one artifact into another; they were more resistant to changes of natural kinds within categories, with the resistance increasing sharply with age, and at all ages they were strongly resistant to cross-ontological category changes. As Keil notes

> This study strongly indicates that kindergartners, and very possibly considerably younger children, are not the pure phenomenologists they appear to be, even when making distinctions between members of the same ontological category. They have beliefs about what sorts of mechanisms underlying characteristic feature changes are relevant to membership in a biological kind and what ones are not; and although many of these reasons may not be correct in the eyes of most adults, they are nonetheless theoretical constructs that may well be specific to biological kinds.[45]

As the comparison of kindergartners, second graders, and fourth graders shows, these theories rapidly become more sophisticated, emphasizing origins, deep as opposed to surface features, what the parents were, what sorts of offspring could be expected, and the basic impossibility of change of kind. In looking at the development of these concepts of natural kinds, what one is seeing is the development of theories in which a variety of characteristics are integrated through underlying causal processes. Keil makes the point explicitly.

> Most concepts are partial theories themselves in that they embody explanations of the relations between their constituents, of their origins, and of their relations to other clusters of features. This is readily apparent for concepts of events but is even more important with regard to objects, since one's full concept of an object (say, a dog or a typewriter) crucially depends on understanding not only the causal relations between its properties and why they cluster as they do, but also the potential causal roles such an object stably and regularly engages in when interacting with other objects.[46]

This does not of course mean that all characteristics associated with the object are fully integrated into such a structure. There remain correlated properties represented in and part of the concept, although related by association rather than by causal connections. But the model of the concept as a bundle of features assembled on the basis of similarity only—whether it is the common property classical view or the match to prototype view— is clearly inadequate to explain the experimental data. The view that theories are built up out of relations among concepts that are themselves atheoretical simply will not wash. Conceptions appear to *be* theories in their own right.

This view of concepts implies that the notion of causality is central to conceptual development, at least with respect to concepts of the natural world, and that it is present even among children of kindergarten age. It is therefore an important question just how early this notion appears among children, and how its presence is to be accounted for. Although Piaget's work on this subject is probably the best known in the literature,[47] the crucial experimental advance was made by Michotte. In a remarkable series of experiments, Michotte showed that adults *perceive* causal relations, and that this perception is often an illusion. The experimental apparatuses used by Michotte were of two sorts: discs rotating behind a screen which contained a viewing slit, and coordinated Kodak projectors. Both created images in which subjects saw squares or other figures perform various sorts of movements. In other words, the subjects were not viewing physical objects like billiard balls, but images only. In what he called "direct launching," Michotte used the rotating disc apparatus so that subjects saw two squares, A and B; A approached B, which was stationary until the two squares appeared to touch; A's motion thereupon ceased, and B moved away from A.

Michotte's subjects perceived A as causing the movement of B. Moreover, the perception of causality was overwhelming in direct launching, even when the subjects knew how the apparatus produced the apparent motions. As Michotte emphasized, "All the causal impressions mentioned in the book have occurred in the presence of observers who knew perfectly well that 'in reality' no causal influence was operating."[48] This point is crucial; observerss's knowledge that no real causality was involved, or that the sequence of events they were seeing was physically impossible, had no effect upon their perception—they perceived the interaction as causal in spite of their knowledge to the contrary.[49] Michotte developed from his experiments a set of rules that enabled him to create this illusion, and to make it vanish by varying certain features of the scene perceived by the subjects. But the central point is that the subjects perceived the interaction of the images as causal even knowing that the perception was an illusion.

In recent years, perceptual illusions have received a great deal of intensive study. Bruner and his coworkers have shown that there are cases in perception where prior knowledge can have a marked effect on what is perceived.[50] To use Pylyshyn's term, in such cases the perceptual system is "cognitively penetrable" by conceptual knowledge.[51] But the existence of perceptual illusions shows that this is not always the case. For example, when subjects look at this figure, they see a white triangle, and the triangle appears to be whiter than the surrounding white background. It makes no difference at all that the subject knows there is in fact no triangle and that the surface within the illusory figure differs in no respect from the rest of the background.[52] In such cases, the perceptual system which yields this illusion is "cognitively impenetrable"; conceptual knowledge has no effect on the perception.

Figure 3

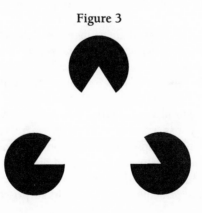

Illusory phenomena are among the data that have led Marr,[53] Fodor,[54] and others to propose that the perceptual system contains "modules"—relatively self-contained perceptual units that process perceptual data "from the bottom up" and then input the results of this processing to more central cognitive systems. The modularity theory has now acquired substantial experimental support. Among other virtues, it offers an explanation for the existence of illusions such as the Muller-Lyre, the triangle illusion, and many others. These result from the automatic action of the module, and the fact that the module processes "from the bottom up" means that higher-level beliefs have no influence on its working. Conversely, illusions that are cognitively impenetrable become clues to the existence of modules. As Leslie has pointed out, the existence of causal illusions of the sort demonstrated by Michotte and the fact that these illusions are cognitively impenetrable provide a strong argument that they result from a modular perceptual system.[55]

If such a modular perceptual system yielding causal perceptions exists, it would be quite reasonable to assume that it exists in infancy. Leslie has carried out a series of experiments on infants 27 weeks old that support the hypothesis that they perceive direct launching as causal. Using the habituation-of-looking method, he has shown that these infants perceive direct launching as having a more complex internal structure than other interactions in which causal perception should not be present. This result is predictable from the hypothesis that they perceive direct launching as a causal process. Leslie has also shown that two-year-old children have a well-developed understanding of causality that enables them to employ causal principles in counterfactual reasoning. To do this, he created "pretend" games with these children—for example, having a pretend birthday party for a toy animal. When the experimenter "accidently" tipped over a cup filled with pretend tea, the children were perfectly able to describe what the effects would be. By using a series of such pretend situations, Leslie showed that the children had an accurate grasp of real-world causal notions, and that they applied them in pretend situations to determine what the consequences of various events and accidents would be.[56]

These results strongly suggest that causal notions are not the end result of learning but its basis—that is, that the infant has a causal perceptual system, probably from birth, which underlies the development of a causal theory of the world as the child grows, and that, by the time the child is two, this theory has reached the point where causal reasoning is employed not only in developing an understanding of the real environment, but also in counterfactual situations. It should therefore be no surprise that concepts developed as part of this enterprise of understanding the world should involve causal principles. One would be surprised if they did not.[57]

Spelke has argued that by the fourth month, the child already has a rudimentary theory of physical objects organized around the notions of substance, cohesion, boundaries, and spatio-temporal continuity. Is this object theory also to be attributed to modular perceptual processes? Spelke thinks not, and Leslie has produced some very remarkable evidence to support her position. Baillargeon's experiment with rotating a screen through the space apparently occupied by a solid block has already been discussed. It is not obvious how this experiment, which involves the notion of substance, could be explained on the basis of perception alone. But more important, Leslie has shown that the Pulfrich double-pendulum illusion actually involves the illusion of one solid rod passing through another. In brief, this illusion involves two pendulums with rigid rods swinging in opposite phase in a frontal plane. Under appropriate viewing conditions, the illusion is produced that the pendulums are following elliptical paths in which they are, as it were, "chasing each other around."[58] But for this illusion to work, the rods from which the bobs are swung must pass through each other, despite the fact they are solid rigid objects. The illusion does work, and the rods do appear to pass through each other. This is strong evidence that the principle of substance (that two objects cannot co-habit in the same space) cannot be based on a perceptual module; it must be a higher-level principle of the cognitive system. It would appear therefore that our view of the world as one of individuated objects is a cognitive theory that, given its extremely early appearance in infancy, is the result of hardwired cognitive processes.[59]

Meaning

The argument to this point has concerned the development of concepts and theories. It is an explicit premise of this argument that language is distinct from thought and that substantial conceptual development takes place in children prior to the acquisition of language. But such a position leaves unexplained the question of the relation of language to thought. Clark's Lexical Contrast Theory seems to provide the most satisfactory answer to this problem currently available.[60] Clark's theory is based on several premises: (1) that concepts are distinct from, and predate, language, (2) that the primary motive for language acquisition is the desire of people to communicate with each other, (3) that "the conventional meanings of every pair of words (or word-formation devices) contrast," and (4) that "for certain meanings, there is a conventional word or word-formation device that should be used in the language community."[61]

From (4) it follows that in language learning, children will look for consistency in word usage across occasions and will modify their own usage to achieve such consistency. From (3) it follows that the child will assume that new words contrast with those he already knows. Both consequences are empirically supported. From (1) through (4) it follows that in acquiring words the learners' goal is to fill lexical gaps—that is, to find words that will enable them to express the concepts they want to use. Thus when children want to talk about an instance of a concept, they will seek an appropriate word with which to do so. Similarly, when children hear new words, they will assume that these contrast with those they already know and will seek a concept to match the new word. Further, given the communicative motive, children should seek most for words related to members of those categories they find most salient. But words once acquired should have a reciprocal function. Thus just as contrasting concepts will lead children to seek appropriately contrasting words, so new words should lead the child to seek appropriately contrasting concepts.

What does this theory imply regarding language acquisition? In view of (2), not only is language acquisition driven by communicative needs, but it is to the intended meanings of the child's linguistic expression that the principle of contrast applies, not always the actual expression used. That is, since children seek to communicate and, by hypothesis, have yet to acquire fully adequate means of doing so, they will try to make the linguistic resources they do have go as far as possible. One predictable result should be overextension of terms, e.g., calling all four-legged animals "doggie." This phenomenon is well known and amply documented.

A second is that children will not overextend a term to cover instances for which they already have an appropriate term. Thus once children have command of the term "cow," they will not extend "doggie" to include cows. It also follows from the desire for communication and the principle of contrast that overextension should diminish as the child acquires more words that make possible more precise communication.

A third consequence is that in the early stages of language learning, the learner will rely heavily on general-purpose words such as demonstratives and deictics and broadly extendable substantives such as "thing." The same phenomenon will be observed with verbs; thus young children use "do," "make," and "go" to cover a wide variety of actions and events. Here too one would predict that as the lexicon expands, the use of these all-purpose words will be restricted.

A fourth consequence is that, lacking words to fill felt gaps, children will invent new words for the purpose. The use of affixes—particularly suffixes, the conversion of words from one category to another (verb to noun or vice versa), and the compounding of words (e.g.," doorknob") are all well-known methods of doing this, and are all used by children. Thus "I goed" for "I went," "I bell it" for "I ring it," "plantman" for "gardener," all are quite reasonable attempts by children to communicate a message for which they lack the necessary words. Generally, these coinages tend to be as simple as possible and transparent in meaning, to use productive devices, and to extend existing paradigms (e.g., "I swimmed" for "I swam"). Here again, it is predictable that these coinages will be abandoned when new words are introduced that do the job of communication and gap filling more adequately.

Finally, Clark notes that lexical gaps can be filled by the figurative use of language. This method, which is of course extensively used by adults, is less commonly used by young children, although it does occur. Young children tend to adhere to literal uses of words, probably because the figurative use seems less transparent.[62]

Clark's theory is complemented by Markman's recent work, which has shown in a number of studies that when children first learn a word applied to an object (usually by ostension), they assume that the word "is likely to refer to the whole object and not to its parts, substance, or other properties."[63] Furthermore, children "constrain word meanings by assuming at first that words are mutually exclusive—that each object will have one and only one label."[64] Thus when children were presented with an object for which they already had a term—a cup, for example—and then were told "See this? It is pewter," they interpreted "pewter" not as another name for the cup but as referring to its substance, whereas when the same procedure was repeated with objects (such as tongs) for which they had no names, they tended to interpret "pewter" as a label for the object.[65] These results indicate both a built-in tendency for children to interpret words as naming objects, and a way in which they subsequently come to learn terms for parts, properties, and substances of objects.[66]

Clark's theory is supported by much data on language acquisition, and it has many advantages. Although there are language learning phenomena that it does not predict—e.g., underextension—these are not incompatible with the theory. Of particular importance is that the theory explains why language should be learned in the first place, and that many of the so-called errors that children make in acquiring language become explicable as attempts to achieve the child's purposes.

But what is less clear in Clark's theory is how word meanings are related to concepts, or, for that matter, what meanings are. Clark says

> But to study concepts and meanings, it is essential to keep them distinct. Words serve to flag or pick out particular categories or,

depending on the context, particular facets of a category. The relation between concepts and meanings, therefore, is necessarily an indirect one. Words (and their meanings) simply evoke concepts; they do not represent them. Thus information pertinent to forming a conceptual category may have no role in the meaning of the word used to pick out that category.[67]

Again,

Children learn that a particular label or flag simply picks out a particular conceptual category. This view of meaning solves the problem of how a word is related to the mass of information that can be linked to a single conceptual category. Speakers depend on the particular linguistic or nonlinguistic context and on mutual knowledge for their listeners to be able, on different occasions, to pick out different pieces from all the information potentially pertinent to a category.[68]

There is every reason to distinguish concepts from words and to assert that concepts can and do exist independently of linguistic expressions. But is there any reason to hold that when words have been acquired that "evoke" concepts, those concepts are not the meanings of the words concerned? Why is a third entity—a "meaning" distinct from the concept—necessary, and, if necessary, what is it? Underlying Clark's refusal to identify meaning with concept seem to be two facts: (1) that concepts involve a "mass of information" that is not part of the meaning, and (2) that linguistic expressions may evoke different portions of this information when used in different contexts. These facts certainly show that the meaning cannot be identical with the whole concept; they do not, however, show that the meaning cannot be the core of the concept.

In recent years the classical notion that the meaning of a term consists in the necessary and sufficient conditions for the application of that term has been roundly criticized. These criticisms are entirely just, for the classical notion involves, among other things, a confusion between meaning and reference fixing. Thus, to use the popular example, being featherless and being biped are necessary and sufficient conditions for the correct application of the term "man," but no one considers them to constitute an adequate definition of that term. Rather, what is wanted when one asks for the meaning of a term such as "man" is knowledge that will enable one fully to understand and predict the character and behavior of the object in question. To understand the meaning of "man" is to know what men are and why; to have, in short, a theory of man which is explanatory. But as we saw above, concepts of kinds, and indeed, I would argue, all concepts, involve theories about the instances of the concept which contain explanations of the properties and relations characterizing those instances. We also have seen that the concept will involve more than this. It will include correlated properties linked to the theoretical core by a variety of associations. But if we call the central theoretical component the "core" of the concept, then I would argue that the core is itself the meaning of the term. Thus when one defines "gold" as "the element having atomic number 79," the significance of this definition is that from a knowledge of the atomic number of an element, all its chemical properties can be derived. The definition encapsulates a causal theory about gold which accounts in a causal fashion for the properties and relations of the metal.

How is one to deal with Clark's point about contextual effects? Certainly she is right; consider (a) Clark's theory is pure gold, (b) this ring is pure gold, (c) she's a golden blond, (d) he a golden boy, (e) he's seeking a pot of gold, etc. With the exception of (b), these statements all tap properties of gold which lie outside the meaning as just defined. But why is it easier to explain contextual effects by invoking a meaning which then (somehow) evokes a concept than by letting the conceptual core be the meaning, which is then evoked whenever any part of the concept is activated? Contextual effects are produced, after all, by embedding a token of an expression in a linguistic context where the "core" meaning is to some degree inappropriate and which therefore requires—on the assumption that communication is intended—accessing some further parts of the conceptual content. There seems to be no reason why this cannot be done as easily by taking meaning as the conceptual core as by postulating an intermediate entity.

One might object to this position by pointing out that (a) and (e) at least involve the notion of gold as valuable, and that valuational properties cannot be derived from physical ones. Nevertheless, the valuational aspect of gold is a context effect—not a component of the meaning. To see this, suppose that gold were suddenly to become as common as sand in our society. The economic value of gold would thereupon vanish (one does not seek a pot of sand). So the notion of gold as being of great worth would also rapidly decline. Yet would one want to say that the definition of "gold" was changed by increasing the amount of it in the world? Indeed, it would make no sense to say that, for if it were so changed, one would no longer be talking about the same thing. The valuational properties of gold are a function not just of its physical properties, including its rarity, but also of its role in the context of human societies. In the view suggested here, conceptual cores—understood as theories that explain the behavior and properties of instances of the concept—are the meanings of concepts. On the assumption that the objective of definition is complete understanding, the ideal or "perfect" definition is exemplified by "gold =df the element whose atomic number is 79."

This ideal definition will seldom be attained, of course; as Keil notes, such conceptual cores are usually partial theories at best. If the definition of "gold" is "perfect" in the sense indicated, it is also exceptional; most definitions will be imperfect. Consider for example the term "knife." Certainly it is a defining property of a knife that it is used to cut and/or puncture. As is true for all artifacts, the definition must give central status to functional properties, but the core would also include the fact of its being made or shaped for this purpose. But these characteristics do not constitute a perfect definition. One can also cut with a laser and puncture with a needle or do both with scissors, none of which are knives. Nor is it easy to see how such core characteristics could be supplemented to create a perfect definition. Swords also have single blades, and there is no clear boundary between a short sword and a long knife. The result is that "knife" cannot be given a perfect definition. Nevertheless, it can be given a sufficiently good definition to allow the term to be used adequately for the purposes of communication.

I suggest that perfect definition represents the further and ideal end of a scale on which rudimentary ostensive definition is the hither end. Definitions for most terms will lie somewhere between these extremes, as the definition of "knife" does. If the attainment of understanding, prediction, and control are among the primary motives for thinking, it follows that we will try to move as far as possible along that scale; hence, from our first introduction to an instance of a concept through ostension, we will try to develop an increasingly adequate concept which will enable us to understand what it is and does, and the core of that concept will be the meaning we give to the term used for it. Sometimes—chiefly as a result of scientific investigation—we will be able to reach a perfect definition. But usually we will have to settle for something considerably short of that. Nevertheless, if we have attained a sufficient understanding so that communication can proceed unimpeded, we have what is essential for ordinary purposes, and here, as elsewhere, we learn to live with our shortcomings.

Thus far, I have referred to conceptual cores as causal theories. But with respect to entities such as numbers and geometrical figures, the core of the concept will not be causal but logical or mathematical. Thus the definition of "even integer" will include being divisible by 2 without remainder, while that of "odd integer" will include not being divisible by 2 without remainder. The point is that a concept is not simply a collection of similar features but that it has an internal structure in which many features are related to each other. Whether the internal structure is causal or logical depends upon the nature of the concept and its instances.

The claim that concepts are theories and that meanings are conceptual cores would appear to lead to the conclusion that meanings are factual beliefs. This thesis has been attacked by Katz on several grounds. First, he argues that it would make descriptions such as "creature with a heart" and "creature with a kidney" synonymous.[69] But even if one wanted to characterize a natural kind by its anatomical characteristics—and that is certainly one possible method—one would want a far more complex description than this. The terms "creature with the heart" and "creature with a kidney" may be coextensional, but that does not make them synonymous. Second, Katz objects that the statement, "There is something about which no one at present has any factual beliefs," is a true statement.[70] But the term "something about which no one at present has any factual beliefs" would be meaningless if the meaning of a term were the core of factual beliefs about its referent. Hence Katz concludes that meanings cannot be factual beliefs. But presumably the sentence, "There is something about which no one at present has any factual beliefs," is a factual statement; how else could Katz claim it to be true? But then there is at least one factual belief about the referent—namely, this one—and this contradicts Katz's hypothesis.

But Katz's main argument is that semantic relations among terms and statements, such as analytic, synthetic, synonymous, redundant, etc., would on this view break down.[71] The force of this objection escapes me. If I believe a sister to be a female sibling—if these properties are part of what I consider the core of the concept of "sister"—then I have no hesitation in saying that the statement, "all sisters are female siblings," is true, and even that it is analytic in the sense that it simply explicates what I believe to be the meaning of "sister." This meaning may be changed, but at present, the inference from

Sarah is John's sister

to

Sarah is female

seems to me unexceptional, but that does not make the statement, "all sisters are female," an eternal truth.

The same argument holds with respect to synonymy. When used as a consanguineal kinship term, "sister" is synonymous with "female sibling" in our culture. The synonymy is clearly restricted to the domain of consanguineal kinship; one does not (usually) refer to a nun as a female sibling. And it is limited to current beliefs; as noted, nature is not bound by our definitions. But within those limits, the terms are synonymous salva anything you like, and there is no reason not to say so.

But the notion that meanings consist of factual beliefs requires qualification. Not all theories are true, and many are known to be false. No one today believes that there is such a thing as phlogiston, but the phlogiston theory is well known and certainly the term "phlogiston" is meaningful. All theories are in some degree hypothetical, and one need not believe a theory to be true to understand how the entities posited by the theory are supposed to behave. We can define "phlogiston" and state its properties and their causal relations as these are described in the theory. One is not required to believe that the theory is true in order to do this. It is quite sufficient to understand what would be the case if the hypothetical theory were true.

Reference

The argument so far obviously assumes that both infants and adults refer to a world of objects. If the conclusions drawn from the psychological studies cited above are correct, human beings are programmed to perceive the world as one of individuated objects. This is the world of naive realism—the common-sense world that semanticists have assumed to be that to which language refers.[72] The existence of this preformation system does not of course give any grounds for assuming that the world really is as we perceive it to be, but such ontological issues need not concern us here. It is sufficient for present purposes to note that the common-sense world is presupposed in ordinary discourse in English.

How do we refer to this world? More exactly, what is meant by saying that we refer to this world? It is true that we often speak of the reference of a word, as if the word were an entity capable of referring. But this is clearly a metonymy; the words of a language we do not understand, such as Harappan, do not now refer, even though we are quite sure that the Harappans once used them to refer. Human beings use signs to refer to objects of interest to them; the "reference of a sign" is simply that which the speakers of that language community use it to direct attention to. As the familiar phenomenon of ciphers shows, a particular group may use any word to refer to anything, provided there is prior agreement on its use. Within a language community generally, there is an agreed-upon reference for a given word, meaning that the word will be used by members of that community to refer to that object. Obviously, the possibility of communication depends upon such standard usage. Neither monologue nor dialogue would otherwise be possible.

Most signs do not refer to only one thing; "dog" refers to all dogs. It is clearly not true that the utterance of "dog" leads the hearer to attend to all dogs simultaneously, but rather that it directs attention to whatever fits the concept of a dog. Reference *per se* does not involve a concept; pointing may direct people's attention to a particular part of their visual field without their knowing what is being pointed at—fortunately, or we could never learn. But the generalization of a sign to refer to like things is not just a matter of conditioning, but of concept formation. If it were not, we should never be able to say much about dogs except that they are called "dog." Thus, although reference is primary, in the sense that being able to direct attention to a subject is a precondition for communication, and indeed for thinking, yet reference and meaning (concepts) develop together and are intrinsic to signhood.

It is an important consequence of this view that reference is an intentional phenomenon. The fact that a particular cloud formation happens to look like a ship does not show that the cloud refers to a ship. Accidently falling off the roof may direct one's attention to the force of gravity, but it is not a symbolic action referring to gravity. Instances of a physical law may cause scientists to think of the law, but they do not refer to the law and are not signs of the law. When one says that a word refers or a picture refers, what is being said is that among a particular group of people it is agreed that the word or picture is being used to refer. That is, when the word is used by members of the group, they intend to refer to something and their audience knows that by using that word they intend to refer to that thing or those things.

Pointing at an object while saying a word or sentence that applies to it is the prototypical case of ostensive definition, although in fact any non-linguistic method of directing attention to the object and associating a word with it is equally a form of ostensive definition. Wittgenstein argued that ostensive definition involved the use of samples.[73] Certainly this is so from the teacher's point of view, but not necessarily from the learners. Indeed, in the case of concrete general terms like "dog," the learner's problem is precisely to learn that the object pointed at is a sample. How does the child do this?

As Katz, Baker, and Macnamara have argued, and as the work of Spelke et al. demonstrates, the infant perceives the world in terms of individuated objects. But some of these objects acquire their salient individuality by virtue of their relations and importance to the child—for example, the caretaker. Other objects—like blocks—do not possess such individuality but are seen as members of a kind. It is those objects whose individuality is quite literally forced upon the child who receive proper names; others receive general, or class, names. In other words, "The reason children are able to learn the distinction between common and proper nouns and the syntactic marking of that distinction is that they have previously made the relevant distinction among the referents."[74] Thus by seventeen months children learn that there are two kinds of names—proper names and common names, and they have already learned that the syntactic indicator for a common noun is the prefixed article "a" or "the." But the understanding of the significance of the syntactic distinction is based upon the differentiation between objects that have peculiar individuality and those that do not. This is shown by the fact that efforts to teach children to identify blocks by proper names based on the use of syntactic cues have not been successful. On the other hand, even at seventeen months, the children are able to grasp that an individual who has a proper name can also have a common name— that is, is a member of a class. As Katz, Baker, and Macnamara conclude,

> What children learn to begin with is that the individuals of certain classes are important as individuals. Thus, individuality is never merely that, but the individuality of a member of a class. The two notions are inextricably related from the start.[75]

Ostensive definition involves many problems which are well known. If an adult points at Fido and says "dog," how does the child know that the reference is to the object rather than to its color or shape? Since the child already views the world as one of objects with various aspects such as color and shape, the reference could be to any of these. The standard view has been that the child does not know which is meant from a single act of ostension, that it will require multiple episodes involving different objects and comparisons among them to sort out matters. Thus "dog" will be found to apply to some animals of different shapes and colors; "brown" to some dogs, some tables, some suits, and so forth. Comparison and contrast are the keys, as Clark notes, that enable the child to zero in on the correct range of application. It has been objected that since the number of properties of any object is infinite, this method can never be determinate, but while this may be theoretically true, it is practically irrelevant. It may be true that Fido is 93 million miles from the sun, but this is not a property taught by ostension, and the method of comparison is certainly adequate to determine what referent is meant. However, if Markman's "whole object assumption" is correct, the child is programmed to give priority to the whole object as the referent of a word, and only arrives at words for properties or parts through the "mutual exclusivity" principle.[76] Either way, the child can clearly determine the reference of an ostensively defined term.

When by comparison we generalize a term such as "dog" or "brown" from a single object to multiple objects, it is obvious that the term must apply to all those objects from which it has been generalized. Thus attribution is in one sense the converse of generalization. The relation between a predicate and its subjects is usually put in term of satisfaction conditions; the subjects must satisfy the predicate. There is no conflict here. If *a* satisfies the propositional function Fx, then F is true of *a*. But if F is true of *a*, F could be generalized from *a* together with similar objects. However, genuine predication involves more than this; it involves knowing not only when a term applies but when it does not. As Evans has shown, for terms of divided reference, predication involves a grasp of the identity conditions of the referent. Thus, where the compound term "white rabbit" is construed as involving predication (i.e., the rabbit is white), it is not enough that there should be some overlap between the properties "white" and "rabbit," for that could be achieved by so arranging multiple cottontails that their tails are contiguous. It must also be the case that satisfying the conditions for "white" is only achieved by something satisfying the identity conditions of "rabbit"—conditions involving at least cohesion, boundaries, and spatio-temporal continuity.[77] But as Spelke has shown, these are among the identity conditions for physical objects generally—conditions met by our fundamental object concept.

However, not all those things that we meet in experience satisfy the basic identity conditions for objects. Water does not; snow does not; air does not. In such cases, there is neither cohesion nor boundaries. Terms for such substances—"mass terms," as they are usually called—can be learned by ostension, since such entities do display at least substantiality and a limited form of spatio-temporal continuity. (Water is subdivisible, all parts—at least those perceptible to a child—remaining water, and can appear or vanish by change of phase, so the spatio-temporal continuity is limited. However, within a broad range of temperatures, a given body of water does exhibit a good deal of continuity. Much the same holds of snow, air, and similar masses.) Predicates such as "cold," "wet," etc. are applicable either to the mass itself, or to particular individuated portions of it—e.g., the water in the tub is hot. It seems to be unclear just when the child learns the distinction between objects and substances, but he certainly has begun to learn it before the age of two and probably well before that. His mastery of terms for masses and objects—of mass nouns and count nouns—is at least partially acquired by that time, although it increases thereafter with age. There is, however, no simple relation between the syntactic distinction of mass noun and count noun and the objectival or substantive nature of the referent. In the first place, many mass nouns in English are semantically collective nouns; thus "furniture," "silverware," and "jewelry" are syntactically mass terms (one cannot say "*a furniture" or "*furnitures") although semantically they refer to collections of individuated objects. Second, as Gordon has shown, young children use syntactic indicators more than semantic ones in mastering the count noun/mass noun distinction, although semantic factors do play some part.[78]

Quine has suggested that once we have the linguistic mechanism of predication, as in "This box is square," we are led by analogy to predications such as "Square is a shape," thereby converting general terms into singular abstract terms.[79] If so, it is the focusing of attention on the property of being square that is crucial, not linguistic usage. Given the fact that general terms imply the recognition of a property, there is no reason why the property itself cannot be made the primary focus of attention and its characteristics analysized. Thus a word like "square" may serve either as a general term, predicating a property of something, or as a singular abstract term, focusing attention on the property itself. Given the range of subjects that we can make objects of attention, it is no surprise that we refer constantly to abstractions and have the linguistic tools to facilitate our doing so.

One apparent implication of Clark's Lexical Contrast Theory is that while there is thought without corresponding words, there should be no words without corresponding thoughts. This implication, however, is apparent only—fortunately so, because there are well-known countercases. Thus the words "round" and "square" have both meaning and reference, but the term "round square" does not refer. The point, obviously, is that the two terms are incompatible, so their conjunction is contradictory; nothing is both round and square. This raises no problem for Clark, since her theory does not imply that all contrasting concepts must permit conjunctions that are consistent. In this case, the contradiction is obvious; in many other cases, it is not. "The class of all classes not members of themselves" is one of the more famous examples; it took Russell to prove that the assumption of the existence of such a class was contradictory. Nevertheless, the term itself is meaningful; certainly it is not nonsense or meaningless. Terms involving contradictions cannot refer to anything, for there can be no object that can serve as their referent, but the statement of the contradiction itself is meaningful; indeed, if the expression were simply meaningless, it is hard to see how it could be said to be a contradiction.

A more difficult case is posed by a term such as "a/the proof of the Continuum Hypothesis." Here we do not know whether there is such a proof. Yet it is quite clear that the term makes sense, and some mathematicians are working very hard on finding just this proof. How is this possible? It is possible because it is one of the characteristics of attention that it can be directed to a hypothetical entity as well as to an existent one. If this were not so, how could we refer to the answer to a problem we have not yet solved? And how could we seek it? Granting that we may have reference-fixing criteria that will enable us to tell whether or not something we have found is such an answer, we need also the capacity to attend to the hypothetical entity before we have found it. Such hypothetical supposition of an entity does not involve a commitment to its actual existence (there may be no proof of the Continuum Hypothesis, and it cannot be proven from the present axioms of set theory), nor to the actual existence of possible entities. There is all the difference in the world between saying, "I am seeking a proof of the Continuum Hypothesis, if there is one," and, "There is a possible proof of the Continuum Hypothesis that I am seeking." The former entertains the existence of the proof as a hypothesis; the latter affirms it as a possible existent. Of course what is supposed as a hypothetical entity must be possible, in the sense that it cannot be contradictory, like a round square, but that is a general condition for existence. But what then is one to do with Russell's case of "the present king of France"?[80] There is no contradiction here—there could be a present king of France, but in fact there is not. Russell's treatment of this case is well known, as are its merits and demerits, and there is no need to review them here. But I see no reason why "the present king of France" cannot be construed as referring to a hypothetical entity. Such a hypothesis is contrary to fact, since there is no present king of France; a statement such as, "The present king of France is bald," is simply a false statement. Similarly, a statement such as, "Nobody lives here," is equivalent to, "It is not the case that there is an x such that x is a person and x lives here." The issue is really no different in the case of such a statement as, "All unicorns are herbivorous"; since there are no unicorns, one might want to call this sentence false, but in its conditional form—(x)(x is a unicorn then x is herbivorous)—it is true. But this is just the general problem of counterfactual conditionals; the antecedent is still false because there is no corresponding referent. At the same time, one can perfectly well talk of unicorns as hypothetical entities that might have existed, although they do not. In that hypothetical sense, all unicorns are herbivorous—that is, if the hypothesis that there are unicorns were true, they would be herbivorous, since our hypothetical Unicorn Theory requires that they have that characteristic. It is not nonsense to discuss the properties of hypothetical entities, even when we know that the hypothesis is false.

The same situation obtains with respect to fictional and mythological entities. Hamlet never existed, yet more has been written about him than about most men who have. Unicorns, Venus, and (probably) Achilles are all creatures of myth and/or fiction. But it is clearly possible to consider these as hypothetical entities that can be discussed and analyzed without our being committed to their existence as real objects. Indeed, such entities do have a kind of reality—Hamlet is a character in a real play, as Achilles is in a real poem. But recognizing that fact neither commits us to saying Hamlet was an actual person nor prevents us from referring to Hamlet as a hypothetical entity.

The referent of a declarative sentence is a state of affairs—namely, that state of affairs described by the sentence. Thus, "John is drunk," refers to the state of affairs in which John is drunk. Imperatives, such as "Shut the door!" refer to the state of affairs that the utterer wishes the hearer to bring about. Interrogatives, such as, "What is the proof of Fermat's last theorem?" refer to the state of affairs that would afford the answer to the question. There are of course a legion of further questions to be raised here—To what do performatives refer? What about indirect discourse?—but these must be postponed for the moment. It is sufficient here to emphasize that these sentences direct our attention and so refer to particular states of affairs.

The thesis that conceptual cores represent the meanings of terms, together with the view of concepts proposed here, implies that there are concepts of individual entities, so that names have a meaning. It is sometimes said that names are pure designators and have no associated meaning. But a name, such as "Napoleon Bonaparte," not only refers to a specific individual person, it also carries with it a concept that involves all one knows about that remarkable man. This may seem odd, for concepts are usually thought of as having some degree of generality, whereas Napoleon Bonaparte was a particular individual. But generality depends upon the dimension being considered. Napoleon Bonaparte did exist over a continuous stretch of time and did a great many things. In that sense the concept of "Napoleon Bonaparte" brings together a multiplicity of properties, acts, events, and relations that centered around him and seeks to integrate those characteristics in a causal and explanatory way. In this sense, individual concepts, such as names, are not different from other concepts.

This view of names may seem opposed to that of Kripke,[81] Putnam,[82] and a number of others, but it is important to be clear just where the differences are. Kripke has put forward a number of theses regarding naming. If one believes, as Kripke does, in possible worlds, then it must be possible to refer to the same individual in different possible worlds. This has led him to define proper names as "rigid designators" thus: "Let's call something a *rigid designator* if in every possible world it designates the same object. . . ."[83] Thus, for Kripke, the name "Napoleon Bonaparte" must designate the same object in every possible world in which the object exists. Kripke then applies the machinery of possible worlds to show that neither the Frege-Russell theory of proper names nor the property cluster theory holds good: Consider any set of properties that might be held to identify a given object X uniquely; then Kripke can specify a possible world in which X does not have those properties. Thus, if "Napoleon" is defined by the properties "Emperor of the French," "victor at Jena and Austerlitz," "exiled to Elba," etc., Kripke can specify a possible world in which Napoleon became a shoemaker and had none of the usually used defining properties. Accordingly, Kripke holds, names cannot have meanings in the sense of sets of properties uniquely specifying the individual named. But how then do names refer? Kripke's answer is the causal chain theory of names. A name is bestowed upon X in some ritual; thereafter those present at the ritual "cause" others to use the name to refer to X, and so the reference is passed from link to link in the causal chain. The name can thus refer, but not through any set of properties.[84]

The basic problem I have with Kripke's theory is with the notion of possible worlds and its heavy reliance upon counterfactuals. With respect to the statement, "Aristotle was fond of dogs," Kripke says,

> A proper understanding of this statement involves an under-
> standing both of the (extensionally correct) conditions under
> which it is in fact true, *and* of the conditions under which a
> counterfactual course of history, resembling the actual course
> in some respects but not in others, would be correctly (par-
> tially) described by (1),

i.e., by the statement "Aristotle was fond of dogs."[85] This claim assumes that we have criteria for saying when counterfactual statements are true or false. But except in the case where the counterfactual is derivable from well confirmed laws of nature or from a well-developed theory, it is at least questionable that we have such criteria or that we can say in this case what is or is not an acceptable "counterfactual course of history." The doctrine of rigid designators is clearly meant to constrain the set of possible worlds, but it is far from clear why one should accept this doctrine or why one should believe that it is adequate to the task.

This objection does not affect the causal theory of names itself. And here there are really two different problems, to both of which the causal theory provides a useful answer. First, how is it that a given person—say, Tom—has a particular name? And second, how is it that in using that name I can refer to that unique person? If one thinks of how individuals actually acquire their names, Kripke is certainly right in saying that there is some sort of baptismal ceremony—what Kaplan calls a "dubbing" ceremony—which gives that name to that person, and that the continued use of the name depends upon a causal process in which the named individuals use the name for themselves and others use it for them. Of course, this process can go awry; as every reader of nineteenth-century fiction knows, the individuals' "true" (i.e., original) names may be hidden and they themselves and others may come to use the wrong names. Nevertheless, it is surely the case that the naming of persons, pets, and even objects does originate in a "dubbing" ceremony and is transmitted by a causal process.[86]

But this leaves unanswered the second question; as Wittgenstein posed it, "What makes my idea of him an idea of *him*?"[87] After all, the name "Tom" is a type that is used to refer to many people in our culture; when I use it to refer to a particular person, why does it designate him? If one considers how one does in fact come to associate a particular name with a particular person, the answer is obviously through some form of ostension— usually, an introduction, or by having him pointed out to you by someone else and identified as "Tom," or by seeing him on TV and being told that he is "Tom," etc. Here again, we have a causal process, although a different one from the original baptism by which he acquired his name. Thus it is perfectly possible that A was baptized "Tom" and is known to you by that name, but that he is introduced to me as "Fred." Then my ideas about this particular Fred refer to the same individual known to you as "Tom"; there are two causal processes involved that pertain to the same individual. My concept of Fred will differ from your concept of Tom, given the different circumstances of our acquaintance. Indeed, I may believe Fred to be a drug dealer, while you believe Tom to be an undercover agent. But in both cases, the same individual is involved; he simply stands in a different causal relation to you than he does to me.

Relativity of Reference

One of the features of what Hao Wang has called Quine's "logical negativism"[88] is his denial that reference is determinate, more exactly, his claim that reference is relative to a particular choice of metalanguage. Quine's most forceful presentation of this claim is made in his famous article, "Ontological Relativity,"[89] published in 1969. Although this paper is well known and has been extensively discussed, it will be described here in some detail because we must understand just what Quine's strategy is. Quine opens on a familiar note—the denial of the existence of mental entities. Mentalistic semantics he compares to a museum in which mental "meanings" are the exhibits and words their labels. But this mental museum is a myth, Quine holds; no such entities exist.[90] Instead, Quine holds that "meaning" must be defined in terms of publicly observable behavior, or more strictly in terms of dispositions to overt behavior. Such dispositions are for Quine sufficiently in the public domain to qualify as empirically observable. But this definition of meaning may, Quine notes, have the effect of creating some indeterminacy, since different expressions may turn out to be behaviorally indistinguishable.

Quine then examines what such indeterminacy might be. Suppose we have an expression from some remote language admitting of two different translations into English which are nevertheless behaviorally equivalent.

> I am supposing that one and the same native use of the expression can be given either of the English translations, each being accommodated by compensating adjustments in the translation of other words. Suppose both translations, along with these accommodations in each case, accord equally well with all observable behavior on the part of speakers of the remote language and speakers of English. Suppose they accord perfectly not only with behavior actually observed, but with all dispositions to behavior on the part of all the speakers concerned. On these assumptions it would be forever impossible to know of one of these translations that it was the right one, and the other wrong.[91]

Indeed, the question of which translation was right would here become meaningless, for once accommodations are reached that render the translations behaviorally equivalent, there is nothing else to appeal to.

Quine uses three examples to illustrate his point. The first is the French expression "ne . . . rien." "Rien" can be translated either as "anything" with "ne" as "not," or as "nothing" with "ne" construed pleonastically. The two translations appear equivalent behaviorally.

The second example is the gavagai argument. Quine himself has expressed regret at the attention that this argument has received, since he feels that it has distracted attention from the fundamentals of his position.[92] Nevertheless, the argument is important and needs to be dealt with. Quine imagines a situation in which an anthropologist meets a native from a hitherto unknown tribe—a case, that is, in which no linguistic community exists between the anthropologist and the native. He further supposes that as the anthropologist and the native stand in a clearing sizing each other up, a rabbit runs by, and the native, pointing at the rabbit, says "Gavagai." The anthropologist infers from this that the native term "gavagai" means "Lo, a rabbit" or "There's a rabbit." (Since Quine considers sentences the basic units of language, he interprets "gavagai" as a sentence rather than a word.) In any case, the anthropologist interprets the expression "gavagai" as referring to the rabbit. (Note that Quine simply assumes recognition of an intention to communicate.)

Of course the anthropologist will test this hypothesis. He will himself point at some other rabbit and utter "gavagai" to see if the native assents.

(Quine also assumes that translations of assent and dissent are already attained.) Assuming native assent to his usage of "gavagai," is the anthropologist's hypothesis justified, that the expression "gavagai" refers to rabbits? According to Quine, it is not. The English term "rabbit" refers to a physical object. But suppose that the native term "gavagai" refers to temporal rabbit slices, or to undivided rabbit parts, or means "Lo, it rabbiteth" in analogy to "Lo, it raineth"? In any of these cases, Quine argues, the native would assent to the anthropologist's use of "gavagai" in just those cases where the speaker of English would use "rabbit."

Now of course it would be possible to ask the native which he meant. It would be possible, that is, if we already had a translation from his language into ours so that terms like "identity," plural forms, articles, and the like were available. But by hypothesis we have in this case no such translation, and must construct one. In doing so we will correlate English sentences to native expressions by what Quine calls "analytical hypotheses." For some terms like "gavagai," translation is facilitated by the fact that those nerve stimulations that elicit "rabbit" from us elicit "gavagai" from the native, but for that multitude of terms like "identity" that are not observation terms, no similar help is available. There is therefore nothing to constrain our making of analytical hypotheses about these words except the desire to find sensible equivalences that will preserve the correlations of stimulations, and this, Quine holds, can be done in multiple ways. Thus if by "gavagai" the native really means temporal rabbit slices, he would take our question, "Is this gavagai identical with yesterday's?" to mean "Is this rabbit slice a member of the same series as yesterday's?" and we would never know the difference. That, for Quine, is just the point. Because analytical hypotheses are underdetermined by stimulus correlations, there are many different mappings from one language onto another that would preserve all stimulus correlations and yet yield different ontologies. We would in fact impute our own ontology of physical objects to the native, since that is how we think, but we would have no grounds other than convenience for doing so. Reference is inscrutable because there is nothing to scrute; all translations are equivalent.[93]

The third example is Japanese classifiers that, used together with a numeral such as "five" and the word for oxen, can be translated either as "five oxen" or as "five head of cattle." In the first case, the classifier indicates that "five" applies to individuated objects such as oxen. In the second, the classifier individuates the mass term "cattle." The translations are equivalent behaviorally in English. As Quine then notes, in these cases the issue has become not one of meaning but of reference. To what does "gavagai" refer? an object? undivided parts? a time-slice? or a mass? And does the Japanese word refer to objects or masses? It appears that we thus discover an indeterminacy of reference. And this indeterminacy Quine holds cannot be eliminated. Why not?

Quine's argument is clearest with respect to radical translation (i.e., the gavagai case), because in this example there is by hypothesis no linguistic commonality between the native and the English speaker. The relation between the expression "gavagai" and its referent is given by direct ostension, that is, by pointing. But Quine argues that what is pointed at could be an object, undivided parts, a time-slice, or a portion of a mass, and we could never tell which, since to point at any of these is to point at all of them. The indeterminacy is irresolvable because Quine holds that individuation is achieved through language. Accordingly to know how the native individuates his world, and so whether he is referring to an individuated object or something else, we must first learn his language, and Quine argues that we can so construe the native's language, by compensating adjustments in translation, as to make any choice of referent fit all dispositions to overt behavior equally well.[94]

Quine then takes up the problem of deferred ostension, illustrated by such examples as pointing at the gas gauge to indicate the gas level in the tank, and pointing at something green to indicate the abstract property "green."[95] Again, the claim is that we could never tell which referent was intended if compensating adjustments are made in the translation, so deferred ostension like direct ostension turns out to be indeterminate.[96]

The introduction of deferred ostension opens the way for Quine to argue that expressions may be paired to Godel numbers so that reference to one is indistinguishable from reference to the other.[97] Quine then brings the argument home by noting that the same indeterminacy of reference which afflicts remote languages exists also among speakers of the same language, and can even be applied to oneself at different times.[98] At this point, Quine has pushed his argument, if not beyond the pale, at least to its edge, and he seeks to resolve the matter by making reference relative to a further language.

Quine draws an analogy between position, which is well known to be specifiable only in terms of a coordinate system, and reference, which he says is determinate only relative to a "background language."[99] Or, as Quine puts it, "It makes no sense to say what the objects of a theory are, beyond saying how to interpret or reinterpret that theory in another."[100] He then goes on to develop the thesis that, to use Tarski's terms, the reference of an object language must be specified in the metalanguage, the reference of the metalanguage must be specified in the metametalanguage, and so on. The argument is developed with respect to mathematical models, drawing on the notions of proxy functions, Godel numbers, the Lowenhein-Skolem theorem, and similar ideas.

I have described this famous paper by Quine in detail to emphasize what Quine is up to here. The basic notion that underlies Quine's argument is that an abstract formal theory admits of multiple models, and that the model being used as an interpretation of the formal theory can only be specified in a metatheory. This thesis is, of course, a well-known proposition of model theory, and its truth is not in question. Quine's strategy is to show that a natural language can be treated as if it were an abstract formal theory, so that it too will admit of interpretation by multiple models and the model actually referred to in a given case can only be stipulated in a metatheory. Thus, in the first twenty-four pages of the paper Quine talks about language, but from there on he talks about theories—in the last eighteen pages of the paper, the word "language" occurs only four times—once on page 52 in the title of Carnap's *Logical Syntax of Language*, once on page 61, once on page 67 in the expression "background language," and once on page 68 in the "Note added in Proof." In other words, by the twenty-fifth page Quine thinks he has shown that natural languages can be treated as can formal theories, and so both may be discussed under the latter heading.

But can natural languages in fact be treated as formal theories? It is not obvious that they can. Granted that philosophers have for years talked of "formal languages," most of them have sharply divided such formal systems from natural languages. Of course, one could simply strip a natural language of all meanings and references and treat it as an uninterpreted system, but obviously the result would no longer be a natural language, and Quine is not guilty of so simpleminded a move. Further, one might have thought that the referential apparatus of a natural language was sufficient to insure determinate reference; certainly many past philosophers have thought so. What Quine undertakes to do is to prove that even the apparently determinate referential apparatus of natural languages admits of sufficient indeterminacy so that alternative models would satisfy all the conditions imposed by the language itself.

Quine presents his argument as if it were derived from his behavioristic definition of meaning. The legitimacy of this definition of meaning is a complex question to which we shall return in the next chapter; for the moment it may be set aside, since the heart of Quine's argument is his attack on the determinacy of ostensive definition. It is by ostensive definitions that natural languages are tied to the natural world; to break this link is to leave their relation to the natural world arbitrary. Quine's strongest argument is in terms of radical translation; ostensive definition, he claims, cannot distinguish between object reference, undivided part reference, time-slice reference, and mass reference. But this claim rests upon a further assumption—that the individuation of the world is achieved solely through linguistic devices. Thus Quine says that *if* we knew the native speaker's plural forms, articles, use of "identity," and the like, we could tell which of the above sorts of things he was referring to; it is because we have no prior access to these linguistic devices, and in learning his language will so construe them as to make his references match ours, that the problem of reference is insolvable. But this claim of Quine's is false. As we have already seen, the individuation of the world into enduring objects is achieved by psychological mechanisms that are hardwired and therefore universal. As the work of Spelke, Baillargeon, and others cited above demonstrates, long before children learn any language at all they have already come to see the world as a world of individuated objects continuous in space and time—therefore, the individuation of the world into enduring objects cannot be determined by language. The child's conceptualization of the world finds expression in language, as one would expect on the basis of Lexical Contrast Theory, and, as Markman has shown, children interpret the first word they learn for an object as applying to the whole object and only later begin to separate out its distinct features. Hence the indeterminacy Quine alleges in the case of "gavagai" is mistaken. The native speaker does conceive the world in terms of enduring individuated objects because all humans so conceive the world. Anthropologists may take this fact for granted and proceed to base their translation of the native tongue upon it without being guilty of making an arbitrary assumption.

Quine is also on less than solid ground in his analysis of Japanese classifiers. As Quine describes the two interpretations, "One way treats the third Japanese word as an individuative term true of each bovine, and the other way treats that word rather as a mass term covering the unindividuated totality of beef on the hoof."[101] Mass terms are differentiated from count nouns syntactically, but from a semantic point of view there are two kinds of mass terms: those which, like "water," "air," and "snow," refer to an unindividuated stuff, and those which, like "furniture," "silverware," and "jewelry," are collective nouns referring to aggregates of individuated objects. "Cattle" belongs in the latter category; it refers to an aggregate of individual bovines. Hence "five bovines" and "five head of cattle" are both terms that refer to collections of individuated objects; the latter expression does not individuate an undifferentiated mass of beef into individual animals. The situation in Japanese is roughly parallel to that in English. The Japanese word for oxen is not a mass term such as "water"; it corresponds most nearly to an English term such as "deer" that takes no plural, can be used with different numerals ("one deer," "five deer"), but when used with a numeral greater than one refers to a collection of individuated animals, not to an unindividuated mass. Syntax here is not an adequate guide to semantics; the individuation is independent of the language although it is expressed in the language.

Quine then attempts to show that the phenomenon of deferred ostension, or deferred reference, permits the substitution of one model for another as the interpretation of a natural language. But his analysis of the way deferred reference actually works in a natural language is faulty. Following Nunberg, let us call the apparent referent (e.g., the gas gauge in Quine's example) the *demonstratum*, and the deferred referent (e.g., the gas level in the tank) the *referent*. Then let us define a "referring function" F that maps the physical demonstratum into the referent. Let *a* be the demonstratum and let *b* be the referent, and let B be the "range of reference" determined by "the nature of the predication, and by the conversational context."[102] That is, to use Nunberg's example, if, pointing at a copy of a newspaper, I say "Hearst bought that for $50,000,000," we know that F must be a function from newspapers to expensive things. Then a given function F: X → Y allows the derivation of a referring function only if:

1. The hearer would be expected to know that $a \varepsilon X$ (and would know that he was expected to know, and so on . . .)

2. The hearer would be expected to know that $Y \cap B \neq \emptyset$.

3. Given a demonstratum *a*, and a range of reference B, and a given function F:X → Y such that $Y \cap B \neq \emptyset$, and an intended reference $b \varepsilon B \cap Y$, F allows the derivation of a RF [referring function] only if the set A of all values of F^{-1} (b) is manifestly discriminable from the set of things that are not values of F^{-1} (b).[103]

Condition 1 simply requires that the hearer know that $a \varepsilon X$, on whatever basis. Condition 2 requires that the intended referent *b* be in Y as well as B. Condition 3 says that for any demonstratum, the hearer must be able to distinguish it from other things like it for which the same function has different values. Thus one can point to a copy of the *New York Times* to refer to the New York Times Company, but one cannot intelligibly point to a magnifying glass made by McLeod to refer to the McLeod Company, because it is not "manifest" from casual inspection who manufactured that particular object.

Nunberg has shown that in certain cases what might be thought to be a perfectly adequate referring function may fail. For example, if one points at a copy of *Bleak House* and says, "He was sent to debtor's prison," intending thereby to refer to the father of Charles Dickens, the reference fails. Yet the function from authors to their fathers satisfies conditions 1, 2, and 3. The reason for the failure, as Nunberg shows, is that the following condition must also hold:

4. Given a demonstratum a ε A, and an intended referent b ε B', and given a possible RF [referring function] F such that F:A → B', F can be used in referring only if

    (a). If F is a prime function, and A ∩ B' ≠ ∅, and F(a) ε A ∩ B', then F = I.

    (b). If F is a composite function G o H such that H:A → C and G:C → B'. and C ∩ B' ≠ ∅ and H(a) ε C ∩ B', then G = I.[104]

where "I" is the identity function, B' is the intersection of B with Y, and a "prime function" may be taken to be one that is not composite. As Nunberg comments, "In fact, this condition is no more than the formalization of what has often been observed about metaphorical word uses: that a metaphorical interpretation is available only when a literal interpretation has been ruled out."[105] Thus whenever the referring function can be interpreted as the identity function, it must be so interpreted. A waitress can point at a ham sandwich on the counter and say "The ham sandwich is sitting at table 21"; here, the demonstratum cannot be the referent and the referring function is from order to orderer. But if she points at the sandwich and says, "The ham sandwich should be on rye," the referring function has to be the identity function because it can be.[106]

Deferred reference does not produce the sort of indeterminacy in a natural language that Quine thinks it does. The priority of the identity function sets strict limits on its use. Direct ostension obtains in all cases where it can obtain, given the context; deferred reference obtains only where direct reference is ruled out. The latter sort of case arises in two situations. The first is where the context makes direct reference impossible. The second is where the priority of the identity function is explicitly suspended, as with ciphers or certain literary uses. But in natural languages the priority of the identity function obtains. Ontological switches through the use of deferred reference, whether in the form of Godel numbers or proxy functions, may be logically possible, but they are not in fact possible in natural languages.

Natural languages are related to the world, conceived as a world of objects continuous in space and time, through ostensive definition. Direct ostension is the primary method of reference, with deferred ostension playing an important but secondary role. Of course, anthropologists must learn a great deal about the indigenous language before they understand those contexts that require deferred reference, but so must the child learner. Both, however, are able to learn the language because they can take determinate direct ostension as primary, and then master the use of deferred ostension as a derivative from direct ostension. Thus reference in natural languages is not indeterminate in the sense Quine claims. Natural languages are not formal theories, and the model theory of formal theories is not applicable to natural languages. Quine's claim for the ontological relativity of natural languages fails.

This, however, does not end the matter, for Quine can still point to multiple cases of ambiguous reference in English such as type-token ambiguities, or ambiguities between an abstract singular term and a concrete general one.[107]Moreover, Nunberg himself argues for the ambiguity of such sentences as, "Hearst bought a newspaper" and "We had chicken for dinner," and further argues that the referring functions available in a given language at a given time depend upon the whole world view of the culture. Referring functions like "publisher of," "author of," "manufacturer of," and the like are derived from the relations and institutions of specific cultures, and can vary from one to another. Relativity is not so easily evaded.[108]

Many philosophers, Quine among them, and most linguists have adhered to Frege's dictum that the sentence is the basic unit for the analysis of both reference and meaning. The reasonableness of this dictum is obvious. It is a commonplace that natural languages contain many words that, taken alone, are ambiguous. Thus, "bear" can refer to a large carnivore or to the act of carrying. It is also a commonplace that we can usually disambiguate a word by looking at its sentential context. Thus, in, "The bear ate the goat," it is obvious that "bear" refers to a large carnivore, while in, "We shall bear any burden . . . ," it is clearly a verb meaning to support or carry. The preference for the sentence over the word is thus well motivated; it reduces the risk of ambiguity. But it does not eliminate ambiguity. Consider, "Mary had a little lamb." This sentence could mean that Mary owned a young animal of a particular sort or that she ate a small portion of a particular kind of meat.[109] Many other examples of this phenomenon are well known: Chomsky's "Flying planes can be dangerous," Nunberg's "Hearst bought a newspaper," and so on. But this does not mean that these sentences are always ambiguous, any more than the problem with "bear" proves that every use of that word is ambiguous. Thus if these sentences are placed in a larger context, the ambiguity can be made to vanish. Consider:

> Mary had a little lamb.
> Its fleece was white as snow.
> And everywhere that Mary went
> The lamb was sure to go.

Here there is certainly no ambiguity. "Lamb" refers to a small, very young animal of a particular species, not a kind of meat. That the same thing is true for the other sentences is easily shown:

(1) You can get killed in a lot of ways. Driving cars can be dangerous. Flying planes can be dangerous.

Compare this to:

(2) Meteorites are not the only threat from the sky. Burned out satellites crash every day. Flying planes can be dangerous.

In the first case, the reference is clearly to the act of flying planes; in the second, to planes as flying objects. Again:

(3) Hearst bought a newspaper. He paid $50 million for it.

Compare it to:

(4) Hearst bought a newspaper. He wanted to check the weather report.

In the first case, the reference is obviously to the newspaper company; in the second to a particular copy of the paper. As these examples show, language is highly contextual. The interpretation of a sentence token depends heavily upon the (linguistic or other) context in which it is uttered.

Spoken language, as opposed to written language, also admits of disambiguation through phonological cues. Consider, for example, the sentence,

(5) Who did Peg want to drive to Vermont?

When the sentence is interpreted as, "Peg wants who to drive to Vermont," the "duration of the segment including 'want to' . . . is significantly longer" than when it is interpreted as "Peg wants to drive whom to Vermont?"[110] Moreover, there is experimental evidence that listeners use such cues in interpreting ambiguous sentences. Thus take the sentence,

(6) The hostess greeted the girl with a smile.

The prepositional phrase can be taken either as modifying "the girl" or as modifying the entire verb phrase.

> Lehiste et al. found that listeners were more likely to perceive the latter reading of this sentence when the interstress interval spanning the boundary between "girl" and "with" was lengthened, by virtue of expanding each segment of the string "girl with a smile."[111]

While not enough research has yet been done to know how effectively phonological cues effect disambiguation,[112] it is clear that they play an important part in this process. Unfortunately, such cues are not as often available for the analysis of written language.

If, with Halliday and Hasan, we understand the word "text" to "refer to any passage, spoken or written, of whatever length, that does form a unified whole," then "a text is best regarded as a *semantic* unit: a unit not of form but of meaning."[113] The multisentence units used above to disambiguate the three sentences are texts in this sense. Halliday and Hasan have given a detailed analysis of the ways in which such texts are unified, but the point here is that the unity of the text is semantic. This is the reason that in content analysis a sentence is never interpreted alone; it is always interpreted in terms of some larger block of sentences of which it is a part.

It is critical to emphasize here that while texts often disambiguate sentences, both with respect to reference and meaning, they need not do so. The text may be ill-formed. It may also be deliberately ambiguous, as is the case with many literary texts, where the author employs ambiguity as a literary device. *Moby Dick* is a mighty block of text, yet it is thoroughly and deliberately ambiguous. Literary critics have dealt extensively with this sort of intentional ambiguity and its uses. But we shall not be concerned here with deliberate ambiguity.

The point that must be stressed in the light of the preceding discussion is that in ordinary human discourse, whether written or spoken, sentences do not occur alone. Not even Faulkner ever wrote a one-sentence book, and spoken English consists of clumps of sentences, not of isolated pronouncements. In written English, the paragraph structure is usually used to deal with a specific topic; while the references of individual sentences within the paragraph may be ambiguous if "taken out of context," they are rarely so when taken in context. In spoken conversation, the turn-taking phenomenon often leads to single utterances by individual participants, but the conversation as a whole is unified by a topic or subject of discussion to which, as Grice has emphasized,[114] the contributions of the participants are expected to be relevant. Any ambiguous sentence can be rendered unambiguous by embedding it in an appropriate context.

But now of course we are off to the races. If the terms of a sentence token can undergo reinterpretation with respect to their reference when embedded in a text, the same is true of the text when embedded in a larger text. Thus

Mary had a little lamb.
Its fleece was white as snow.
And everywhere that Mary went
The lamb was sure to go.

Mary went to heaven;
The lamb went there before her.
Now she sits upon a throne
While angels all adore her.

The lamb has now become Jesus and Mary, the Virgin. Clearly, this sort of trick can be played endlessly by choosing suitable linguistic contexts in which to embed the given text. Thus we appear to achieve stability of reference only within the context of the total world view of the culture. This result was of course already suggested by Nunberg's theory of referring functions, but it should be made explicit. The "frame of reference," if one may borrow Quine's term, seems to be the world view, of which the language is only one part.

These considerations certainly appear to make overpowering the case for relativity. Nevertheless, I believe that this conclusion is false. We have in fact several very powerful tools for dealing with this problem. Suppose we return to Quine's case of the native and the anthropologist. We now know that they both confront a world of individuated objects that exhibit identity through time and space. We know this because we know that this way of conceptualizing the world is hardwired into the brain. Recalling Wittgenstein's remark—"The common behavior of mankind is the system of reference by means of which we interpret an unknown language"[115]—we know that the native speaks a natural language that is related to the world by ostensive definitions. Of course, the anthropologist recognizes that some of the native speaker's references may be deferred, but the privileged character of the identity function limits such deferrals to exceptional cases. Given that the usual ostensive reference is not deferred, the anthropologist can work out those that are, just as we do in English.

Thus to recur to the example of the gas gauge, if the reference were to the gauge, one would be surprised to see the driver pouring gas into the other end of the car. The fact that this action changes the reading of the gauge without the instrument itself being touched makes it quite clear that the gauge is an indicator of the amount of gas in the tank and that the reference is deferred. Similar considerations obtain with respect to such examples as the rabbit fly (which always accompanies rabbits in this land). True, when the native points at the fly and cries "gavagai," the anthropologist may be mightily confused. But when the native spears a rabbit rather than swatting a fly, our quick-witted scholar will suspect the truth. Furthermore, our anthropologist knows that since the natives are human, there will be many activities they must do (eating, drinking, sleeping, nursing, etc.) and about which they must communicate; hence, the anthropologist knows that their language will contain words for such activities. There is, in short, a very large area of commonality between the native and the anthropologist, which includes their biological and physical nature, a primitive conceptualization of the environment, certain uses to which objects must be put to satisfy basic needs, and the fact that their language must function in ways that permit them to describe their world and organize action with respect to it.

The point is not that the anthropologist has acquired a master key to the native's language, for he or she has not. The point is that the anthropologist has a place to start. Quite clearly, the anthropologist will have to learn the native's culture before ever hoping to master the various referring functions that obtain in it, and he will have to build up, step by step, an interpretation of the native language, starting with the most basic object, event, situation, and property terms and going on from there. But it is not true that everything is in the wind. Indeed this could not be true, or else no infant born into any society could ever master its culture or its language. If a language is to be learnable by an outsider—and an infant is an outsider to the linguistic system—it cannot be the case that one must know the whole language before one can learn any part of it. There has to be a place to start, and so indeed there is—objects, primitive object identity, ostensions, and the identity function as a privileged referring function. Add to that what the anthropologist knows of the common behavior that characterizes humankind as a matter of biological, physical, and cultural necessity, and the anthropologist has a foundation from which to build. Thus, in interpreting the native term as "identity of an object over time," which for Quine would be an arbitrary analytical hypothesis, the anthropologist can proceed on the assurance that the native has just such a concept of object identity and that the task is to identify it.

That the native speaker may elaborate the concept in ways strange to the anthropologist, as for example the Dorze of Ethiopia hold that the were-hyena can be in two different places simultaneously,[116] will create problems which will require adding more complex explanations to the gloss, but it should not be forgotten that speakers of English have believed God to be everywhere at once, so the idea is hardly unintelligible to them. Of course, it will take a long time to master metaphorical uses, humor, puns, irony, and the like, but it takes a child a long time to master such usages in its own language, too.

There is, however, a problem about learning a language which needs to be taken into account. Recent studies have shown that the optimal period for language learning is very early in life, and that one's mastery of a language varies inversely with the age at which the language was learned. This phenomenon has been demonstrated for the learning of both primary and secondary languages. The reason, as Newport has argued, is not that some magical childhood ability withers with age, but that the increase of cognitive and memory ability with age makes language learning harder. As Newport put it,

> In short, the hypothesis suggests that, because of age differences in perceptual and memorial abilities, young children and adults exposed to similar linguistic environments may nevertheless have very different internal data bases on which to perform a linguistic analysis. The young child's representation of the linguistic input will include many *pieces* of the complex forms to which she has been exposed. In contrast, the adult's representation of the linguistic input will include many more whole complex linguistic stimuli. The limitations of perception and memory in the child will make the analysis of at least certain parts of this system easier to perform. The adult's greater capabilities, and the resulting more complete storage of complex words and sentences, may make the crucial internal components and their organization more difficult to locate and may thereby be a counterproductive skill.[117]

The advantage of the child does not extend to all linguistic features; word order, for example, is as well learned late as early. The advantage seems to lie in those features of language which require analysis into components. Newport's argument is that the child, in learning to decompose the stream of acoustic stimuli from which language is learned, first picks out components rather than whole structures. "Young . . . children . . . typically produce only one or a few morphemes of a complex sign. This type of selective production and omission is characteristic of the child learner."[118] Thus, many words involve multiple components of form that must be mapped by the learner onto the components of meaning.

> With words that have even a small number of components of form and meaning, figuring out the right sized units of the linguistic pairing (that is, which components of form, or combination of components of form, consistently map onto which components, or combination of components, of meaning) is a surprisingly complex computational problem."[119]

The child, with more limited memorial and conceptual resources, perceives and stores only a limited number of components of form and meaning, greatly reducing the computational difficulties involved, while the adult, who perceives and stores whole words with all their components, faces a much more difficult problem. "If the system to be learned actually is morphological (that is, the system is one with morphemes smaller than the whole word . . .), it will be learned more readily with limited storage than with full storage of the whole word and its meaning."[120] As a result, late learners tend to acquire unanalyzed whole-word signs, which are then used inappropriately in "contexts where morphologically constructed forms are required."[121] They also show variable and inconsistent use of structures in which incorrect replacement of morphemes has occurred. Both sorts of errors point to problems of late learners in analyzing complex language structures. At the same time, late learners show much greater variability in success of language learning than do early learners.[122]

While the evidence supporting these finding is solid, it should be noted that the late learners studied were ordinary people without linguistic training. Our anthropologist, on the other hand, may be assumed to have studied linguistics and language acquisition, and so to be able to correct against the usual sorts of errors made by late learners. Newport's work does not show that late language learning is impossible; it shows that late learners, precisely because they have greater cognitive and memory ability, tend to make certain sorts of errors. The process of learning a second language may be more difficult for the adult than for the child, but it can be done, particularly when the learner understands what the difficulties are.

It is fashionable to view the relation of linguistic component to linguistic text in terms of what is called the "hermeneutic circle": that the meaning of a word (sentence, text) depends on the total linguistic context, and the meaning of the linguistic context depends on the meanings of the individual words (sentences, texts) that compose it. If this were the case in a strict sense—if a word had no meaning except as a part of the context and the context no meaning except that derived from its constituents—then it would be impossible to learn the language at all.

But the term "circle" is misapplied here. Consider again the case used for illustration above. A child learns the meaning of the word "lamb" first by ostension as a way of referring to an animal (or more usually these days as a way of referring to an animal referred to by a picture). The meaning of "lamb" as a kind of meat is parasitic on its use to refer to the animal; strictly, it means "meat of a lamb," and also depends on the use of "had" to mean "ate," as in, "I had eggs for breakfast." This use of "lamb" builds on the use learned by ostension. The tertiary meaning that appears in the longer poem is metaphoric. That interpretation depends on the alleged common attributes of a lamb and Christ and on the reading of "had" as "gave birth to," as in "Mary had a baby." What one sees happening here is an extension of the meaning and reference of a term by embedding it in contexts where the identity function cannot be the referring function. But the critical point is that a primary meaning of the word is acquired by ostension which can then be modified by embedding it in various linguistic contexts. It is not therefore true that the word has no meaning outside of its linguistic context.

It may be countered that the ostensive learning of a word is learning in a context. Quite so, but the ostensive learning context need not itself be a *linguistic* context. Pointing at an animal at which a child is looking and saying "lamb" is teaching the use of a linguistic sign, but the context itself is not linguistic. Animals and pointing fingers are not linguistic entities. Nor—by the definition given above—is reference itself either solely or primarily a linguistic phenomenon. One can refer to an object by pointing to it, gazing at it, reaching for it, drawing pictures of it, and in a variety of other ways. We first learn words by substituting them into non-linguistic contexts as more efficient ways of referring. Then we develop linguistic contexts by combining words. There is no circularity here; rather there is a process of learning by which we in time master the complexity of a language.

It seems, therefore, that in natural languages names and pronouns (and variables of a first-order language, if they are taken to be included in a natural language) can refer to, among other things, physical objects in the environment. The individuation of such objects does not depend upon language; the concept of the individuated object predates the acquisition of language and is determined by hardwired characteristics of the mind. Wholesale ontological permutations are ruled out by the role of ostensive definition and the privileged role of the identity function as a referring function. Most referring functions depend upon cultural knowledge, but given the priority of the identity function, the others are derivative; these arise in cases where the demonstratum cannot be the referent. Nothing prevents language learners from acquiring a basic stock of referential functions as they learn the beliefs of the culture. Contextual variations in reference presuppose literal understanding of the expressions in question, and are generated by the imperative in communication that sentences be intelligible.

In the foregoing I have treated the question of reference as a relation between a sign, a mind, and real objects. The assumption of real objects is fairly standard in semantics; most linguists have openly adopted the position of naive realism.[123] But this is surely not true of philosophers. Quine, for example, treats real objects as postulates to account for nerve stimulations; for him, contact with the "external world" boils down to nerve stimulations.[124] I agree with Quine as to the postulational character of real objects, but I disagree with his attempt to use nerve stimulations in this fashion. Indeed, Quine is here seeking to have the benefits of a sense-data theory without the suggestion of internal representations which sense data involves, and he tries to do it by translating sense data into nerve stimulations, which are, at least theoretically, observable in his behavioristic and physicalist sense. This move is not a successful one, for the real question is not which nerves are stimulated, because we are constantly besieged by nerve stimulations, but which stimulations we pay attention to. As I write, I am receiving nerve stimulations from every point on my body, and many points in it; 99 percent of these I ignore in order to concentrate on the paper in front of me. As James pointed out a century ago, attention is selective, and attention is not observable in a behavioristic sense. Two people, receiving identical nerve stimulations in a physical sense, may have quite different experiences because they attend to different stimuli. There is no way to define human experience in terms of nerve stimulations, and there is no way to make sense of human action without dealing with human experience.

Perceptual Judgments

Perception constitutes our interface with the world. Whatever the nature of the interaction between thought and external reality, it is mediated through perception. But human perception is no mere copying of what is "out there." Many philosophers and psychologists have held that perception is an inferential process. But this claim is ambiguous; it can refer to the process by which the percept is derived from neural stimulations, or to the status of the percept once it has been derived. If the former is meant, the claim is at least doubtful. We do not know the exact process by which the percept is created, but there seems to be no reason to hold that it conforms to any particular logical rules. Certainly a transformation occurs; the neural inputs are processed to yield the percept. As we have seen, there is evidence that a good deal of perception is carried out by modules that function automatically from the bottom up. But the fact that a mental process is at work does not mean that the process is an inferential process or that it has any logical character. The fact that so many perceptual processes seem constrained to yield a particular result is an argument against perception being a form of hypothetical inference.[125]

It is true that perception does not always yield a unique result. Two different sorts of cases need to be distinguished here. On the one hand, there are cases where perception appears to be cognitively penetrable. To cite one well-known example, Bruner did a tachistoscopic experiment using fake playing cards—spades colored bright red and hearts colored black. A mixture of fake and real cards was shown by tachistoscope for progressively longer periods until either they were correctly identified or a certain maximum exposure time was reached. As expected, subjects had a hard time with the fake cards, but what is particularly interesting is that some subjects reported seeing a purple spade or heart. Thus their cognitive knowledge regarding the true colors of such cards interacted with the actual stimulus to produce a percept representing a compromise between expectation and reality. As Bruner emphasized, exposure times were very short but the role of cognitive hypotheses, or "sets," in the resulting formation of the percept was clearly demonstrated.[126]

The other type of case is that of reversible figures—figures that can be seen alternately as either one of two quite distinct shapes, but that at any given moment are seen as either one or the other. For many subjects, these figures do not spontaneously reverse; as Rock has pointed out, some subjects have great difficulty in achieving a reversal.[127] But the point is that reversibility is possible. The duck–rabbit and the rat–man are well-known examples; the old woman–young woman is a somewhat more difficult one. These cases are interesting because they show that some perceptual stimuli admit of dual interpretations, although only alternately, not simultaneously. But they are arresting precisely because the phenomenon is rare; normally, the perceptual process results in a unique interpretation.

But the second interpretation of the claim that perception is inferential has considerably more foundation. First, as we have seen, perception sometimes produces illusions. What is important here is not that the illusions occur, but that we can tell that they are illusions. In the triangle illusion, for example, we see a white triangle, but we can and do reject the claim that there is a real triangle there. In these cases, therefore, the perceptual system presents us with a percept that we can treat as a hypothesis about the world and can reject. Second, suppose one enters a room and perceives a table standing in its center. There is no doubt that one does in fact perceive the table. Suppose further that one presses on the table, and find that one's hands pass through it without encountering resistance. One now has contradictory evidence, and can try further experiments, such as trying to walk through the table. Suppose one does walk through it without resistance. One will then reject the perceptual judgment that there is a table in the center of this room. But in doing so one affirms certain perceptual statements—that one felt no resistance from the table surface, that one experienced no resistance in walking through it. And one is also compelled to affirm that one saw a table of a given form and color at a given place in the room. These statements of what one did in fact experience at a given time one cannot reject; but one can and does reject the perceptual statement that there is a real table there. Nothing better shows the hypothetical character of the object than the fact that under these rather bizarre conditions one would reject its existence.

As this argument shows, there is a logical relation between our perceptual judgments of what is real (in the naive-realist sense) and our perceptual judgments about our own experience. If we assume that the objects we perceive are real, that assumption—together with certain physical laws—yields an explanation of our perceptual experience. Since our perceptions are normally perceptions of a world of solid objects in three dimensional space, our experience generally fits the naive-realist view of the world. Indeed, as we have already seen, there is good reason to believe that we are programmed to perceive a world of solid enduring physical objects. So long as our experience fits this view, we have no reason to question it, and do not. But when something goes wrong with that fit, we fall back on the analysis of what we have actually experienced. This is not an attempt to resurrect the given; there is no suggestion here that hypotheses may not have influenced our experience, as in the case of the purple spades, they obviously did. There is nothing more or less sensuous about one type of perceptual report than another. But there is a logical difference. Real-object statements explain our perceptual experience on the assumption that what we see is really there and causes the experience we have. This inference is automatic and uncontrollable in the usual case. But it is an inference nonetheless, and can be wrong.

Does it follow that every perceptual statement can be rejected? It does not, for one cannot reject the statements as to what one actually experienced at a given time. This has nothing to do with any questions of conditions of perception. Sellars's point that to say, "X is red," requires the stipulation of conditions of perception is here irrelevant,[128] for the type of statement that is in question is, "I see a red X now," and the truth or falsity of this statement is independent of any conditions of perception. When, for example, Bruner's subjects reported that they saw a purple spade, they were telling the truth, even though there was in fact no purple spade to be seen.

I know of only one argument that claims that reports of perceptual experience can be false, namely, Goodman's argument in "Sense and Certainty."[129] Goodman argues that on the basis of observation we can assert the following statements.

1. This patch is red at time t1.
2. This patch is blue at time t2.
3. This patch has not changed color from t1 to t2.

But Goodman says that these three sentences cannot all be true. Therefore, at least one of them must be false. We shall ignore here the issue of the time coordinates, since it seems clear that the sentences could be rephrased to avoid them. But note that for Goodman's argument to hold, all three statements must be perceptual reports. Then it is certainly true that the three statements are inconsistent, *if color matching is a transitive relation.* But if color matching is not a transitive relation, the moment-to-moment changes in the color of the patch may all lie below the threshold for a just-noticeable difference so that no change in color is perceived, yet the end points of the continuum may be easily discriminable. And Goodman himself has demonstrated that color matching is not a transitive relation.[130] Hence the argument from "Sense and Certainty" fails.

The point is not a trivial one. Experimental work on perception assumes that subjects can accurately report their perceptions. When Bruner's subjects found out that they had really been looking at a red spade, they did not deny that they had in fact seen the card as a purple spade. Similarly, when one sees a figure as a duck's head at one time, and subsequently sees it as a rabbit's head, one cannot truthfully deny that one had previously seen it as a duck's head. Such reports of what is experienced are indubitable, quite apart from any conditions of perception. Of course, it may turn out that what one saw was not there, but one cannot deny what one saw.

Or can one? What guarantees that such statements are beyond doubt? In one sense, they clearly are not; one could lie. But one cannot lie to oneself as one experiences one's own experience, and we may, under suitable conditions, assume that our subjects are not lying. How then are perceptual judgments related to experience? Perceptual experience, like all experience, simply *is*; taken as it is, it cannot be said to "correspond to the world" or to be right or wrong. Preformed or theory-laden as it may be, it is what we start from in inquiry; the problem is to explain it. Perceptual judgments are reports of what our experience is or was at a particular time.

Such judgments, taken not as statements about the "world" but as reports of experience, are attempts to formulate in language the character of our experience. Since any language has at most a finite vocabulary, perceptual judgments are always incomplete; we can say, "I saw a purple spade," but the exact shade of purple is not thereby captured. Such statements admit of refinement; one might correct the statement "I see a red chair" to "I see a rust-colored chair," thus getting a closer fit to the actual experience. Nevertheless, within the limits of language as a tool for description, we can and do formulate reports of our experiences such that, even if they do not tell everything we experienced, they do tell something. And since a perceptual judgment reports what one experienced at a particular time, what could contradict it? Any contradictory statement would have to deny that that experience occurred at that time. But what other evidence could there be as to one's experience at a particular time than one's own report of that experience? There can of course be a problem about our memories of such experiences, but that is a different problem.

Nothing said here should be taken as suggesting that such perceptual judgments are accurate descriptions of the "world." Goodman and many others have cited cases of apparent motion where for example two separate images flashed in quick succession are perceived as one figure in motion.[131] My point is that the judgment that one saw a single figure in motion is indubitable. That is a judgment about one's experience—about what one saw, not about the "world."

Natural languages are anchored in the perceptual world. We learn words for what we perceive, whatever the sensory modality. Our actions are planned in terms of this world, and our communication is based on the human necessity of coordinating action to deal with it. But the perceptual world is also a cultural world; we not only perceive rocks and plants and stars but cars, clothes, houses, stoves, and the things and behaviors of our culture. Granted that there is a hardwired base to perception, nevertheless the elaboration of that base is done by the culture, and the existence of cultural variation in belief, practice, artifacts, and feeling is beyond question.

Notes

1. Quine, "Epistemology Naturalized," 89–90.

2. Hilary Putnam, *Realism and Reason* (Cambridge: Cambridge University Press, 1985), 240–247.

3. William James, *The Principles of Psychology* (New York: Henry Holt and Co., 1910), vol. 1, ch. 9.

4. Quine, *Word and Object*, 223–225. W. V. Quine, "Mind and Verbal Dispositions" in Samuel Guttenplan, ed., *Mind and Language* (Oxford: Clarendon Press, 1975), 92–95.

5. W. V. Quine, *The Roots of Reference* (LaSalle, Ill.: Open Court, 1973), 35.

6. John M. Pearce, "Stimulus Generalization and the Acquisition of Categories by Pigeons" in L. Weiskrantz, ed., *Thought Without Language* (Oxford: Clarendon Press, 1988), 132–155. David Premack, "Minds With and Without Language" in Weiskrantz, *Thought*, 46–65.

7. Bernadette Bresard, "Primate Cognition of Space and Shapes" in Weiskrantz, *Thought*, 396–415.

8. Catherine Thinus-Blanc, "Animal Spatial Cognition" and Bresard, "Pri-

mate Cognition of Space and Shapes," in Weiskrantz, *Thought*, 371–395 and 396–415, respectively.

9. Premack, "Minds With and Without Language."

10. David Premack, *Gavagai!* (Cambridge, Mass.: MIT Press, 1986), 27.

11. Prosopagnosia in an inability to recognize faces, which can be congenital or due to brain damage.

12. Andrew W. Young, "Functional Organization of Visual Recognition" in Weiskrantz, *Thought*, 78–107.

13. Daniel L. Schacter, Mary Pat McAndrews, and Morris Moscovitch, "Access to Consciousness: Dissociations Between Implicit and Explicit Knowledge in Neuropsychological Syndromes" in Weiskrantz, *Thought*, 242–278.

14. Andrew Kertesz, "Cognitive function in Severe Aphasia" in Weiskrantz, *Thought*, 459.

15. Edoardo Bisiach, "Language Without Thought" in Weiskrantz, *Thought*, 465–466.

16. Eve V. Clark, "Meanings and Concepts" in John H. Flavell and Ellen M. Markman, eds., *Cognitive Development*, vol. 3 of Paul H. Mussen, gen. ed., *Handbook of Child Psychology* (New York: Wiley, 1983), 787–840.

17. Clark, "Meanings and Concepts," 788.

18. Elizabeth Spelke, "The Origins of Physical Knowledge" in Weiskrantz, *Thought*, 168–184.

19. Richard Held, "Binocular Vision—Behavioral and Neuronal Development" in Jacques Mehler and Robin Fox, eds., *Neonate Cognition* (Hillsdale, N.J.: Lawrence Erlbaum, 1985), 37–44. Michel Imbert, "Physiological Underpinnings of Perceptual Development" in Mehler and Fox, *Neonate Cognition*, 69–88.

20. Marc H. Bornstein, "Infant into Adult: Unity to Diversity in the Development of Visual Categorization" in Mehler and Fox, *Neonate Cognition*, 115–138.

21. Patricia K. Kuhl, "Categorization of Speech by Infants" in Mehler and Fox, *Neonate Cognition*, 231–262.

22. Jean Piaget, *The Construction of Reality in The Child* (New York: Basic Books, 1954), ch.1.

23. Adele Diamond, "Differences Between Adult and Infant Cognition: Is the Crucial Variable Presence or Absence of Language?" in Weiskrantz, *Thought*, 337–370.

24. Spelke, "Origins of Physical Knowledge," 176.

25. Elizabeth S. Spelke, "Perception of Unity, Persistence, and Identity: Thoughts on Infants' Conceptions of Objects" in Mehler and Fox, *Neonate Cognition*, 89–113. Renee Baillargeon, "Representing the Existence and the Location of Hidden Objects: Object Permanence in 6- and 8-Month Old Infants," *Cognition* 23:21–41 (1986). Claes von Hofsten and Elizabeth S. Spelke, "Object Perception and Object-Directed Reaching in Infancy," *Journal of Experimental Psychology: General* 114:198–212 (1985). Philip J. Kellman, Elizabeth S. Spelke, and Kenneth R. Short, "Infant Perception of Object Unity from Translatory Motion in Depth and Vertical Translation," *Child Development* 57:72–86 (1986). Renee Baillargeon, Elizabeth S. Spelke, and Stanley Wasserman, "Object Permanence in Five-Month Old Infants," *Cognition* 20:191–208 (1985).

26. Spelke, "Origins of Physical Knowledge," 180.

27. Ibid., 181.

28. Weiskrantz, *Thought*, 496.

29. Kalvis M. Jansons, "A Personal View of Dyslexia and of Thought Without Language" in Weiskrantz, *Thought*, 498–503.

30. Anne Roe, *The Making of a Scientist* (New York: Dodd, Mead and Co., 1953).

31. Nelson Goodman, *Languages of Art* (Indianapolis: Bobbs-Merrill, 1968).

32. Ludwig Wittgenstein, *Philosophical Investigations* (Oxford: Basil Blackwell, 1953), Part 1, §§68–71.

33. Eleanor Rosch and Carolyn B. Mervis, "Family Resemblances: Studies in the Internal Structure of Categories," *Cognitive Psychology* 7:573–605 (1975). Eleanor Rosch, "On the Internal Structure of Perceptual and Semantic Categories" in Timothy E. Moore, ed. *Cognitive Development and the Acquisition of Language* (New York; Academic Press, 1973), 111–144. Daniel N. Osherson and Edward E. Smith, "On the Adequacy of Prototype Theory as a Theory of Concepts," *Cognition* 9:35–58(1981). Edward E. Smith and Daniel N. Osherson, "Conceptual Combination with Prototype Concepts," *Cognitive Science* 8:337–361 (1984).

34. Hilary Putnam, *Mind Language and Reality* (Cambridge: Cambridge University Press, 1984), 249.

35. Edward E. Smith and Douglas L. Medin, *Categories and Concepts* (Cambridge, Mass.: Harvard University Press, 1981), 83–84.

36. Sharon Lee Armstrong, Lila R. Gleitman and Henry Gleitman, "What Some Concepts Might Not Be," *Cognition* 13:263–308 (1983).

37. Armstrong, Gleitman, and Gleitman also used "female" as a concept for which a classical definition should be well known. However, the actual examples used are roles more or less commonly associated with females. It is not clear that a graded response should not have been expected in this case.

38. Ibid., 290.

39. David Kelley and Janet Krueger, "The Psychology of Abstraction," *Journal for the Theory of Social Behavior* 14:43–67 (1984).

40. Armstrong et al., "What Some Concepts," 291.

41. Quine, *Roots of Reference*, 19.

42. Nelson Goodman, *The Structure of Appearance* (Cambridge, Mass.: Harvard University Press, 1951), 237.

43. Frank C. Keil, *Concepts, Kinds, and Cognitive Development* (Cambridge, Mass.: MIT Press, 1989), chs. 8–11.

44. Ibid., 200.

45. Ibid., 230.

46. Ibid., 281.

47. Jean Piaget, *The Child's Conception of Physical Causality* (New York: Harcourt Brace and Co., 1930).

48. A. Michotte, *The Perception of Causality* (New York: Basic Books, 1963), 85–86.

49. Ibid., 85, 109, 159.

50. Jerome S. Bruner, *Beyond the Information Given* (New York: W. W. Norton and Co., 1973), 68–82.

51. Zenon W. Pylyshyn, *Computation and Cognition* (Cambridge, Mass.: MIT Press, 1986), 134–135.

52. Irvin Rock, *The Logic of Perception* (Cambridge, Mass.: MIT Press, 1985), 104ff.

53. David Marr, *Vision* (New York: W. H. Freeman and Co., 1982), ch. 3.

54. Jerry A. Fodor, *Modularity of Mind* (Cambridge, Mass.: MIT Press, 1983).

55. Alan M. Leslie, "The Necessity of Illusion: Perception and Thought in Infancy" in Weiskrantz, *Thought*, 185–210.

56. Ibid.

57. Ibid.

58. Ibid., 198.

59. Ibid. Spelke, "Origins of Physical Knowledge."

60. Clark, "Meanings and Concepts."

61. Ibid., 820.

62. Ibid., 820–832.

63. Ellen M. Markman, "Constraints Children Place on Word Meanings," *Cognitive Science* 14:57–77 (1990), 59.

64. Ibid., 66.

65. Ibid., 72.

66. There are unresolved problems here about levels of generality. "Basic level" terms (e.g., "dog") are acquired before terms of either greater generality (animal) or lesser generality (spaniel), yet all of these terms may apply to the same object. See Lila R. Gleitman, Henry Gleitman, Barbara Landau, and Eric Wanner, "Where Learning Begins: Initial Representations for Language Learning" in F. J. Newmeyer, ed., *Linguistics: The Cambridge Survey, vol. 3. Language: Psychological and Biological Aspects* (New York: Cambridge University Press, 1988), 172ff.

67. Clark, "Meanings and Concepts," 831.

68. Ibid., 825.

69. Jerrold J. Katz, *Semantic Theory* (New York: Harper and Row, 1972), 74.

70. Ibid., 74.

71. Ibid., 74–76.

72. John Lyons, *Semantics* (Cambridge: Cambridge University Press, 1986), vol. 2, 442.

73. Wittgenstein, *Philosophical Investigations*, Part 1, §16.

74. Nancy Katz, Erica Baker and John Macnamara, "What's in a Name? A Study of How Children Learn Common and Proper Names," *Child Development* 45:469–473 (1974), 469.

75. Ibid., 473.

76. Markman, "Constraints."

77. Gareth Evans, "Identity and Predication," *Journal of Philosophy* 72:343–363 (1975).

78. Peter Gordon, "Evaluating the Semantic Categories Hypothesis: The Case of the Count/Mass Distinction," *Cognition* 20:209–242 (1985). Peter Gordon, "Count/Mass Category Acquisition: Distributional Distinctions in Children's Speech," *Journal of Child Language* 15:109–128 (1988).

79. Quine, *Roots of Reference*, 86.

80. Bertrand Russell, "On Denoting," *Mind* 14:479–493(1905).

81. Saul A. Kripke, *Naming and Necessity* (Cambridge, Mass.: Harvard University Press, 1980), 48.

82. Putnam, *Mind*, 198ff.

83. Kripke, *Naming and Necessity*, 48.

84. Ibid., 91–93, 135–136.

85. Ibid., 6.

86. David Kaplan, "Quantifying In," *Synthese* 19:178–214 (1968).

87. Wittgenstein, *Philosophical Investigations*, Part 2, §iii. See Roderick M. Chisholm, *The First Person* (Minneapolis: University of Minnesota Press, 1981), 3, n1).

88. Hao Wang, *Beyond Analytic Philosophy* (Cambridge, Mass.: MIT Press,1986), 8.

89. Quine, "Ontological Relativity," 26–68.

90. Ibid., 28.

91. Ibid., 29.

92. W. V. Quine, "On the Reasons for Indeterminacy of Translation," *Journal of Philosophy* 67:178–183 (1970).

93. Quine, *Word and Object*, ch. 2. W. V. Quine, "Ontological Relativity."

94. Ibid., 35.

95. Ibid., 38–40.

96. Ibid., 41.

97. Ibid., 42.

98. Ibid., 47–48.

99. Ibid., 49.

100. Ibid., 50.

101. Ibid., 37.

102. Geoffrey D. Nunberg, "The Pragmatics of Reference," Ph.D. diss., City University of New York, 1977, 56.

103. Ibid., 57–59.

104. Ibid., 69.

105. Ibid., 121n4.

106. Ibid., 63.

107. Quine, "Ontological Relativity," 40.

108. Nunberg, *Pragmatics of Reference*, 10–13 and ch. 3.

109. The example is Quine's, *Word and Object*, 91.

110. William E. Cooper and Jeanne Paccia-Cooper, *Syntax and Speech* (Cambridge, Mass.: Harvard University Press, 1980), 159–160.

111. Ibid., 214.

112. Ibid., 213.

113. M. A. K. Halliday and Ruqaiya Hasan, *Cohesion in English* (London: Longman Group, 1976), 1–2.

114. Paul Grice, "Logic and Conversation," in *Syntax and Semantics* vol. 3, Peter Cole and Jerry L. Morgan, eds., *Speech Acts* (New York: Academic Press, 1975), 47–48.

115. Wittgenstein, *Philosophical Investigations*, Part 1, §206.

116. Dan Sperber, *Rethinking Symbolism* (Cambridge: Cambridge University Press, 1974), 131.

117. Elissa L. Newport, "Maturational Constraints on Language Learning," *Cognitive Science* 14:26 (1990).

118. Ibid., 23.

119. Ibid., 24.

120. Ibid., 25.

121. Ibid., 23.

122. Ibid., 11–28. Jacqueline S. Johnson and Elissa L. Newport, "Critical Period Effects in Second Language Learning: The Influence of Maturational State on the Acquisition of English as a Second Language," *Cognitive Psychology* 21: 60–99 (1989).

123. Lyons, *Semantics*, vol. 2, 442.

124. Quine, *Word and Object*, 31–35.

125. Cf. David Kelley, *The Evidence of the Senses* (Baton Rouge: Louisiana State University Press, 1986).

126. Bruner, *Beyond the Information Given*, 68–82.

127. Rock, *Logic of Perception*, 78.

128. Wilfrid Sellars, *Science, Perception and Reality* (London: Routledge and Kegan Paul, 1963), 147.

129. Nelson Goodman, "Sense and Certainty" in *Problems and Projects* (Indianapolis: Bobbs-Merrill, 1972), 60–68.

130. Goodman, *Structure of Appearance*, 237.

131. Nelson Goodman, *Ways of Worldmaking* (Indianapolis: Hackett Publishing Co., 1978), 15–16.

Chapter 2

Other Minds and
Intersubjective Knowledge

Even if the theories advanced in Chapter 1 are granted, Premises (3) and (4) are hardly secure; both assume the truth of Premise (2): "There are other persons who have minds." Part of the issue here is what "mind" means. In the present chapter, we explore the child's development of a theory of mind, which is very much the theory of mind of our common-sense so-called "folk psychology." Young children learn to think about minds in terms of mental states, such as beliefs, which they understand as playing causal roles in the explanation of behavior—their own as well as that of others. In other words, their concept of mind is not egocentric; there is no problem of "other" minds in this theory because the theory of mind as it is developed applies to both the self and other persons. This theory holds mental states to be real and causally effective, so that support for the theory as a whole is support for these claims.

Nevertheless, the problem of intersubjective knowledge—of how we know what others feel and think—remains a genuine issue. I argue that, the privacy of experience notwithstanding, intersubjective knowledge is possible although it is to a considerable extent theoretical knowledge, and is also in part a matter of degree. A mental state such as pain is not less intersubjectively knowable than that something is red or hard; phenomena such as dreams and visions are also describable in a public language and can be objects of intersubjective knowledge, although assertions about them are less secure than those concerning pain. I also argue that thoughts expressed in language are intersubjectively knowable. The most powerful argument against this possibility is Quine's claim of the Indeterminacy of Translation. As I argue at some length, I believe that Quine's argument is erroneous. Thus I hope that this and the preceding chapter serve to warrant Premises (2), (3), and (4), and, at least in part, (7).

A Theory of Mind

The cognitive revolution in psychology, which led to the development of "cognitive science" and "cognitive psychology," has been an attempt "to demonstrate that behavior is a function of representations of the world rather than of the world directly."[1] This attempt has led to the formulation of theories of cognitive functioning—of "mind"—in which mental states such as beliefs, desires, intentions, and feelings, and mental processes such as perception, thinking, and inference, play causal roles in the explanation of what people do and say. Such theories are a far cry from the sort of behaviorism which at one time held so great a sway in psychology.[2] They are mentalist theories in that they assert the existence of mental states and processes that are causally effective.

Such theories have been derided by some on the ground that they are "folk psychology." In so far as such remarks are intended to suggest that these theories are not scientific, they are mistaken. Unless one holds on dogmatic grounds that any theory postulating mental entities is unscientific, careful examination of the literature in this field should be sufficient to refute such a charge.

But there is another sense in which the charge has some truth to it, for one finding of cognitive science is that people do employ mentalist theories in their efforts to explain and predict the behavior of others and of themselves. Such "meta-cognitive" studies—studies of the theories people hold about cognition and mental functioning—are relatively new, but a great deal of work has been done since 1975 on these issues, much of it focusing on the development of such theories in children. These studies have a particular interest. Insofar as our goal is to find out how we know what we know, these studies fulfill that objective. They show when and how such theories first emerge and how they are used. They further show that quite young children have concepts of the mental states of themselves and others. Moreover, these studies demonstrate that such theories are used to explain and predict behavior. And they show that the process of development of such theories of mind is not egocentric; explaining others's mental states and explaining one's own are part of one enterprise. The development of a theory of mind is also the development of a theory of other minds; there is no separate problem of the existence of other minds.

At the same time, this psychological work leaves certain questions unanswered. It may be true, as these studies show, that mental states—one's own or those of others—are postulated to explain and predict speech and behavior, but one also seems to have an access to one's own mental phenomena which one does not have to that of others. When I have a toothache, it would be idiotic to say that I only surmise that I have the pain from observing my own behavior and speech. In other words, there appears to be a difference in the empirical basis on which one attributes mental states to oneself and to others. This is of course the hoary philosophic problem of intersubjective knowledge; how can one know that what one knows or feels is similar to what another knows or feels? The problem is inescapable because the possibility of communication depends upon its solution. But before plunging into this philosophic quicksand, it is important to examine some of the psychological work that has been done on the development of theories of mind.

One of the most important experimental results in this field is the false-belief experiment. Suppose two children, Sue and Ann, are in a room where there is a table on which there are two boxes, A and B, and a marble. Sue places the marble in Box A and leaves the room. The experimenter, with Ann watching, takes the marble out of Box A and places it in Box B. Ann is then asked to predict in which box Sue will look for the marble when she re-enters the room. Note what this experiment requires of Ann: She must be able to predict Sue's behavior, not on the basis of where the marble really is, but on the basis of where Sue believes the marble is. That is, Ann must attribute to Sue a belief that does not correspond to the facts, and predict Sue's behavior on the basis of that attributed belief state. Children as young as four are able to succeed in this experiment; children younger than four are not. Why not?[3]

Alan Leslie has been one of the leaders in the work on the cognitive development of young children. Leslie has shown that by the age of two, children are capable of pretending. Not only do they pretend in their own play, but they understand that they are pretending. When a child pretends that her doll has a dirty face and proceeds to wash it, the child understands that the doll's face is not really dirty, and that the pretend situation is not the real situation. Moreover, two-year-olds understand that others pretend. When the mother pretends that a banana is a telephone, the child recognizes that mother is pretending and cheerfully joins the game.[4] It is therefore quite clear that by age two, the child is capable of differentiating a pretend situation from a real one, recognizing the pretense as such, and of recognizing pretense in another. The structural analogy to the false-belief situation is obvious. Why then cannot the two-year-old pass the false-belief test?

Leslie comments,

> My proposals for understanding these phenomena come down to two points: First, that the development of a theory of mind depends on *specific* innate mechanisms, and, second, that these mechanisms are at work very early in life in generating *pretend* play.[5]

Leslie points out that there are three basic types of pretense: object substitution (a banana for a telephone), pretend attribution of properties (the doll's face is dirty), and imaginary objects (a pretend companion). These three forms involve distortions of normal reference, truth, and existence relations. These distortions correspond to the semantic properties of propositions that express the content of mental states: they are referentially opaque, truth–falsehood implications are suspended, and existence is not implied. Thus in, "John believed that the cat was ill," the sentence in indirect discourse is referentially opaque, neither its truth nor its falsity is asserted, and the existence of the cat is not implied. This correspondence leads Leslie to propose that the child has "meta-representations" of the form "agent—informational relation—'expression'"[6] where the quotation marks indicate that the expression is "decoupled"—i.e., removed from its normal semantic relations, just as expressions in indirect discourse are. In short,

> The meta-representational theory defines the ability to pretend (and understand pretense in others) as the power to compute a three-term function *pretend* $(a, "e_i," e_j)$, where a ranges over agents, "e_i" is a decoupled expression and e_j a primary representation (e.g., of the current perceived situation to which "e_i" is related).[7]

It is the decoupling mechanism that Leslie takes to be innate.

How is this mechanism activated? Leslie points to certain "mannerisms" which seem to be critical for engaging in shared pretense. Among these are "knowing looks and smiles," certain vocal intonations, and certain very exaggerated gestures.[8] Little attention has been given to these mannerisms nor to how they are acquired, if indeed they are acquired. Even less seems to be known about the conditions that lead to individual pretense. As Leslie notes, telling children to pretend does not produce the desired activity.[9] But it is important to note that by two years of age children are able to recognize pretend behavior in others and to enter into shared pretend activities. The development of the decoupling mechanism seems to involve the recognition of its existence and function in others.

By the age of three, Leslie argues, the child not only can pretend but also can make its pretense an object of thought. Furthermore, it can recognize that some of its prior beliefs are false. Yet the child still fails the false belief test described above. This is not because children at that age lack the notion of causality, for as we saw above Leslie has shown that two-year-olds understand the idea of causation and employ it in pretend play.[10] The critical point, Leslie believes, is that until the age of approximately four, the child does not recognize mental states as causes of behavior. Because children first develop the notion of causation as applying to material objects, it is difficult for them to recognize that mental states also can be causally effective in the physical world, and can be caused by events in the physical world. Leslie suggests that it is the child's developing understanding of perception that creates these connections. What four-year-old Ann must recognize is that Sue's belief that the marble is in Box A is the result of her having placed it there but not having seen it moved. It is the understanding that Sue's beliefs are a consequence of her perceptions and that her actions are consequences of her beliefs that are crucial for passing the false-belief text. As Leslie urges, too, it is important that at four the child is first able to make the distinction between appearance and reality, which also depends upon the recognition that beliefs are caused by perception.[11]

By age four, Leslie believes, the child has at least a rudimentary theory of mind in which mental states, taken as real, function as part of the causal structure of the world. Of course, this theory will be enriched and elaborated as the child grows, but the basic elements are there by four years of age. Leslie draws no great distinction between the child's coming to understand its own mental states and its coming to understand those of others; these occur simultaneously, and as part of the general process of coming to understand that mental states are real and part of the causal order. It is, however, important to note that for Leslie the term "meta-representation" is defined by the schema "agent—informational relation—'expression'." This is a different use of the term than occurs in some of the alternative theories, to which we must now turn.

Heinz Wimmer and his colleagues take a somewhat different view. According to them, "The capability for meta-representation implies an understanding that representations can be true or false, and an explicit conceptualization of at least some of the relationships a person can take toward representations (e.g., pretending that x or wanting that x)."[12] Children in their view have this capacity by the age of two, but until the age of four children "have no idea of where knowledge or belief come from."[13] It is this lack of an understanding of the informational origins of belief that Wimmer et al. see as underlying the failure of younger children to pass the false-belief test or to distinguish appearance from reality. This does not mean that children under four do not understand that people see, hear, touch, etc. But Wimmer and his colleagues emphasize the difference between seeing, hearing, etc., as physical processes and as epistemic processes. Two-year-olds can see that someone is looking at an object; they understand that noises are heard and that others also hear; they can observe when someone touches an object, or sniffs it, or licks it. But this is a recognition of a physical relation between objects. What the two-year-olds do not understand is that these relations are sources of information, of knowledge for the observed.[14]

Wimmer and his co-researchers describe an experiment in which two children were seated on opposite sides of a table on which there was a closed box containing an ordinary object. The pairs of children were ages three, four, and five. One of the two children was given access to the contents of the box, either by being allowed to look into it or by having the information whispered to him. When the information was then given to the other child, the first subject observed the process by which it was given, knew what the process was, and knew what was in the box. The subject children were asked, "Does (name of other child) know what is in the box or does she not know that?"[15] Most of the three-year-olds and some four-year-olds said the other child did not know what was in the box, even when the other had either looked into it or been told by the experimenter. Some three year olds who had had no informational access and did not know what was in the box themselves also claimed to know. Five-year-olds, on the other hand, were able to answer these questions correctly.

These results Wimmer et al. interpret as showing that the children did not understand the informational origins of belief. The fact that the children were more often right about their own knowledge than about the other child's knowledge Wimmer sees as due to the fact that being right about one's own knowledge only requires the functioning of perception, whereas being right about another's knowledge requires understanding the relation of perception to knowledge.[16] One should note here that children first discover the informational origins of belief in other children and then apply this discovery to themselves. It is having to account for what another does that makes children aware of their own mental processes.

This theory does account for the false-belief test. If Ann does not understand the origin of Sue's belief that the marble is in A, there is no reason for her not to think Sue will look for the marble in B, where it really is.

The theory can also be used to account for the emergence of the appearance–reality distinction at the same age that the false-belief test is passed. Flavell's famous experiment, in which a child is shown a sponge that looks like a rock, is for Wimmer et al. a question of understanding that a belief derived from visual perception can be falsified by information acquired by touch.[17] But Wimmer and colleagues also explored when children recognize that belief can be acquired by inference. In an experiment that contrasted obtaining knowledge by perception with obtaining it by inference, both by the subject and by the other child, four-year-olds denied the other child's knowledge unless the other child had had perceptual access, while six-year-olds attributed knowledge to others when there was inferential access but not perceptual access. Again, children more readily claimed knowledge for themselves than for the other, because according to Wimmer the former required only the functioning of inference whereas the latter required understanding the relation between inference and belief.[18]

In numerous articles and a recent book, Henry Wellman has advanced a theory of the development of children's theory of mind which is able to deal with the false-belief problem but which is more comprehensive than those of Leslie and Wimmer. According to Wellman, two-year-old children do not understand the concept of belief;[19] however, they do have a concept of desire, but a non-representational one—desire is construed simply as someone wanting an object.[20] They also understand that desire causes action.[21] By the age of three, the child has acquired the concept of belief[22] and understands both belief and desire as representational. Moreover, by age three, according to Wellman, the child can both predict and explain actions on the basis of belief and desire,[23] so its notion of the causal role of belief and desire is well established.[24] Furthermore, as against Wimmer, Wellman holds that the three-year-old does understand the informational origin of belief in perception.[25]

But Wellman believes that the three-year-old child's representational theory of belief and desire is a copy theory—that is, the child understands that his representation of an object is an entity distinct from the referent, but one that "copies" it and so can stand for the referent. At the same time, the child can form representations of hypothetical or fictional entities (e.g., unicorns), although it is not entirely clear in these cases in what sense the representation is a copy. This concept of representation as a copy permits also a concept of misrepresentation, but only in the sense that the representation fails to provide a copy of the intended object—what Wellman calls "hit or miss" representation. Thus Wellman describes the three-year-old's understanding of mental phenomena as follows:

My contention is that three-year-olds understand ideas, beliefs, mental images, dreams, and such to be representational. They understand some of these to be fictional and some to be reality-oriented representations, but in each case representational. Hence it is incorrect to say they do not have a representational understanding of mind. However, their representational understanding of reality-oriented representations is a copy understanding.[26]

The three-year-old accordingly has a genuine theory of mind of the belief and desire variety, but despite this considerable accomplishment it still lacks the full understanding of representations which characterizes the older child and the adult.

Why then do three-year-olds fail the false-belief test? Wellman's answer is because they have a direct copy understanding of belief.

Children were shown a Smarties box (a distinctive candy box well known to British children) and asked what it contained. All said Smarties. They were then shown they were wrong and that the box actually contained a pencil. Next they were asked about a friend waiting in the hall. "What will she think is in here?" Notice that in this task no desire is attributed to the friend . . . and if anything the child is likely to think the friend will want Smarties, not a pencil. Second, the child is not asked to predict action; he is simply asked to say what his friend will think. Three-year-olds (M = 3–5, range 3–1 to 3–9) failed this task; they were correct only 45% of the time. . . . I think they fail because they have a direct copy understanding of belief. When asked about the content of their friend's belief, they know that belief is a reality-oriented representation, and hence a direct copy of reality; therefore their friend thinks there is a pencil in the box.[27]

Knowing what is really in the Smarties box, the three-year-old assumes his friend's belief about the contents of the box will match the real contents— hence he fails to understand that his friend upon seeing the box will think it contains Smarties.

The transition from this early theory of mind, which cannot deal with the false-belief problem, to the more adequate theory of mind which can do this comes, according to Wellman, at about four years of age, and involves a shift both in the child's conceptualization of the mind itself and in its understanding of representation. As Wellman puts it, "The earliest theory of mind—that of three-year-olds—can be seen as having a containerlike nature; the later theory of mind—that of somewhat older children and adults—can be seen as having a homunculuslike nature."[28] The "homunculus" model Wellman considers as the everyday way of describing an information-processing view of mind.[29] This change in turn is the product of a new understanding of representation, in which an interpretative concept of representation replaces the earlier copy theory.[30] The mind is now viewed as an active interpreter of reality, which processes information to create a construal of what is there. It is this development that enables children to understand that their friend's belief can be false since his friend interprets the Smarties box as having a different content than they do.

Josef Perner has advanced a rather different theory of the mental development of children, one which is also adequate for dealing with the false-belief problem. Perner emphasizes the difference between what he calls a "situation" theory and a representational theory. Drawing upon Frege and Goodman, Perner defines a representation as having both a reference and a sense—that is, it is not only a representation *of* something but it represents its referent *as* something.[31] A primary-level representation or model is a representation of the situation that the child perceives; for the very young child, it *is* itself the real situation. This model does not permit discrepant information; a change in the real situation leads to the updating of the model by incorporating new information and discarding old.[32] But by one and a half years of age, the child begins to employ multiple models that include representations of other situations—past situations and hypothetical situations such as arise in pretense. These secondary-level representations are still representations of situations, but those situations can be distinguished from and contrasted with the real situation. Such ability to manipulate multiple models enables the child—even the very young child—to distinguish between true and false statements, but, according to Perner, the child's understanding of "true" and "false" is not metarepresentational but situational.

> My contention is that young children are not aware of (do not model) the fact that the statement has an interpretation and a referent. All they know is how to treat a yes-no question, namely, by comparing the described situation with reality. . . . These examples are intended to demonstrate that the child need not understand her "No" answer as a meta-representational judgment of truth on a false statement. From her point of view the "No" simply marks disagreement between the situation described by the statement and the perceived situation.[33]

As Perner understands the term "metarepresentation," a representation can only be a metarepresentation if it is a representation that refers to the relation between a representation and its referent.[34] Thus the sort of representations discussed above are not metarepresentational in this sense, because although they refer to particular situations, they are not models of the representation relation itself; they do not refer to the relation of the model to its referent, but only to the referent. For Perner, a metarepresentation is about representations conceived as representations. Such metarepresentations, Perner believes, are achieved by the child at about the age of four, and it is the development of this capacity to use metarepresentations which Perner sees as critical for the passage of the false-belief test. Thus, referring to what he calls "the *puzzle of false belief*," Perner says

> The representational view of mind solves this puzzle in an elegant way. For instance, in our experiments the child can understand that Maxi experiencing himself putting the chocolate inside the green cupboard forms a representation of the chocolate as being there. Then the chocolate is moved without Maxi being informed about it. Lacking information about its new location, Maxi keeps representing the chocolate as being in its original location. When Maxi looks for the chocolate, the representational view implies that when he is aiming at acting according to the real situation, he will be guided by his *representation of the real situation* and not by the real situation directly. But Maxi's mental representation misrepresents the real situation as a different situation ("chocolate still in GREEN cupboard"), which explains why he acts as-if the real situation were a different one despite his aiming at the real situation.[35]

Children before the age of four—before they develop metarepresentations—are for Perner situation theorists, but do not have a genuine theory of mind, for although the children use mental representations, they do not conceptualize them as representations. The advent of metarepresentations, however, means that the children can now think about their own representations and processes of thinking; at that point Perner believes it is proper to say that the child does have a real theory of mind.[36]

These examples are by no means exhaustive of the literature in this highly controversial field. Other theories argue that the development of the child's theory of mind begins earlier and is completed later than the theories here discussed allow.[37] Still others argue that recursion is the key to understanding mental life.[38] But these four studies should be sufficient to bring out certain essential points. First, whether or not the development of a theory of mind is based on innate mechanisms of the sort postulated by Leslie, everyone agrees on approximately the same sequence in the child's development—that is, that the abilities emerge at specifiable ages. It may well be, as Chandler argues,[39] that psychologists have been so concerned with not ascribing to children more capacities than they actually have that they have tended to make the requirements for attribution too strict, thus failing to credit children with capacities as early as these actually appear. Nevertheless, there is very high agreement among the researchers on the actual experimental findings as to what capacities the child has and at what age.

Second, although before the end of the second year, a child differentiates animate objects from inanimate ones and understands the capacity of the former to operate on their own,[40] there is at least no very hard evidence of the child's understanding mental states until roughly the age of two, by which time language is being acquired. Young children use terms for mental states, e.g., "think," "know," etc., very early, but it is not clear what two-year-olds mean by these terms.

Third, children's development of a theory of mind is not egocentric; rather, their grasp of the relevant concepts involves their application both to themselves and to others at roughly the same time. In fact, as we have seen, it is arguable that in certain cases the child first becomes aware of a given mental phenomenon in others and then uses that knowledge to understand himself. Thus between four and six children learn to distinguish between real and apparent emotions. Harris and Gross believe that this distinction is first brought home to children by discovering that another's beliefs about their emotions can be in error, and can be manipulated by such methods as facial display.[41] But whether metacognitive concepts are first learned with respect to others and then applied to oneself, or vice versa, or whether some are acquired in the former way and some in the latter, it is clear that these concepts are applied to both the self and to others at approximately the same time.

As Olson, Astington, and Harris put it

> So what is a theory of mind? The events to be explained and predicted are talk and action (some would say behavior). The theoretical concepts are those of *belief, desire, intention,* and *feeling.* And third, these concepts may be used to explain and predict the events in the referential domain, namely, talk and action. Finally, if the theory provides the best explanation and prediction of the events in the referential domain, the entities specified by the theoretical terms may be treated as real entities.[42]

The work here described shows that children do very rapidly acquire such a theory of mind, which is the basic common-sense theory of mind used by adults. While it is not possible at this point to say how much of this development is due to innate factors and how much is learned, what cross-cultural data there are indicate that the timetable of emergence is very robust.[43] Everything currently known suggest that, in forming their theories of mind, children draw both upon their own experience and upon the need to explain what others do and say, and that the resulting theory is not a theory of their own mind or of any one mind but of mind in general. For such a theory there is no problem about other minds. The fact that children develop this theory of mind at a very early age, of course, does not prove that the theory is true. That is a question of how successful it is in explaining what human beings do. We shall return to this problem in Chapter 4.

Intersubjective Experience

Underlying this sort of common-sense theory of mind there are problems that have long disturbed philosophers. The claim that other minds exist is a claim by the theory of mind, and is warranted to the degree that the theory is successful. But granted the existence of other minds, there remain classic problems of the degree to which we can know what others think and feel—that is, the degree to which our knowledge of mental states can be said to be intersubjective. Even within the general framework of the theory of mind described above, to what extent can we have intersubjective knowledge, given the apparent difference in the empirical basis for self-knowledge and for knowledge of others?

Consider the situation in which Teacher A and Student B both confront a particular stimulus object—say, a cup. A points to the cup and says, "cup." A can see that B looks at the cup, so that he has grounds for believing that he has focused B's attention on that object. B then says, "cup." Can A know that B's perception of the cup matches his own? Clearly he cannot. A's perception of the cup is private to A; B's perception of the cup is private to B. There is no way A can compare B's perception with his own, nor can B compare his percept with A's.

But can we even assume that when A says "cup," B hears the same thing A says? After all, hearing is private too. In this case, however, there is a difference. A can both hear himself and hear B, so when B replies with "cup," A can know directly that B used the same word that he used. B's use of the word could of course be accidental—that is, not related to A's—but if B consistently uses A's labels appropriately, the probability of the match being accidental becomes vanishingly small. Of course the acoustic stimuli for A and B differ; one cannot even hear one's own voice as others hear it, and B's voice certainly will not match A's. But as we have already seen, even infants can form equivalence classes of acoustic stimuli that are phonetically similar. There are therefore good grounds for saying that A and B can know that they are using the same word. This does not amount to a sharing of experience; neither A nor B can hear what the other hears. But if B utters the same word A uttered, it is reasonable for A to infer that B did hear what A heard, and if B does this repeatedly, the inference becomes virtually certain. Thus there can be intersubjective knowledge, in the sense that A can know that B heard what A heard, although there cannot be shared experience.

The situation here described, where A teaches B through ostension that an object X in the visual field of both is designated by a certain term, is precisely the sort of situation classically cited as one that permits intersubjectivity. But as we have seen, actual intersubjectivity is not achieved; the nearest approach to it concerns the word applied to that object. Even the belief that A and B are both focusing attention on the same stimulus object is a hypothesis. This situation is not changed if A and B are deaf, for sign languages have the same characteristic, that the utterer can both see his own sign and his respondent's. What is not shared is the private sensory experience of the object, and since there is no sharing of that experience, there is no shared observation of the stimulus object at all, for although A can see that B is looking at X, he has no way of knowing what B sees.

To get beyond this point, we have to add an additional premise, namely, that like stimuli have like effects on perceivers who attend to them, *ceteris paribus*. This is of course a hypothesis; it is supported to the extent that A and B act toward X in similar ways, that what they say about X makes sense to each other, etc. I am not suggesting that either A or B is aware of making this hypothesis at that time, or ever, for that matter—the issue here is one of the logic of the situation, not of what A and B think they know. The hypothesis may of course be wrong; B may be severely nearsighted or colorblind and his visual experience may be quite different from A's. But in such a case we maintain the hypothesis and attribute the difference to B's defective receptors. Indeed, insofar as one can speak of "standard observers," what one means is observers for whom the hypothesis is true; all others are by definition non-standard.

I have belabored this point because I want to emphasize that even in the prototypical case of scientific observation, where observers of normal eyesight stand side by side observing the same stimulus X, intersubjectivity is an inference. The most that can be said to be shared on the basis of observation alone is language use; that even attention is shared is a hypothesis. It is therefore not true that shared language creates an intersubjective world;

it may be a necessary condition for such a world but not a sufficient one. Causal assumptions are also necessary, and without those causal hypotheses there would be no intersubjectivity with respect to the observation of objects. As Leslie and others have pointed out, it is by fitting mental states into the causal structure of the world that we are able to make sense of their relations.

If, as is generally agreed, the primary function of language is the coordination of human action through communication, it must be possible for us to achieve intersubjective agreement about our experience. As we have just seen, such agreement can be attained with respect to our experience of the world around us through language supplemented by appropriate hypotheses concerning attention and causality. That it is in fact achieved is shown by our success in coordinating action, including our ability to predict and control interpersonal conduct. But is this sort of intersubjectivity, as we usually call it, limited to our experience of the world we know through our five senses, or does it extend to other kinds of experience—specifically, to those that take place within us?

Consider the problem of pain, about which so much has been written in recent years.[44] Pain is not a disposition to use certain words, nor to moan and groan, or to roll on the floor—it is an internal state of the organism. It is therefore private, as is one's experience of red. Yet we have intersubjective knowledge of pain. This, of course, does not mean that you can experience my pain or I, yours, but you cannot experience my red either, nor I, yours. "Pain," like "red," is a word in the public English language, and is learned like any other word. The teacher knows that certain stimuli produce pain in all normal people—a hot object that the skin contacts, a sharp object that breaks the skin, a fall from beyond a certain height, etc. Children are taught that what they feel as a result of these events is called "pain." And this is confirmed by the fact that the teacher admits to pain under the same stimuli that produce it in children. The underlying principle is the same as in other perceptions—like stimuli when attended to by the subjects produce like effects, *ceteris paribus*. The *"ceteris paribus"* clause is necessary to cover cases of anesthesia, nerve damage, and similar exceptional cases.

If I go to my doctor and say, "I have a pain in my lower chest," my doctor—fortunately for me—does not dismiss this as a statement regarding a private state about which we cannot intelligently converse. Quite the contrary, being a doctor, she knows a variety of conditions which can cause pain in that location, and she proceeds to search for the appropriate cause by a process of elimination until she either finds a cause adequate to account for the pain I report or she does not. But even if she does not find such a physical cause, she does not dismiss my claim that I have a pain there as false. There are such things as psychosomatic pains, and where no physical cause can be found she will seek a psychological one. In short, in everyday communication, we deal with pains as real internal states of organisms about which we can have intersubjective knowledge. The difference between "pain" and "red" is actually minimal; both are private experiences. They are made intersubjective by language together with the appropriate supplementary hypotheses. The fact that I am in pain and my doctor is not whereas we both see a red book is irrelevant; from the causal hypothesis it follows that if my doctor were experiencing the same stimuli I am, she would feel a pain similar to mine.

The notion that one escapes the privacy of experience by limiting one's talk to the intersubjectively observable properties of objects in the positivist sense is nonsense. All experience is private; no one can experience what another person experiences. But private experience can be made a public topic, and the method for doing this is through the causal hypothesis and language. The causal hypothesis grounds the belief that we have similar experiences under similar conditions; language enables us to communicate about those experiences. Pain is no more or less private than the experience of seeing red or hearing middle C.

But to communicate about internal states, we have to be able to attend to them, identify them, and describe them. How can we know such inner states? To this there is a relatively obvious answer. Whatever constitutes the "knower" in human beings, it is either the central nervous system, and particularly the brain, or it is some function of the central nervous system. The neurophysiological data supporting this view are so overwhelming and so well known that they hardly need to be reviewed here. Even though we do not at present know how the activities of various systems of neurons produce the particular sensations we have, we do know that the stimulation of certain nerves will produce certain sensations, that lesions at specific points in the brain will affect certain functions,—speech, memory, cognition, the motor control of certain parts of the body. There is also clear evidence that the severance of certain nerves can deprive certain areas of the body of the capacity to feel, and that degenerative diseases of the central nervous system may deprive their victims of both feeling and motor control of specific parts of the body. In short, our ability to feel, act, perceive, and think are functions of the central nervous system.

This being the case, it is hardly a cause for surprise that our nerves can be stimulated from within the body as well as from without. But it is a peculiarity of the central nervous system that not all internal processes produce stimulation of the nerves which translates into sensations or feelings or anything else of which we are aware. We are not immediately aware of the functioning of our kidneys, nor of the growth of our hair, nor of innumerable other processes taking place within us. Why should it be the case that we actually feel some processes or states and not others? Undoubtedly the answer has to do with our evolutionary history; it is not hard to see that awareness of pain, or of hunger, would have survival value. But such answers merely translate our ignorance into Greek, and it may well be that the question itself is unanswerable and pointless. How it happens that at least some states and processes produce sensations of which we are aware while others do not is quite another matter, but the answer, if and when it comes, will have to come from neurophysiology, and we do not at present seem to be very close to having it. What can be said is that we do have some awareness of some internal states and processes, and that there is nothing very surprising about that. As Michael Levin has put it, we are "hooked up" to our own nervous system but not to those of others.[45] Given that fact, we have a privileged access to some of our own internal states and processes that others cannot have.

Nevertheless, as we have just seen, we can describe and communicate about these internal states such as pain. Language learning is no different in this case than in any other case of sensory experience. From our experiences of pain, we develop a concept of pain just as we do of red. Not all pains are alike; a burn, a cut, a blow, an infected tooth, all produce pains that differ in quality. We integrate these into a general concept of pain which includes the causes of pain. And because pain is a subject of intense interest, we have words to communicate about it, as Lexical Contrast Theory proposes. Indeed, the English language is filled with words referring to internal states—love, hate, guilt, fear, shame, pride, rage, etc. One who denies the existence of such internal states faces the rather daunting task of explaining why the public language should contain so rich a vocabulary of this sort.

One attempt to answer this problem that has achieved some popularity has been the argument that all internal states must be dispositionally defined. If this means that internal states have causes, and so occur only when caused, the point is granted. But that is not the usual meaning; rather, the usual claim is that the internal state consists of a disposition to respond to an "external" or "observable" cause with "observable behavior." For some, notably Ryle, the "inner state" is nothing but a conditional that links stimuli observable by others to behavior observable by others. This is I believe a false claim. First, it denies any internal processing of the stimuli which might lead to differential responses. Second, to the extent that it succeeds at all, it does so by making its description of both the alleged causes and the alleged behavioral effects so vague that they are essentially useless. Thus Ryle "unpacks" "vain" as "whenever situations of certain sorts have arisen, he has always or usually tried to make himself prominent."[46] This tells us nothing about the stimulus situation, and little about the response; vanity may affect behavior in many ways, and Ryle made not the slightest attempt to find out what these ways are. There is, of course, an alternative type of dispositional analysis, used for example by Quine.[47] Here a disposition is analyzed in terms of an observable stimulus, an inner physical state or structure of the organism, and an observable effect.[48] But although this view concedes the causal role of internal states, they are states about which nothing at all is known. It also denies on purely dogmatic grounds that the stimulus may be internal, and it is uninteresting, since the occurrence of the behavioral effect can never be predicted from the stimulus alone but only from the joint occurrence of the stimulus and the unknown and therefore inscrutable internal state.

It is of course true that internal states do have causes, and usually behavioral consequences. But it is simply not true that the relation of internal states to behavioral consequences is one to one. Even a state like pain, which often does lead to quite visible behavioral effects, does not always do so. Each of such states as guilt, love, shame, etc., may be caused by widely varied sorts of factors and may affect observable behavior in a bewildering multitude of ways, or may even not affect it at all. They may have quite different sorts of consequences, e.g., physical states such as stomach ulcers, cognitive processes such as rationalizations, or other emotional states such as hatred. There are behaviors that we all recognize as symptomatic of certain internal states—although the relation is probabilistic only—and these symptoms are very often important in identifying the internal states, our own or others. But to identify the internal state with such behavioral symptoms is as false as identifying a disease with a symptom—indeed more so, because the relation of disease and symptom is at least likely to be much more constant than that between internal state and physical manifestation.

Now consider dreams. It may be that there are people who never dream, but recent research on dreaming suggests that the phenomenon is very nearly universal. Dreaming poses an extraordinarily complex problem of internal experience. There is, first, the problem of when and why dreams occur; second, there is the problem of recalling the dream; and third, there is the problem of dream content. The first two issues have been subjects of intensive research, particularly because they are not independent. Since dreams occur during sleep, they cannot be directly reported as they occur; accordingly, access to dreams is through recall only. If there is no recall of the dream, there is no indication that the dream ever existed; if the dream existed, why should it be so difficult to recall it? The correlation of Rapid Eye Movements during sleep with dreaming has provided a partial answer to the question of when dreams occur. While one cannot say that REM invariably indicate that the subject is dreaming, there is substantial evi-

dence to support that hypothesis—dream recall is much higher among subjects awakened during REM periods than at other times in the sleep cycle.
Thus REM appears to provide a physiological indicator (if only a probabilistic one) of the occurrence of the internal dream state.[49]

Dream recall is notoriously difficult; reports must be obtained immediately upon awakening or the likelihood of obtaining them declines drastically. The problem here however is not simply one of recalling dreams;
experiments have shown that recall of many types of events occurring during sleep is very poor, and the difficulty in the retrieval of dreams may be
simply a part of a more general phenomenon about sleep, the reasons for
which are at present very obscure.[50] Nevertheless, despite all the difficulties, reports of dreams are obtainable in sufficient quantity to make possible
the study of dream content.

It will be noted that in the preceding remarks, the real existence of
dreams as inner states is taken for granted. The correlation of REM with
dreams assumes that the reports given by the awakened subjects are recalls
of dream events—not something produced by the act of awakening or by
some other cause. The extensive research on the problem of dream recall
similarly assumes the reality of the dream experience and focuses on why it
is more easily retrieved under some conditions than under others. Yet the
dream itself is a totally private experience; no one but the dreamer can
know the content of the dream when it occurs, and dreamers rarely know
during the dream that they are dreaming. Moreover, dream content (at least
in our culture) is often bizarre, judged from the standpoint of ordinary
waking experience. Dreams often involve apparent contradictions (as when
a boy appears in the dream as a girl) and fantastic events that often violate
the laws of nature, and the dream is often fragmentary and chaotic. Why
then do we so readily accept the reality of dreams? And why do we accept
such bizarre accounts as true accounts of what was dreamed?

The answer to the first question seems obvious. We believe that others dream because we dream; we do not find it bizarre that others have
experiences similar to our own. This is not a case, like pain, where we can
identify the causes that produce the internal state; we do not know even
now what causes people to dream. Rather, the acceptance of dreams as real
events rests upon their universality. If everyone attests to having at some
time a given type of experience, we accept as true the claim that such experience really occurs. The content of the dream may not be accepted as true,
but the existence of dreams as real events is accepted.

It should be emphasized that dream content can be and is described
in the public language. Because dream experience is largely perceptual in
character, visual or tactile, the vocabulary that serves to describe perception serves also relatively well for dreams. The same is true for the emo-

tions that usually accompany dreams; they are the same emotions of fear, anger, sorrow, etc., that accompany life in general. It is true that dreams sometimes involve states not describable in the public language, and the dreamer is forced to use metaphors—often unsuccessfully—to convey what he felt or saw, but usually a verbal description is constructed that is understandable by others. Accordingly, dreams are a type of private experience that occurs during sleep, that is practically universal, and that is publicly describable. These factors make it possible to discuss dreams, to compare accounts of them, and to accept them as real occurrences to which the dreamer has some degree of private access.

It is also important to note that in our culture there are virtually no constraints upon what the content of a dream can be. If a subject reports that he dreamed he raped his mother, or murdered his brother, or flew to Mars, or had sex with an octopus, our usual response is, how quaint! What we do not do is say that he must be lying because he could not have dreamed that. One reason surely for this is that, aside from Freudians, we attach no meaning to dreams, so that literally anything is possible, and Freudians will always find a meaning they like, no matter what we dream. In this sense, our dreaming experience is completely unconstrained; anything goes.

This situation is not universal. Dreams in some cultures have (or have had) very specific meanings. Among the Ojibwa, for example, dreams were regarded as true experiences of the self, which according to Ojibwa theory was capable of leaving the body during sleep and traveling about the environment. Thus the Ojibwa drew no distinction in kind between the experiences of the self when awake and its experiences in dreams; both were conceived as veridical. It was therefore possible for the Ojibwa to meet with, talk to, and even have sexual intercourse with non-human persons such as thunderbirds, to see and fight with cannibal giants and great snakes, to encounter the "bosses" of the various species, and in short to have what they took to be sensory contact with what we would call "supernatural entities." The significance of this definition of dream experience for the Ojibwa culture has been beautifully described and analysized by Hallowell.[51] The world view of the Ojibwa differed profoundly from that of European-Americans, in large part because of their broader concept of experience. Further, as Hallowell has shown (and there are many anthropological studies that support this), the content of dreams is culturally variable and will reflect the beliefs and attitudes of the people in whose culture they occur. It may even be that dreams themselves have a different character depending on the culture; Hallowell always believed (although he could not prove) that Ojibwa dreams were much more similar to Ojibwa waking experience than is the case with dreams in our culture.[52] Thus among the

Ojibwa it might well have been the case that a dream report would have been rejected as impossible if it deviated too radically from the expectations of the culture.

Consider now the case of visions. Visions are surely private. Moreover, unlike dreams, the occurrence of visions is not universal. But visions are of various sorts and have at least some known causes. It is not news in our culture that visions can be induced by the use of such drugs as LSD. It is also known that visions can be caused by physiological conditions, such as fasting and certain diseases, e.g., epilepsy. The fact that visions do occur is therefore generally accepted by scientists, even though the vision experience itself is private and its content is not (in our culture) usually taken as true. But again it needs to be stressed that other interpretations are possible in other cultures. Among the Ojibwa, Winnebago, Menomini, and many other Native American tribes, the puberty vision quest has been widely practiced. Presumably most male adolescents had such visions, so that in those cultures they were a universal type of experience for males. On the other hand, the causal factors were conceived in a manner very different from ours.[53] In many cultures epilepsy has been associated with access to the divine through visions—that is presumably what happened to Paul on the road to Damascus. In different cultures there may be different views of the causes of visions, and the experience itself may be rare or common.

What one comes down to, then, is that we accept as really occurring a wide variety of internal experiences, and that the interpretation of those experiences varies dramatically from one culture to another, sometimes being regarded as veridical experiences of reality, sometimes as hallucinations induced by disease, drugs, or other abnormal physiological states. At one extreme is a phenomenon such as pain that can be produced at will in anyone by certain standard procedures and that is experienced by everyone sometime. Such a phenomenon is no less intersubjectively observable than seeing red. At the other extreme are states such as spirit possession or mystical union. The causes of these phenomena are not clearly understood, although in a given culture there may be accepted causal explanations, and the incidence of such phenomena is enormously variable, being common in some cultures and rare in others.[54]

Attitudes toward the phenomena will vary from one culture to another. Where they are common and there is an accepted causal theory that leads members of the society to accept the content of the experience as veridical, even though that content is private, the account of it will usually be believed as an account of something real. In other cases, as, for example, with possession in the United States, where few people have the experience and its causes are not known, the occurrence of the experience itself may be hidden or it may be classed as pathological. Thus, it appears that the notion of intersubjectivity is a matter of degree rather than the sort of all-or-nothing distinction traditionally made by positivists and other believers in the myth of "hard data." Crucial to the way that experience will be interpreted are the beliefs of the culture concerning its causes and nature, the degree to which experiences of that type are common among members of the society, the degree to which the experiences are describable in the public language, and the degree to which the causes are known and/or manipulable by members of the society.

But a special warning is in order here. Members of the Indian peyote cults understand that their visions occur only when they take peyote. But they do not attribute the vision to the peyote in the way we attribute hallucinations to LSD. Rather, they think the peyote is "medicine," in the Indian sense—that there are spiritual powers associated with it, and that the causality lies in the spiritual powers, not in the chemical properties of the substance.[55]

Finally, note that it undoubtedly is possible to induce a very wide range of experiences, many of them unknown in the Western world, by the use of various disciplines, rituals, substances, and meditative practices. There is here a yet-to-be explored territory about which anthropology has a lot more to say than psychology. Indeed, one reason for the astonishing poverty of the psychology of religion has been the unwillingness of psychologists to address such experiences and the difficulty of using experimental methods to study them.[56] No doubt, psychological principles underlie all of these types of experience but so do cultural beliefs and practices. For the student of other cultures and other times, this is certainly one of the most difficult and important areas of research.

Thus, even if it is granted that we have private access to some of our own inner states, as it seems obvious we do, the attribution of corresponding states to others rests on a theoretical basis. Whether it is the sensation of red or the sensation of pain, the attribution depends upon hypotheses regarding causality, attention, and the state of the other's perceptual apparatus. In the case of dreams, attribution is based not only on the other's speech (e.g., dream report) but also on the hypothesis that dreaming is a universal human phenomenon, even though dream content is culturally variable. Visions, too, are accepted as real events on the basis of certain causal hypotheses, as well as verbal reports. Thus, intersubjective knowledge is a form of theoretical knowledge even though knowledge of our own internal states may be partly observational. We can know what others experience because we have theories about human experience that are supported by empirical evidence.

Translation and the Intersubjectivity of Thought

The argument so far has been concerned with the degree to which we can have knowledge of another's experience, or equivalently the degree to which such experiences can be considered intersubjective. But what about another's thoughts? Can we know what concepts and theories others hold? It should be obvious what is at stake here. If in fact we cannot know—at least with reasonable assurance—what concepts and theories others hold, then the whole notion of communication becomes vacuous, for what else is communicated except the thoughts and experiences of another? Such a position would not be solipsism, for it would not deny the existence of things or even persons other than the speaker, but it would lead to a kind of linguistic monadology, in which each of us has a language that is, so far as we can know, wholly private and in which the noises and inscriptions made by others may mean very nearly whatever we choose to have them mean.

The principal argument against the possibility of knowing what others mean is Quine's argument for the indeterminacy of translation. Quine's argument has two basic premises, one epistemological and one ontological. The epistemological premise is the Underdetermination Thesis, namely, the thesis that scientific theories are underdetermined by all possible observations, and that therefore if there were any one scientific theory that accounted for all possible observations, there would be other scientific theories, logically incompatible with the first, that account equally well for all possible observations. This thesis is clearly of fundamental importance, but its discussion must be postponed to a later point.

The ontological premise is that there are no mental entities, and therefore all talk of reference and meaning must be based upon the observed verbal behavior of physical bodies, or, more accurately, upon their dispositions to verbal behavior. Any translation, whether from one language to another or from one speaker to another within a single language community, must therefore rest upon a matching of dispositions to verbal behavior.

Quine admits that some matchings of sentences in one language to those of another are not arbitrary. By an "occasion sentence" he means a sentence that a speaker will regard as true or false on a particular occasion on the basis of "nerve stimulations." Thus when we find a person from a hitherto unknown jungle tribe who assents to the occasion sentence, "gavagai," under the same stimulations that would lead us to assent to the occasion sentence, "Lo, a rabbit," and dissents from it under just the stimulations where we would dissent from the English occasion sentence, Quine regards "gavagai" and "lo, a rabbit" as "stimulus synonymous." Here one is dealing with the conditioning of a verbal response to specific sensory stimuli, and Quine believes that such conditioned responses are suitably dispositional and objective. But as soon as we go beyond "stimulus synonymy" of this sort to "standing sentences" (e.g., "All men are mortal"), we exceed what such conditioning can ground. We must therefore rely upon "analytical hypotheses" that correlate the words and sentences of others to our own, and these hypotheses are "theoretical," that is, their truth values are not fixed by specific "nerve stimulations." It follows from the Underdetermination Thesis that any such translation is underdetermined by all possible observations of speech behavior, so that given any one translation scheme that matches A's dispositions to verbal behavior with B's, there will exist alternative translation schemes that are equally adequate and plausible.

So far, the underdetermination of scientific theories and the indeterminacy of translation stand on the same basis. But they differ in that, whereas in scientific theories there is something to be right or wrong about, namely, what physical objects exist and how they interact, in translation there is nothing to be right or wrong about, for there are no mental entities, no meanings or references beyond dispositions to verbal behavior. In this sense, there is no fact of the matter to the question of translation, for once A's dispositions are matched to B's, there is nothing further to argue about, no matter how many alternative translation schemes there are. To ask which translation is right presupposes that there are meanings and references which underly and determine dispositions to verbal behavior. But this is just what Quine denies; for him, meanings and references *are* the dispositions. Given alternative translation schemes (matchings of dispositions), there is nothing further to appeal to, no "fact of the matter" as to which is right.[57]

This doctrine of Quine's is certainly one of the most radical forms of skepticism ever seriously proposed by a major philosopher. As Kirk comments:

> Like all skeptical doctrines, it feeds our craving for radically disturbing, mystifying ideas. It takes us to an abyss where we cannot possibly know what others think or feel—and not for the reassuring reason that the contents of everyone's thoughts and feelings are inaccessible to outsiders, but for the utterly disorienting reason that it is never a matter of fact what those contents are.[58]

Confronting a doctrine so bizarre, one looks first for some arcane and complex argument underlying it. But the actual grounds of Quine's argument seem to be neither arcane nor particularly complex. The basic principle that supports the argument is Quine's commitment to physics as the fundamental arbiter of what there is. It is Quine's view that physics is, if not our first philosophy, at least our first science—the discipline that decides what is or is not, what is a fact and what is not a fact.[59] Of course, Quine recognizes that current theories of physics may be in error and may require revision; he is not claiming that our present physical theories give us absolute truth. But he does hold that our present physical theories are our best estimate of what the world is, and, moreover, that physics as a discipline is the field whose authority on such questions must override all others.

This view of Quine's does not amount to an old-fashioned reductionism. Quine does not claim that every statement of every science is reducible to statements of physics, in the sense of being logically deducible from the axioms of physics. Rather, he holds that statements in *every* science are true or false depending on what truths are stateable in terms of physics. In other words, it is physics that determines what the facts are, and so to say that a statement of biology or chemistry is true because it corresponds to the facts is to say it corresponds to the facts as stated by physics.[60] Ultimately, it is subatomic particles and their behavior that are the reality to which sentences in other disciplines must conform. This is clearly a metaphysical or ontological doctrine; it is not an epistemological claim, but a claim about the constitution of reality.

It is this metaphysic that grounds Quine's antimentalism. Quine does not believe that statements about concepts, meanings, beliefs, intentions, and the like correspond to any physical realities. There is no state of the world as described by physics that corresponds to "bachelors" meaning "unmarried males." Hence when Quine says that translation—that is, the equating of two expressions as having the same meaning—involves no fact of the matter, this is not because there is something peculiar about translation, but because meanings have no factual correlates. Quine would therefore jettison all talk of mental entities on the ground that there is no state of the physical world which makes statements about such entities either true or false.[61]

How then can Quine talk of language? He can do so insofar as language consists of physical states—noises or inscriptions. But of course that is, as Quine understands perfectly, a hopelessly inadequate way of dealing with language. Accordingly, Quine resorts, somewhat reluctantly one feels, to talk of dispositions to verbal behavior. The use of dispositional concepts in science is perfectly standard—solubility, for example—but in such cases the disposition is based on the molecular structure of the body in question.

In analysizing verbal behavior dispositionally, Quine follows the analogy of the hard sciences as far as it will take him, but that is not very far. Thus, Quine would analyze dispositions to verbal behavior as involving some set of stimuli, some neurophysiological state of the organism, and an observable verbal response. The problem is that the relevant neurophysiological state is wholly unknown. When, for example, the verbal stimulus "Good morning," uttered by one person, evokes the verbal response "Good morning" from another, Quine assumes that the respondent's behavior is caused by both the verbal stimulus and by some physiological state of that person. But neither Quine nor anyone else knows at present what that state is, nor has anyone at present a clue how it might be described in terms of quantum mechanics. That, of course, makes dispositional analysis totally useless for either explanatory or predictive purposes; one might as well speak of a "greeting virtue" on analogy to the "dormative virtue" that scholastics used to explain why opium puts people to sleep.

Nevertheless, Quine thinks dispositions to verbal behavior are sufficiently within the pale of physical facts to be used to define language. A language is, for Quine, a system of dispositions to verbal behavior, where this system is understood to include second-order dispositions, that is, dispositions to acquire or lose first-order dispositions.[62] Hence it is dispositions to verbal behavior which define for Quine the "facts" of language. Therefore, if there should exist two languages, L_1 and L_2, and two alternative translations of sentence S_1 of L_1, one of which maps S_1 of L_1 into S_2 of L_2 while the other maps S_1 of L_1 into S_3 of L_2, where S_2 and S_3 are not equivalent sentences in L_2, but nevertheless the correlation of dispositions to linguistic behavior between L_1 and L_2 is unaffected by which translation is used, then there is for Quine no fact of the matter as between the two translations. Hence, the translation is indeterminate.

The privileged role Quine assigns to physics is not a matter of pure dogmatism. In epistemology, Quine is an empiricist. But it should be recalled that he is also an advocate of "naturalized epistemology," that is, he holds that epistemology is a part of natural science, the part that explains how we know what we know. The appearance of circularity here is real and fully admitted by Quine, but it is also a non-vicious circle, for Quine does not claim that ontology is deduced from epistemology nor vice versa. Quine construes epistemology's problem as explaining how, from nerve stimulations caused by physical objects impinging on our sensory surfaces, we come to project the world we do; he is an empiricist in admitting only sensory stimulation as evidence. And Quine believes that naturalized epistemology warrants our current theories of physics, thereby warranting the assertion that "the facts of the matter" are those stateable in terms of physics. Epistemology and ontology thus lie within science; there is no transcendental viewpoint from which to evaluate these disciplines, no higher knowledge beyond what science itself provides.[63]

When Quine talks about a translation of language L_1 into language L_2 (and vice versa), what exactly is he talking about? Quine has described a translation in terms of a "translation manual."

> The linguist's finished jungle-to-English manual has as its net yield an infinite *semantic correlation* of sentences: the implicit specification of an English sentence, or various roughly interchangeable English sentences, for every one of the infinitely many possible jungle sentences.[64]

As Kirk has argued, Quine cannot be required to provide for all the variant interpretations of sentence tokens due to context—no conceivable translation manual could do that. The most that should be required is a manual of "*theoretical* or *pure* translation—translation of words, phrases, and whole sentences which are not actually being used, and for which no special context of use is envisaged."[65] After all, that is what cross-language dictionaries seek to do. Is a manual, so conceived, a statement of semantic truths? Evans argued that a translation need involve no reference to meanings at all—that what it does is simply to correlate expressions or sentences that are mentioned rather than used, for example, "garçon" = "boy."[66] This is in one sense true. It is conceivable that one could have a manual translating Harappan into Elamite, and know that the document was such a translation (one might have a Sumerian text that so identified it), yet, since neither Harappan nor Elamite is currently translatable into any modern tongue, one would have no idea what any of the correlated expressions meant. But obviously such a manual would be of no use whatever. As Kirk notes, to be used it would have to be "semantically based and justified."[67] That it seems to me is an understatement. To say that an expression S in L_1 is a translation (in the pure sense) of expression S' in L_2 is to say that the two expressions have the same meaning. When one puts "garçon" = "boy," one is saying that "garçon" means what "boy" means. A translation manual is, as Quine said, a semantic correlation.

In his recent book, Kirk has produced an extremely interesting argument that he believes refutes Quine's doctrine of the indeterminacy of translation. Kirk first argues that indeterminacy of translation between languages depends upon indeterminacy of translation within a language, that is, unless there is intralinguistic indeterminacy, there is no interlinguistic indeterminacy. He then tries to prove that there need not be intralinguistic indeterminacy. The argument is based on the claim that language learning proceeds by small and semantically indivisible steps. Kirk first tries to show that two children starting to learn English and a variant English called Martian could be taught an initial small vocabulary in both languages by methods that would permit no indeterminacy between the two variants. Then he argues that, given any stage of English (E_n) and Martian (M_n) such that there is no indeterminacy of translation between them, any extension of these by addition of a predicate or predicate cluster that creates new stages E_{n+1} and M_{n+1} will introduce no indeterminacy. By induction, therefore, English and Martian are intertranslatable ideolects of English which are determinately translatable.[68]

Kirk's argument is the most ingenious attempt yet made to refute the Indeterminacy of Translation thesis.[69] Whether or not it succeeds is an open question. There is no doubt that he is right that intralinguistic indeterminacy is the fundamental doctrine. Quine himself says this, and further says that he invoked the gavagai argument merely as a heuristic aid to get the basic intralinguistic point across.[70] The more difficult question is whether or not the inductive argument holds—specifically, whether the steps of language learning are reducible to the acquisition of new predicates and predicate clusters. Peter Smith has noted that such acquisition also involves steps that give children new semantic structures, and it is at least arguable that steps of that sort might introduce indeterminacy.[71] But my objection to Kirk's approach is somewhat different. Kirk is willing to grant Quine's other major doctrines and then tries to show that they do not support the Indeterminacy of Translation thesis. Since I find some of these other doctrines unacceptable, this seems to me a dubious strategy. The place to challenge Quine's thesis is at its premises.

Quine's ontological claim is that physics defines what constitutes matters of fact. Among his epistemological claims is that a purely naturalized epistemology is empiricism, construed as a theory of evidence.[72] Quine refers to it as a theory of "warranted belief," and says of it, "It has both a descriptive and a normative aspect."[73] Naturalized epistemology describes the evidence upon which scientific theories rest, but it is also normative in that the "empiricist discipline" requires scientific theories to be responsive to empirical evidence.

> Where empiricist discipline persists is partly in the relative firmness of this link between a goodly store of occasion sentences and concurrent stimulations, and partly in a high degree of dependence upon these occasion sentences on the part of sentences in the interior of the fabric [of theory]. It is a matter of degree of responsiveness, a matter of more or less responsible science, of better and worse.[74]

In this sense, naturalized epistemology may be said to warrant physics. Since, as is well known, physics postulates a number of entities that are in no sense reducible to sensory stimulations (e.g., subatomic particles), and since Quine believes naturalized epistemology warrants physics, it is obvious that Quine has no objection to such postulates. But the epistemology underlying naturalized epistemology is no different from that underlying physics. That is, if naturalized epistemology is a part of science, then the same epistemology that warrants physics warrants naturalized epistemology. If this is circular, it is the same circularity that Quine already has cheerfully embraced, and it is clearly implied by the claim that epistemology is a part of science rather than its foundation.

Quine's claim of the interlocking nature of this relationship between naturalized epistemology and ontology, however, is based upon the assumption that naturalized epistemology is behavioristic—that the only ontological posits made by naturalized epistemology are physical objects such as nerve endings. But in naturalized epistemology, at least as it is currently practiced, entities such as concepts and meanings are postulated. In Chapter 1, we reviewed a variety of studies from various specialties within cognitive science which converge on the conclusion that mental representations such as concepts and meanings do exist. Obviously, such entities are, at the present state of inquiry, theoretical constructs. But Quine has no objection to theoretical constructs in physics, so he can hardly object—at least in principle—to such constructs in cognitive science. And if cognitive scientists find it necessary—as they do—to make such postulates, why are they not matters of fact? How is it that the epistemology that warrants such postulates in physics cannot do so in psychology? It cannot be because the epistemologies are different, for they are asserted by Quine to be the same. It cannot be an objection to constructs *per se*, for Quine considers them legitimate in physics. The answer appears to be that Quine regards physics as true and mentalist theories as false.

A true theory, for Quine, defines what is ontologically real. In view of the Underdetermination Thesis, Quine happily admits that alternative theories involving incompatible ontological postulates can be equally warranted. Nevertheless, he believes that only one such theory can be true, so that we must take a sectarian view in favor of that theory within whose tradition we stand. This cheerful sectarianism may resolve for Quine the dilemma of multiple but conflicting theories of physics, but it does not resolve the problem that the naturalized epistemology that warrants all theories of physics itself involves ontological posits such as concepts and meanings. I do not think that Quine can, or would, take the position that philosophers should dictate to scientists what postulates they may make, and insofar as epistemology is naturalized—that is, insofar as it lies within science—it is the cognitive scientists who must decide what entities it is necessary to postulate in their science. The result is that Quine's theory commits him to two quite different ontologies—that of quantum mechanics and that of cognitive science. But these ontologies are inconsistent, it should be emphasized, only if one insists that only one can be affirmed at a given time.

Why should one insist upon this? Quine's antimentalism is notorious, but philosophers do not make such decisions on the basis of prejudice. Quine takes the claim that only the entities postulated by physics are real to be a claim of physics itself; hence to admit other sorts of entities would be for him contradictory. And it may be granted—although Quine would not—that in an ultimate sense, there can be only one true ontological theory, an issue to which we will return later. But the history of science does not warrant the claim that at every stage of scientific development one should insist upon ontological consistency.

The virtues of the division of labor are nowhere more obvious than in the sciences. The social structure of science shows a continual proliferation of specialties that develop increasingly arcane theories. It often happens that the theories in different fields are not ontologically consistent with each other. Field theory was not consistent with Newtonian mechanics; surely no one would hold that field theory should have been abandoned for that reason. In fact, such conflicts are inevitable, and one trusts will ultimately prove to be resolvable, but at any given time one has to live with a less tidy ontological zoo than one might like. Indeed, it is sometimes just those conflicts over ontology which provide the spur to further scientific advance. It would therefore be counterproductive to try to legislate against them, even if one could.

Quine's aversion to allowing psychological constructs such as concepts and meanings as legitimate seems to be based on the belief that such entities are "spiritual" or "immaterial," rather like goblins and demons. This is certainly not the view of most cognitive scientists, among whom it is taken for granted that such entities must be somehow grounded in the electrochemical nature of the brain. At present, no one knows just how such psychological entities as beliefs, intentions, concepts, meanings, and so forth, are related to the functioning brain; therefore they must be treated—for now—as autonomous, although there is every expectation that in due course the nature of these relationships will be discovered. But meanwhile cognitive scientists must pursue their own science as their scientific judgments and intuitions dictate. Any regulative principle that says cognitive scientists must restrict their ontological posits to those of quantum mechanics is a dogma warranted neither by science nor by the history of science nor by naturalized epistemology.

If the forgoing argument is correct, Quine has no legitimate ground for denying that concepts, beliefs, meanings, and so on, are legitimate scientific constructs. That being so, relations among meanings are matters of fact, just as much as are relations among electrons. A translation manual, whether intralinguistic or interlinguistic, is therefore a theory about how meanings are in fact related, and there is no reason to hold that such a theory is any more or any less indeterminate than a theory about electrons. The argument that translation is subject to some type of indeterminacy beyond that affecting theories of physics therefore collapses; there is indeed a fact of the matter.

In order not to confuse the issue, I have followed Quine in viewing the problem of understanding another's thought as one of translation. In fact, there are two quite different problems—those of translation and of interpretation—which Quine lumps together under his rubric of "translation." Thus, Quine's "gavagai" example is really a question of interpretation rather than translation[75] and his concept of translation is one no professional translator would accept. We will return to this distinction and its consequences in Chapter 6. But both correct interpretation and correct translation depend upon the basic principle that meanings are real entities that stand in determinate relations. There are practical difficulties in translating a text from one language into an "equivalent" text in another language, which arise from differences between the two languages. Different languages often lack coreferential terms. And there are complex problems involved in satisfying syntactic constraints. These problems, and others, will occupy us below, but they do not affect the general point at issue here, namely, that there are determinate relations among meanings that make possible both intralinguistic and interlinguistic understanding. That being so, it is clear that intersubjectivity with respect to meanings, beliefs, theories, and the rest, can be attained through communication, and primarily through linguistic communication. Indeed, it is hard to understand how anyone could ever have seriously doubted this. That Russian, Japanese, and Chinese scientists are thorough masters of the same science that we ourselves believe and practice is a claim that I believe no sane person would challenge.

Notes

1. David R. Olson, "On the Origin of Beliefs and Other Intentional States in Children" in Janet W. Astington, Paul L. Harris, and David R. Olson, eds., *Developing Theories of Mind* (New York: Cambridge University Press, 1988), 417.

2. Lynd Forguson and Alison Gopnik, "The Ontogeny of Common Sense" in Astington et al. *Theories of Mind*, 226–227.

3. Alan M. Leslie, "Some Implications of Pretense for Mechanisms Underlying the Child's Theory of Mind" in Astington et al., *Theories of Mind*, 19–20.

4. Ibid., 22–23.

5. Ibid., 20. (Emphasis in original)

6. Ibid., 28.

7. Ibid., 30.

8. Ibid., 31.

9. Ibid., 32.

10. Alan M. Leslie, "The Necessity of Illusion" in Weiskrantz, *Thought*, 185–210.

11. Leslie, "Some Implications," 37.

12. Heinz Wimmer, Jurgen Hogrefe, and Beate Sodian, "A Second Stage in Children's Conception of Mental Life: Understanding Informational Accesses as Origins of Knowledge and Belief" in Astington et al., *Theories of Mind*, 173.

13. Ibid., 173.

14. Ibid., 174.

15. Ibid., 175.

16. Ibid., 175–179.

17. Ibid., 188.

18. Ibid., 179–182.

19. Henry M. Wellman, *The Child's Theory of Mind* (Cambridge, Mass.: MIT Press, 1990), 208.

20. Ibid., 210.

21. Ibid., 216–217.

22. Ibid., ch. 3.

23. Ibid., ch. 6.

24. Ibid., 91, 118, 183.

25. Ibid., 186.

26. Ibid., 248–249.

27. Ibid., 262

28. Ibid., 268–269.

29. Ibid., 270.

30. Ibid., 268.

31. Josef Perner, *Understanding the Representational Mind* (Cambridge, Mass.: MIT Press, 1991),16–21.

32. Ibid., 45.

33. Ibid., 77–78.

34. Ibid., 41.

35. Ibid., 181. (Emphasis in original)

36. Ibid., 240–255.

37. Michael Chandler, "Doubt and Developing Theories of Mind" in Astington et al., *Theories of Mind*, 387–413.

38. Carol Fleisher Feldman, "Early Forms of Thought About Thoughts: Some Simple Linguistic Expressions of Mental State" in Astington et al., *Theories of Mind*, 126–137.

39. Chandler, "Doubt," 191–198.

40. Diane Poulin-Dubois and Thomas R. Shultz, "The Development of the Understanding of Human Behavior: From Agency to Intentionality" in Astington et al., *Theories of Mind*, 109–125.

41. Paul L. Harris and Dana Gross, "Children's Understanding of Real and Apparent Emotion" in Astington et al., *Theories of Mind*, 295–314.

42. David R. Olson, Janet W. Astington, and Paul L. Harris, "Introduction" in Astington et al., *Theories of Mind*, 3.

43. Ibid., 14; John H. Flavell, "The Development of Children's Knowledge About the Mind: From Cognitive Connections to Mental Representations" in Ibid., 249; Harris and Gross, "Children's Understanding" in Ibid., 302.

44. Wittgenstein, *Philosophical Investigations*, Part 1, §244ff. Sidney Shoemaker, *Self-Knowledge and Self-Identity* (Ithaca, N.Y.: Cornell University Press, 1963), 168.

45. Michael E. Levin, *Metaphysics and the Mind-Body Problem* (Oxford: Clarendon Press, 1979), 139.

46. Gilbert Ryle, *The Concept of Mind* (New York: Barnes and Noble, 1949), 85.

47. Quine, "Mental and Verbal Dispositions," 83–95.

48. William Lyons, *Gilbert Ryle: An Introduction to His Philosophy* (Sussex: Harvester Press, 1980), 50–51.

49. John W. Herman, Steven J. Ellman, and Howard P. Roffwarg, "The Problem of NREM Dream Recall Re-examined" in Arthur M. Arkin, John S. Antrobus, and Steven J. Ellman, eds., *The Mind in Sleep: Psychology and Psychophysiology* (Hillsdale, N.J.: Lawrence Erlbaum, 1978), 59–92.

50. Donald R. Goodenough, "Dream Recall: History and Current Status of the Field" in Arkin et al., *The Mind in Sleep*, 113–140.

51. A. Irving Hallowell, *Culture and Experience* (Philadelphia: University of Pennsylvania Press, 1955).

52. A. Irving Hallowell, personal communication.

53. Ruth Benedict, *The Concept of the Guardian Spirit in North America* (Menasha, Wis.: American Anthropological Association Memoirs 29, 1923). Hallowell, "The Self and Its Behavioral Environment" in *Culture and Experience*, 75–110.

54. Clifford Geertz, *The Interpretation of Cultures* (New York: Basic Books, 1973), Part 2.

55. George D. Spindler, *Sociocultural and Psychological Processes In Menomini Acculturation* (Berkeley and Los Angeles: University of California Press, 1955), 85f.

56. Murray G. Murphey, "On The Scientific Study of Religion in the United States, 1870–1980" in Michael J. Lacey, ed., *Religion and Twentieth-Century American Intellectual Life* (New York: Cambridge University Press, 1989), 136–171.

57. Quine, *Word and Object*, 73–79. Quine, "Ontological Relativity." Roger F. Gibson, Jr., "Translation, Physics, and Facts of the Matter" in Lewis Edwin Hahn and Paul Arthur Schilpp, eds., *The Philosophy of W. V. Quine* (LaSalle, Ill.: Open Court, 1986), 139–154. W. V. Quine, "Reply to Roger F. Gibson, Jr." Ibid., 155–157.

58. Robert Kirk, *Translation Determined* (Oxford: Clarendon Press, 1986), 250.

59. W. V. Quine, "Replies" in Donald Davidson and Jaakko Hintikka, eds., *Words and Objections: Essays on the Work of W. V. Quine* (Dordrecht: D. Reidel Co., 1969), 303. Kirk, *Translation*, 135–138.

60. Kirk, *Translation*, 19, 135–138.

61. Ibid., 156–157. Quine, *Word and Object*, 264–265. Quine, "Mind and Verbal Dispositions," 83–95.

62. Quine, *Word and Object*, 26–30. Quine, "Mind and Verbal Dispositions." Kirk, *Translation*, 252–258.

63. Gibson, "Translation," 139–154. Gibson's paper is of particular importance as an exposition of Quine's position because Quine himself approves of it— Quine, "Reply to Gibson," Ibid., 155. See also W. V. Quine, "The Nature of Natural Knowledge" in Guttenplan, *Mind and Language*, 67–81.

64. Quine, *Word and Object*, 71. (Emphasis in original)

65. Kirk, *Translation*, 34. (Emphasis in original)

66. Evans, "Identity and Predication."

67. Kirk, *Translation*, 33.

68. Ibid., chs. 10, 11.

69. Ken Genes has recently published an article that seeks to show that Quine's statement of the Indeterminacy Thesis is inconsistent. Whatever the merits of Genes' argument, his grounds for rejecting Quine's formulation are quite different from those presented here. Ken Genes, "The Indeterminacy Thesis Reformulated," *Journal of Philosophy* 88:91–108 (1991).

70. Quine, "Reasons for Indeterminacy." Quine, *Word and Object*, 27.

71. Peter Smith, "Review of Robert Kirk, *Translation Determined*," *Philosophical Books* 28:220–224 (1987).

72. Gibson, "Translation," 149.

73. W. V. Quine, *Theories and Things* (Cambridge, Mass.: Harvard University Press, 1981), 39.

74. Ibid., 41.

75. Thomas S. Kuhn, "Commensurability, Comparability, Communicability" in Peter D. Asquith and Thomas Nickles, eds. *PSA 1982* (East Lansing: Philosophy of Science Association, 1983), 672.

Chapter 3

Causation and Explanation

In this chapter, we begin the examination of Premise (8): "Human action is causally explainable"—an examination that will continue through the succeeding two chapters. The first problem is to come to an understanding of what a causal explanation is, and it is that task to which the present chapter is devoted. Our starting point is Hempel's famous analysis of explanation, which has dominated the field for the past fifty years. Hempel's "covering law" model of explanation is analyzed and some of the many objections that have been raised against it are discussed—particularly the claim by philosophers of history that causal explanation must be by single causal statements. This argument leads inevitably to the problem of what causality is, which takes us to an analysis of Hume's position and of the problems that have beset the classical empiricist doctrine of causation. I conclude that neither the nature of the causal relation nor of the entities that can enter into this relation are entirely clear. I then examine Salmon's views on the nature of causal explanation, and conclude that despite the undoubted merits of his analysis, Salmon's notion of causal process is inadequate as a basis for a theory of causal explanation. Next, I examine Railton's theory of explanation, which seems to be the best and most comprehensive thus far developed. As I emphasize, Railton's theory offers a nice way of resolving the conflict between the advocates of the covering law theory and the proponents of the single causal statement theory. Even so, it is clear that causality itself remains a less-than–clear concept. I conclude that causal relations are ontologically real features of the world, but that their nature is a question for science, not philosophy.

The Hempelian Theory

The problem of explaining what humans do and why they do it is surely as old as the human race itself. It commanded the attention of the ancients, as such works as Aristotle's *Politics* and Thucydides's *History* demonstrate, and has continued to be a central focus of inquiry ever since. The triumphs of science since the Renaissance have led to efforts to develop a science, or sciences, of human behavior; with the emergence of the modern panoply of social sciences in the nineteenth century, these efforts have intensified. During the last fifty years, philosophers and social scientists have written extensively on the problem of explaining human conduct, without achieving notable success. In fact, there is probably less agreement on this issue now than there was half a century ago.

As Salmon has pointed out,[1] the modern era of controversy over the nature of explanation began with the famous Hempel and Oppenheim paper, "Studies in the Logic of Explanation."[2] In that paper, Hempel and Oppenheim presented what has become known as the Deductive-Nomological (DN) model of scientific explanation. According to this view, the occurrence of a particular event of type E is explained if it is logically deducible from premises that include one or more general laws relating the occurrence of certain types of conditions to the occurrence of an E-type event, and factual statements asserting that in the case in question each of the specified conditions was realized. Then the simplest schema is:

DN: $C_1, C_2, \ldots C_k$ Statements of antecedent conditions

$L_1, L_2, \ldots L_n$ General laws
_____

E Description of the empirical phenomenon to be explained.[3]

This is an explanation of the occurrence of a particular event, but the schematic letters "C_i" and "E" refer to types of events. The explanatory power of the schema lies in the fact that the conclusion is a logical consequence of the premises. The law or laws are deterministic, so that given the premises, it is logically true that the conclusion follows.

This model has come to be known as the "covering law" model of explanation, from the metaphorical idea that the general law "covers" the particular case. It involves certain presuppositions that should be noted. One is that all laws are general, that is, the law cannot contain any reference to a particular. This was seen as necessary to rule out "general" statements such as "All chairs in this room are made of wood." For the same reason, Hempel and Oppenheim stipulated that laws could contain only purely qualitative properties, so that properties referring to particulars (e.g., "earthly") are proscribed. They further claimed that explanation and prediction have identical logical structures, so that if the E-type event has occurred we have an explanation, and if it will occur, we have a prediction; they were then led to claim that every prediction is an explanation once the predicted event has occurred and every explanation is a prediction if the explained event has yet to occur. This symmetry of explanation and prediction underlies the claim of "nomic expectability"—that an event is explained if its occurrence was to be expected, given the laws and conditions stated in the premises.[4]

The extension of the Deductive–Nomological (DN) model to the explanation of general laws would appear to be straightforward. However, as Hempel and Oppenheim note, this is not the case. One can derive a law from other laws by a strictly logical argument; the problem arises with regard to the premises of the argument. A deduction of Kepler's laws from the conjunction of Kepler's laws and Boyle's Law would hardly constitute an explanation of Kepler's laws, whereas their deduction from Newton's laws would. The problem, then, is to rule out examples such as the former, where despite the fact that the argument is logically valid, nothing is really explained.[5] Assuming that this can be done, there is no problem with extending the DN model also to the deduction of statistical laws if the premises are probabilistic. But there is a major problem with the extension of the model to the explanation of particular events when one or more of the covering laws are probabilistic in character. This problem was dealt with by Hempel in 1962[6] and more fully in 1965[7] in what he called the Inductive-Statistical (IS) model of explanation.[8] Let

$$P(F/G) = r$$

be a probability law that asserts that the probability that x is an F, given that x is an G, is r. Then the IS model is

$$
\begin{array}{l}
P \quad (F/G) = r \\
Gx \\
\rule{4cm}{0.4pt} \quad r \\
Fx
\end{array}
$$

where "x" is an event, "Gx" means "x is a G," "Fx" means "x is an F," and the double line indicates that the argument is not a deduction—rather, Fx follows only with probability r. In this formulation of the model, Hempel required that r be close to 1 in order for the "argument" to constitute an explanation. Furthermore, the probability is relative to our knowledge at the time. Accordingly, Hempel requires that the reference class be maximally specific in that no further partitioning by relevant variables be possible in the state of our knowledge. Thus unlike the DN model, the IS model is explicitly epistemic.[9]

Hempel's work thus provided a comprehensive view of explanation, including four major types—explanation of particular events by general laws, explanation of particular facts by statistical laws, explanation of determinate general laws, and explanation of statistical laws. As Salmon has shown in his history, Hempel's program established a basic view of explanation which has dominated discussion of the issue ever since. But there were problems with Hempel's view, which occasioned sharp controversy, and it is from those controversies that the present work in scientific explanation has largely sprung. It is not necessary here to review this controversy; Salmon has provided a very good account of it. What is important is to point out certain specific problems with the Hempelian view which are relevant to our purposes.

First, one of the problems with the DN model is the stipulation that no law can contain a reference to any particular. This restriction is too strong; it rules out Galileo's Law of Falling Bodies, which refers to the earth, and Kepler's laws, which refer to the sun. Granting the importance of eliminating pseudo-laws such as "all chairs in this room are made of wood," the demand for total generality is not an acceptable way of achieving this objective. There are even some generalizations about individuals, such as, "Whenever John eats strawberries, he gets a stomach ache," which qualify as genuine laws.

Second, Watkins has shown how the problem of explaining laws can be solved within Hempel's general deductivist model by developing a more adequate understanding of what constitutes a theory. Let T be a finite set of k axioms (k>1) and C(T) the set of singular predictive implications that follow from T. Then what Watkins calls the "organic fertility requirement" is that for every partition of T into exclusive and exhaustive subsets T' and T", T is a genuine theory iff C(T) > C(T') ∪ C(T"). Otherwise, T would be merely some collection of axioms that have no more power together than they do separately. As Watkins puts it, "the idea behind the organic fertility requirement is that if T is a genuine theory, then however we partition its axioms, we shall always find that their conjunction is organically fertile in the sense that the whole has more testable content than the sum of the testable contents of its two parts."[10] Much here will depend on how the theory T is axiomitized, and Watkins sets out five rules governing that axiomitization. The fourth rule is

> Wajsberg's requirement: an axiom is impermissible if it contains
> a (proper) component that is a theorem of the axiom set, or
> *becomes one when its variables are bound by the quantifiers that*
> *bind them in the axioms.*[11]

This constraint eliminates the problem of deriving Kepler's laws from the conjunction of Kepler's laws and Boyle's Law.

But Hempel's program faced more fundamental problems. The IS model particularly has drawn heavy fire. As Jeffrey and Salmon have both pointed out,[12] the requirement that r be nearly 1 is dubious. Thus suppose we roll a pair of fair dice. The probability that the sum of the faces of the dice will be greater than 2 is .97. If in fact the outcome is a sum greater than 2, we have what is according to Hempel an explanation:

P (sum of the faces > 2/ two fair dice are rolled) = .97
In this case, two fair dice are rolled.

$$\overline{\rule{4in}{0pt}} \quad r = .97$$

In this case, the sum of the faces is > 2.

But suppose we roll snake-eyes. That outcome would not be explained by the argument, since the probability of that outcome is only .03. But why not? After all, if the probability that the sum is greater than 2 is .97, that very statement implies that the probability of the sum equalling 2 is .03. The "explanation" here appears to be simply the probability law governing the behavior of the dice. It is, as both Jeffrey and Salmon point out, this inability to deal with low or moderate probability events which is fatal to Hempel's position. Indeed, both Jeffrey and Salmon are led to deny that statistical inference provides any explanation at all as applied to events.[13] If this is true, then the heart of the Hempelian position—that it is the logical relation of premises to conclusion which provides the explanatory power of an explanation—is destroyed.

Hempel's program also evoked a very strong reaction from philosophers of history and historians, who considered the DN model and the IS model simply irrelevant to history and who were irritated by Hempel's abrasive insistence that historical "explanations" deserved the name only insofar as they could be assimilated to the covering law model.[14] Hempel and many other philosophers of science thought that the DN and IS models applied universally. Obviously, these models are derived from the physical sciences; for Hempel, the ideal of explanation is best exemplified in physics, and other fields can be ranked in order of degree of "development" by how closely they approximate the ideal. So Platonic a view is seriously jeopardized if different kinds of explanations are used by different disciplines. But this is exactly what the philosophers of history argued.

In 1957, Dray presented an argument that action explanations should be in terms of reasons rather than of laws or causes, and that to explain why an agent A did X, one should argue

> Agent A was in a situation of kind C.
> When in a situation of kind C, the thing to do is X.
> Therefore, agent A did X.[15]

A more detailed and sophisticated form of the rational action theory has been elaborated by Martin, which makes acting for reasons constitutive of rational action and rejects the covering law analysis.[16] The attack on the covering law model of explanation received a considerable boost from the publication in 1959 of Hart and Honore's *Causation in the Law*.[17] In law, as in history, explanation often takes the form of singular causal statements, and this is often the case in situations where there is no apparent way to support such statements by general laws. Given the close relation between legal reasoning and historical reasoning,[18] problems arising in legal philosophy have had a significant impact on how philosophers of history think about cause, and have helped to lead to a reconsideration of the nature of causal explanation in history.[19]

Among philosophers, Scriven has been one of the most outspoken opponents of the covering law model. Scriven holds that causality is "the most important explanatory notion in history"[20] and one that is primitive; it cannot be explicated in Humean terms nor in terms of necessary and sufficient conditions.[21] A cause cannot be identified with sufficient conditions, since it could not then be distinguished from a reliable indicator constantly conjoined to the effect (e.g., a fever is an indicator but not the cause of an infection). It cannot be identified with a necessary condition, for in cases where an effect is overdetermined (i.e., has multiple causes) no one condition is necessary. As Scriven presents it, causality must therefore be regarded as a basic indefinable notion that underlies all explanation. Mandelbaum also has assailed the covering law model and the Humean analysis of causality. For Mandelbaum, causation is a continuous process that can be directly observed. For him, laws are descriptions of these continuous causal processes, but the explanatory power lies in the processes, not the laws.[22]

Among historians themselves, the argument has taken a somewhat different form. The covering law model is rarely discussed as such; rather, the debate centers on the issue of whether or not history is (or can be) a science. Among partisans of the history-as-science school, it has generally been assumed that scientific explanations must be of the covering law sort, while their opponents believe that history is a "humanistic" discipline that does not employ covering laws. An excellent review of this controversy up to 1977 has been written by Lawrence Stone.[23] In chapter 7, we shall return to the later stages of this debate.

It was certainly one of the great virtues of Hempel's theory of explanation that it seemed to combine a Humean empiricism with respect to cause with the power of deductive logic. Hempel explicitly described the DN model as a model of causal explanation,[24] and recent debates concerning explanation have come increasingly to center on the concept of causality. Indeed, the idea of causation seems to lie at the very heart of the enterprise of accounting for one fact or event in terms of another. It is therefore important to look closely at this concept.

Causation

The idea of causation appears to have dual roots. On the one hand, there is the perceptual illusion of causation which was discussed in Chapter 1. Instances of physical contact among bodies which approximate the paradigm of direct launching are perceived as involving causation, no matter how they are produced. On the other hand, Richard Miller has argued that causation is a concept built up by extension from certain core or elementary notions:

> The elementary varieties include pushing (for example, the wind's blowing leaves), giving sensations or feelings (for example, a sting's hurting), and motivating action (for example, fear's motivating flight). Someone who does not recognize any of the elementary varieties, or someone who is not led by growing experience of them to group these varieties under the same label does not have the concept of cause.[25]

These elementary forms of causation are well known to people from their own experiences of doing things and having things happen to them. It is just a fact that we can move things by pushing (if they are not too massive), that things that act upon us can produce feelings and sensations of impact, pain, irritation, and so on, and that motives move us to action. Certainly all human beings have these capacities and experiences and derive from them the ideas of effort, agency, power, and production. These are universal experiences of humankind, and are intersubjective in the sense discussed in Chapter 2—a point that should be evident from the fact that the public language contains so many terms for them.

But efforts to synthesize these different strains of thought have not produced satisfactory results. The imputation of ideas of effort, agency, power, and production to inanimate objects such as machines or billiard balls has not been very successful, nor has it been clear how the apparently causal interactions among such objects can be related to human experience of agency. Certainly the most important early writer on this subject was Aristotle, and his view contains a mixture of elements, some based on analogy to human experience, some on observations of external events, and some on more theoretical considerations. As Edel remarks,

> Clearly Aristotle's notion of efficient cause is a complex one, not to be equated simply, as it often is, with our later notion of the "pushing cause." Its function varies from being a stimulator, to providing the initial material of being, to shaping, to being an agent, according to different examples.[26]

It was Hume who took the radical step of trying to analyze causation solely on the basis of actual sensory observation. In what must be one of the most widely quoted passages in the philosophical literature, but one which will be quoted here once more, Hume wrote:

> Here is a billiard ball lying on the table, and another ball moving toward it with rapidity. They strike; the ball which was formerly at rest now acquires a motion. This is as perfect an instance of the relations of cause and effect as any which we know either by sensation or reflection. Let us therefore examine it. It is evident that the two balls touched one another before the motion was communicated, and that there was no interval betwixt the shock and the motion. *Contiguity* in time and place is therefore a requisite circumstance to the operation of all causes. It is evident, likewise, that the motion which was the cause is prior to the motion which was the effect. *Priority* in time is, therefore, another requisite circumstance in every cause. But this is not all. Let us try any other balls of the same kind in a like situation, and we shall always find that the impulse of the one produces motion in the other. Here, therefore, is a *third* circumstance, viz., that of *constant conjunction* betwixt the cause and the effect. Every object like the cause produces always some object like the effect. Beyond these three circumstances of contiguity, priority, and constant conjunction I can discover nothing in this cause.[27]

The billiard ball case exemplifies what Michotte called "direct launching," in which as we saw in Chapter 1 the perceptual illusion of causation is overwhelming. It is a mark of the singular acuity of David Hume that in spite of that illusion, he was able to provide so penetrating an analysis of what is actually seen. However, Hume does not mean that contiguity, priority, and constant conjunction are all there is to the notion of causality; what he means is that in those cases we consider to be instances of causal connection in nature, contiguity, priority, and constant conjunction are all that we can actually observe. This left him with the problem of accounting for the seeming necessity of the relation. But following Locke, Hume admitted reflection as well as sensation as a source of impressions, so that we may have impressions of reflection. Events associated in the world by contiguity, priority, and constant conjunction become connected in the mind, Hume held, by a natural law of mental association so that the connection between them becomes habitual. It is from our observation of this habitual connection—from our "impression of reflection"[28]—that we derive our idea of causality as a necessary connection among events. Thus, despite the perceptual illusion of causality, nature itself exhibits nothing but the three criteria of contiguity, priority, and constant conjunction; it is we who contribute the belief in a causal relation and its necessity.

But this view, once stated as a thesis concerning the nature of causality in general, was then turned back upon human experience. This of course leaves us with the problem of how to account for those experiences of effort, agency, power, and production from which the notion of cause was partially derived. Certainly there appears to be a *prima facie* incompatibility between the Humean concept of cause and the human experiences of agency, efficiency and freedom, and no attempt to deal with the nature of human behavior can avoid this problem.

Hume's analysis of causation is justly regarded as one of the great achievements of empiricism. But as it stands it is far from being a satisfactory thesis. None of the three criteria—the observable features—cited by Hume are adequate as a basis for imputing causality to natural events. In the first place, temporal priority is not an invariable correlate of causation. Many writers have pointed out that cause and effect can be simultaneous. Thus consider a law such as $f = ma$. Although some have questioned whether such a "Law of Correlation" is a causal law, no one would deny that the force is responsible for the acceleration rather than the acceleration producing the force. There is no temporal difference between the application of the force and the acceleration of the body. All causal relations represented in the form of equations (unless a time lag is explicitly introduced) raise this problem. Further, some writers even argue that causal priority need not coincide with temporal priority and that, since there is no logical inconsistency in time-reversed causation, it is an empirical question whether or not a later event can cause an earlier one.[29]

In the second place, whether or not contiguity in space is a necessary condition for a causal relation depends on which physical theory one holds. In Newtonian physics, there is action at a distance and contiguity is unnecessary; in Einsteinian physics, there is no action at a distance and contiguity is necessary; in quantum mechanics, the issue is unresolved, but there are some phenomena that appear to show action at a distance. Salmon discusses this point at length and is forced to conclude that his theory, which does require contiguity, may not be applicable to quantum mechanics for just this reason.[30]

Finally, there are well-known cases of constant conjunctions that are clearly not cases of causal relations—for example, day always precedes night, but no one supposes that day causes night. Indeed, one of the arguments made by Dray and others against Hempel's claim of symmetry between explanation and prediction was that correct predictions may be made on the basis of indicators that are not causes. Thus from a certain pattern of skin eruptions, a physician can predict that further symptoms will appear, but the skin eruptions are not causes of the later symptoms. Whenever there are phenomena that are joint effects of an underlying cause, the conjunction of the effects may be perfect and so permit unfailing prediction. Clearly, then, constant conjunction is not a sufficient condition for the presence of a causal relation.

But is constant conjunction, if not a sufficient condition, at least a necessary condition for a causal relation? The obvious objection to this claim is that it would make all unique events causeless. To this it has been replied that whether or not an event is unique is a question of how that event is classified; every event is unique in some respects but not necessarily in others. Hence it is not clear that there are unique events in any causally significant sense. Nevertheless, there are events that do appear to be unique in the sense that no presently imaginable classification could bring them under a law-like generalization. The Big Bang in which our universe began is a unique event, and certainly it is obvious that none of the Humean criteria can be applied to the Big Bang, at least as it is currently understood. Whether there are other such events is not clear, but this one is at least sufficient to refute the claim that every event has a cause in the specific Humean sense.

The claim that constant conjunctions or regularities are required for causality has also been criticized on the ground that an effect may be overdetermined—there may be several factors that can independently cause the effect. But although there certainly are such cases, it is still the case that there is a constant conjunction between the effect and each of the separate causal factors. All that the existence of overdetermination shows is that from the occurrence of the effect, one cannot infer which causal factor operated; it remains true that each cause is constantly conjoined to the effect. In somewhat more detail, if something C is a cause of something E, it may well be the case that E would have occurred even if C did not; there might be multiple factors that cause E, so that although the occurrence of C is sufficient for the occurrence of E, it is not necessary. Similarly, C might be a part of a complex of factors K that together cause E; C would then be a necessary but not sufficient condition of E, if E is caused by K. Let these conditions that in conjunction with C are necessary for the production of the effect E be called the "causal field."[31] For example, it is a necessary condition for a man dying that he was born alive. But if one is seeking to explain why he died, one would not normally cite his being born alive as a cause of his death. All such conditions may be said to belong to the causal field. Thus if we believe that in a causal field, C causes E, and that there are no other combinations of factors that would cause E in the absence of C, we should be willing to accept

> In F [the causal field] in this case, had not C occurred,
> E would not have occurred.

That is, if we know the causes of E, and if none of them obtain, then E should not occur. Thus, it seems to be true that a belief in constant conjunction as a criterion of causality implies the assertion of counterfactuals.

A similar conclusion seems to follow from cases of causal pre-emption. Suppose that a cause C is constantly conjoined to an effect E, and that there is a second cause C* that is also constantly conjoined to E. Suppose a case where C is realized, but before E occurs, C* is realized, so that the occurrence of E is actually due to C*. Thus for example consider a man dying of AIDS who decides not to wait for the inevitable and takes poison. Certainly the actual event of his dying is due to the poison. Nevertheless, it is also true that, had he not taken poison, he would have died of AIDS. In this case, the causal role of AIDS in producing his death was pre-empted by his taking the poison. But even to state that causal pre-emption occurred clearly involves the counterfactual that had pre-emption not occurred, the pre-empted cause would have brought about the effect anyway.

As these examples should make clear, it is difficult to defend the constant conjunction or regularity thesis without resorting to counterfactuals. Attempts have accordingly been made to supplement Humean analysis by accepting as law-like only those statements of regularities which can support subjunctive conditionals. Certainly this requirement captures a criterion that one would want any attribution of causality to meet, but it also involves the rejection of just the sort of radical empiricism that Hume sought to defend. The truth or falsity of subjunctive conditionals cannot be verified by observation alone.

How can one know that a counterfactual is true? One answer is that a counterfactual is true if it follows from a true law. Thus if a baseball traveling in a given direction with a particular velocity suddenly changes direction and velocity, we account for that (in Newtonian physics) by the action of some force on the ball, and given the first and second laws of motion we feel certain that had that force not acted on that ball, it would not have acquired its new direction and velocity. But this answer does little to support the Humean analysis. If the law is simply a statement of a regularity—a constant conjunction—what grounds are there for projecting it into the future, or onto cases which have not in fact occurred? Goodman's analysis of projectibility makes it a consequence of past projections; predicates are projectible if they are better entrenched than rival predicates.[32] This does not solve the problem; it merely restates it in terms of predicates. To project a law into the future, or to use it to support a counterfactual, builds upon past usage, but the underlying assumptions are that past usage is the result of successes, and that past successes will be followed by future successes. This is to say that projectible regularities of the sorts asserted in a law are not matters of chance but that there is some ontologically real connection between the factors referred to in the antecedent and those referred to in the consequent for the existence of which successful predictions can be regarded as confirming evidence. To take this view is to abandon the Humean analysis of causality. Hume's three criteria of priority, contiguity and constant conjunction must then be seen simply as indicators, albeit fallible ones, of the presence of causal connections in nature. Wherever a process exhibits these features, we have some grounds for believing that causality is involved.

What are the entities which enter into causal relations? Hume's own account is ambiguous as between objects, types of objects, and events. Davidson has argued strongly for events as the only entities which can be causes or effects,[33] but this claim has been challenged on several counts. First, to define causation as a relation holding among events only, and events as the sole entities which can stand in causal relations, involves a circularity unless there is some independent identification of events, or of causation, neither of which Davidson provides. Second, Davidson's criterion for the identity of events—"events are identical if and only if they have exactly the same causes and effects"[34]—involves a regress. According to this criterion, events e and e' are identical only if, for every c and every f, c is a cause of e iff c is a cause of e', and f is caused by e iff f is caused by e'. But suppose a cause

c_1 of e and a cause c_2 of e'; how do we know that these causes are identical? Since all c's must be events if they are causes, we can only prove their identity by showing that *they* have the same causes and effects. Obviously we have a regress here with respect to both causes and effects.

Kim argues that an event should be conceptualized as $[x, P, t]$, which means the object referred to by "x" has the property referred to by "P" at the time indicated by "t." Then two monadic events $[x, P, t]$ and $[z, Q, t']$ are identical if and only if $x = z$, $P = Q$, and $t = t'$. The event schema and the identity criterion can be adapted to deal with dyadic or n-adic events without difficulty. But what exactly is an event as Kim describes it? Kim takes his schema as referring to events, states, processes, conditions, "and the like."[35] Clearly, what is required is some thing having a property at a time, but the time may be an interval as well as a point, and there is no apparent restriction on what sort of thing "x" may refer to. There is also the well known problem of determining when properties are identical, and the fact that times are relative to a frame of reference.

Most writers on causation and events hold that events involve in some way the notion of change. It is however quite unclear what changes, or that change is essential to the concept of event. Suppose a body moving in a straight line at uniform velocity; is this motion an event? There is certainly change—of position; there is also uniformity—of velocity and direction. Or suppose a body falling with constant acceleration; there is both change—of velocity, and uniformity—of acceleration. Again, suppose a balloon constantly expanding, even if the rate of expansion is diminishing. There is change—of volume, and uniformity—the balloon continues to expand. Are these events, or processes, or states, or what? I do not know the answers to these questions and so far as I can see no one else does either. It would seem therefore that the difference between change and uniformity is not an adequate criterion for distinguishing events from states or processes.

Among the Humean criteria for causation are spatio-temporal contiguity and temporal priority. Brand, who believes causes and effects are events, argues that an event has the form

(2) x Fing occupies r.

where "x" is an object, "F" a predicate expression, and "r" refers to a spatio-temporal region.[36] But the notion of the spatial extent of an event raises complicated problems, as Needham points out.

Quinton[37] conjures up a picture of the scene in a church as a couple are married, and wonders how far the marriage extends

into the rafters! Where does an eclipse of the sun by the moon
occur? How are the spatial boundaries of the location determined? Does the region include, for example, every point from
which an influence traveling no faster than the speed of light
could reach one of the bodies involved within some given interval of time?[38]

The spatial volume of r is, at the very least, ill-defined. Furthermore,
the criterion of spatial contiguity raises the further difficulty that it rules
out the possibility of causal action at a distance. As we saw above, this is a
matter that must be resolved by physicists, not by philosophers, and it
would be senseless to insist on this particular Humean criterion until the
problem within physics is settled.

The criteria of temporal contiguity and temporal priority also raise
serious difficulties. Some writers have held that there are "point events,"
that is, instantaneous events.[39] Davidson thinks not, and with good reason.[40] As Steiner notes, instantaneous events (instantaneous acceleration, if
that is an event) are definable only as limits of a series of intervals, which
raises serious doubts as to whether they are suitable entities to play a causal
role.[41] Most writers take events as enduring through some interval of time.
But how long an interval of time? Consider, for example,

(3) The physical universe expanding for 20 billion years.

This fits Brand's schema, and Kim's, but is this an event? If an event can last
for twenty billion years, what is not an event? And how would an event be
differentiated from a state or process? I know of no criterion by which one
could set a maximum temporal duration for events or a minimum temporal
duration for states or processes. Hence the distinction seems to be at best
ill-defined.

Finally, there is the problem of how an event e (or any other entity)
that is temporally prior to an effect e' can possibly act upon e'. Suppose that
e terminates at time t. In view of the continuity of time, there is no instant
next after t. Yet temporal contiguity seems to require that there be no interval between e and e', and our common-sense notions of causal action seem
to demand that t must have a successor.[42] But if there is no temporal difference between e and e', are they really different events? Thus we seem to
find unexpected difficulties in these criteria wherever we turn.

Salmon takes events and processes to be only arbitrarily distinct:

An event is something that happens in a fairly restricted region
of spacetime. The context determines how large or small that

region may be. A process is something that, in the context, has greater temporal duration than an event. From the standpoint of cosmology a supernova explosion . . . could be considered an event; the travel of a photon or neutrino from the explosion to earth (requiring thousands of years) would be a process.[43]

Thus for him events and processes alike can be terms of causal relations. Since states and, on Salmon's view, objects can be construed as processes, and since there appears to be no clear criterion for ruling out any of these from standing in causal relations, I shall adopt this latitudinarian perspective.

Salmon's Theory

Of recent works on the philosophy of science, Salmon's *Statistical Explanation and the Causal Structure of the World* is certainly one of the most important and one that presents an alternative to the Hempelian model of explanation. In his earlier work, Salmon argued for what he called the statistical relevance view of explanation.[44] In his latest work, he takes a somewhat different position. As he describes it,

It now seems to me that explanation is a two-tiered affair. At the most basic level, it is necessary, for purposes of explanation, to subsume the event-to-be-explained under an appropriate set of statistical relevance relations. . . . At the second level, it seems to me, the statistical relevance relations that are invoked at the first level must be explained in terms of causal relations.[45]

Salmon spells out the two tiers of the explanatory structure he proposes in considerable detail. The first, or statistical tier, is illustrated by the following example. Suppose that the event to be explained is that a particular boy—Joe—stole a car. We look first for an appropriate reference class of which Joe is a member—in this case, say, that of American teenager (call it A)—and an appropriate description of the car theft—say, a delinquent action. The original question is now transformed into the question of why this American teenager committed a delinquent act. If we partition the class of delinquents into B_1, those with no prior criminal convictions, B_2, those with convictions for minor infractions only, and B_3, those with convictions for a major offence, we have what Salmon calls an "explanandum partition" that will define the sample space for the explanation. Accordingly, we obtain the prior probabilities $P(B_1/A)$, $P(B_2/A)$ and $P(B_3/A)$, or in general $P(B_i/A) = p_i$ for $i = 1 \ldots m$. We then look for those factors that are, according to our criminological theories, relevant to the commission of such a crime (e.g., sex, religion, parents's marital status, socio-economic status). Each of these factors admits of partition (male, female; Protestant, Catholic, Jew; parents never married, parents divorced, etc.; upper class, middle class, lower class, and so on). Combining all these variables, we get a matrix of cells such as male-Protestant-parents married-lower class; female-Catholic-parents divorced-middle class, etc. Call these cells the Cs. Then $A.C_1$, $A.C_2$, $A.C_3 \ldots A.C_j$ form the explanans partition, and we must obtain the complete set of posterior probabilities $P(B_i/A.C_j) = p_{ij}$ for $i = 1 \ldots$ m and $j = 1 \ldots s$. We must also make sure that the cells $A.C_i$ are homogeneous so that none of them can be further divided in a way that is relevant to the occurrence of any B_i (in short, that we have included all the relevant variables). We determine the marginal probabilities $P(C_j/A) = q_j$ so that we can separate out the influence of the particular explanatory variables; and we further require that p_{ij} not equal p_{jk} (i.e., that we include only relevant variables). Finally we determine into which cell $A.C_j$ Joe falls. To the degree that $P(B_i/A)$ is not equal to $P(B_i/A.C_j)$, the variables lumped under C are statistically relevant to Joe's delinquency; if $P(B_i/A) < P(B_i/A.C_j)$, then the difference $P(B_i/A.C_j) - P(B_i/A)$ shows the degree to which those variables increase the probability of Joe's being delinquent; if $P(B_i/A) > P(B_i/A.C_j)$, the difference shows the degree to which those variables decrease that probability. In either case, the variables are statistically relevant to the degree that they change the prior probability, and the difference between the prior and posterior probabilities is the measure of the relevance.[46]

Obviously, what Salmon is describing here is an ideal; we never know that all relevant variables have been taken into account, and irrelevant variables have a way of sneaking in no matter what we do. But the central claim is that it is not the absolute probability of the event that is explanatory but the difference between the prior and the posterior probabilities. If a variable is relevant to the occurrence of a given type of event, different values for that variable should make a difference in the probability of that type of event occurring. And, although few methodology books would describe statistical explanation in as Bayesian terms as Salmon does, what he has outlined is acceptable in the social sciences as a valid form of statistical explanation.

The statistical relevance model is not an argument. Salmon is explicit on that point:

> According to the S-R [statistical relevance] approach . . . the statistical basis of scientific explanation consists, not in an argument, but in an assemblage of relevant considerations. High

probability is not the desideratum; rather the amount of relevant information is what counts. According to this approach, the S-R basis of statistical explanation consists of a probability distribution over a homogeneous partition of an initial reference class. A homogeneous partition, it will be recalled, is one that does not admit of further relevant subdivision. The subclasses in the partition must also be maximal—that is, the partition must not involve any irrelevant subdivisions. The goodness, or epistemic value, of such an explanation is measured . . . by the gain in information provided by the probability distribution over the explanandum-partition relative to the explanans-partition.[47]

It is not the logical relation of premise to conclusion but the difference between prior and posterior probabilities that is important here.

But does such an S-R explanation explain? At one time, Salmon thought so, but he has now revised his view. What the S-R approach does is describe the relations among a variety of random variables and show which variables are statistically relevant to the dependent variable in question, that is, it provides us with correlations among these variables. These statistical relations therefore become evidence to be accounted for by the second, or causal, tier of the explanation. But they do something more than that. Insofar as the relationships found are statistically significant—are great enough so that they cannot reasonably be attributed to chance—their existence shows that the independent variables have some relation, direct or indirect, to the dependent variable. They thus demonstrate that a causal process must be operating, but they do not indicate what that process is. That is the task of the second tier.

The most radical aspect of Salmon's new theory is his claim that we must invoke causal processes to account for these statistical relations of relevance. This is no minor change. It involves the claim that processes are the fundamental ontological constituents of the world.[48] Process ontologies are not exactly new; Whitehead labored to construct such a system, but as Rescher has remarked, there are a host of problems about such entities that remain to be worked out.[49] Salmon makes little attempt to do this. He does tell us that "a given process . . . has a certain degree of uniformity—we may say, somewhat loosely, that it exhibits a certain structure."[50] He also says, "What I mean by a process is similar to what Russell characterized as a causal line"[51] and then quotes Russell to the effect that "a person, a table, a photon" are causal lines, and hence, for Salmon, processes. Thus any entity that endures over some time interval is a process, although in what other than uniformity its structure consists is left unclear.

Salmon is chiefly concerned with distinguishing between causal processes and pseudo-processes. This is done in terms of Reichenbach's notion of mark transmission. In *The Philosophy of Space and Time*, Reichenbach used the notion of mark transmission as a way of determining when one event is the cause of another. For any two events, E_1, and E_2, Reichenbach holds,

> If E_1 is the cause of E_2, then a small variation (a mark) in E_1 is associated with a small variation in E_2, whereas small variations in E_2 are not associated with variations in E_1.[52]

This asymmetry of the causal order Reichenbach then used to define the unidirectional order of time. Reichenbach's use of the mark criterion pertains to events rather than processes, but Salmon employs it as a way of distinguishing between those processes that are truly causal and those that are not:

> Let P be a process that, in the absence of interactions with other processes, would remain uniform with respect to a characteristic Q, which it would manifest consistently over an interval that includes both of the space-time points A and B (A $\neq$ B). Then, a mark (consisting of a modification of Q into Q'), which has been introduced into process P by means of a single local interaction at point A, is transmitted to point B if P manifests the modification Q' at B and at all stages of the process between A and B without additional interventions.[53]

Salmon gives two illustrations to demonstrate the difference between causal- and pseudo-processes. First, suppose a large circular building with a spotlight mounted at the center. The light beam going from the spotlight to the building wall is a causal process. A red filter intercepting the beam at any point will mark the beam by changing its color, and that mark will be transmitted to the wall. But now let the spotlight rotate; the spot of light on the wall will also rotate around the circumference of the building. The moving spot is a process, but not a causal process, for no mark introduced at a given point on the wall will be transmitted. Second, suppose a car traversing a road as an example of a genuine causal process, and its shadow running along beside it as an example of a pseudo-process.[54] What makes the shadow a pseudo-process is that it is parasitic on the genuine process. While a scratch to the car as a result of grazing a wall will be a transmissible mark of the car, there is Salmon holds, no similar transmissible mark of the shadow.

This definition has drawn some fire, and justly so. As Kitcher remarks, under this definition the shadow *is* a causal process, because "when the car grazes the wall its shadow acquires, and continues to have, a new characteristic—*being the shadow of a scratched car.*"[55] Part of the trouble here is that Salmon's definition does not capture his own insight. Thus he remarks "A causal process is one that is self-determined and not parasitic upon other causal influences."[56] Obviously, "being the shadow of a scratched car" is parasitic on another causal process, but Salmon does not manage to rule this out in his formal definition of mark transmission given above.

At a deeper level, Salmon owes us an analysis of the structure of a process which he has not given. Thus he says,

> The difference between a causal process and a pseudo-process, I am suggesting, is that the causal process transmits its own structure, while the pseudo-process does not. The distinction between processes that do and those that do not transmit their own structures is revealed by the mark criterion. If a process— a causal process—is transmitting its own structure, then it will be capable of transmitting certain modifications in that structure.[57]

But as Kitcher's example shows, mark transmission alone does not define the structure of the process; rather, the notion of the structure of a process must be clarified before it will be possible to distinguish between marks that are and those that are not parasitic upon another causal process.

Granting Salmon his notions of process and mark transmission, he is then able to deal with the explanation of statistical relevance relations by arguing that "the basic causal mechanism . . . is a causal process that carries with it probability distributions for various types of interactions."[58] To make this more precise, he defines the notions of "direct causal relevance" that holds between two events if they are connected by a causal process, and "if that causal process is responsible for the transmission of causal influence from one to the other"[59] and "indirect causal relevance" if two events are the results of a common cause, or if the two processes modify each other as a result of interaction.[60] But both direct and indirect causal relevance involve genuine causal relations that have explanatory power. On this basis, then, Salmon argues that statistical relevance relations are to be explained by causal relevance relations.[61]

As Salmon points out, his is an updated version of the mechanical philosophy. "Scientific explanation . . . consists in exhibiting the phenomena-to-be-explained as occupying their places in the patterns and regularities which structure the world. Causal relations lie at the foundations of these patterns and regularities."[62] We do not, Salmon thinks, understand a phenomenon until we can construct a causal account of why it occurred. This does not require going back to Newtonian mechanics, but it does require models that involve causal processes, not just correlations.

Hempel's position on explanation, including both the deductive-nomological and the inductive-statistical versions, has generally been referred to as a "covering law" position. In this case, it seems very clear what is meant. In both models there must be among the premises at least one general law or law-like statement—in the deductive-nomological model a statement of the form $(x) (Fx \rightarrow Gx)$, and in the inductive-statistical model a statement of the form $P (F/G) = r$. Although Salmon has attacked Hempel's view of explanation as an inference, he nevertheless considers his own view to also be a covering law position. On this point, he is very explicit.

> Causal processes and causal interactions are governed by basic laws of nature. Photons, for instance, travel in null geodesic paths unless they are scattered or absorbed upon encountering material particles. Freely falling material particles follow paths that are non-null geodesics. Linear and angular momentum are conserved when particles interact with one another. Energy is conserved in isolated physical systems. *The causal/mechanical version of the ontic conception of scientific explanation is as much a covering-law conception as is any version of the epistemic conception.*[63]

Why should an explanation have to be of the covering law type? For Hempel the answer is obvious: If an explanation is an inference, it must involve a universal premise; otherwise no conclusion can be deduced. In the inductive-statistical model this requirement is compromised, but only just. The law that serves as a premise is not indeed universal, but the condition that r must be close to 1 makes it approximately universal, and clearly Hempel regards the strength of the explanation as depending on r.

For Salmon, on the other hand, the answer is not so obvious, and much of the trouble comes from the problem of how causal processes are related to laws. In describing the "ontic" conception of explanation (and Salmon says his own theory is ontic), Salmon says that laws are natural regularities that are described by law statements.[64] But Salmon also says that laws "govern" causal processes: "Causal processes and causal interactions are governed by basic laws of nature,"[65] and he further says that, "causal relations lie at the foundations of these patterns and regularities [in nature]"[66] Since Salmon says that entities (photons, electrons, etc.) are causal processes, it is unclear whether the causal process is the regularity described by the law, is governed by the law, or is the cause of the law. In what sense can a law "govern" a causal process, if both the process and the law are regularities? And what does it mean to say the electron is a causal process? One can understand that the behavior of an electron might exhibit a regularity, so that it would be true that under conditions C, all electrons exhibit a given behavior. But how does the continued existence of the electron over some time interval exhibit a regularity? Or, to put the matter differently, suppose an entity to come into existence which is unique, endures for some period, and is then destroyed. Is that entity a causal process? Salmon would apparently have to say that it is. Then the claim that the ontic conception of explanation is a covering law theory apparently means that there cannot be any such unique entity. But why not? Certainly the physical universe is a physically existent entity, and it is apparently unique. Here again one comes up against the vagueness that infests Salmon's concept of process.

Even more troubling is the question of what in Salmon's theory constitutes causation. Salmon says that a process that can transmit its own structure can transmit "causal influence." But Salmon's theory of transmission is the at-at theory of Russell.[67] As Salmon puts it, "The transmission of a mark from point A in a causal process to point B in the same process *is* the fact that it appears at each point between A and B *without further interactions*."[68] Again, "according to the 'at-at' theory, to move from A to B is simply to occupy the intervening points at the intervening instants. It consists in being *at* particular points of space *at* corresponding moments."[69] What the at-at theory does is to give a satisfactory answer to Zeno's Paradox of the Arrow. It allows something to move continuously through space and time. This solution obviously can be applied to the simple persistence of stationary objects in time as well as to motions in space-time. But when Salmon says, "A process that transmits its own structure is capable of propagating a causal influence from one space-time locale to another,"[70] one would think that some concept such as energy or force would be required. Salmon explicitly denies this; causal influence is distinct from motion, momentum, or energy.[71] The reason, Salmon says, is that there is "a fundamental problem involved in employing this fact [energy transmission] as a basic criterion—namely, we must have some basis for distinguishing situations in which energy is transmitted from those in which it merely appears in some regular fashion."[72]

The example given to illustrate this problem is the spot of light projected on the wall of the circular building by the rotating spotlight. At each point on the spot's path along the wall there is energy from the light beam, but that energy is not transmitted from spot to spot. This seems like an odd example to give, since on Salmon's analysis two different light spots on the wall are independent effects of a common cause. Since Salmon uses this example to show that transmission of the energy cannot be distinguished from appearance of the energy, he evidently does not regard being effects of a common cause as involving "further interaction." But if Salmon considers it illegitimate to look beyond the "process" of the moving spot itself, he is open to a similar problem respecting mark transmission. Consider a melody, played on an instrument such as a clarinet. Suppose that after the first ten bars, the melody is transposed from the key of C to the key of G, and is finished in that latter key. The key of C is here Salmon's characteristic, Q, and the key of G is the mark, Q'. Does it follow that, because at each moment after the transposition, the melody is in the key of G, the melody is a causal process? Surely on any reasonable interpretation the notes are independent effects of the musician's actions; no note transmits "causal influence" to its successor. Problems of this sort are inherent in the use of the at-at theory to describe causal transmission. The at-at theory makes it impossible to distinguish the transmission of a mark from A to B from its simply appearing at every point of the closed interval from A to B; it is indeed the point of the at-at theory that no such distinction *can* be made. But since the presence of a mark in a process at every point from A to B can be due to a common cause, Salmon's theory cannot distinguish a genuine causal process from a pseudo-process.

The root problem here, it seems to me, is that Salmon is trying to combine two incompatible notions. On the one hand, he regards causal processes as ontologically real entities of some sort; on the other, he wants them to be Humean regularities. But they cannot be both, and the attempt to make them both leads to the ambiguities in their relation to laws and to the attempt to make the at-at theory do something it cannot do. This problem cannot be resolved without some greater clarity on just what the nature of a causal process is.

That a process ontology can be adequate for the general theory of relativity has been shown;[73] whether the same is true of quantum mechanics Salmon considers an open question. But the specific theory of processes which Salmon proposes is inadequate. Mark transmission is not a satisfactory way of identifying those processes that are causal. Given the fact that mark-bearing processes can be effects of other processes, it is doubtful that a causal process can be identified by any feature of that process itself.

If there is a way of identifying causal processes absolutely, it would seem that the "structure" of the process must be the key. Thus when Salmon says, "A process that transmits its own structure is capable of propagating a causal influence from one space-time locale to another,"[74] he seems to regard "structure" as the determining factor. But Salmon gives us almost nothing beyond the mark transmission criterion as a definition of the structure, and it is not clear what other sorts of structure his processes can have. Thus, Salmon cites photons and electrons as examples of genuine causal processes. But since these are presumably irreducible or ultimate particles, they cannot have a "structure" in the sense of being composed of more basic constituents. They do have properties—an electron has a mass and a charge—and perhaps one can talk about a "structure" of properties, but then one needs a criterion for sorting properties into those that can be parasitic on other processes and those that cannot, and this brings us full circle.

As these considerations show, one major objective of Salmon's theory has not been achieved—Salmon has not been able to provide a way of discriminating causal processes from pseudo-processes on the basis of identifiable characteristics of the process alone. These problems do not show that Salmon's ontic theory of causal processes is false, but they do show that substantial refinement of the theory is necessary.

But whatever the short comings of Salmon's theory, I think he is right about the relation between statistical relevance and causal relevance. One need not adopt his Bayesian view to agree with him on this point. Statistical associations among variables that are strong enough so that they cannot be reasonably attributed to chance alone are *prima facie* evidence of the existence of causal processes. It does not matter if the value of the correlation coefficient is low as long as it is significant in the statistical sense. In saying that the correlation is not due to chance, one is asserting that there is some underlying causal process that is responsible for it. The correlation itself may be spurious, owing to an unknown common cause, but the fact that a significant correlation exists implies the existence of *some* underlying causal mechanism. Thus as Salmon says, statistical relevance—a significant statistical relationship—is evidence for the existence of a causal process, whether or not we know what that process is.

Railton's Theory

Peter Railton's theory of explanation stands in rather marked contrast to those of Hempel and Salmon. Railton's theory is nomothetic; he regards scientific explanations as fundamentally law-based.

> A nomothetic ideal emphasizes that an understanding of the world must be theoretical, at least to the extent of reflecting some conception of what is necessary (or lawful) and general as

opposed to accidental and particular, some conception, that is, of what the *organizing principles* of the world are (even if these principles embody randomness) which we must grasp in order to know the *how* and *why* of things.[75]

Railton's position is thus a covering law position, but it is not a purely deductivist one, as Hempel's DN model is, nor is it based on nomic expectability, but rather upon theoretical comprehension. His theory is a realistic—what Salmon calls an "ontic"—rather than epistemic theory, and it is explicitly an attempt to account for the explanations that are actually used in science. Thus Railton offers an alternative form of the covering law theory which has many of the virtues of the other versions without some of their problems.

As we saw above, both Hempel's various schemata and Salmon's outline of explanation represent ideal forms that will not be realized in practice. Railton explicitly develops his theory in terms of an ideal explanatory text:

Imagine them [scientific explanations] in an idealized form, purged of mistakes or gaps, carried to the highest level of theoretical generality, bringing all the relevant laws and principles to bear on the explanandum down to the most basic truths of physics. Call such accounts *ideal (explanatory) texts*. Now consider merely the complicated *structure* of such ideal texts, the ways in which laws are brought to bear, regularities or particular facts derived, etc. Call this structure an *Ideal (explanatory) form*. Many ideal texts, then, will share a given ideal form. If the motivation given for a covering law approach to explanation is well-grounded, then the backbone of an ideal form will consist of covering law arguments. Is there only one ideal form for explanation? I think not. Rather there are several definite kinds of explanation recognized in science—causal, probabilistic, and structural particular-fact explanations, theoretical explanations, etc.—, and to these correspond several definite ideal forms. . . . All of these forms, if the covering-law approach is sound, are structured basically along covering-law lines.[76]

Thus all ideal forms of explanation are for Railton covering-law forms, but there are different kinds of covering-law explanations. We must therefore look briefly at what these different forms are.

The first type of ideal explanatory form is causal explanation of particular events. Railton describes what such an ideal explanatory text would be:

The ideal form of causal explanation . . . involves more than just finding some law under which *a* and *b* [events] can (under some description and along with some statement of antecedent conditions) be subsumed, difficult as that job may be. To fill out an ideal explanatory text for a causal explanation of *b* we must also bring to bear all relevant theory, and give a full account of the workings of the causal mechanisms that led to *b*, tracing these workings down to the most fundamental levels of physical description, and exhibiting along the way all the laws that govern these workings. Thus the ideal form for causal explanation demands completeness not just in the sense of filling in all the connections and nodes of the causal network culminating in the explanandum event, but also in the sense of fully exposing the underlying processes and principles that figure in this network, and showing how these phenomena derive from basic properties of the universe.[77]

It is important to see that the ideal causal explanatory text is not just a deductive argument. Railton is explicit that "the basic structure of paradigm explanations in science *is* that of an extended deductive argument from laws"; but the ideal text contains in addition to such an argument a description of the basic causal mechanisms involved—"scientific explanations are not merely *arguments* or *demonstrations*, they are *accounts, analyses* of what happens and why."[78] Thus in causal explanation, mere subsumption under general laws is not enough; the ideal text must involve causal laws; there must be "no ineliminable sub-part of the chain of reasoning that involves non-causal laws,"[79] and the causes involved must be the actual causes that produced the phenomenon in question. Causality is thus, in Railton's view, a basic category of explanation, and causal explanations are a fundamental type of scientific explanation.

Railton's second type of ideal explanatory text is that for the probabilistic explanation of particular events. The schema for the deductive-nomological-probabilistic (DNP) text is:

(a) A theoretical derivation of law (b1), below, from basic physical theory, embedded in an account of the probabilistic mechanisms to which (b1) applies.

(b) An irreducibly probabilistic law of the form:

(b1) (t) (x)[Fxt $\rightarrow$ Prob (G)xt = p]
"At any time, anything that is F has probability p to be G."

The relevant particular fact(s) about the case at hand, e:

(b2) F_{eto}
"e is F at time t_0."

And the obvious conclusion:

(b3) Prob $(G)_{eto} = p$.
"e has probability p to be G at time t_0."

(c) To which we append a parenthetic addendum to the effect that e did become G at t_0.[80]

From (a) through (b3), this is a deductive argument that shows that e has a certain probability of being G at time t_0. But the addendum, (c), does not follow from this argument; it is a matter of chance that e did become G at t_0, although it is chance constrained by the probability p.

Railton's interpretation of probability is a propensity interpretation; he takes propensities to be real physical tendencies in objects to behave in a particular way.[81] Hence the DNP model is taken to be a true description of an objective situation; the probability is objective rather than epistemic. This view avoids one of the major asymmetries of the Hempelian position. Furthermore, in Railton's view, the DNP model applies only in cases where the occurrence of the particular event in question is objectively indeterminate (e.g., alpha decay of U^{238}). Statistical explanations where the underlying situation is really deterministic (e.g., classical statistical mechanics) Railton sees as providing clues or insights into the underlying causal mechanisms involved, but not a true probability explanation: "If the underlying physics of the theory is deterministic, and relative frequencies of outcomes are due only to scattered initial conditions, then it stands to reason that classical statistical mechanics offers solely causal, deterministic explanations."[82] Quantum mechanics, on the other hand, provides cases of phenomena that are fundamentally indeterminate and can therefore be described only by probabilistic statements.

The causal and probabilistic ideal explanatory texts both focus upon "giving an account of the mechanism(s) actually responsible for bringing about the explanandum."[83] But Railton has a third type of ideal explanatory text for particular events—what he calls structural explanation. Laws such as the Heisenberg Uncertainty Principle, the Pauli Exclusion Principle, Gibbs's Phase Rule, conservation laws, and the Principle of Least Action fall into this category. These are physical laws that limit the possible states or state-evolutions of physical systems.[84] These laws can be used to explain particular events, but they do not provide causal explanations, Railton argues, unless the notion of causation is made so broad that it includes everything. If one explains "why an electron entering the orbits of an ion takes on a spin of -1 in terms of the Pauli Exclusion Principle,"[85] what is the cause? One could, Railton says, point to a principle or a structure, but certainly not to something that we would ordinarily recognize as a cause.[86] Similarly, Railton argues that explanation by reduction is not causal: "Whatever the relationship between reduced and reducing phenomena, it *cannot* be one of effect and cause, since the two are not properly distinct, and a minimum requirement for a causal relation . . . is that cause and effect be distinct."[87] Thus Railton holds that structural explanations form a distinct third type of ideal explanatory text.

The three ideal types just outlined may constitute distinct sorts of explanatory texts, but in particular cases they are very often combined. Such a combined text Railton calls an "encyclopedic ideal text."[88] Thus causal, probabilistic, and structural laws may all be invoked in a complete explanation for a particular case, with some portion of the ideal encyclopedic text being of each type.

As one might expect, Railton holds that laws can be explained by accounts that involve causal, probabilistic, and structural factors. "As in nomothetic particular-fact explanation, so in nomothetic theoretical explanation: we build up ideal encyclopedic texts by amalgamating various explanations, often of various forms."[89]

There are, as Railton emphasizes, certain restrictions on the freedom with which such amalgamations can be made. If the law to be explained is fundamentally probabilistic, as is the case with certain laws of quantum mechanics, then there can be no explanation of the regularity which shows that it "*had to* obtain."[90] Similarly, "one may . . . give a structural and a causal explanation of the same explanandum, but one cannot give both a structural and a causal account *of the same explanatory relationship*." Thus there are what Railton calls "exclusion principles" governing the creation of an ideal encyclopedic text for a theoretical explanation.[91]

One of the most attractive features of Railton's theory is that it offers a very simple and very reasonable account of the relation between nomothetic explanation and explanations offered in the form of singular causal statements. The basic argument is this: If ideal explanatory texts constitute the ideal forms of explanation for a given phenomenon, they are clearly an ideal that is never actually attained. This in itself is not an objection; Salmon's description of a statistical relevance explanation is also an ideal that will never be realized. But once such an ideal is accepted, it is then possible to rate actual explanations offered by someone for a phenomenon as better or worse, depending on the degree to which they approximate the ideal. An actual explanation, of course, may fall short for many reasons: "it may leave things out, include irrelevancies, contain misrepresentations, be logically inconclusive, be vague, and so on."[92] But despite its failings, a proffered explanation may be explanatory to the degree that it gives information about the ideal explanatory text:

> Let us imagine that we seek a scientific explanation of some phenomenon p; let us now assume that we are in the following "standard condition" of knowledge and ignorance—we do not know any of the details of the ideal explanatory text for p, but we have some firm notion of the relevant ideal form for the explanation of p, and moreover we have good familiarity both with the kinds of scientific concepts involved in filling out that form, and with common-sense language of explanation and its links to more scientific explanatory language; against this "standard background" of interest, partial ignorance, and partial knowledge, a proffered explanation may convey explanatory information by reducing uncertainty about the relevant ideal text, i.e., by enabling us to *reconstruct* at least some of this text. To the extent that, against a standard background, a proffered explanation conveys information about the relevant ideal text, we can say that it *contains* more or less *explanatory information*. And the more explanatory information a proffered explanation contains, the higher the degree of scientific understanding it exhibits.[93]

Thus, to use the example that Railton uses—Scriven's famous ink bottle—the lawless explanation for "Why is the ink-bottle on its side?—Because Scriven knocked it over," "points to a causal process that is responsible for the explanandum fact, it eliminates myriad other explanations (a sure sign that explanatory information is being conveyed); and it gives us an idea of where to look for further explanation."[94] Thus the singular causal statement is explanatory in the sense that it conveys explanatory information, but it can be improved by filling in more of the ideal explanatory text, including the relevant covering laws.

This thesis of Railton's also helps to resolve the problem of the relations between the pragmatics of explanation and explanation as a description of true relations existing in the world. Railton conceives ideal explanatory texts in the latter sense; they are true if they accurately describe the relations holding in the world, false otherwise. But in a given condition of knowledge, when one asks for an explanation of some phenomenon, it may be quite sufficient in that context to provide only a singular causal statement or some other truncated version of the ideal text. Thus, in a particular context of knowledge, the question, "Why did the car engine stop?" may be satisfactorily answered by the statement "The fuel line is blocked."

The fact that some partial explanations are pragmatically acceptable does not therefore create difficulties for Railton's account; rather Railton's account shows why, against a particular background of knowledge such partial explanations are acceptable. They convey enough explanatory information appropriate to the particular situation to permit a specific problem to be dealt with.[95]

Railton's theory is by no means free of problems. The propensity theory of probability is a subject of considerable controversy, and Railton does not resolve those issues. Similarly, although Railton insists that the ideal explanatory text must include a full description of the causal mechanisms involved, he does not provide the sort of elucidation of the concept of causality which would seem necessary to fulfill this injunction. Moreover, his attitude toward deductivism is ambiguous. He states that the basic framework of the ideal explanatory text is a deductive argument, but he insists that it must contain more than that—it is an "account" rather than an argument. But what sort of account? It is not a narrative;[96] apparently it is a description of objective relations in the world that shows which phenomena are due to other phenomena, and how.

If this description seems vague, nevertheless I think that Railton is right in claiming that this is what scientists seek to do in the formulating of explanations, and that he is also right in holding that to "explain explanation" is to seek to explain what scientists actually do, or try to do, not to generate an abstract model divorced from scientific practice.[97] For a naturalized epistemology, it is difficult to see how the study of scientific explanation could take any other course.

Furthermore, Railton's theory has many virtues. It does justice to both causal explanation and probabilistic explanation within the nomothetic framework; there is no such asymmetry as between Hempel's DN and IS models. In including structural explanations as a distinct type, the theory avoids the difficulties involved in giving either a causal or a probabilistic account of laws like the Pauli Exclusion Principle. The concept of the ideal explanatory text sets out clearly the ideal of scientific explanatory efforts, and the notion of explanatory information offers a simple way of relating partial explanations, including singular causal statements, to the ideal text. On balance, the virtues of Railton's theory seem considerably to outweigh its failings.

Causation Again

But we are still left with the problem of causality. If not all laws are causal laws—and it is certainly difficult to see how the Pauli Exclusion Principle can be considered as causal[98]—do all causes exhibit lawful regularities?

That is, need all causal relations conform to Hume's criterion of constant conjunction? If, as I have argued, Hume's criteria are seen as indicators (and fallible ones) of causal relations in the world, then there is no contradiction in supposing that some causal connections exhibit invariable sequences while others do not. There is no *a priori* reason for excluding unique events from the domain of caused events, and events such as the Big Bang provide some incentives for including them. We certainly have at present no lawlike explanation of the Big Bang, and to leave it as the uncaused creation of all there is does not advance us much beyond, "Let there be light!"

But if we accept the claim that there are unique occurrences that are caused, or more generally that, even if in a given causal field c causes e in a particular case, it need not do so in any other case, then it would appear that every occurrence can legitimately be said to be caused. This would make chance events indistinguishable from caused events; every occurrence could be said to be causally related to any other occurrence, and such a claim could neither be confirmed nor denied, since one could never show that two occurrences were not related by a unique causal relation. One could no longer say that occurrences falling under significant statistical regularities were causally determined, since the concept of statistical significance would become meaningless. Unless there is some peculiar characteristic of causal processes by which they can be directly identified without reference to occurrences at other times and places—and as we have seen mark transmission will not suffice for this purpose—then causal determination can only be distinguished by contrast to chance, that is, by lack of causal determination. If this distinction cannot be made, talk of causality becomes vacuous.

But the distinction between those things that exhibit an orderly dependency and those that do not is a fundamental distinction among the elements of our experience. Whatever we may choose to call it, such a distinction must be marked, since all planning and prediction, not to mention understanding, depend upon it. And the dependence of A upon B is very hard to establish except by determining that when B occurs A occurs. It seems therefore reasonable to adopt, as a basic principle of causality, the following:

> P: In a causal field F, if any A-type occurrence is ever a cause of a B-type occurrence, such that the A-type occurrence causes the B-type occurrence with a significant probability r, then in F, every A-type occurrence always causes a B-type occurrence with probability r.

Unless some such principle as P holds, then either everything causes everything or nothing causes anything. Thus causality cannot be divorced from the notion of regularity or law. And clearly P legitimizes the use of counterfactual conditionals based on such laws. Causes, laws, and counterfactuals are inseparable.

This discussion of theories of causality and their problems should suffice to bring out certain features of our notion of causality. Clearly, "causality" is a very vague notion; after several thousand years of efforts to clarify the concept, we still have no adequate theory of its nature, nor is there complete agreement on what observations should be taken as indicators of causal relations. We are not even certain what sorts of things the terms of a causal relation refer to. What I think can be said is that causality is a common-sense notion that attempts to bring together a variety of types of dependencies we find in the world. It is possible, as the work of Michotte, Leslie, and others suggests, that our proclivity to interpret certain phenomena as involving cause has an innate basis, but if so that is merely the initial impetus, the first clue, as it were, to seeing causal dependencies in the world. As Miller has argued, our notion of causality seems to originate in certain core experiences and to be extended step by step to other cases, more or less as such notions as number and a work of art are developed.[99] As I have already suggested, the basic experiences seem to be those of direct launching, agency, and being made to feel something (e.g., being hurt or hit). From these we extend the concept by including more and more cases. What seems to be common to these cases is the recognition of dependency—that one thing happening depends upon another. Such a recognition is only possible by contrast with situations in which such dependency does not exist—in other words, by contrast to chance. If the motions of the child's arm bore only a random relation to his efforts to move it, if billiard balls in contact moved or did not move at random, if hurts came and went at random, regardless of what children did, there would be no concept of causality. Doubtless it is those regularities which are the most nearly constant conjunctions upon which we first build this distinction, and it was these that Hume remarked. More complex sorts of statistical dependencies are more difficult to discern, and may require very complex analytic techniques for their discovery. But it is "significant" associations—associations too strong to be due to chance—that are the clue to causation, whether the underlying process is deterministic or not. Certainly it is true that we do impute causality on the basis of a variety of experiential indicators. Some of these Hume detected, but he missed others. Since his time, quantitative analyses, and particularly statistical analyses, have enlarged the range of indicators. None are entirely adequate, since exceptions can be found for all. But the underlying intuition that the world we know is not a random chaos, and that some distinction must be drawn between phenomena that are somehow dependent on other phenomena and those that are not seems to be irrefutable.

What then is the status of causality? Is it merely a subjective proclivity on our part to see order in chaos, or are there real connections among phenomena such that some determine others? Both Salmon's theory and Railton's agree that there are real causal relations in the world. Indeed, if there is order in the world, that fact requires explanation, and such an explanation must involve real causal processes. What those processes may be is clearly a problem for science rather than for philosophy.

Quine has argued that a causal process should be conceived in terms of energy transmission.[100] Hume, of course, denied that we can perceive any such transmission, but as Aronson has noted, Hume paid attention only to qualitative impressions and his argument collapses as soon as quantitative characteristics of bodies are introduced.

> We now have an answer to the question: is there an element to the causal relation in addition to mere sequence of events? The answer is "Yes!"—the causal relation is more than sequence in that the cause and effect are not only objects or events which are constantly conjoined, but the cause object possesses a quantity (momentum, energy, force, *etc.*) which is transferred to the effect object. Again, as in the case of *a* and *b* [billiard balls], *a*'s momentum was transferred to *b* at the instant it made contact with *b*. Since such a process involves numerical identity of that particular quantity throughout the sequence of events, it can be seen that, ontologically, this type of causation is more than mere sequence of events.[101]

In fact, Hume's argument, if fully developed, seems inconsistent with fundamental conservation laws of physics.[102] Moreover, the definition of causation as energy transmission provides a reasonable explanation of why an object such as an electron is a causal process in Salmon's sense: Since matter is a form of energy, the object is energy transmitted through time.

Yet as Michotte demonstrated, an experimental device that simulates the interaction of billiard balls produces the illusion of momentum transmission even when subjects know that no transfer is taking place. And we seem to have in quantum mechanics cases in which the energy transmission model either does not apply or where the application thus far eludes us. Moreover, it is difficult to see how the energy transmission model can account for the causal role of triggers. When I flip a switch, the light goes on. Certainly in flipping the switch I expend energy, but the energy is mechanical, not electrical, and it is surely not converted into electrical energy. Yet this does appear to be a case of my action causing the light to go on. Even more puzzling is the problem of information triggers. A message sent from one person to another may initiate an action, for example, a battle. No doubt the writing of the message involved an expenditure of energy. But how is that energy transmitted so as to produce the battle? And surely the energy expended in writing the message is wholly disproportionate to the energy involved in the battle.[103] Obviously, trigger phenomena involve energy systems in some type of interaction, but it is not clear at present how these should be conceptualized and whether or not they can be assimilated to the energy transmission model.

I take it that when Railton talks of the ideal explanatory text containing, in addition to causal laws, descriptions of causal mechanisms, it is such "mechanisms" as the transmission of momentum between billiard balls that he has in mind. Whatever the inadequacies of the energy transmission model may be, we do know of a number of such cases where an appropriate "mechanism" of this sort can be specified, and surely descriptions of them should be included in the ideal explanatory text. What really is the "cement of the universe" is, after all, a scientific question, not a philosophic one. The imperfections of our current theories can only be remedied by the scientific determination of just how the basic processes of nature take place, and as energy appears to be the fundamental "stuff" of the universe, it will hardly come as a surprise if those basic processes involve some sort of energy transformation. Meantime, we must build our theories as best we can, using such laws and such causal mechanisms as are known to us, imperfect though our knowledge may be. Imperfect knowledge is better than no knowledge, and it will only be made more perfect by building on what we already have.

Notes

1. Wesley C. Salmon, "Four Decades of Scientific Explanation" in *Minnesota Studies in the Philosophy of Science*, Philip Kitcher and Wesley C. Salmon, eds. (Minneapolis: University of Minnesota Press, 1989), 3–4.

2. Carl G. Hempel and Paul Oppenheim, "Studies in the Logic of Explanation," *Philosophy of Science* 15:135–175 (1948).

3. Ibid., 138.

4. Peter Albert Railton, "Explaining Explanation: A Realist Account of Scientific Explanation and Understanding," Ph.D. dissertation, Princeton University, 1980, 46–70. Hempel has accepted some modifications of this claim; see Railton's discussion.

5. Hempel and Oppenheim, "Studies," 159n28; Salmon, "Four Decades," 9–10.

6. Carl G. Hempel, "Deductive-Nomological vs. Statistical Explanation" in H. Feigl and G. Maxwell, eds., *Scientific Explanation, Space, and Time, Minnesota Studies in the Philosophy of Science* 3 (Minneapolis: University of Minnesota Press, 1962), 98–169.

7. Carl G. Hempel, *Aspects of Scientific Explanation and Other Essays in the Philosophy of Science* (New York: Free Press, 1965).

8. Salmon, "Four Decades," 8–9.

9. Hempel, *Aspects*, 381–403. Salmon, "Four Decades," 51–58.

10. John Watkins, *Science and Scepticism* (Princeton, N.J.: Princeton University Press, 1984), 205.

11. Ibid., 208–209. (Emphasis in original)

12. Richard Jeffrey, "Statistical Explanation vs. Statistical Inference" in N. Rescher, ed., *Essays in Honor of Carl G. Hempel* (Dordrecht: D. Reidel Publishing Co., 1970), 104–113. Wesley C. Salmon, *Scientific Explanation and the Causal Structure of The World* (Princeton, N.J.: Princeton University Press, 1984), 85–97.

13. Jeffrey, "Statistical Explanation," 108. Salmon, *Scientific Explanation*, 88.

14. Carl G. Hempel, "The Function of General Laws in History," *Journal of Philosophy* 39:35–48 (1942).

15. William Dray, *Laws and Explanation in History* (London: Oxford University Press, 1957), ch. 5.

16. Rex Martin, *Historical Explanation* (Ithaca, N.Y.: Cornell University Press, 1977), 158–159, 198–201.

17. H. L. A. Hart and A. M. Honore, *Causation in the Law* (Oxford: Clarendon Press, 1959).

18. Robert William Fogel and G. R. Elton, *Which Road to the Past?* (New Haven, Conn.: Yale University Press, 1983), 13.

19. Murray G. Murphey, "Explanation, Causes, and Covering Laws," *History and Theory* Beiheft 25, 43–57 (1986).

20. Michael Scriven, "Causes, Connections and Conditions in History" in William H. Dray, ed., *Philosophical Analysis and History* (New York: Harper and Row, 1966), 238.

21. Michael Scriven, "The Logic of Cause," *Theory and Decision* 2:49–66 (1971).

22. Maurice Mandelbaum, *The Anatomy of Historical Knowledge* (Baltimore: The Johns Hopkins University Press, 1977), 56–7, 69, 93, 98–105.

23. Lawrence Stone, "History and the Social Sciences in the Twentieth Century" in Charles F. Delzell, ed., *The Future of History* (Nashville, Tenn.: Vanderbilt University Press, 1977), 3–42.

24. Hempel and Oppenheim, "Studies," 139–140.

25. Richard W. Miller, *Fact and Method* (Princeton, N.J.: Princeton University Press, 1987), 78.

26. Abraham Edel, *Aristotle and His Philosophy* (Chapel Hill: University of North Carolina Press, 1982), 414.

27. David Hume, quoted in Salmon, *Scientific Explanation*, 136–137. (Emphasis in original)

28. David Hume, *A Treatise of Human Nature* (Oxford: Clarendon Press, 1949), 165.

29. J. L. Mackie, *The Cement of the Universe* (Oxford: Clarendon Press, 1986), 186–187.

30. Salmon, *Scientific Explanation*, 242–259.

31. Mackie, *Cement*, 35.

32. Nelson Goodman, *Fact, Fiction, and Forecast* (Cambridge, Mass.: Harvard University Press, 1955), 95–107.

33. Donald Davidson, *Essays on Actions and Events* (Oxford: Clarendon Press, 1980), Essay 7.

34. Ibid., 179.

35. Jaegwon Kim, "Causes and Events: Mackie on Causation," *Journal of Philosophy* 68:427–441 (1971). Jaegwon Kim, "Causation, Nomic Subsumption, and the Concept of Event," *Journal of Philosophy* 70:217–236 (1973), 222. Jaegwon Kim, "Events and Their Descriptions: Some Considerations" in Rescher, *Essays*, 198–215.

36. Myles Brand, *Intending and Acting* (Cambridge, Mass.: MIT Press, 1984), 73.

37. Anthony Quinton, "Objects and Events," *Mind* 88:197–214 (1979).

38. Paul Needham, "Causation: Relation or Connective?" *Dialectica* 42:201–219 (1988), 212.

39. Jan Frederick Andrus, "The Time Variable," *The Southern Journal of Philosophy* 25:1–12 (1987).

40. Davidson, *Essays*, 177.

41. Mark Steiner, "Events and Causality," *Journal of Philosophy* 83:249–264 (1986).

42. Ibid.

43. Salmon, "Four Decades," 108.

44. Wesley C. Salmon, *Statistical Explanation and Statistical Relevance* (Pittsburgh, Pa.: University of Pittsburgh Press, 1971)

45. Salmon, *Scientific Explanation*, 22.

46. Ibid., 37–41.

47. Ibid., 88–89.

48. Ibid., 139–146.

49. Nicholas Rescher, "On the Promise of Process Philosophy," paper delivered at Texas A&M University Conference on "Frontiers of American Philosophy," May 12, 1988.

50. Salmon, *Scientific Explanation*, 144.

51. Ibid., 140.

52. Hans Reichenbach, *The Philosophy of Space and Time* (New York: Dover Press, 1958), 136.

53. Salmon, *Scientific Explanation*, 148.

54. Ibid., 143–144.

55. Philip Kitcher, "Two Approaches to Explanation," *Journal of Philosophy* 82:632–639 (1985), 638. (Emphasis in original)

56. Salmon, *Scientific Explanation*, 146.

57. Ibid., 144.

58. Ibid., 203.

59. Ibid., 207.

60. Ibid., 158–168, 170–174.

61. Ibid., 208.

62. Ibid., 239.

63. Ibid., 262. (Emphasis in original)

64. Ibid., 17.

65. Ibid., 262.

66. Ibid., 239.

67. Ibid., 147–157.

68. Ibid., 148. (Emphasis in original)

69. Ibid., 153.

70. Ibid., 155

71. Ibid., 146, 169.

72. Ibid., 146.

73. Ibid., 140–141.

74. Ibid., 155.

75. Railton, *Explanation*, 117–118. (Emphasis in original)

76. Ibid., 128–129. (Emphasis in original)

77. Ibid., 129–130.

78. Ibid., 168. (Emphasis in original)

79. Ibid., 216.

80. Ibid., 275.

81. Ibid., 295–300.

82. Ibid., 317.

83. Ibid., 341.

84. Ibid., 350–353.

85. Ibid., 364

86. Ibid., 364–366.

87. Ibid., 369. (Emphasis in original)

88. Ibid., 382–383.

89. Ibid., 433–434.

90. Ibid., 434. (Emphasis in original)

91. Ibid., 435–436. (Emphasis in original)

92. Ibid., 131.

93. Ibid., 134. (Emphasis in original)

94. Ibid., 138.

95. Ibid., 151ff.

96. Ibid., 413.

97. Ibid., 493–496, 520.

98. Salmon, "Four Decades," 165.

99. Miller, *Fact and Method*, 73–83.

100. Quine, *Roots of Reference*, 4–8.

101. Jerrold Aronson, "The Legacy of Hume's Analysis of Causation," *Studies in History and Philosophy of Science* 2:135–156 (1971), 145.

102. Ibid., 149.

103. Andrew Newman, "The Causal Relation and Its Terms," *Mind* 97:529–550 (1988).

Chapter 4

Action

In this chapter, the theory of explanation described in the preceding chapter is applied to the problem of explaining human action. The first step is to develop an adequate definition of action—no small matter in view of all the controversy that has surrounded this endeavor. I then consider the attempts by philosophers to give causal accounts of action. Following Davidson, we arrive at a model in which action is explained by the combination of belief and desire. The objections of Castaneda and Chisholm to the usual "s believes that p" model of belief are considered, and the issue of whether desires or intentions are the motives of action is discussed at some length.

Having hopefully gained some enlightenment on these matters, we confront again the issue of whether action explanations should be by covering laws or single causal statements. I argue that attempts by philosophers to solve this problem have been less than successful, and that no adequate philosophical answer has been given to the question of whether human action is causally determined or free. Accordingly, I turn to current work in psychology. Our feelings of freedom and self-determination when we act turn out to be the results of causal processes describable by social learning theory. This is not a denial of human freedom, but an explanation of what produces the feelings of free self-efficacy that we have. Further, psychologists have developed theories of action which, while considerably more sophisticated than those of "folk psychology" or of the philosophers, utilize the concepts of belief and desire as basic explanatory variables. These theories have acquired very solid experimental support, and demonstrate that causal explanations of human action can be given in terms of

135

mental states of the sort postulated in cognitivist theories of mind. There is therefore good reason to accept the existence of such mental states as real causally efficient agents in terms of which human action can be explained.

In recent years, philosophic arguments about the explanation of human conduct have tended to center around the notion of action. On the one hand, many writers have argued for a causal theory of action and have accordingly believed that human action can be causally explained. On the other, many writers have argued that human action is free and cannot be explained on causal grounds. Since these two positions contradict each other, it is necessary to decide between them. We will look first at the causal theory proposed by philosophers, then at its denial, and then return to the issue of the causes of action.

Definition of Action

Action theorists distinguish sharply between behavior and action. The term "behavior" is generally used to refer to whatever people do, and it is in that sense that I will use it here. Thus physical movements, speech, thinking, perceiving, and so on, are behaviors in this very wide sense of the term. On the other hand, the term does not normally refer to the circulation of the blood or digestion or similar processes. The differentiating factor is not consciousness, for one often moves without being aware of doing so and one is certainly aware of indigestion. Nor is it intention, for behavior may be unintentional. Rather, "behavior" seems to refer to doings other than those comprised in the purely biological functioning of the organism. Thus eating, drinking, and sighing are behaviors because, although biologically based, their performance is culturally shaped, whereas the physiological processes of digesting, aging, and growing are not behaviors as the term is usually used.

Behavior forms a continuous stream, for people never stop behaving from birth to death. We normally divide up the behavioral stream in quite arbitrary ways, so that lifting one's arm, scratching one's head, and rubbing one's hands together are treated as distinguishable segments of the behavioral continuum, whereas the various motions that constitute rubbing one's hands together are not. There are therefore no atomic behaviors out of which the behavioral stream is constructed; the division into segments is arbitrary and any segment could be further subdivided.

I shall define "action" as follows

D1: Let {B} be a partially ordered sequence of behaviors performed by a person S, G a goal held by S, and E S's expectation that performing {B} will contribute to the attainment of G in an expected way. Then the ordered triple <{B},G,E> is an action.

{B} alone cannot be the action because identical behaviors may be performed as parts of different actions (e.g., walking or running). G alone is not an act since people usually have goals that they do not act to realize, and E cannot be the action since one may have such expectations without acting upon them. It is the combination of these elements that constitutes an action.

The term "sequence" used in D1 refers to a set of behaviors that are at least partially ordered temporally. It is not implied that every behavior that S performs during the course of the action is a member of the action: One may light a cigarette while driving a car without the lighting of the cigarette thereby becoming part of the act of driving. Nor does anything in D1 preclude the set of behaviors from having only one member. Simultaneous behaviors—moving the gear shift while pushing in the clutch—are included, since the temporal ordering is partial. The unity of the behaviors in the set consists in their relations to goals and expectations, not in temporal juxtaposition or the inclusion of all S's behaviors during a given temporal interval.

The goal and expectation included in the schema $A = <\{B\},G,E>$ may be said to be "internal" to A. But A may itself be related to a further goal G' by further expectations E' that relate A to G' as a means. In such a case, one can consider the ordered triple $A' = <A,G',E'>$ as a single action, but whether or not one wishes to do so is largely a pragmatic matter. If one intends to relate A' to yet further goals and expectations G" and E", it may make sense to conceive A' as an action; if not, perhaps not. The point is that some actions are composed of more elementary actions, although not all are, but there is no recursive action formation operator such that every action A^n is related by some set of expectations E^{n+1} to a goal G^{n+1} so that $<A^n,G^{n+1},E^{n+1}>$ automatically forms a new action A^{n+1}. If such were the case, one would either have an unexplained "greatest action" or an endless series.

D1 clearly rules out behaviors that are not performed for a purpose from being actions. This is an objection only if there is reason to hold that there are non-purposive actions. Consider the case in which a child, while playing with a gun, inadvertently pulls the trigger and thereby kills a playmate. We would say without hesitation that the child shot his friend although he did not do so purposely and did not expect to do so. In law, one who does something is held responsible for those consequences of his behavior that could have been expected to occur on the basis of ordinary foresight. But according to D1, the child's shooting of his friend was not an action. The child's pulling of the trigger was inadvertent and the shooting, although a consequence of his behavior, was accidental. The problem of the law is to control behavior, and it does so in part by sanctions that encourage foresight and prudence. Our problem is to understand what humans do, and distinguishing a particular structure of behaviors by its causes is a step toward that goal, whether it deviates from legal usage or not.

Consider now the case of a man who shoots at what he takes to be a deer and finds that he has shot his friend instead. It can be argued that he did not purposely shoot his friend and did not expect to shoot his friend, and surely this is true. But he did shoot at a target and he did hit it as he expected to; he therefore performed an action even though he erroneously believed the target was a deer. It is common to point out in such cases that what is an action under one description is not so under another and to stipulate that a behavior is an action if it is so under some description. But this seems to me too loose, for in fact any behavior is an action under some description. Rather, I think the range of admissible descriptions must be limited to those that correctly describe S's goals and beliefs. Thus hitting a home run is an action although few hitters intend to hit a home run when they do so. But they do have as their goal hitting the ball so as to score the most runs they can, and that purpose clearly covers hitting a home run.

But what about the man who means to shoot a deer that is really there, aims at the deer, fires, misses the deer and hits his friend instead? Shooting at the deer is an action; the man had a purpose, which was to kill the deer; he fired in the expectation that doing so would kill the deer, since he expected the bullet to follow the line of sight from the gun to the target. But shooting his friend is not an action; he did not hit the target at which he aimed. There is a crucial difference between attempting to perform an action and failing, and actually performing the action. Both are actions, but they are different sorts of actions. An attempted murder is an action, but it is not the same as committing a murder.

Nevertheless, this case brings out two important points. An action can be described in terms of its consequences as well as its causes. Thus consider the policeman who shoots a burglar. Suppose the bullet passes through the burglar's body and breaks a window. One could describe the act as shooting the burglar or as breaking the window. Both descriptions involve causal results of firing the gun; the former involves the purpose for which the gun was fired, the latter does not. As D1 makes clear, what is required is that the behavior (firing the gun) must have been for *a* purpose, but it need not have been for the purpose of attaining every particular consequence that might be used to describe the act. What then of the way the consequence was produced? D1 requires that the behaviors {B} be expected to contribute in an expected way to the attainment of the purpose for which the act was performed. Nothing in D1 requires that {B} should be expected to contribute to the production of some other consequence of {B} that may not have been foreseen at the time the action was taken. Clearly the fact that an action can be described in terms of some particular consequence does not imply that the consequence is a goal of the action.

The second problem is the problem of control. Philosophical discussions of action have been largely limited to cases where the actor has total control over the performance of the act (e.g., raising one's arm). Not all actions are of this sort. Hitting a target requires a degree of skill and a conjunction of circumstances not always within the command of the actor. One may try to perform an action yet fail because one has incomplete control of the situation. As the case above shows, trying to hit a target in an expected way is not the same as hitting it. This is a difficulty that, I believe, has not been adequately resolved by philosophic action theories.

I think it will be found that D1, although stringent, still manages to embrace those behaviors that have normally been called "actions." And I think it will also be found that it manages to rule out most of those celebrated cases of wayward causal chains that we do not want to call "actions." Brand has cited examples of four types of such cases that seem quite representative.

Case 1. Abel, who is attending a party, wants to spill his drink because he wants to signal to his confederates to begin the robbery and he believes, in virtue of their prearrangements, that spilling his drink will accomplish that. But Abel is inexperienced in crime and this leads him to be very anxious. His anxiety makes his hand tremble, and so his glass spills. . . .

Case 2. Bob finds himself in a difficult position while climbing. He is supporting another man on the rope. He wants to rid himself of the danger of holding that man, and he thinks that he can do so by loosening his grip. His belief and want unnerve him, and as a result cause him to loosen his hold. . . .

Case 3. Carl wants to kill his rich uncle because he wants to inherit the family fortune. He believes that his uncle is home and drives toward his house. His desire to kill his uncle agitates him and he drives recklessly. On the way he hits and kills a pedestrian, who, as luck would have it, is his uncle. . . .

Case 4. Dan, the sheriff, sees the bankrobber riding down Main-
street. He wants to shoot him and believes that by taking
careful aim, the bullet from his gun will directly hit the robber. Dan, however, is a terrible shot. The bullet goes in the
wrong direction; but as luck would have it, the bullet hits a
spittoon and ricochets, hitting the bank robber.[1]

Case 1 is clearly ruled out by D1. Abel did not actually spill his drink
with the expectation of signaling; he did it inadvertently as a result of his
anxiety. Case 2 is ruled out in the same way; Bob does perform the behavior
of loosening his hold on the rope but not actually with the expectation of
dropping his partner. Similarly, in Case 3, Carl does not hit the pedestrian
with the expectation of killing his uncle; indeed, he does not even know
that the pedestrian is his uncle when he kills him. In Case 4, unlike the first
three, the wayward causal chain is a chain of consequences, not antecedent
causes. Dan, the sheriff who can't shoot straight, does perform an action in
shooting at the bank robber; all the requirements of D1 are fulfilled. But he
does not perform an action in shooting the bank robber because the actual
behavior of shooting the spittoon was not expected to contribute to the
goal of shooting the robber; the outcome is a matter of pure luck. On the
other hand, had Dan been a trick shot artist who deliberate banked the bullet off the spittoon with the expectation of hitting the robber, the shooting
of the robber would have been an action.

Philosophic Theories of the Causes of Action

With this understanding of what an action is, we may turn to the question of what causes actions. It has been argued that human action is
determined, not by causes, but by reasons. As Dray put it, we explain why
S A'd by showing that given the circumstances, Aing was the thing to do.[2]
Or in other formulations, action is the outcome of a practical syllogism: We
do what we do because it is the rational thing to do.[3] I think this view has
been pretty well laid to rest by Davidson. Explanations of action by reasons
require a distinction between two senses of the word "reasons." In one
sense, reasons are rationalizations of an actions—justifications, if you
will—and need have no relation to why the action was done. In the second
sense of "reason" (e.g., the reason for which he did it was to earn a dollar)
the reason is being cited as a cause and has explanatory force. More exactly,
Davidson defines a primary reason as a pair consisting of a "pro-attitude"
(want, desire, etc.) toward actions having certain properties and a belief by
the agent that the action (suitably described) has that property.[4] Then he

holds that, "A primary reason for an action is its cause."[5] Primary reasons therefore provide a causal explanation of action.[6] This view does not compromise the intentionality of action, for Davidson holds that, "to know a primary reason why some one acted as he did is to know an intention with which the action was done."[7] Since Davidson's article, it has generally been accepted that where actions are explained by reasons, reasons function as causes. It should also be noted, in view of the emphasis on rationality involved in some of these arguments, that not all actions are rational, by any definition of rationality. Thus, going to the movies tonight is surely an action. But in the circumstances it may be thoroughly irrational: One may not be able to afford the money or the time; one may know one can't afford it, and reprimand oneself that going to a movie tonight is stupid; and then go anyway! We are not always rational.[8]

That belief is a necessary condition of action is obvious I think in view of D1 above. The relation of the behavior sequence {B} to the goal G is given by the belief that {B} is a means to obtaining G. This belief may be true or false; there may or may not really be such a relation between {B} and G that the performance of {B} by S will enable S to achieve G—but so long as S believes that there is such a relation, he has a reason to do {B}. It is therefore clear that without beliefs there is no action. Certainly, beliefs are not the sole causes of action, but they are necessary conditions of actions.

Belief itself is an internal state of the organism. It is conceptual in nature but is normally expressed in language. It has been common to take as the canonical form of such an expression "S believes that p," where "S" refers to the agent and "p" to a statement. There is, however, an important objection to this view. As Hector-Neri Castaneda has pointed out,[9] statements of the form

(1) I believe that I will die;

and

(2) John believes that he will die;

cannot be made to conform to this schema. In (1) and (2) the apparent object of belief is not a statement; in (1) it is an occasion sentence and in (2) a sentential function. This seems at first a rather trivial point, but in fact what Castaneda has done is to expose a profound truth about sentences containing psychological verbs such as "believes" and constructions in indirect discourse.

Note first that (1) and (2) are not as similar as they seem. (1) is an occasion sentence in the sense that its truth or falsity depends on who the believer is; nevertheless, the pronoun "I" has an invariable reference to the author of the sentence. "I" does not necessarily refer to the subject of the "psychological" verb; thus in

(1') John believes that I will die,

"I" does not refer to John but to the author (utterer, writer) of the sentence. This restrictive reference applies to both occurrences of "I" in (1). "I will die" necessarily refers to the utterer of the sentence, and is as it stands as much an occasion sentence as (1) of which it is a part. (2), however, has a somewhat different structure. "John," being a proper name, refers to a specific individual who has a belief; in that sense (2) is a standing sentence. But the "he" in (2) has no determinate reference; it can refer to John or to any other male. Therefore, "he" is a free variable and "He will die" is truly a sentential function. Whereas (1) could be put in the form, "I believe that p," if "p" is permitted to be the occasion sentence "I will die," (2) cannot; (2) would come out as "John believes that Dx," which is nonsense.

What has gone wrong here? Why is it that a sentence such as "John believes that grass is green" goes easily into the form "John believes that p" whereas "John believes that he will die" does not? The answer carries us back to the issue of how one can know what it is that another believes. The issue is not obvious, but it emerges from the analysis of how beliefs are communicated.

Whenever one sincerely utters a fact-stating sentence in a fact-stating context, one is stating what one believes. Thus when I utter the sentence, "Grass is green," I am stating a belief that I hold. In doing so, I do not have to state that I believe the sentence; my utterance of it in a fact-stating context is quite sufficient to make that clear. Specifically, uttering a sentence "p" in a fact-stating context does not involve a reference to the speaker; the sentence "Grass is green" is about grass being green, not about me or my belief. The illocutionary act involved indicates that the utterance expresses my belief that grass is green, but there is no explicit reference to me.

What is true of uttering is also true of believing, intending, wishing, and so on. My belief that grass is green is expressed in the corresponding sentence, but to believe the sentence is not to believe that I believe it, or to think about myself at all. Beliefs such as that grass is green are about a state of affairs believed to obtain, not about the believer. We can think, believe, intend, and so forth, without simultaneously thinking, believing, intending, and so on, that we do so. Thinking of something is not equivalent to thinking about thinking of something. The inequivalence of the negations of the two sentences should make that obvious.

Nevertheless, what one believes, thinks, and the rest, can be made the object of one's thought. Thus, for any belief I have, I can think that I believe it. This clearly applies to most other psychological states. Nor is this a trivial matter, for all my beliefs represent my peculiar view of the world; they are a view from a particular perspective, that may or may not be shared by another. This is dramatically clear with respect to beliefs involving indicators such as the personal and demonstrative pronouns, and adverbs of time and place. Such indicators play a critical role in the referential system, and one that locates things referred to in terms of the speaker as point of origin. What is "here" to me may be "there" to another; my "now" may be another's "then"; but my "I" can never be another's "I." One's beliefs are in this sense primarily one's own, and so it becomes a question as to how they can be made known to another and so made sharable, or at least understandable.

Consider the sentence:

(3) Mary is smart.

Suppose I now believe that I believe (3), that is,

(4) I believe that Mary is smart.

What is the relation between (3) and (4)? Obviously, they are not logically equivalent, for their negations are quite different; the negation of (3) may be false, although (4) is true. (3) is what Quine calls a standing sentence; (4) is what he calls an occasion sentence, since its truth or falsity depends upon who the believer is and when it is uttered. But this is a difference between (3) and (4) as types; as a token, (4) is entirely determinate, since "I" can only refer to the author. Both (3) and (4) admit of existential generalization: (3) yields:

(3') $(Ex) (x$ is smart$)$.
(4) gives
(4') $(Ex) (x = I$ & x believes $(Ey) (y$ is smart$))$.

Note that these schemata do not involve quantifying into an opaque context; all occurrences of "x" are outside the belief context, and "y" lies wholly within that context, since if x believes (4) he must also believe (4'). (3) of course admits of substitution; if:

(5) Mary = Jane,

then:

(6) Jane is smart,

follows from (3) and (5). What about (4)? Clearly, from (4) and (5) it does not follow that:

(7) I believe that Jane is smart,

for I may not know that Jane and Mary are the same person. However, from (4) and

(8) I believe that Mary = Jane,
(7) does follow.

Complications set in when beliefs become reflexive. Consider:

(9) I believe that I am wise.

"I" must always refer to the author. If it be granted that only an existing being can believe, then from (9) we have

(9') (Ex) (x = I & x believes that x is wise).

Suppose that

(10) I = John.

It does not follow from (9') and (10) that:

(11) John believes that John is wise.

I may be an amnesiac and not know that I am John. If, however, we have:

(10') I believe that I = John,

then from (9') and (10'), (11) does follow.
Consider, however:

(12) John believes that he is wise.

To what does "he" refer? It is not obvious that "he" refers to John; unlike "I," which must refer to the author, "he" can refer to anyone. This ambiguity can be remedied by rephrasing (12) as

(12') John believes that he himself is wise.

But what now is the status of "he himself is wise"? This is not a complete sentence but a sentential function, yet in this context it can refer only to the antecedent "John." Thus, unlike (4) and (8), and even (9), (12) cannot be put in the form, "S believes that p" for some complete sentence token p.

Castaneda has proposed treating quasi-indicators (such as "he himself") as bound variables with the antecedent as quantifier.[10] This is not an ordinary form of quantification, and I propose to call the antecedent so used a *quasi-quantifier*. The standard theory of quantification involves three distinct notions—bondage, quantity, and existence. Quasi-quantification does not involve either quantity or existence; it is a mechanism of bondage only. Thus, following Castaneda's notation, if we represent "he himself" by "he*," (12') becomes

(12")John believes that he* is wise.

To avoid ambiguity, I will use the "*" operator to signal both the quasi-quantifier and the quasi-indicator, and where there is more than one such, I will use subscripts on the operator to show what binds which.

It is important here to distinguish, as Castaneda does, between the clause in indirect discourse and the prefix. Thus in (12"), "He* is wise" is in indirect discourse, and the prefix is "John believes that." If the belief sentence is to be unambiguous, the prefix must contain a quasi-quantifier corresponding to each quasi-indicator. Thus consider:

(13) $Paul^{*1}$ believes that Sue^{*2} believes that she^{*2} was seduced by him^{*1} there* then*.

There is no quasi-quantifier for "there*" or "then*," and Sue^{*2} occurs in indirect discourse. The speaker who advances the sentence therefore may not know when or where the event occurred or that Sue exists. To remedy this, one would need (13) to be rephrased as:

(13') About Sue^{*2}, in that $place^{*3}$, at that $time^{*4}$, $Paul^{*1}$ believed that she^{*2} believed that she^{*2} was seduced by him^{*1} $there^{*3}$ $then^{*4}$.

Note that what this does is to permit the description of Paul's beliefs in terms of entities in my—the speaker's—frame of reference. The utterer thus knows what, in his belief-world, Paul's beliefs refer to.

It is, however, an important fact that Paul may believe in the existence of entities that I do not. For example, Paul might subscribe to:

(14) $Paul^{*1}$ believes that $Aphrodite^{*2}$ believes that he^{*1} insulted her^{*2}.

Unless I am willing to countenance the existence of Aphrodite, she should not appear in the prefix; otherwise existential generalization with respect to Aphrodite would be possible. Thus, it is quite possible to say that Paul believes in Aphrodite without being committed oneself to Aphrodite's existence—so:

(14') $Paul^{*1}$ believes that (Ex) (x = $Aphrodite^{*2}$ & x^{*2} believes that he^{*1} insulted her^{*2}).

Quasi-quantification involves quantifying into opaque contexts. This practice leads to trouble. Thus from (14') and

(15) Paul = Sam,

we can apparently derive:

(16) Sam^{*1} believes that (Ex) (x = Aphrodite^{*2}, & x^{*2} believes that Sam^{*1} insulted her^{*2}.

But Paul may not know that he is Sam—hence although the substitution is legitimate in the prefix, it is not legitimate within the belief context, since Paul does not believe that Aphrodite believes that Sam insulted her. Hence substitution within the belief context requires:

(17) Paul believes that Paul = Sam.

What is essential is that any substitution of identicals within a belief context must be a substitution of terms that the believer believes refer to entities that he thinks exist and he thinks are identical, whether they are so in fact or not.

An alternative theory for dealing with these problems has been proposed by Chisholm. Chisholm assumes,

> First, a believer can take himself as his intentional object; that is to say, he can direct his thought upon himself. And, secondly, in so doing, grasps or conceives a certain property which he attributes to himself.[11]

Thus with respect to first-person statements such as:

(20) I believe that I will die,

Chisholm employs what he calls "direct attribution"—a form of attribution taken as primitive by which one attributes a property to oneself. Thus:

> For every x, every y and every z, if x directly attributes z to y, then x is identical with y.[12]

The content of this attribution, z, is a property. Thus (20) becomes:

(21) x believes that he himself will die =df the property of being such that one will die is such that x directly attributes it to x,[13]

or

> I believe that I will die =df I directly attribute to myself the property of being such that I will die.

Beliefs about others are then explicated in terms of what Chisholm calls "indirect attribution." This requires that there be a relation, R, that I bear only to a third person or thing z, that I directly attribute to myself the property of bearing R to z, and that z have the property F.

> Whenever we have indirect attribution, then the believer attributes a property to the object, *as* the thing to which he bears a certain identifying relation.[14]

Chisholm's model for R is an identifying relation, or reference fixing relation, that the speaker bears to the designatum.[15] There may be many such relations, so that the speaker can refer to the object in varying ways, and so also that the speaker and hearer may each identify the same object, although they use different identifying relations to do it.[16] Thus when Chisholm identifies Tom as "the person who lives in the house at which I am looking," he explicates the relation as, "I attribute to myself the property of being a thing which is such that there is just one person who lives in the house at which that thing is looking."[17] The property is attributed to the speaker rather than the object, but the relation serves to identify the object.[18]

As Kim points out, Chisholm's theory has advantages; it exhibits a logical structure for sentences with quasi-indicators, which involves only standard quantification and admits of existential generalization and substitution of identicals.[19] Nevertheless, Chisholm's theory seems to me unacceptable. First, it makes all reference a form of self-reference. But from a psychological point of view, this is false. When people refer to other objects, they do not thereby think of themselves as referring to those objects; they think of the object referred to. A child is taught to refer to something as a dog, not by attributing something to himself, but by attributing a property to another object.

Second, Chisholm's theory seems to be aimed at maintaining certain ontological doctrines about properties and propositions—specifically, that no property can involve an essential reference to a contingent ("No property is such that it can be conceived only by reference to some individual thing"[20]) and that there are no first-person propositions. I can see no advantage to Chisholm's Platonic ontology and therefore no reason to accept an analysis designed to support it.

Third, and most important, Chisholm's theory loses Castaneda's central insight that the problem of quasi-indicators is the problem of describing one believer's system of belief in terms of another's. This is the crucial insight Castaneda has given us, and it needs to be preserved.

To return to the issue of what a belief state is, it should now be clear why the form, "S believes that p" is inadequate. Instances of this schema are sentences that, like all sentences, are written or spoken by someone—call him Z. If the referring expressions contained in p (i.e., in S's belief system) are properly matched to those of Z's belief system, the canonical form is adequate, e.g., "S believes that grass is green." But the referring expressions in p may not match those of Z.

Two sorts of cases arise here. First, S may believe in the existence of entities whose existence is denied by Z, and these entities may be referred to by expressions in p. Quantification in this case must be internal to p. Second, although S and Z may agree on what entities exist, their apparatuses for referring to these entities may differ; for example, they may use different names for the same object. This situation becomes particularly salient where p contains demonstratives, personal pronouns, and adverbs of time and place, since these indicators are always relative to the position of the speaker. Here the references of expressions in p must be identified by expressions in the prefix and by quasi-quantification that links these expressions across belief systems. It is still correct to say that S believes that p, but for Z to know what S believes, the references in p must be equated to Z's or wholly restricted to S; they cannot be left ambiguous. It thus appears that the general case is that in which S's references must be matched with Z's, and that the special case is that in which matching may be taken for granted (e.g., S believes that grass is green).

The second component of what Davidson calls a primary reason is desire. If the Davidsonian scheme is to hold, desire must be a cause not only of some actions but of all actions. Yet even if it is granted that desires do cause some actions, there would appear to be cases in which this is not so. Thus I may desire to smoke, and yet not smoke. As all smokers, and ex-smokers, know, the desire for a cigarette can amount to a positive craving, and yet one can refrain from smoking. How is this possible if desire causes action? One answer is that this is a case of a conflict of desires; I desire to smoke, and I also desire health, and the two desires are not consistent. Hence it is held the stronger desire wins. But unless there is some way of determining the strength of a desire independently of the action it is said to cause, this claim becomes vacuous because irrefutable. Similar problems arise with the conflict between desire and duty. One may perform acts from a feeling of duty or obligation which one does not desire to perform. Thus one may advance under fire from a feeling of duty when one very much desires to move rapidly in the opposite direction. Again, it can be countered that the conflict is between a desire to do one's duty and a desire to save one's life, but some argument is required to substantiate the claim.

No one denies that desires have motive force, and that they are somehow involved in producing action. But some writers have held that it is intentions that cause action, and that desires serve as determiners of intentions. Brand in particular has drawn a sharp contrast between desire and intention, and has argued that intentions cause action. According to Brand, desires and intentions must be distinguished on the following scores. First, one can intend actions that one does not desire.[21] One can intend to eat spinach, although one hates the stuff. One may also very strongly desire to do something, yet have absolutely no intention of doing it. Intention here seems to be a resolution to act formed as a result of desires and beliefs rather than simply a combination of desires and beliefs.

Second, Brand argues that being compelled to do something is consistent with intending to do it but not with desiring to do it.[22] Thus the cleptomaniac may be compelled to steal, intend to steal, even plan to steal, yet desire not to steal. But the cleptomaniac may also intend not to steal, yet do it anyway, so intention does not always prevail. Further, the cleptomaniac may intend to steal and also desire to steal; one can enjoy one's compulsions. It seems clear that Brand has established a distinction here.

Third, Brand argues that a desire is satisfied if the end is attained, but an intention is satisfied only if the end is attained through one's own efforts.[23] But this distinction is doubtful. Being satisfied only if I obtain the end by my own efforts seems to be a case of not only desiring the attainment of the end but also desiring that it be attained by a particular means. It is not clear that we have a distinction here.

Fourth, Brand holds that desires have variable strength while intentions do not.[24] But there seems to be a confusion here between an intention as a plan and the strength of commitment to an intention. Obviously an intention as a plan of action does not admit of strength; it is or is not a plan. But one's adherence to the intention does admit of variation. Thus one can say, "I firmly intend to A" or "I more or less intend to A"; certainly these common locutions convey different degrees of commitment to the intention as a plan.

Fifth, Brand holds that we can have incompatible desires but not incompatible intentions.[25] I presume that what this means is that if I have incompatible desires and act on one of them, the other may continue to be present at least to some degree. Thus I may smoke because I desire to smoke, but feel badly about what I am doing because I also desire not to smoke. But if I intend to smoke and do so, it makes no sense to say that I simultaneously intend not to smoke. I may feel guilty about my action, but that seems to be a case of conflict between an intention and a desire. Brand does seem to be right here, and there does appear to be a real distinction.

Sixth, Brand argues that if one intends an end, one also intends the means for achieving the end, whereas one can desire the end but not desire the means.[26] This does seem to be true, for even if one uses the undesired means to obtain the more desired end, the distaste for the means remains, whereas one can hardly say that in adopting means to an intended end, one somehow intends the means less than the end.

Finally, Brand argues that whereas one can desire to perform an action oneself, or to have another perform it, one can only intend one's own action, not that of another.[27] One can, of course, intend that another should intend to do something; for example, one can so act as to create an intention in another which would produce an action. But as Brand points out, any intention that another act involves at least two actions—one's own and the other's—whereas one's own intention to act involves only one action. Clearly there is a difference here between intention and desire.

It does appear, then, that there is a difference between intention and desire. Brand holds that intentions have both a cognitive and a conative element, but that an intention cannot be equated to what Davidson calls a "primary reason." In Brand's view, intentions may be caused by desires and beliefs, but they are not reducible to desires and beliefs. Davidson would apparently disagree with that, since in his paper on intending, he describes an intention as an all-out judgment that an action is desirable, "given the rest of what I believe about the immediate future."[28] But while an intention may be some sort of judgment, it does not seem to be a judgment that something is desirable, for judging that an action is flat-out desirable does not in itself appear to involve any intention of doing it. If one accepts Brand's claim that an intention involves a plan, which clearly consists of beliefs, the "conative" aspect is some sort of resolution to execute the plan. I would suggest therefore that:

D2: I intend to do A =df I have a plan for doing A and I commit myself to following that plan.

On D2, one can clearly have an intention contrary to one's desires. One can also have an intention to do what one must do. Intention will involve a commitment to a whole plan, even if the means are distasteful, and the strength of the commitment can be variable. One cannot simultaneously carry out two intentions that require contradictory courses of action, and one can only intend one's own action. Thus, the criteria specified above seem to be met.

But what does it mean to "commit" oneself to a plan? This is a matter that will require further discussion, but for now we can take commitment to be an obligating of oneself by oneself to do something. It involves motive power in the same sense that any promise or obligation does, except that the obligation is to oneself rather than others. Hence failure to fulfill an intention will produce disappointment in oneself or remorse, or even embarrassment or guilt, depending on the intention and the circumstances. There are thus sanctions involved, but sanctions applied by the self to the self.

It would appear then that both desires and intentions can cause actions; nevertheless, there is an important difference in their causal functions which needs to be brought out. If I desire to smoke, and I also desire not to smoke, I obviously have a conflict of desires. There are several ways in which such a conflict may be resolved; I may decide to smoke in spite of the contrary desire, or not to smoke despite wanting to. Or I may objectify the desires and pose the question of whether I desire to desire to smoke or desire to desire not to. The point is that the resolution clearly requires a decision between conflicting alternatives; after all, how else could such a conflict be resolved except by deciding on one alternative or the other?

A decision is an action. What is the cause of a decision? It is very difficult to see how such a cause can be an intention. True, I may intend to make a decision. If I have a problem, I may set aside a particular time to make the decision, or fix upon a specific place where it will be made—after dinner I'll go sit in the garden. But that is not what is meant when one talks of the cause of a decision; one means in fact why one decided in favor of a particular desire or course of action. How could an intention be the cause of such an action? If I intend to choose not to smoke rather than to smoke, I have already made the decision. An intention seems to be the result of a decision, not the cause of one. But if that is so, what does determine decisions? The standard decision theory model holds that at least *rational* decisions are the product of desire and belief—more exactly, of preferences or desires along with probabilities expressing my degree of belief that a course of action will be successful. The qualification that the decision is "rational" has to do, not with the causal role of belief and desire, but with the choice between different courses of action. For a given set of desires (utilities), a rational decision requires that all possible courses of action be represented in the choice, that the subject assign to each a utility and a probability of success representing his belief that the course of action will yield the desired result, and then that the expected utility of each course be calculated. If the decision rule is to maximize expected utility, if there is a unique maximum, the choice is then determined. But not all decisions are rational in this sense. Often it is the case that few of the possible alternative courses of action are considered, different decision rules may be employed, or the assignment of probabilities and utilities may not be consistent. But none of these considerations change the fact that belief and desire play causal roles in decision making; they only qualify the way those factors operate. Accordingly, it does seem clear that beliefs and desires are the factors that determine decisions, rational or not.

What then of obligation or duty? Cannot these too determine the outcome of decision? Apparently not. An obligation or a duty has the form of an ethical imperative—you ought to care for your sick wife. But the question is, how binding is the obligation? When one decides between one's obligation to one's sick wife or going on holiday, the choice seems to be between one's desire to honor one's marital obligation or one's desire to enjoy oneself. The same is true of duty, if duty is really distinct from obligation. It is my duty to serve on a jury when called; it also requires a substantial sacrifice of time. When I must decide between the two, the question seems to be how much I desire to do my duty as opposed to how much I desire to spend that time in other ways.

If this argument is correct, it is necessary to distinguish between two kinds of actions, which may be called decisions and executions. Executions are those actions in which a chosen course of behavior (action) is carried out. Decisions are those actions in which the course to be carried out is chosen. Executions are usually determined by beliefs and by intentions that are the results of decisions, while decisions are determined by beliefs and desires, not by intentions.

Yet the same problem arises with intentions that arises with desires; there seem to be cases in which one can intend to do A and yet, even when the other conditions are met, not do A. One can, for example, intend to cut the grass today. One can decide to do so in the morning, intend to do so throughout the day, and still go to bed without having done so. And when asked the next day why one did not cut the grass, one can honestly reply, "But I intended to!" And one did! And one didn't do it. How then can intention be the cause of action?

If actions are causally determined, it seems clear that they can be causally explained. What would such an explanation be? In the light of D1, it should be clear that an action is not a simple phenomenon; the action A = <{B},G,E> has an internal structure that is complex, and this creates problems for the explanation of actions. Each of the components of an action admits of an explanation that is not an explanation of the others. Thus {B} may be explained in terms of both G and E; the behaviors were performed as means to the attainment of the goal, and that they were seen as means is guaranteed by E. Explaining G is explaining why S holds a certain goal. This will involve biological, psychological, or cultural factors quite distinct from either E or {B}. Explaining E is explaining why S holds certain beliefs. Such an explanation obviously presupposes a knowledge of G and {B}, but it does not explain why {B} was performed. Thus explaining an action is a complex business and requests for explanations of actions are often ambiguous because they can be addressed to various constituents of the action. "Why did he do *that*?" is often a request for an explanation of a particular behavior; "*Why* did he do that?" is apt to be a request for an explanation of a goal or of the relation of behavior to a goal, that is, of an expectation. In short, to ask for an explanation of an action may mean asking for an explanation of some component of an action, or of the action as a whole, and these are not the same.

When we explain an action as a whole by citing beliefs (expectations) and desires (goals) as causes, the beliefs and desires cited obviously cannot be those internal to the action. Thus consider the action of signing a letter. The behavior is the making of a linear inscription on the paper. The internal goal is to identify oneself as the author to the recipient; the internal expectation is that by making the inscription one will communicate the desired information to the recipient. So much is involved simply in the act of signing, as distinct from the behavior. But to explain the action of signing the letter, one must cite further beliefs and desires external to the act itself. Someone might desire to make clear a stand on raising taxes, and believes that by signing this letter this could be done. If this distinction is not kept in mind, one's explanation is likely to be circular.

What is the logical form of an action explanation for the causal theory of action? There are two candidates: the singular causal statement model or the covering law model. The most common type of explanation given is the singular causal statement. As we saw above, singular causal statements carry explanatory information when they are true, and tell us something about the ideal explanatory text. But the claim is often made in action theory that singular causal statements provide explanations of action without reference to covering laws or to anything like an ideal explanatory text. This claim requires examination.

Consider the sorts of singular causal statements usually offered in action explanations. Such statements would have the form:

(23) S A'd because he believed Y and desired Z.

or

(23') S A'd because he believed Y and intended Z.

Thus for example one might say:

(24) He threw the pass because he wanted his team to score and he believed that throwing a pass was an effective means of achieving that goal.

or

(24') He threw the pass because he intended to score and believed that throwing a pass was an effective means of achieving that goal.

Let us first ask under what conditions a statement of the form (23) is true or false. Clearly such a statement will be false if S does not believe Y, or if S does not desire Z, or both. But does it follow that (23) is true if S believes Y and desires Z, and that (23') is true if S believes Y and intends Z?

Suppose one has the singular causal statement,

> (25) Jones cut his own throat because his prime goal was to have a long life and he believed that by cutting his own throat he could best attain that goal.

Certainly one would require considerable convincing before accepting the claim that Jones both desired this goal and held this belief. But suppose there is convincing evidence for both; what would we say about (25)? It seems to me that on the standard theory, we should have no choice but to accept (25) as true. That fact is worrisome, because it suggests that statements like (25) cannot be false if in fact the subject has the stipulated beliefs and desires. But the truth or falsity of a causal statement should depend upon its referring to a real causal connection. What kind of a causal statement is (25) if it cannot be wrong about a causal connection?

Davidson comments:

> When a person acts with an intention, the following seems to be a true, if rough and incomplete, description of what goes on: he sets a positive value on some state of affairs (an end, or the performance by himself of an action satisfying certain conditions); he believes (or knows or perceives) that an action, of a kind open to him to perform, will promote or produce or realize the valued state of affairs; and so he acts (that is, he acts *because* of his value or desire and his belief).[29]

As Davidson says, this is "a very persuasive view of the nature of intentional action."[30] But why is it so persuasive? This is the psychological theory that children develop within the first two years of life and that dominates our common-sense thinking about human action from that point on.[31] It also fits our experience of our own actions since we act intentionally to obtain things that we desire, and in so acting we do what we do because we believe the action will bring us what we desire. Because this experience is so universal, we refuse to accept the possibility of a countercase. Therefore, if we were to perform some action, and having done so, were to find that we could cite no reason for it—that it was prompted by no desire and guided by no belief— we would find that experience impossible. We would insist that there was a cause, although we could not say what it was. Whether the cause was repressed, or was due to a second personality lurking in our psychic depths, or whatever, we would insist that there was something that produced that action. And being convinced of this in our own case, we take it for granted that this must be true of all others. People do not act without reasons.

It is not difficult to understand why Davidson's scheme seems so plausible. Yet the problem raised by (25) remains. If there is a causal relation between beliefs, desires, intentions, and actions, then a singular causal statement would seem to be true when it refers to that causal relation, and false otherwise. If Davidson's scheme is correct, it must always be the case that when a particular desire and belief, or intention and belief, are held by an actor S, then S A's. That is, we seem driven to say that the truth of a singular statement such as (25) depends upon the existence of some sort of general law. As we saw in the preceding chapter, causality always involves law. Therefore, the singular causal statement does not really stand alone as an explanation of action.

It is true that in a given context, against a given background of knowledge, such a singular causal statement may be pragmatically adequate as an explanation. To the degree that a singular causal statement carries explanatory information, it serves an explanatory function, whether we are able to fill in the rest of the ideal text or not. But however inadequate our present knowledge of the ideal explanatory text may be, the explanatory power of the singular causal statement depends ultimately upon its relation to that text.

The second alternative usually cited is the covering law model of explanation for action. I believe there is no real doubt that the covering law model does provide an explanation for an action, if we have the covering law. The problem, as opponents of the covering law model have frequently pointed out, is that we seem not to have such laws. Clearly, the model cannot be taken seriously if there are few if any covering laws to serve as premises. Davidson has sought a middle way here by arguing that while explanations by singular causal statements need not exhibit covering laws, the truth of such singular causal statements implies that a relevant covering law exists, whether we can exhibit it or not:

> It does not follow that we must be able to dredge up a law if we know a singular causal statement to be true; all that follows is that we know there must be a covering law. And very often, I think, our justification for accepting a singular causal statement is that we have reason to believe an appropriate causal law exists, though we do not know what it is. Generalizations like "If you strike a well-made match hard enough against a properly prepared surface, then, other things being favorable, it will light" owe their importance not to the fact that we can hope eventually to render them untendentious and exceptionless,

but rather to the fact that they summarize much of our evidence for believing that full-fledged causal laws exist covering events we wish to explain.[32]

But since we do not know what the relevant covering law is, we do not have a covering law explanation of action. If it is the truth of a singular causal statement that guarantees the existence of the invisible covering law, how do we know that the singular causal statement is true? As we saw above, the truth of the singular causal statement seems to presuppose a true covering law. If so, the whole argument becomes circular, with the truth of singular causal statements depending upon true but mysterious covering laws, the existence of which depends on the truth of the singular causal statement. The problem is not solved by referring to Railton's ideal explanatory texts, for the question is precisely whether or not such texts exist for action explanations. If there are in fact no covering laws, then Railton's approach, like Hempel's, will not work. Something seems to be wrong with this approach. Let us therefore examine the criticisms that have been brought against it.

The causal theory of action has been criticized on a number of grounds. One is the argument that the theory leads to a regress. If action is determined by beliefs and desires (we may ignore intentions here, since they are determined by desires and beliefs), what determines beliefs and desires? Am I free to choose my own beliefs and desires? So far as belief is concerned, the answer appears to be no, at least if conscious choice is meant. The contrary has of course been argued; Pascal's wager is certainly one of the most famous examples. But I have never met anyone who was actually led to believe by Pascal's wager. I think it is beyond question that at some unconscious level our desires and other beliefs do affect how we believe, but I do not think it is possible to just decide to believe something and thereupon to believe it. Of course, one can decide to question a belief; one can wish it were not true, and try to find reasons for rejecting it. But notoriously we often fail in such endeavors; the questioning may lead to increased conviction of the truth of the belief even when one wanted to disprove it.

The situation with respect to desire is much more complex. Biologically based desires are not subject to choice; one may decide where or when or how they are or are not to be expressed or satisfied, but not whether or not one will have them. Even anorexics get hungry. But in the case of acquired desires, the case is different; to a considerable degree one can choose one's desires. Consider again the case of smokers. The smokers desire to smoke; otherwise, they would not smoke. But suppose that the smokers learn of the carcinogenic effects of cigarette smoke. Since they also desire a long and healthy life, they have a conflict between desires. Can they choose which desire they will have? I pick this example precisely because it is well known that smoking is addictive, so that there is a real physiological base to the smoker's desire. Yet it is manifestly the case that one can choose not to smoke, and further that one can choose to rid oneself of the desire to smoke. And not only can one choose to do this, one can do it, as thousands of ex-smokers can testify. It therefore seems quite clear that at least with respect to a wide range of acquired desires, one can in fact choose one's own desires.

When one chooses what one desires, the choice itself of course is motivated. That is, what one chooses depends upon one's beliefs and one's desires. One has here what looks like a regress; insofar as desires are chosen, the choice itself is determined by beliefs and desires, and since those desires can be chosen, there is a prior choice determined by beliefs and desires, and so on. But there is no genuine regress. The fact that some desires can be chosen does not imply that all are. If in a given case, one chooses to have a particular desire, and that choice itself is caused by beliefs and desires, it does not follow that the latter desires were also chosen by an act of decision. Even though one can choose some desires, it is quite clear that most of our desires are not deliberately chosen.

But this conclusion raises the issue of freedom in quite a strong form, for if neither beliefs nor desires are ultimately chosen freely, there would appear to be no freedom at all. To claim that an individual so determined is still free would be to accept the principle that we are free when we do what we desire, or, put differently, that we cannot be coerced by our own wants. Levin has put the point more generally.

> Attempting to construe your wants as forcing you to act leads to absurdity; it represents your wants as leading you to do what you don't want to. . . . My desires and decisions can be thought of as forces acting on me only if they are thought of as distinct from the self on which they act, as external forces impinging on the self. But the correct elaboration of the metaphor is that I *am* the totality of my desires.[33]

But this argument is not right. The smoker who wants to stop smoking and cannot in fact is constrained by his desire to smoke, just as the alcoholic who wants to be rid of his desire for alcohol, but cannot, is constrained by his desire. This situation is not confined to desires that, like those just mentioned, have a physiological basis. A man may be so fearful of others that he cannot establish social relationships, even though he knows this about himself and desires to change his fear. Extreme cases of this sort are well understood to involve not only irrationality, but a degree of psychological malfunctioning that requires medical treatment. When a desire reaches the point that it becomes impervious to counterdesires (when it is what Levin calls "reason insensitive"[34]) we are no longer dealing with normal desires but with addictions or obsessions that lie beyond the normal range. That such cases do occur is a fact, but it is also a fact that they represent an abnormal extreme. We may indeed define the normal as those cases where our desires can be influenced (either positively or negatively) by other desires or by information that leads us to revise our estimate of the likelihood that following them will yield as desirable results as we had thought.

But ruling out as psychopathic such cases of irresistible impulse does not eliminate cases of resistible and unwanted desires. Conflict among desires is the normal situation of human beings, and conduct is usually the result of a compromise among these conflicting desires. Everybody has some desires that the person condemns but which pose a problem, constant or intermittent, of control. It is not clear on the theory so far considered how such control is possible or in what it consists. Without an answer to that question, the theory that you are your desires is inadequate.

The most common criticism of the causal theory of action is the prediction paradox. Suppose we have a theory about an agent S that predicts that in specific circumstances she will perform an action A—call this theory T_0. Assuming such a theory to exist, there is no reason why S may not learn about the theory; suppose she does. Then S could so act in the specific circumstances as to prove the theory false; that is, she could deliberately not do A. Therefore, it is held, there cannot be such a theory T_0.

In answer to this paradox, Levin has given the following argument. T_0 presumably predicts what S will do under certain circumstances that do not include her knowledge of T_0. Accordingly, when S learns about T_0, the antecedent conditions are changed and T_0 no longer applies; rather, we now need a new theory T_1 that includes S's knowledge of T_0 among the antecedent conditions. Obviously, this process can lead to an infinite series of theories predicting S's actions, such that if T_n is any theory of the series, T_{n+1} is T_n so altered as to include S's knowledge of T_n among the antecedent conditions of action. Of course, in practical terms S cannot regress very far in this series, but in principle there is no reason why she must stop at any given point. But Levin argues that the regress so described is not vicious, because the series $\{T_n\}$ will contain a fixed point T_a such that S's behavior on learning of T_a will be no different than her behavior without knowing of T_a.

Why should this be so? The argument draws on a fixed-point result due to Simon. The problem with which Simon deals is the effect prior to an election of publishing a poll predicting that a certain percentage of the voters will vote for a particular candidate, C. Let I be the percentage of voters who would have voted for C if the poll had not been published, V the percentage who actually vote for C, and P the percentage that the poll predicts will vote for C. Taking I as given, and assuming that the poll shows C winning, the function $V = f(I,P)$ can be graphed as:

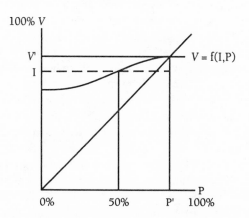

The rise in $V = f(I,P)$ is the bandwagon effect caused by the publication of the poll. The diagonal gives the set of points where $V = P$ (i.e., where the actual vote equals that predicted by the poll). Thus the point (V', P') is a fixed point; if the poll predicts that P' percent of the voters will vote for C, it will be correct, since $V' = P'$. Such a fixed point will always exist if $V = f(I,P)$ is continuous.[35] Drawing on this result of Simon's, Levin argues that if T_{n+1} differs from T_n only in including S's awareness of T_n and the consequences of that fact, there will be a "fixed point theory" about S's action such that S's knowing T_n will produce no change in his conduct.[36]

Levin's argument is related to Simon's only by analogy. First, Simon is dealing with aggregate data, Levin with an individual case. As Simon notes, his own argument assumes that the function $V = f(I,P)$ is continuous. Although strictly the function is probably not continuous, yet if the number of cases is large, the approximation will be close enough so that it can be treated as continuous. But there is no corresponding continuous function for the individual case. Furthermore, Simon's argument deals with a single act—voting—and assumes that the effect of knowing the prediction is only to change the candidate for whom the voters vote. But in the individual case, the effect may well be not to vote at all, or to assassinate the candidate, or any of a number of other distinct actions. Simon's result clearly has no direct application to the case of a particular individual.[37]

Nevertheless, it seems to me that Levin's intuition is correct—that beyond some point in the series S's action will not be changed by knowledge of a prediction. After all, why should it change? Presumably, it would change for either of two reasons: (a) S objects to having her actions predicted, or (b) S objects to the action that T_n predicts that she will perform. In the latter case, S could presumably then choose an alternative action that she desired (i.e., of which she approved), and having done so would have no objection to carrying it out even if T_{n+1} predicted that she would do it.

Only if, for all x, T_x always predicted that S will do something of which she would disapprove if she knew T_x, would there be no point at which S's action would not be changed by further regression in the series. The only cases I can think of where this could happen would be ones in which S objects to having her actions predicted, which brings us back to the first reason, above. But in point of fact, people do not usually object to predictions that they will do something in particular circumstances, provided that the action is one of which they approve. To be known as the sort of person who acts consistently with standards one approves should be gratifying to the individual and would therefore not be grounds for changing one's actions.[38]

About the only cases in which it seems plausible that prediction would always be resented would be cases where the success of the action depends upon secrecy (e.g., action by a criminal or a spy). But even here, it is not so much a case of predictability as of who has access to the knowledge necessary to make the prediction. Both criminals and spies must have reputations of meeting certain self-approved and other-approved standards if they are to function successfully with colleagues and superiors in their chosen lines of endeavor; their concern would be with the possibility that their enemies might be able to predict their course of action. So even here there is no reason to think that one's own knowledge of a theory predicting one's action would be cause for a change in one's actions; such a change would only be expected if the wrong ones among the others had access to the theory. The so-called prediction paradox therefore does not seem to be a genuine paradox.

Psychological Theories of the Causes of Action

Thus far we have been discussing theories formulated by philosophers. Neither with respect to the causes of action, the explanation of action, nor the problem of freedom do these theories seem to take us very far. It is therefore necessary to turn to what psychologists have been doing in the study of such matters, if further progress is to be made. Let us take first the problem of freedom. I take it that the basic fact here is beyond question: People do believe they freely choose much of what they do. Given that fact, it would seem one must either hold they are right and so really are "free," or else one must hold our experience of freedom to be an illusion.

But this is an incorrect formulation of the problem. When one experiences oneself as freely choosing to act in a given way, one is certainly not hallucinating. The real question is, what is it that is being experienced when one feels oneself to be acting freely? DeCharms argued that persons are in fact agents who initiate causal processes. As he put it: "Man's primary motivational propensity is to be effective in producing changes in his environment."[39] According to DeCharms, this "propensity" is innate, and may therefore be said to be hardwired into the person, but this does not diminish for DeCharms the fact that humans cause their own behavior.

> The most basic postulate that we wish to present is that a man is the origin of his behavior. He is a unique locus of causality. Heider (1944,1958) has developed the proposition that man is perceived as a locus of causality under certain conditions and it is a commonplace that men *feel* that their behavior is caused ultimately by them. Our postulate states more, i.e., that man *is* the locus of causality for his behavior.[40]

Building on DeCharms, Deci has carried that argument a step further. Deci argues that humans have an innate need to be competent and self-determining in their relations with their environment:

> Intrinsic motivation is innate. All humans are born with the basic and undifferentiated need for feeling competent and self-determining. Humans are active organisms in continual interaction with their environment, and the basic intrinsic need provides much of the motivation for this interaction.[41]

From this Deci argues that "intrinsically motivated behaviors are characterized by *internal* causality. The cause of the behavior is the intent to receive the internal rewards of the activity, i.e., feelings of competence and self-determination."[42] Thus Deci in effect holds that our feelings of freedom and self-determination are caused by the innate need for such feelings, or put differently a need to be gratified by experiencing such feelings. This is a need that Deci sees as rooted in the evolutionary necessity for effective action in the environment. But whatever the origin of the need, the result is that our sense of personal freedom and self-determination is the effect of causal processes that take place in us—basically, of our successfully solving problems and overcoming obstacles set by the environment.[43]

A much more comprehensive and, I believe, more satisfactory theory has been developed by Bandura. His theory involves neither an innate drive of the sort postulated by Deci nor the prime cause thesis of DeCharms; in fact Bandura regards behavior as the result of an interaction between the environment, the person, and the person's behavior, and considers problems of ultimate causality unanswerable. Our interest here, however, is in his theory of self-efficacy. Bandura has shown that from the observation of others we learn generalized standards of how to behave to achieve desired results. These standards are acquired by induction from observing how others behave and what the outcomes of their behavior are; when their behavior leads to outcomes we value, we model our behavior on theirs in the expectation that similar blessings will accrue to us.[44] These standards are general and generative; we can apply them successfully in new situations in which we have not previously seen them used. We then attempt to act according to these standards, and evaluate our own performance according to the degree to which it matches the standard. Achieving a satisfactory match between behavior and standard is rewarding, producing in us feelings of self-efficacy and self-satisfaction.[45] Our capacity for self-evaluation and self-reward create a general ability to regulate our own behavior in terms of anticipated rewards.[46]

As Bandura notes,

> Although both external and self-directed procedures alter behavior, the practice of self-reward can have the added advantage of developing a generalizable skill in self-regulation that can be used continually. It is perhaps for this reason that self-rewarded behavior tends to be maintained more effectively than if it had been externally reinforced. Moreover, personal changes achieved mainly through one's own efforts increase a sense of personal causality.[47]

Feelings of self-efficacy arise from multiple sources; we learn from experience that we can produce changes in the environment, that we can do things to obtain anticipated rewards.[48] We learn the same lesson from others, either by direct teaching or by observing their behavior.[49] And we learn it from our capacity to regulate our own behavior through internal standards, the evaluation of our own behavior based on information derived from feedback from our enactments, and the correction of our own behavior to match our standards. Thus we perceive ourselves to be effective causes because we learn from our behavior that we are indeed effective causes[50] and this conviction about our self-efficacy then becomes an important determinant of our behavior. As Bandura and his associates have demonstrated experimentally in detail, our self-efficacy beliefs play a causal role in what we do.

It is this capacity for self-regulation that provides the answer to the threatened tyranny of undesirable desires. To the degree that we acquire internal standards and the ability to control our own action so as to conform to them, unwanted desires are controlled although rarely eliminated. And much of what we normally think of as human freedom, and of what we experience as self-efficacy or personal causation, lies in our ability to resolve the conflict of desires in favor of those we approve and against those we disapprove. Much of human history has revolved around the contest between what people have perceived as their nobler and their baser desires. Without both the capacity and the need for self-regulation, there would be no sense of personal freedom.

The critical point in Bandura's work for our present purposes is that our belief in our own "freedom"—that is, our ability to regulate our own behavior and to motivate ourselves to do what we wish to do—is no illusion; it is instead a causal result of a complex learned process by which we can and do regulate our own behavior. Certainly innate factors are involved; Bandura remarks that the capacity to acquire standards from the observation of others and then to use those standards to shape and motivate our own behavior through self-evaluation and self-reward seems to be a uniquely human capacity. But there is no need to postulate an innate drive for personal causation nor is it necessary to go beyond social learning theory to account for our experiences of and beliefs in our own freedom. So understood, there is no contradiction between freedom as thus described and determinism of the sort discussed above. When we act on the basis of our own decisions, motivated by our own desires, we are free; we can regulate our own behavior and we do so by using causally effective methods of self-reward and self-evaluation. There is, in short, no problem of freedom because our experience of freedom and our belief that we are free are the products of causally effective psychological processes.

None of the objections to the causal theory of action seem to hold up under examination. Yet as we saw above, the philosopher's causal theories of action do not appear to be very satisfactory. This has led some critics of action theories to claim that any psychological theory that utilizes concepts such as "belief" or "intention" is a "folk psychological theory" and by definition unscientific.[51] This view, however, is mistaken. Within the last two decades there has been a very substantial amount of work in psychology on intentional action, and some of the theories that have been developed have now acquired impressive experimental support. Locke, Shaw, Saari, and Latham have reviewed the experimental literature on the relation of goals and behavior.[52] As they point out, there is a fairly large body of experimental data to show that goals ("what an individual is trying to accomplish") do affect behavior. Goals clearly direct attention and action; they mobilize effort to achieve the goal sought, and determine the duration with which that effort is sustained. They also motivate the development of strategies or plans for the achieving of goals. It is therefore quite wrong to dismiss intentional explanations as being purely a matter of "folk" beliefs; contemporary psychology is a science, and it provides substantial support for the explanatory character of intentional theories.[53]

It will be useful to present here a sketch of two of the more impressive of these theories, although the treatment must necessarily be very brief and incomplete. Fishbein and Ajzen have advanced a theory that relates belief, attitude, intention, and behavior, and that has proven very successful. They define belief as a relation between an "object" (i.e., referent) and an attribute, value, concept, or other object to which a subjective probability is given.[54] The approach they take "is essentially based on an information processing model, and a person's beliefs represent the information he has about himself and his social and physical environment."[55] The processing of this information they show can be described to a reasonable approximation by probability models. "Thus man may be viewed as a fairly rational processor of information available to him. His descriptive and inferential beliefs are not capricious, nor are they systematically distorted by motivational or emotional biases."[56] This is not a claim for strict rationality in the sense of the practical syllogism, but rather a finding that in general "various quantitative probability models provide fairly accurate descriptions and predictions of inferential belief formations."[57]

By an "attitude," Fishbein and Ajzen mean an individual's feeling of favorableness or unfavorableness toward an object, attribute, or act.[58] In their view, attitudes are based upon and determined by beliefs; when one believes that an object has an attribute or that an act has a consequence, one will also form a favorable or unfavorable attitude toward that object or act. Obviously, any individual will have multiple beliefs about almost any object or act, each of which will involve some evaluation, positive, negative, or zero—and therefore the individual's attitude must be the resultant of these multiple elements. Fortunately, not every belief held by individuals about a given referent needs to be entered into the equation; it is sufficient to deal with their salient beliefs, which are defined operationally as the first ten to twelve beliefs elicited in a free response format, and the strength of those beliefs as measured by their subjective probability. This yields an equation for attitudes:

$$(26) \quad A = \sum_{i=1}^{n} b_i \, e_i,$$

where i ranges over the n salient beliefs considered, b_i is the strength of the individual's belief that an object has an attribute or an act has a given consequence, and e_i is the evaluation, on a favorable-unfavorable scale, of the attribute or consequence.

> Thus, according to the model, a person's attitude toward an object can be estimated by multiplying his evaluation of each attribute associated with the object by his subjective probability that the object has that attribute and then summing the products for the total set of [salient] beliefs. Similarly, a person's attitude toward a behavior can be estimated by multiplying his evaluation of each of the behavior's consequences by his subjective probability that performing the behavior will lead to that consequence and then summing the products for the total set of [salient] beliefs.[59]

The limitation to salient beliefs is justified not only by practical reasons but because experiments have shown that beyond the first few beliefs elicited, successive additional beliefs contribute less and less to the total, so that the total levels off after the first ten beliefs or so.[60]

By a "behavioral intention," Fishbein and Ajzen mean an individual's subjective probability that he will perform a behavior.[61] Intention involves four elements—the behavior, the "target" object at which the behavior is directed, the situation in which the behavior is to be performed, and the time at which the behavior is to be carried out. As a result, intentions can vary in specificity with respect to all four of these elements. An intention to buy coffee at the Acme at 3 p.m. this afternoon is very specific on all four counts; an intention to go shopping this week is very general. Not surprisingly, a close relation between attitude and intention is found only when both are measured at the same level of specificity.[62]

Behavioral intentions, according to Fishbein and Ajzen, are determined by the weighted sum of two components. The first is the actor's attitude toward the behavior involved—not, it should be noted, the object toward which the behavior is directed, but the behavior itself. As noted above, this attitude, A_B (B referring to the behavior) is given by:

$$(27) \quad A_B = \sum_{i=1}^{n} = b_i\, e_i,$$

where b_i is the belief that performing behavior B leads to consequence i, e_i is the actor's evaluation of i, and n is the number of salient beliefs.[63]

The second factor is the actor's perception that reference individuals or groups—that is, persons or groups with respect to whose standards and expectations the actor evaluates himself and his own behavior—think he should or should not perform the behavior. This factor may be computed by

$$(28) \quad SN = \sum_{i=1}^{n} = b'_i \, m_i,$$

where b'_i is the individual's belief that the reference individual or group i thinks he should or should not perform behavior B, m_i is his motivation to comply with referent i, n is the number of relevant referents, and "SN" stands for "subjective norm." SN is thus determined by the sum of products of normative beliefs—more strictly, the subjective probabilities of those beliefs—multiplied by the strength of the motivation to comply with them.[64] Thus we have that I, the intention to perform B, is given by

$$(29) \quad I = (A_B) \, w_1 + (SN) \, w_2,[65]$$

where w_1 and w_2 are standardized multiple regression coefficients. Intention is then used as the predictor of behavior.

It will be observed that the Fishbein and Ajzen theory involves not only the determinants of belief and desire usually employed in the action theories of philosophers but also social determinants that philosophers have generally ignored. It should also be stressed that whereas philosophic theories of action have usually stressed attitudes toward the target object,[66] the Fishbein and Ajzen theory specifies the determinant as attitudes toward the behavior. This does not mean that the attitudes toward the object are irrelevant, but that they affect intention only through affecting attitudes toward behavior. Thus, consequences of performing a given behavior toward a liked person may differ from those of performing it toward a disliked person; the effect here will be registered in A_B. But there are also cases where one is expected to perform the same behavior toward both liked and disliked persons; here, attitude toward the target object will be irrelevant.[67]

How well do intentions, defined as above, predict behavior? Assuming that behavior is defined at the same level of specificity as intention, that the intention is stable (that is, does not change between the measurement of intention and the observation of behavior), and that the performance of the behavior is under the control of the actor, the answer is, very well indeed. Correlations in the .7 to .8 range have been obtained under these conditions in a number of experiments.[68] There is then very substantial empirical evidence that this model does predict and explain behavior. This is not a matter of "folk" psychology but of scientific psychology, employing a model involving concepts of belief, attitude, and intention. As Tesser and Shaffer comment in a recent review of the psychological literature, "The Fishbein & Ajzen model has been extremely fruitful. We suspect that the theory will undergo even further refinement and will remain an influential approach for years to come."[69]

In discussing the Fishbein and Ajzen theory, I have used the terms "behavior" and "action" interchangeably, as is the practice in the psychological literature. But when one looks at the actual "behaviors" that the model is used to explain, it is clear that they are limited to what philosophers call "actions." Thus among those to which the model is applied are attending church, contributing money to a church, attending a social event, owning a copy of a book, performing actions in a Prisoner's Dilemma game, performance in a war game, attending football games, signing up for an alcoholic treatment program, voting for a political candidate, and so on.[70] It should therefore be clear that the model is one that predicts, and provides causal explanations for, actions in terms of beliefs, attitudes, and intentions.

More recently, Ajzen and his coworkers have further developed this theory into what they call a "theory of planned behavior." We noted above the difficulties that are introduced into philosophical theories of action when the action in question is not completely under the control of the actor. The Fishbein and Ajzen theory assumes that the actor has total control. For some actions, this is a reasonable assumption, but reflection shows that it is less often reasonable than one might at first think. Even a simple action such as going to the store may depend upon the weather, one's car starting, not having a traffic accident on the way, not getting a flat, and so forth. This has led Ajzen further to refine the Fishbein and Ajzen theory by introducing the concept of perceived control as a determinant of action.

Since performing an action depends on the agent's control of the situation as well as his intention, Ajzen takes as the predictor of behavior both the agent's intention to try to perform the behavior, I_t, and his actual control over the factors involved in executing the action. However, since actual control is rarely predictable—one cannot predict individual traffic accidents—Ajzen instead has used the agent's perception of control. But this substitution has far-reaching effects, for quite apart from the accuracy of the agent's perceptions of control, the fact that the agent believes them will affect his intentions and attitudes. Thus if in (29) one substitutes A_t—attitude toward trying—for A_B, it is necessary to distinguish between attitude toward the successful performance of the action, A_s, and attitude toward the failed performance of the action, A_f. A_t then becomes:

(30) $A_t = [P_s A_s + P_f A_f], P_s + P_f = 1,$

where p_s is the subjective probability of successful performance and p_f the subjective probability of unsuccessful performance.

Similarly, SN must be modified by multiplying it by p_r—the subjective probability of the belief that the agent will successfully perform the action that the agent attributes to the reference individuals or groups. Thus we have:

$$(31) \quad I_t = [w_1 \{p_s \sum_{i=1}^{n} b_{s_i} e_i + p_f \sum_{i=1}^{n} b_{f_i} e_i\} + w_2 \, p_r \sum_{i=1}^{n} b'_i \, m_i]$$

or

$$(32) \quad I_t = [w_1 A_t + w_2 SN_t].$$

(31) captures the effect of introducing the agent's perception of control on the intention to try, which is what is causally relevant to the agent's performance of the action. Experiments confirm that the theory of planned behavior is a better predictor of action than the original Fishbein and Ajzen theory of reasoned action in those cases when the agent's control is not complete; where it is complete, the former theory reduces to the latter.[71] But prediction is further improved by adding to the model "behavioral expectation," defined as the agent's estimate of what he actually will do as opposed to what he intends to do. Behavioral expectation is given by $I_t b_c$, where b_c is the subjective probability of the agent's belief that he can control the action. This interesting result shows that the agent's perception of his actual control over the performance of the action is usually more realistic than one would guess, based on his intention to try to perform it.[72] Of course, behavioral expectation is not a causal factor in explaining the agent's action; it is the agent's actual control that is causally relevant. Nevertheless, to the extent that behavioral expectations are accurate, they can be used to improve prediction.[73] Clearly, where the agent perceives his control to be total, (32) reduces to (29).

It is not intended here to suggest that the theories of Fishbein and Ajzen are perfect, or that they have said the last word on these matters, nor have they made any such claims. There are problems yet to be solved. For example, Fazio has shown that attitudes, defined as "an association between a given object and a given evaluation," once activated can generalize to affect the processing of information concerning unrelated objects or topics.[74] This finding would seem inconsistent with Fishbein and Ajzen's theory of the relation between belief and attitude. It is not that Fishbein and Ajzen ignore the possibility of feedback, but that Fazio's results indicate that actors are less objective processors of information than their model requires. Clearly, as Tesser and Shaffer have emphasized, there is much work to be done.[75] Nevertheless, it is clear that Fishbein and Ajzen's theory of reasoned action and Ajzen's theory of planned behavior are theories that do provide causal explanations and predictions of action well supported by empirical evidence. Whatever the refinements that must be made, there is no substantial doubt that these theories provide causal explanations of action in terms of beliefs, attitudes, and intentions.

The bearing of this psychological work on the issue of the explanation of action should be obvious. As we have seen, the objection to the singular causal statement explanation was that it took for granted the very point at issue, namely, the existence of a real causal process connecting action to beliefs, desires, and intentions, while the objection to the covering law theory was that covering laws seemed to be in embarrassingly short supply. What the work of Fishbein and Ajzen, and of other psychologists working in this field, has shown is that there are real causal relations connecting belief, attitude, intention, and action. Whether these relations are simply referred to by singular causal statements or are more fully developed by explicitly stating the model used and the values for its variables, in either case we have genuine causal explanations of action.

Undoubtedly, we are still a long way from being able to construct an ideal explanatory text for the explanation of actions, but the claim that no such text can exist because there are no covering laws is clearly false. So seen, the philosophic theory of action may be regarded as a first approximation toward an adequate psychological theory, which psychologists are now developing. The shortcomings of the philosophical theories are not trivial; it is a matter of importance that it is attitudes toward behavior rather than target objects that are critical, and philosophers have generally ignored the role of social norms in action and the problem of perceptions of control. But these corrections can be made without throwing out the major contention of action theory that the explanation of action must be in intentional terms and must involve cognitive and attitudinal factors. None of this, I trust we now see, is in any way opposed to the thesis that action can be causally explained. There is no contradiction between a scientific causal explanation of action and an intentional explanation.

The picture of action presented here remains seriously incomplete, for it leaves out of account—or at least does not deal adequately with—some of the most important explanatory concepts involved in the theory of human action. These are rules and complex plans. To these subjects we must now turn.

Notes

1. Brand, *Intending*, 17–18.

2. Dray, *Laws and Explanation in History*, 124.

3. G. E. M. Anscombe, *Intention* (Ithaca, N.Y.: Cornell University Press, 1969).

4. Davidson, *Essays*, 5.

5. Ibid., 12.

6. Ibid., 8–9.

7. Ibid., 7.

8. Ibid., 22, 42.

9. Hector-Neri Castaneda, *Thinking, Language, and Experience* (Minneapolis: University of Minnesota Press, 1989), ch. 12. My treatment of the first and third person quasi-indicators differs somewhat from Castaneda's.

10. Ibid., 218–226.

11. Chisholm, *First Person*, 28.

12. Ibid., 28.

13. Ibid., 28.

14. Ibid., 30. (Emphasis in original)

15. Ibid., 58–59.

16. Ibid., 59–60.

17. Ibid., 59.

18. Ibid., 35–37.

19. Jaegwon Kim, "Critical Notices: *The First Person*," *Philosophy and Phenomenological Research* 46:483–507(1986).

20. Chisholm, *First Person*, 7.

21. Brand, *Intending*, 122.

22. Ibid., 123.

23. Ibid., 124.

24. Ibid., 125.

25. Ibid.

26. Ibid., 126.

27. Ibid.

28. Davidson, *Essays*, 99.

29. Ibid., 31. (Emphasis in original)

30. Ibid.

31. Wellman, *Child's Theory of Mind*, ch. 4.

32. Davidson, *Essays*, 160. Cf. 16–18.

33. Levin, *Metaphysics*, 239. (Emphasis in original)

34. Ibid., 246–252.

35. Herbert A. Simon, "The Effect of Predictions" in May Brodbeck, ed., *Readings in the Philosophy of the Social Sciences* (London: Macmillan, 1969), 447–455.

36. Levin, *Metaphysics*, 258–269.

37. Simon, "Effect."

38. Levin makes this argument (*Metaphysics*, 266–269).

39. Richard DeCharms, *Personal Causation* (New York: Academic Press, 1968), 269.

40. Ibid., 272–273. (Emphasis in original)

41. Edward L. Deci, *Intrinsic Motivation* (New York: Plenum Press, 1975), 65.

42. Ibid., 253. (Emphasis in original)

43. Ibid., 56–62, 139–141, 148–154.

44. Albert Bandura, *Social Foundations of Thought and Action* (Englewood Cliffs, N.J.: Prentice-Hall Co., 1986), 100, 323, 341–345.

45. Ibid., 354ff, ch. 9.

46. Ibid., 344, 354ff.

47. Albert Bandura, *Social Learning Theory* (Englewood Cliffs: Prentice-Hall Co., 1977), 144.

48. Bandura, *Social Foundations*, 259–261.

49. Ibid., 210–211.

50. Ibid., 391.

51. Paul Churchland, "Eliminative Materialism and the Propositional Attitudes," *Journal of Philosophy* 78:67–90 (1981).

52. Edwin A. Locke, Karyll N. Shaw, Lise M. Saari, and Gary P. Latham, "Goal Setting and Task Performance: 1969–1980," *Psychological Bulletin* 90:125–152 (1981).

53. Fred Vollmer, "Intentional Explanation and Its Place in Psychology," *Journal for the Theory of Social Behavior* 16:285–298 (1986).

54. Martin Fishbein and Icek Ajzen, *Belief, Attitude, Intention and Behavior* (Reading, Mass.: Addison-Wesley Co., 1975), 131.

55. Ibid., 135.

56. Ibid., 215.

57. Ibid., 214.

58. Ibid., 216–217.

59. Ibid., 223.

60. Ibid.

61. Ibid., 288.

62. Ibid., 296–303.

63. Ibid., 301.

64. Ibid., 302. On the concept of reference groups, see Robert K. Merton, *Social Theory and Social Structure* (Glencoe: Free Press, 1957), chs. 8, 9.

65. Fishbein and Ajzen, *Belief*, 301.

66. This criticism does *not* apply to Davidson, whose "pro-attitude" is an attitude toward behaviors or actions.

67. Fishbein and Ajzen, *Beliefs*, 307–308.

68. Ibid., 352–383.

69. Abraham Tesser and David R. Shaffer, "Attitudes and Attitude Change," *Annual Review of Psychology* 41:479–523 (1990), 491.

70. Fishbein and Ajzen, *Beliefs*, 355, 373–374.

71. Deborah E. Schifter and Icek Ajzen, "Intention, Perceived Control, and Weight Loss: An Application of the Theory of Planned Behavior," *Journal of Personality and Social Psychology* 49:843–851 (1985). Icek Ajzen and Thomas J. Madden, "Prediction of Goal-Directed Behavior: Attitudes, Intentions, and Perceived Behavioral Control," *Journal of Experimental Social Psychology* 22:453–474 (1986).

72. Icek Ajzen, "From Intentions to Actions: A Theory of Planned Behavior" in Julius Kuhl and Jurgen Beckmann eds., *Action Control: From Cognition to Behavior* (Berlin: Springer-Verlag, 1985), 11–39. Icek Ajzen, *Attitudes, Personality, and Behavior* (Chicago: Dorsey Press, 1988). Icek Ajzen, "Attitude Structure and Behavior" in Anthony R. Pratkanis, Steven J. Breckler and Anthony G. Greenwald, eds. *Attitude Structure and Function* (Hillsdale, N.J.: Lawrence Erlbaum Associates, 1989), 241–274.

73. Ajzen and Madden, "Predictions," 472.

74. Russell H. Fazio, David M. Sanbonmatsu, Martha C. Powell, and Frank R. Kardes, "On the Automatic Activation of Attitudes," *Journal of Personality and Social Psychology* 50:229–238 (1986). Russell H. Fazio, "On the Power and Functionality of Attitudes: The Role of Attitude Accessibility" in Pratkanis et al., *Attitude Structure and Function*, 153–179.

75. Tesser and Shaffer, "Attitudes and Attitude Change," 491.

Chapter 5

Rules

This chapter concludes the treatment of explanations of human action by examining the role of rules and plans. After describing the chief properties of rules, the crucial distinction between satisfying a rule and following a rule is discussed. I seek to show that the concept of rule following is applicable to both rules of which we are explicitly aware and those of which we are not explicitly conscious. A rule is described here as a normative belief; following a rule needs a commitment to the rule and so requires a motive for following the rule. The explanatory and predictive force of rules depends upon their being followed and so upon the motives for following them. Issues of rule change, rule deviation, rule violation, and rule learning are treated in terms of this analysis of rule following. The treatment of plans closely parallels that of rules.

Of course, any discussion of rules and rule following must deal with Wittgenstein's famous paradox and the skeptical solution to it that he proposed. I argue that Wittgenstein's skepticism is unjustified. This leads naturally to a discussion of the private language argument, in which again I take issue with Wittgenstein's position. Once we are free of these skeptical doubts, rules and plans may be used as components of causal explanations of human action, and schemata for such explanations are suggested. It is hoped that this and the two preceding chapters suffice to establish the truth of our initial Premise (8).

Rules

The psychological models discussed in the preceding chapter have been applied chiefly to the explanation and prediction of highly specific actions. Although the theory of levels of specificity contains a mechanism for dealing with repeated actions and more complex structures, there is evidence that the addition of other variables will be required for this purpose.[1] The philosophic theories of action also have been concerned with simple specific actions such as raising one's arm. Important as this sort of explanation and prediction is, it is also important to consider the problem of explaining and predicting repeated actions and action sequences.

It is a truism that human behavior is often rule-governed behavior. But the content of this claim depends upon what is meant by a "rule," and the sense in which rules may govern behavior. Accordingly, we must look first at the notion of a rule. Some examples may help to fix ideas. Consider:

1. Drive on the right hand side of a two way street.
2. $(x)^2 = y$
3. Pick only green things.
4. White moves first.
5. Subject and verb always agree in number.

These sentences exhibit considerable differences in linguistic form. (1) and (3) appear to be imperatives; (2), (4), and (5) can be read either as descriptions of states of affairs or as rules for performing actions. Thus as Ganz notes, (4) can be taken as describing what happens in chess or as a rule prescribing how chess is to be played.[2] If (5) were taken as a description of English speech, it would be false; much actual speech behavior does not conform to it. (2) may seem more puzzling, but it should not be. Read as a description, it says that to any value of x there corresponds a value of y that is the square of x. Read as a rule it says, to find y, square x. Hence it seems quite clear that although many rules can be linguistically formulated (but not all, as Wittgenstein's example of the signpost reminds us[3]), they can be formulated in quite different ways, so that one cannot tell from the linguistic form of a sentence whether it formulates a rule or not.[4]

Is there, then, an underlying logical structure peculiar to rules? It has been argued that rules are always conditional. Thus Ganz holds that rules apply to activities, and are conditional upon engaging in the relevant activity. So (1) obviously obtains only if one is driving a vehicle, (4) if one is playing chess, (5) if one is speaking or writing English.[5] In this respect, rules are similar to laws. When conditionally formulated, the antecedent stipulates the ontological conditions for the application of the rule, and the consequent formulates an invariant relationship among variables referring to elements of an action. These are not truth functional conditionals, since they embrace unrealized as well as realized situations. The logical form of rules is therefore not different from that of laws.[6]

It is the use to which a sentence or other symbolic structure is put that determines whether or not it formulates a rule. Used as a description of chess-playing behavior, (4) is not a rule; used as a prescription, it is.[7] The same is true for all the other sentences. It does not follow that any sentence can be used as a rule. It is hard to see how

(6) Joe stubbed his big toe,

could be employed as a rule, and harder yet to see how interrogatives could so function. But we can at least say that various types of sentences can be used as rules or rule formulations.

Distinguishing between a rule and a rule formulation is made necessary by the fact that, as we have seen above, different sentences can be formulations of the same rule. Thus "$(x)^2 = y$" and "to find the value of y, square x" formulate the same rule in quite different symbols. A rule therefore cannot be identified with a linguistic inscription or with a particular linguistic or symbolic formulation. I shall understand a rule to be conceptual—that is, a particular sort of relation among concepts—that can be expressed in a variety of symbolic forms, not all of which need be linguistic.

It is a property of rules that they are normative. Thus (5) formulates the correct way to speak English, not necessarily what actual speakers do. (1) formulates a rule of the U.S. automobile driving code that prescribes the approved (and in the United States the legal) mode of behavior with respect to the operation of a motor vehicle. This normative character of rules is well recognized and generally accepted. What needs special emphasis is certain consequences of this characteristic. First, rules have no truth value, for a normative statement is neither true nor false. Second, because they are normative, rules can be violated. Third, rules form a basis for the evaluation of behavior. All three of these consequences are of major importance and require discussion.

A rule is normative; it defines or specifies what is correct or appropriate to do in a given circumstance. A rule therefore can be violated, but it cannot be falsified or disconfirmed. If one says, "The President are not a crook," one has violated (5) above, but this does not jeopardize the rule status of (5); rather, it shows that one has made an ungrammatical statement. Rules and rule sentences therefore cannot have a truth value, for the predicates "true" and "false" do not apply to them. In this sense, rules are categorically distinct from laws; "F = ma" is a law that can be true or false (confirmed or disconfirmed); "Pick only green things," is a rule that admits of neither of these predicates. However, the statement that someone's behavior is governed by a rule is a descriptive statement that can be true or false. But the difference between stating a norm and stating that someone is observing that norm is obvious, and not likely to lead to confusion. Nevertheless, the distinction requires emphasis, for a rule or rule formulation by itself cannot explain an action or behavior, whereas the statement that someone is observing a certain rule may be explanatory.

Rules are prescriptive. Whether being prescriptive is entirely distinct from being normative is a matter into which we need not enter; the point is that rules are both. The rule says that in situation S, one should do A. The prescriptive character of the rule makes doing A obligatory. Just how the prescriptiveness is enforced will depend upon the sorts of sanctions involved. If the rule is backed by an external authority, the sanctions can be formidable indeed. And in this lies the solution to the problem of one's following a rule of which one strongly disapproves. A convict is subject to many rules that he would cheerfully disobey. Those rules are still norms and the convict will follow them in the full sense of consciously conforming his behavior to them and evaluating his behavior in terms of them, although he may negatively evaluate both the rules and himself for conforming. But if the sanctions for non-conformity are severe enough (as in prison they are) he will follow the prescriptions to avoid the punishment. One need not approve a rule to follow it or think it good to understand its normative character.

Many philosophers have discussed the critical distinction between satisfying a rule and following a rule.[8] Suppose that in sorting colored candies, one happens to pick out one green candy after another; does that fact show that one is following rule (3): Pick only green things? It does not; it might be the case that one likes mints and only the green candies are mints. One's sorting behavior here *satisfies* rule (3) in the sense that it is consistent with the rule, but one could not say one is *following* the rule, since in reality one is following a quite different rule: Pick mints. Ganz has argued that to *follow* a rule, (a) one must know the rule, (b) one's behavior must satisfy the rule, and (c) one must be seeing to it that one's behavior satisfies the rule.[9]

Ganz's formulation however is subject to a crucial objection. The first condition and certainly the third seem to imply that anyone following a rule must be explicitly conscious of the rule being followed. The formulation therefore appears to eliminate the possibility that social actors could follow an unconscious rule, that is, a rule of which they were not explicitly conscious. But there are two sorts of cases in which it is commonly held that people do follow rules of which they are not explicitly conscious: rules governing linguistic behavior and rules governing automatic behavior.

Ganz is aware of these problems, and in her fourth chapter she argues that, although grammatical behavior is rule-like and rule-describable, it is neither rule-directed nor rule-guided.[10] Instead, Ganz holds that, "Grammars originate as laws"—that is, as regularities in linguistic behavior—that are subsequently adopted as rules or "standards for correct speech."[11] Linguistic behavior, she argues, is better conceived as a matter of abilities rather than rules, as a skill comparable to other skills, or more strictly as the output of a combination of "natural" skills such a pattern recognition and extrapolation.[12] But Ganz remains convinced that speaking cannot be a matter of following unconscious rules, because by her definition one cannot follow a rule without being explicitly conscious of it.[13]

Ganz's argument is not convincing, however. First, it is quite clear that rule induction is an induction of rules directly; what one learns in observing models is a rule, not a law.[14] There is simply no evidence for any such intermediate stage of law learning as Ganz supposes. Second, linguistic phenomena are not law-like. It is a characteristic of rules, but not of laws, that they can be violated. And grammatical rules are constantly violated, particularly in speech. Listen to any conversation and you will hear repeated violations of the rules of grammar. But in that case, whatever governs linguistic behavior cannot be laws. Third, while learning a language certainly involves natural abilities, linguists are unanimous in holding that "the mystery of the learning feat derives from two crucial facts about the human use of language: It is rule governed, and it is creative."[15] One cannot evade the fact that linguistic behavior is rule-governed behavior.

Granting that linguistic behavior involves following rules, there is overwhelming evidence for the claim that many rules of language are followed without the speakers being explicitly conscious of those rules. Although recent studies have shown that explicit metalinguistic consciousness occurs earlier than was once thought,[16] it is clear that the child language learner acquires an ability to employ linguistic structures in a rule-governed way before it is able to articulate the rules. How this is achieved remains at present a hotly debated topic of extensive research.

Most psycholinguists agree on the importance of innate constraints, but there are multiple theories about just how acquisition takes place. Karmiloff-Smith has proposed a multiphase model of acquisition that may serve as an example here. In phase one, she argues, "surface output for a particular linguistic form is predominantly (although of course not exclusively) driven by external stimuli. Second, representations of that form are stored independently of others."[17] The child here seeks to match adult linguistic performance, as perceived by the child, and is largely successful in achieving communicative adequacy. "Phase 2 is characterized by the fact that the child now ignores to a great extent the external stimulus and concentrates on gaining control over the organization of those internal representations which had hitherto been stored independently."[18] This process, which is unconscious, redescribes the already stored representations and permits the substitution of plurifunctional forms for the "plethora of unifunctional form-function pairs" of phase one.[19] Thus the transformations occurring in this phase are chiefly in linguistic organization. "Phase 3 is characterized by an intricate balance between the reconsideration of external stimuli (the adult model) and the internal representational links established during phase 2."[20] Only at the completion of these three phases can the linguistic structures so achieved become accessible to consciousness.[21] This model is not a stage model; the phases may occur at different chronological points with respect to different aspects of the language system.

Karmiloff-Smith's evidence for this model draws very heavily upon repair data, that is, the child's corrections of its errors, and changes made by the child in its statements that are not corrections but that show sensitivity to the linguistic system. These types of repairs demonstrate that the child is using linguistic organizations—rules—of which it is not explicitly aware but that nevertheless play a role in determining its speech. In other words, it is following unconscious rules.

Thus it is clear that Ganz's criteria for rule following must be modified. Her first condition—one must know the rule—requires a distinction between knowing and knowing that one knows. As Perner has argued effectively,[22] a child can have a representation of the perceived situation without being aware that he has such a representation. If "know" is given this latitudinarian sense, the first condition is acceptable, for children who follow the rule know the rule in this broad sense whether they know that they know it or not. The second condition—one's behavior must satisfy the rule—poses no problem. It is the third condition—one must see to it that one's behavior satisfies the rule—that creates the trouble, since Ganz clearly intends this to mean that one is explicitly conscious of the rule.

Certainly one way of "seeing to it" does consist in deliberately controlling one's behavior so that it conforms to standards of which one is explicitly conscious; but that is not the only possible interpretation of "seeing to it." Children's repair data show that a broader interpretation is necessary. As Clark points out, young children learning language acquire the ability to comprehend linguistic utterances before they are able to produce them. The child first acquires a representation of the utterance from adult speech, and stores it in memory. That representation is then used as the standard to which the child tries to match its own production. This process of coordination takes place over time, with the child progressively approximating the standard until it is achieved. Such a process, Clark notes, requires

a) A *monitor* to keep track of the sequences of sounds and larger units uttered on each occasion;

b) A *checker* to see that the sequences uttered match the sequences intended;

c) A *repairer* for reproducing the requisite elements whenever there is a mismatch between the form intended and the form actually produced.[23]

That such capacities exist in the young child is shown by the occurrence of repairs.

What is the status of repairs in children's speech?

> First, if repairs occur (whether self- or other-initiated), they offer evidence for the existence of a monitoring system. Second, they also provide evidence for an ability to detect mismatches between some representation of what an utterance should have sounded like and the child's own version. Otherwise, children would be unable to repair on demand, and repair appropriately, when asked to. Third, if children also make repairs spontaneously, those repairs would be evidence that monitoring, checking, and repairing play a direct role in the acquisition process: They allow children to coordinate comprehension and production, and thereby introduce changes into their language.[24]

Such repairs, both spontaneous and on demand, are observed in children even at two years of age, well before the child is explicitly conscious of the process involved.[25]

The processes of monitoring, checking, and repairing described by Clark certainly amount to the child's "seeing to it" that its linguistic performance conforms to a standard. When a three-year-old child spontaneously corrects itself, as e.g., in:

> She had a silly putty like *me had*—like *I*—like *I did*;
>
> There *isn't* any—there *aren't* any;
>
> I *sticked* it in—I *stuck* it in.[26]

the child is obviously "seeing to it" that its utterances conform to a grammatical standard. Moreover, as Karmiloff-Smith emphasizes, some repair data show not only deliberate conformity to a single rule or standard but an understanding of a larger syntactic structure. Thus when, in a game involving several toy cars, only one of which belongs to the child, it says, "I'll park *a* car—I'll park *my* car here," the child's repair is not a correction of an error (since "*a* car" is grammatically correct) but a choice made in terms of the determiner system to increase specificity.[27] There seems, therefore, to be convincing evidence that young children are able to follow rules in the sense of "seeing to it" that their behavior conforms to the standard prescribed by the rule without having an explicit consciousness of the rule in question such as would be required for them to state the rule itself. One may therefore accept Ganz's third condition with the understanding that "seeing to it" does not require explicit consciousness of the rule in question.

Such a modification is also required with respect to many cases of adult behavior. Consider a non-literate society. Such a society will have a spoken language that has a grammar; that is, combinations of words in the native language are not arbitrary but show definite patterns. Moreover, the natives themselves distinguish between correct and incorrect speech; certain sequences of words are considered acceptable, others are not. Thus the native linguistic behavior gives the appearance of being rule governed. Yet the natives are unable to state what these rules are. This is not because the rule is somehow hidden. When Hallowell pointed out to Chief Barens that the Ojibwa pronominal system distinguished between animate and inanimate things, the Chief immediately recognized that this was so although he had never thought of it before.[28] Here again repair data can be marshalled to show that the natives are "seeing to it" that their linguistic behavior conforms to the rules of their grammar without their having an explicit awareness of what those rules are.

The issue of unconscious rule following also arises with respect to automatic behavior. When one learns to drive a car, one is taught a set of rules about operating the car. These are highly conscious and take some time to master. But once one has become a reasonably accomplished driver, one is able to drive "automatically," that is, without paying much attention to the rules. Is one then still following the rules? and if so, are the rules unconscious? It is a commonplace that the acquisition of a skill—driving, boxing, cycling, whatever—involves an initial stage of instruction in which one is very conscious of what one is doing and why, and a later stage when performance becomes habitual. This is indeed one of the most fortunate features of our cognitive structure, since it permits the development of highly complex organizations of behavior. But to say that behavior that is learned as rule-governed behavior ceases to be so when it becomes habitual or "automatic" is an error. When one drives, one is of course aware of what one is doing, as will be instantly apparent if one makes an mistake. The difference is not between conscious and unconscious behavior; it is a difference in the amount of attention one has to devote to the activity in first learning it and after it is mastered. Once behavior has been mastered to the degree that it becomes habitual, it can be performed with minimal attention; that does not mean that it is unconscious. When one "automatically" brakes on approaching a red light, one is following a rule in the full conscious sense of "follow," however little attention one must devote to doing so.[29] Automated rules are not unconscious rules in the sense that the young child's linguistic rules are; they are simply conscious rules that have become habitual.[30]

How are rules learned? The most common way is by being taught; one is taught a rule by others who already know the rule. This is quite clear in child rearing. Children are repeatedly instructed as to what they should or should not do. It is no accident that one of the first words a child learns is "no." But rules can also be learned by induction. When an individual observes others whose behavior in a given situation illustrates a rule, and the outcomes of their behavior are such that the individual seeks to model performance on theirs, he or she is capable of abstracting from their behavior the rule by which they operate. The basic processes involved are those of abstracting the relevant attributes from the exemplars, integrating this information into a composite rule, and using the rule to produce new instances of the behavior. The problem of extracting the relevant attributes may be lessened if the learning situation is designed for teaching purposes by various methods of directing the learner's attention to the significant attributes, but whether this is the case or not the learner will proceed to develop hypotheses as to the nature of the rule, which will then be tested in further situations to see if the rule works.

Since social rules usually involve a combination of multiple attributes, often with differing weights for different attributes, considerable testing is usually required before the right combination is found. Moreover, grasping the rule, particularly if the rule is rather abstract, may not at once lead to successful application of the rule in one's own performance. Knowledge and skill (knowing that and knowing how) are not the same. Nevertheless, experiments demonstrate that learners can and do acquire rules by induction from observing the behavior of others, and that they are then able to apply those rules successfully in new situations differing from the ones in which the rules were learned.[31]

Rule induction thus confronts the standard problem of induction; how does the learner identify the relevant attributes? It must be emphasized that although this problem is philosophically of great importance, it is not of great practical moment. Most rule learning occurs in natural settings where direct teaching is involved; either the rule is communicated verbally to the learner, or it is demonstrated by a model with accompanying verbal commentary designed explicitly to aid the learner in identifying the relevant properties. Very little of our actual rule learning takes place by pure induction, that is, by observing the performance of others without any effort by the models to communicate the rule to the observer.

Nevertheless, such cases can and do arise and should not be ignored. As Goodman has taught us, prior knowledge certainly accounts for much of our success here.[32] Children learn very quickly that attributes such as gender and age play a significant part in rules, while eye and hair color do not. The entrenchment of predicates encapsulates this prior knowledge, much of it derived from teaching, and guides the learner's projections in seeking to form hypotheses concerning new rules. But if there is no difference in kind between the purely inductive problem for rules and for laws, there is a very important difference in degree. Nature does not tell us which of her attributes are important for the discovery of her laws; human beings do. It is a mistake to model the situation of the rule learner on that of a scientist seeking to understand physical phenomena. Only in the most exceptional cases would rule learners find themselves confronting as bitchy a teacher as Mother Nature, and as we all know even the inherent bitchiness of nature has not prevented the discovery of the laws of science.[33]

How do rules guide behavior? What is it for behavior to be governed by a rule? Wittgenstein long ago pointed out how complex these questions are, but they are critical. Probably the first point to be made is that by itself a rule does not guide behavior. A rule is a norm, a statement or symbol of what should be done under certain circumstances. The rule in this sense is a belief. But there are many norms; few are followed. Ganz argues that for a norm to function as a rule-guiding behavior, it must be *adopted* as a rule, and that the defining characteristic of adoption is that performers will evaluate those of their behaviors that conform to the rule as correct and those that do not as incorrect.[34] "Adoption" here need not mean a conscious decision; it is enough that the rule be taken as a standard. The critical point here is that if one understands rule guidance as a concept-matching activity—matching one's behavior to that prescribed by the rule—one must be motivated to make one's behavior match the rule. That one is following a rule shows that there is some motive, some desire, that leads one to see to it that the match obtains, but it says nothing about the nature of this motive.

Why should one follow a rule? Obviously, there can be many reasons. But since rule-governed behavior is action, it is clear that two quite different questions are involved. One is the question of explaining some specific rule-governed behavior, the other is the question of explaining why the rule itself is followed. To explain the former, one must cite not only the specific rule involved but also the fact that the actor is following the rule. It is the fact that the rule is being followed—that the actors are conforming their action to the rule—that explains why, in the given circumstances, the appropriate action was performed. This explanatory pattern is often illustrated by using the example of games. The example is ill-chosen because many game rules are deliberately designed not to permit the prediction of specific acts—otherwise, the activity would not constitute a game. If the rules of chess required that when white moves king's pawn to king's fourth, black must counter with the same move, who would play? Much better examples are to be found in social behavior such as greeting rituals. When two members of our society meet and one extends the right hand waist-high, thumb up, it is obligatory, if the other is following the rules of common courtesy, to respond so as to complete the handshake.

But why should the rule itself be followed? Consider first the case of what may be called "cultural rules." In this case, there is a set of actors, A, a class of situations, S, a set of people, E, who expect that members of A will, when in a situation of type S, follow a rule R, and sets of sanctioners, $X_1 \ldots X_n$, who will sanction members of A positively or negatively as they do or do not follow the rule. Obviously, A and the Xs are subsets of E; A will be an X since members of A sanction themselves through self-evaluation for following or not following R. This rather standard situation is illustrated by the rule (1): Drive on the right hand side of a two-way street. A is the set of drivers, E the population in general, X the police, S the situation of driving a car on a two-way street. Because in such cases at least some of the sanctions enforcing the following of the rule are publicly known, and those sanctions are deliberately made severe enough to ensure a high degree of conformity, it is quite easy to explain why on a given occasion on Colorado Boulevard in Denver, Jones drove on the right-hand side of the street. This does not of course explain why Jones drove at all, but it does explain why, given that he drove on that two-way street, he drove on the right.

This is an extreme case. Consider the opposite extreme. In walking to the pitcher's mound, Jones never steps on the white line defining the base path. Here there is a rule: When taking the field to pitch, never step on the line. No one expects this of Jones, and probably most people are not aware of the existence of the rule. No person sanctions Jones for following or not following the rule, except Jones himself. One might observe Jones in many games and never notice that his behavior satisfied this rule. But suppose one did notice this peculiar behavior on Jones's part. How would one know Jones was following a rule? The obvious way would be to ask him why he behaved thus, but Jones might lie, or it might not be possible to ask him. What evidence would persuade you that following a rule was the explanation of Jones's behavior?

It seems to me the reasoning would be this. First, there is no known reason for not stepping on the line; there is no physical barrier, and no rule of baseball mandates this behavior. Second, pitchers are well known to be superstitious and to follow private rules they believe bring them good luck. But third, there would have to be some acts indicating that Jones's behavior in not stepping on the line is the result of following a rule. Thus, there would have to be cases in which Jones breaks stride to avoid having his foot touch the line. Such cases would correspond to acts of correction in the case of linguistic rules. One would still not know for sure that Jones was following a rule, but the hypothesis that he was doing so would be the best available explanation, given the evidence at hand. In this case, Jones would be the only sanctioner, but he would still be following the rule because he believed doing so would bring him luck to help him win and because he desired to win.

It is a characteristic of rules that they can be violated. It is also a characteristic of rules that they can be changed. Given that not all behavior that is supposed to be rule governed actually satisfies the rule, and that behavior that violates one rule may be the result of following a different rule, how can one tell which is which? Some have concluded that these facts render rules useless for prediction. Clearly, these questions are fundamental and must be answered.

Consider first what a rule requires. A rule does not tell precisely what is to be done in a given situation. What the rule prescribes is behavior of a certain type. Commonly, this "type" is an equivalence class of behaviors that differ quite widely in many attributes. Thus greeting rules in our society permit a wide range of verbal expressions to serve as greetings: "Hello," "How are you?," "How nice to meet you," etc. One may shake hands, bow, nod, smile, etc. Other rules are less latitudinarian. But all rules admit a certain acceptable range of variation in their performance. Even where the acceptable range is narrow and so structured that there is an ideal performance, as in ballet, still a reasonable approximation to the ideal will be regarded as acceptable.

It follows that deviations from the prescribed behavior will be of various kinds. There is, first, simple failure to attain the standard of acceptability. This is essentially an error rate; one tried and missed. People do misspeak and utter ungrammatical sentences even though they know the rules and follow them. Such error rates can be expected to vary from person to person, but for a given person the rate should be relatively stable over time (assuming the rule is already learned, and barring some impairment that renders performance more difficult). Moreover, where it is possible to measure degrees of deviance—how much the incorrect performance deviates from acceptability (obviously it will not always be possible to do so)—the distribution of errors should show a characteristic pattern, with the frequency of errors decreasing with distance from the boundary of acceptability.

Whenever rates of deviance change markedly or systematically, something interesting is going on. Let us assume for the moment the highly idealized case in which one can neglect errors of reporting, so that reported deviance equals real deviance. (Obviously, this is an idealized situation; reported deviance usually varies from real deviance for a number of well-known reasons). An increase in deviance means either that motivation for following the rule is weakening or that deviance is no longer due merely to error, or both. If the deviance represents rejection of the rules in question, then, assuming enforcement to be constant, not only should the amount of deviance increase but its severity should increase, that is, the frequency of highly deviant acts should increase. In fact, a rise in deviance owing to rule rejection will usually prompt stricter and more severe enforcement sanctions, but in any case such a change in conformity is usually detectable either by direct observation or by historical records, since enforcement of sanctions against extreme deviance is usually done by an institution that generates a record, and will in any event attract attention.

What then about the case of rule change? Clearly, for many cultural rules, change involves action by some official institution, and the nature of the change will be overt. But where it is not an official change (e.g., changes in dress or in food ways) the important point is that the deviation will be systematic. Take for example the change in Western women's attire from skirts to men's-style pants. Not only does the rate of deviance from the old rule that women should wear only skirts show a steady increase, but there is a progression in the kinds of situations in which women wear pants. The trend is first apparent in leisure activities, particularly those involving physical exertion—horsebackriding, cycling, hiking, and so forth. It then moves to other sorts of situations—informal entertainment or socializing, and some occupational situations where pants have advantages over skirts, as in working around machinery. It grows most slowly in highly formalized situations and in activities where women are new entrants into the field (e.g., her wedding, or interviewing for an executive business position). Thus the nature of the deviance here—both its increase and the systematic patterns it shows—are indications of rule change, not simply of rebellion or of error.

These comments obviously pertain to deviance at the aggregate level; what about the individual level? Similar factors are involved. No one always succeeds in following a rule. Although people differ in their susceptibility to error, and will show different rates of conformity for different rules, an individual following a rule should show a relatively constant error rate. Rule rejection by individuals may be sudden or slow; they may stop following a rule once and for all at a given time, or gradually abandon it. In either case, the deviations will increase markedly. If they simply reject an old rule without adopting a substitute rule, one would expect their behavior in the situations previously covered by the old rule to become increasingly random. If on the other hand they adopt a new rule, the deviant behavior (from the standpoint of the old rule) will be systematic in ways that will pose the usual problems of rule induction. But in all these cases, we have something more than the pattern of the deviations to work with; we have the corrective behavior to conform to the new rule. While in the aggregate case this will be evident in the activities of sanctioners, in the individual case it will also show in the actor's corrective actions. And there is no better criterion of rule following than corrective behavior.

But can we distinguish systematic deviations from random ones? Wittgenstein wrote, "There is no sharp distinction between a random mistake and a systematic one. That is, between what you are inclined to call 'random' and what 'systematic'."[35] Surely, the first sentence of this quote is incorrect; there are mathematical tests for randomness. But perhaps what Wittgenstein meant is that one is inclined to call errors "random" whenever one does not perceive an order to them, and "systematic" when one does; that is, perhaps Wittgenstein's remark is a psychological observation rather than a mathematical one. The context of the quote offers little help here and is consistent with either interpretation. Without trying to guess what he meant, the important point is that there is an objective difference between a random distribution of errors and a systematic one, and that the difference can be detected.

Wittgenstein

Any attempt to deal with rules must confront the issues raised by Wittgenstein in the *Philosophical Investigations*. It should be obvious that the position taken here differs from his. As I understand the matter, a rule is a belief that is taken by individuals as a standard or criterion to which they seek to conform their behavior and by which they evaluate their performances. On this view, a rule is not a causal process, but following a rule is. Clearly, this is not Wittgenstein's position.

Kripke has provided an incisive exposition of Wittgenstein's views, which, although it has aroused the usual protests from Wittgensteinians, seems to me an admirable statement of Wittgenstein's position. Kripke emphasizes that the central issue of the *Philosophical Investigations* is the paradox that Wittgenstein states in paragraph 201, as follows:

> This was our paradox: no course of action could be determined by a rule, because every course of action can be made out to accord with the rule. The answer was: if everything can be made out to accord with the rule, then it can also be made out to conflict with it. And so there would be neither accord nor conflict here.
>
> It can be seen that there is a misunderstanding here from the mere fact that in the course of our argument we give one interpretation after another; as if each one contented us at least for a moment, until we thought of yet another standing behind it. What this shews is that there is a way of grasping a rule which is *not* an *interpretation*, but which is exhibited in what we call "obeying the rule" and "going against it" in actual cases.[36]

Kripke explicates Wittgenstein's position by using the following example. Suppose we know the usual meaning of "plus" and its application—namely, how to add. Let it be the case that all the numbers I have ever added are less than 57. (The choice of 57 is obviously arbitrary, but since there is an infinity of numbers, there exists a number so large that numbers greater than that have never been added by anyone. Hence, in using 56 as the greatest number to which we have yet applied addition, no generality is lost.) Define the function "quus"—symbolized by +!—as follows:

$$x +! \; y = x + y, \text{ if } x,y < 57$$
$$= 5 \text{ otherwise.}[37]$$

Now the Wittgensteinian skeptic says, "Who is to say that this [quus] is not the function I previously meant by '+'?"[38] Since up to the time the question is posed, all the additions I have ever performed will be finite in number and concern numbers less than 57, there is no basis in my past behavior for deciding between "plus" and "quus." Indeed, given any finite series of numbers, there will be many different formulae that will both yield that finite series as past applications and different continuations of the series in future applications. How then can I know that I actually used plus in the past? Furthermore, if I cannot know the answer to this question with respect to the past, I also cannot know its answer with respect to the present.[39]

Kripke's example is an illustration of Wittgenstein's general position. Wittgenstein regards all rules as open to this challenge, including all rules of word usage. Thus the fact that up to now I have always called a type of object a "table" proves nothing about my use of "table" tomorrow. Or, to use Goodman's well-known case, the fact that I have always before referred to things having colors in a certain part of the color spectrum as "green" does not prove that I did not really mean they were "grue," where "grue" means:

Green up to time t; blue thereafter.[40]

The skeptical paradox is therefore general, and applies to all language, all mathematics, and all rules.

Kripke emphasizes that,

An answer to the sceptic must satisfy two conditions. First, it must give an account of what fact it is (about my mental state) that constitutes my meaning plus, not quus. But further, there is a condition that any putative candidate for such a fact must satisfy. It must, in some sense, show how I am justified in giving the answer "125" for "68 + 57."[41]

Unless one is to accept Wittgenstein's own skeptical solution to this paradox—that the only justification lies in the agreement of the group,[42] so that the individual alone acts blindly and without justification—then an answer must be provided that meets these conditions. The question is, can this be done?

In Kripke's example, the issue is whether, in my past "additions," I have followed the plus rule or the quus rule. The claim is that there is no fact about my mental history that will decide the matter. So far as my history of actual additions is concerned, this is obviously true; by hypothesis, I have never added numbers larger than 56 and therefore every act of adding I have done satisfies both the plus and the quus rules. But the claim goes beyond this; it is also claimed that there is no fact about my mental states, past or present, which would enable me to tell whether I meant "plus" or "quus." This claim rests on Wittgenstein's analysis of introspection. For Wittgenstein, introspection must be the "observation"—in a very wide sense of that term—of something "sensible," where "sensible" is extended to include not only inputs through the five exterior senses but feelings, aches, tickles, twinges, and other sensations. These may be images, or "pictures" as he calls them, or simple tingles, but whatever they are they must be something sensible, in this very broad sense that, in more classical terms, involves both sensation and sensibility.[43] As Kripke has noted, this is a classical view of empiricism.[44] Further, Wittgenstein holds that there is no distinctive feeling of remembering.[45] Hence according to him there is no introspective evidence as to whether I formerly meant plus or quus. Indeed, for Wittgenstein, there is no introspective evidence regarding meaning or belief or intentions, or any of the mental states that are conceptual. Therefore he thinks there is no fact of the matter regarding a person's mental history with respect to any of these conceptual states or processes.

The issue of introspective access to one's "thoughts" is one that has vexed philosophy since Descartes and that is currently the center of sharp debate.[46] Fortunately, it is not necessary for our purposes here to review this debate or to enter into it. The points that do need to be established are that (1) beliefs are mental states, and that (2) people do know what at least some of their beliefs are. That beliefs are mental states is one of the basic premises of cognitive psychology and is supported by an enormous amount of experimental literature. The cognitive revolution in psychology is based on the claim that human behavior is best explained in terms of how humans represent the world rather than in terms of how the world really is.[47], and these representations are mental states.[48] That they exist is a postulate of the theory,[49] and to the degree that the theory is well confirmed, their existence is a fact. It is therefore a fact of our mental histories that such states have existed and do exist.

Do people know their own beliefs? It will suffice to show that people do have conscious knowledge of some of their beliefs. Chapter 2 described some of the more recent work that has been done on children's acquisition of a representational theory of mind, and particularly on the problem of false belief.[50] It should be clear that by the age of approximately four, normal children have a concept of belief, and understand that people act in terms of their beliefs. But is this a concept of belief in others, or in themselves? The answer is both, although the evidence suggests that children may acquire the concept of belief first with respect to others and then apply it to themselves. Thus Astington and Gopnik found that not until it was approximately five years of age was a child able to recognize that its own prior beliefs had been false. As they comment: "This is a nicely Vygotskyan explanation: The child first arrives at a concept of false belief from social interaction, and is then able to apply the concept to the self, to understand the process of representational change."[51]

Metacognitive studies leave no doubt that children—and adults—do know, with respect to a very large class of their beliefs, what they believe.[52] There is then a fact about the mental history of Kripke's "adder," namely, that he believes the rule for "addition" to be the plus rule, or that he believes it to be the quus rule. The fact consists in his having had the belief (whichever it was) at a particular time or during a particular period of time.

But Kripke's second condition remains to be dealt with: How does this fact about my mental history "show how I am justified in giving the answer '125' for '68 + 57'"? There are actually two different issues here: How do I know that I remember correctly? And how do I know that what I remember as "plus" is the same as what I now think of as "plus"? These questions are not the same. I might remember a street scene exactly as it once was, yet mistakenly conclude that the remembered scene was the same as what I now see. Both must be addressed.

In *An Analysis of Knowledge and Valuation*, C. I. Lewis presented a penetrating analysis of the problem of memory.[53] Lewis points out that part of our faith in our memories comes from the fact that our memories hang together in a consistent fashion. The relation, Lewis holds, is actually stronger than consistency; our memorial statements are "congruent," meaning that the probability of any one is increased if the rest are taken as premises. Nevertheless, congruent systems of statements need not be true; some further validation is required. One might think that this could be done by testing the system of memorial statements against empirical evidence, as one tests systems such as quantum mechanics. But as Lewis shows, this is not possible, for it assumes that we have true cognitions against which the system can be tested. Lewis's point is that without veridical memorial knowledge, there are no true cognitions, for what else is cognized in a cognition but the similarity of a current sensible presentation to remembered sensible presentations, taken as indices for some thing or character? Without memorial knowledge, we could not classify a current presentation as anything; we should simply confront a phantasmagoria of stimulations with which we would have no way to deal. Any cognition therefore assumes the truth of some memorial knowledge; therefore we cannot use cognitions to prove the truth of memorial knowledge.

Accordingly, Lewis holds, we must either accept a total skepticism of the moment, or we must grant to memorial statements *prima facie* credibility. The latter gives us a sufficient basis to warrant cognition while still permitting the truth of any individual memorial statement to be impeached. Where we find particular memories to be inconsistent with our other memories, or with the testimony of others, or with physical evidence of appropriate kinds, we can reject or correct those memories. But we cannot reject all memorial knowledge without falling into a total skepticism of the moment—a fate which Wittgenstein would be the last man to accept.

That human memory is not perfectly accurate has been demonstrated beyond any doubt. Psychologists in recent years have done extensive research on human memory and have sought to develop models of how information is coded, stored in memory, and retrieved.[54] Because so much work in cognitive psychology has been stimulated by analogies between the human brain and the computer, the phenomenon of memory errors has been of particular interest to psychologists, since this is an area where the analogy of the brain to the digital computer seems to break down. But nothing in this research demonstrates that *all* our memories are inaccurate; indeed, it is only against the admitted background of accurate memories that the phenomenon of inaccurate memory has been so striking. The existence of such errors of memory in no way invalidates Lewis's argument about the necessity of granting *prima facie* credibility to our memorial statements. In fact, we could not know that some memorial statements were inaccurate if we did not accept others as being accurate.

This view of memory has three important effects. First, the fact that memorial statements have *prima facie* credibility provides the justification for my saying that I have always meant "plus" and not "quus" when I have added numbers in the past, for if my recognition of the plus rule as the rule I have always followed in the past is *prima facie* credible, then it is also *prima facie* credible that I know this rule, satisfy it, and am seeing to it that my behavior conforms to this rule. Note that what this does is to shift the burden of proof from me to the skeptics. I no longer have to prove that I have always added by "plus"; they have to prove that I have not. And how would the skeptics prove that I have always added by "quus"? They cannot prove it from my past actions, since by hypothesis these satisfy the plus rule. They cannot prove it from my mental states, since I recognize the plus rule and not the quus rule. They have therefore no legitimate grounds for challenging my claim to be following the plus rule. The skeptical challenge collapses.

Second, if the rule I have followed, and am following, is the plus rule, then I *ought* to give "125" for "68 + 57." Rules are normative and prescriptive; they tell us what ought to be done when the conditions are such that the rule applies. If I am following the plus rule, then I am justified in giving this answer, rather than "5" because that is what the rule prescribes as the correct answer.

Third, this view blocks any attempt by skeptics to raise further challenges through reinterpretation. Thus the plus rule can be expressed as:

$$n + 0 = n$$

$$n + k' = (n + k)',$$

where the prime sign stands for the successor function, and n and k are integers. (Actually, what most people would consider as the plus rule is a certain algorithm for calculating sums, but the point can be made equally with either form of the rule.) So one might expect the skeptics to raise the question, "How do you know that what you now mean by 'successor' is what you previously meant?" But this move is now blocked by the *prima facie* credibility of my memories. I am justified in saying that my memory of what I previously meant by "successor" is correct unless there is some evidence to the contrary. The skeptics can no longer demand proof that I am using every word as I did before; they must show cause for believing that I am not. Hence the teeth of the skeptic are pulled.

But what about "the same"? Wittgenstein believes that we must justify saying that any two things "are the same." In at least one sense, we cannot. The capacity to recognize similarity, to identify two presentations of an object or situation as the same, is constitutive of thought—all thought. This is not simply a human capacity; it is clearly present in at least all animals. Without such a capacity, learning would be impossible, for if a rat in a maze is to learn which way to turn at the T, he must recognize the situation as like the prior case in which he was rewarded for turning right or left. The ability to recognize things as the same is thus prior to any rule for the use of words, for without it the rule could never have been learned. Indeed, without this ability, conceptual thought would be impossible. As William James once put it, "A polyp would be a conceptual thinker if the feeling of 'Hollo! thing-umbob again!' ever flitted through its mind."[55]

Given this basic notion of sameness, it is possible to extend it to cover greater or lesser degrees of similarity as we choose, so that there is nothing vacuous in Wittgenstein's question, "What counts as the same here?" We can, and do, develop rules on the basis of which remarkably unlike things are treated as the same—equivalence classes in mathematics, for example. But these extensions are matters of rules, and rest on the same basis as other rules—the primitive recognition of sameness and the *prima facie* credibility of memory which enables us to compare prior and present instances. Rules regarding sameness raise no new possibilities for skepticism beyond those already addressed.

There is a further peculiarity of Wittgenstein's view that is worth pointing out. Wittgenstein holds that the only justification for believing one is following a rule is the consensus of the community. Of course, this does not mean that one cannot follow a rule individually but that in doing so one acts blindly—that is, without justification. But Wittgenstein takes as his prime example of rules the use of words. There is something peculiar about this, for the community to which Wittgenstein appeals—what he calls a "form of life"—is a linguistic community. Of course there is consensus on linguistic usage in a linguistic community: that is what defines the linguistic community. But what about other sorts of rules for which this consensus does not exist? Consider, for example, rules of dress in our own culture. Here there is currently an extraordinary degree of variation. If a woman follows her own rules of dress and goes to her wedding in blue jeans, was she right or wrong in doing so? The community does not agree. Is the question meaningless? Suppose, to take a more serious example, Adolph Eichmann's rule-following performances were approved by his Nazi colleagues, as doubtless they were: Was Eichmann justified in doing what he did? The issue here is one of ethics as much as rule following (and since rules are normative, these are not wholly distinct), but the point I want to bring out is that Wittgenstein has so chosen his community that by definition there will be agreement on the rules, and so language consensus may not be an adequate model for analyzing rule following in general.

As Kripke points out, Wittgenstein's private language argument represents an application of his skeptical solution to the paradox of rules.[56] As I find Wittgenstein's rule skepticism unwarranted, so I think his argument against private languages defective. Actually, Wittgenstein's argument involves two rather different claims. The first is that there can be no such thing as a private language, and the second is that there cannot be a private name for a sensation that no one else could know. Clearly, the second claim could be false although the first is true. I agree that there are not private languages, but I disagree with Wittgenstein's second claim. Wittgenstein put it as follows:

> Let us imagine the following case. I want to keep a diary about the recurrence of a certain sensation. To this end I associate it with the sign "E" and write this sign in the calendar for every day on which I have the sensation.—I will remark first of all that a definition of the sign cannot be formulated.—But still I can give myself a kind of ostensive definition.—How? Can I point to the sensation? Not in the ordinary sense. But I speak, or write the sign down, and at the same time I concentrate my attention on the sensation—and so, as it were, point to it inwardly.—But what is this ceremony for? for that is all it seems to be! A definition surely serves to establish the meaning of a sign.—Well, that is done precisely by the concentrating of my attention; for in this way I impress on myself the connexion between the sign and the sensation.—But "I impress it on myself" can only mean: this process brings it about that I remember the connexion *right* in the future. But in the present case I have no criterion of correctness. One would like to say: whatever is going to seem right to me is right. And that only means that here we can't talk about 'right'.[57]

It is essential to bear in mind that "E" is a word in a "private language." "The individual words of this language are to refer to what can only be known to the person speaking; to his immediate private sensations. So another person cannot understand the language."58

Wittgenstein, of course, is denying the possibility not only of such a private language but of such a private name as "E." I believe that this is a mistake, and in making my case I hope to be pardoned for using myself as an example: As the question is one of a private language, there is really no other choice. For the past fifteen years, I have suffered from a condition for which the medical profession has been able to find no demonstrable cause. It consists in the periodic recurrence of a set of curious sensations, a peculiar and indescribable oddness in the visual field, and a feeling of losing contact with the world. In Wittgenstein's honor, I call it "E." Efforts to describe E to assorted medical practitioners have been uniformly unsuccessful: I can tell them little more in the public language than I have said above, which is a hopelessly inadequate and inaccurate description. With the doctors I talk about "E" as "dizziness," although it has never involved any actual dizziness in the usual sense of that word. It is my own conclusion that E is an allergic reaction to the ingestion of certain substances, but for years the doctors rejected my view on the ground that the attacks of E (which often last as long as three weeks) could not possibly have been produced by the tiny amounts of these substances that have led to some of the episodes. The doctors, having run innumerable tests and found nothing, have given up on it, and since I have not yet died of it they no longer consider it serious. Now this is a sensation of just the sort Wittgenstein described; there is no English word for it; I cannot describe it to others in such a way that they can identify it or understand what I am experiencing, and so it cannot be shared. "E" is a wholly private name for a wholly private experience. And of course I have kept just such a diary as Wittgenstein described in an effort to find some correlation between E and something else.

As I read Wittgenstein's passage 258, what he is saying is that E cannot be ostensively defined to refer to my sensation because I would have no criterion for using E correctly. For suppose I had another sensation A; how would I know that A was not E? The only criterion would be what seems to me to be the case, so if A seems to be E, it is E. But, Wittgenstein holds, if whatever seems to me to be right is right, then "right" becomes meaningless here. In other words, the crucial fact is that I could have no justification for saying that the statement "A = E" is wrong, and therefore no justification for saying that it is right. Hence I can have no justification for trusting my memory of E, or for the judgement that the E experience I remember is the same as, or different from, what I now have.

But this claim fails on several counts. First, since memorial state-ments have *prima facie* credibility, I am justified in trusting my memory unless there is reason not to, and the same holds of the justification of judg-ments of similarity or difference. The statement "A = E" has *prima facie* jus-tification and it would be up to the Wittgensteinian skeptic to provide grounds for calling it into question.

Second, as Wittgenstein noted, consistency among memories does not prove them true.[59] But inconsistency among memorial statements does prove that at least one of them is false. I have many other memories closely associated with E (e.g., I vividly recall the fear of passing out which accom-panied E). If therefore I had an experience A that did not arouse the associ-ated memories or aroused contradictory ones, it would be evidence against A being the same as E. Doubtless the contradiction could be removed by altering other memorial statements, but Quinean holism has limited appli-cation in this case. Memorial statements concerning episodes are not theo-retical statements such as, "Phlogiston has negative weight"; they are state-ments about remembered experience and are therefore largely observational in character. Even though memory usually loses a good deal of detail over time, this does not mean that the retained detail is false. If the statement "A = E" does not fit with other memorial statements of which I feel confi-dent, it is "A = E" that will be rejected. In other words, memories, as Lewis pointed out, must be congruent, and if they are not, we have strong reason to reject some of them.

Third, E has empirical correlates that can be used to test "A = E." As noted, I long ago formulated a theory that E is an allergic reaction to certain substances. Obviously, this theory could not have been formulated cor-rectly if I could not have accurately identified recurrences of E. But if my theory is true, then whenever E occurs I must have ingested one of those substances. Several years ago I spoke at a conference in Texas. At the clos-ing banquet we were served a dessert. The next morning I had a recurrence of E. Having reviewed everything I had eaten or drunk during the preced-ing day, I began to wonder about that dessert. Inquiries made to the hotel kitchen staff revealed that it did indeed contain one of the substances that I had previously identified as a cause of E. I take that fact to be confirmation both of my theory about the causes of E and of my ability to use the private name "E" correctly. I conclude therefore that the private language argu-ment, so far as it concerns a private name, is mistaken.

This being said, it should be pointed out that private *languages* are unlikely to occur. If the primary use of language is communication, there is little point in a private language or a private name, except for unusual cases such as mine where the private sensations were first thought to be symp-toms of some mysterious disease. Moreover, languages of the sort we all speak are certainly not the creations of individuals. Whenever and wherever language first appeared (if it permissible to speak of a first appearance of language at all), it was surely the result of a long course of development involving many people over many generations. If one considers the complexity of any natural language, it seems quite impossible that a single individual could develop an entire new language by himself, and certainly it would be pointless to do so.

Rules and Plans

It is frequently said that rules—more exactly, rule following—can explain behavior but not predict it.[60] This is claimed to be so, not because of performance errors (which simply show that the predictions would be probability statements), but because we have no guarantee people will continue in the future to follow a rule they have followed in the past. But this is not entirely true. Whether or not a person will continue to follow a rule in the future depends on the motives and sanctions for following or not following it.

Consider the case of cultural rules. One has here a complex structure consisting of actors, A, who follow the rule, R, situations, S, in which the rule is to be followed, expecters, E, who expect members of A to follow R in any S, and sets of sanctioners, $X_1 \ldots X_n$, who sanction members of A positively or negatively as they do or do not obey R when in S. It is quite true that any member of A may decide at any time not to follow R when in an S-type situation, even though he or she has previously conformed to it. But if there is no change in the structural relations among A, S, E, and $X_1 \ldots X_n$, such a change is unlikely to occur.

Changes in rule following are much more likely to result from changes in the relations among these sets—especially changes in relations among the Xs or in S. It should be noted that performances of cultural rules are usually subject to sanctions from different groups that often have different interests. Thus teachers have as sanctioning groups an administration—more strictly, a variety of administrators who may not agree among themselves—their own colleagues (again, a sum set of sets), their students, and, depending on the situation, quite possibly the parents of their students. The members of each of these categories have conflicting interests and varying degrees of power. Moreover, the levying of sanctions is often itself a rule-governed behavior; it is part of a dean's job to levy sanctions on the faculty and students. Changes in rule following are much more likely to result from changes in power or interests on the part of sanctioners than from independent decisions on the part of the actors. Moreover, situations change. The rules that should be followed in teaching classes of twelve will not be the same as in teaching classes of twelve hundred. But, conversely, where the structural relations among these sets are stable and situations do not change, one would be quite surprised to find significant change in rule following. In such cases, prediction (at least probabilistic prediction) would be thoroughly warranted.

The case of a purely private rule is not subject to these sorts of structural constraints. But there again it is important to emphasize that rule following is motivated—it is not just a case of inertia or whim. Predictability will therefore depend on understanding the motives underlying rule following. The pitcher who never steps on the line does not follow this rule arbitrarily; he has reasons, no doubt including his belief that following this rule helps him win games. But if he has a run of poor performances in spite of following this rule, his faith in it may evaporate and he may well give it up. The point, then, is that rule following is something done for reasons, and that the degree to which one can predict a continuance of rule following depends upon the degree to which one can predict a continuance of the motives that determine rule following and the constancy of the situation. It is too glib to say one either can or cannot predict behavior from the fact that a rule has been followed. Rule following is not arbitrary; one must look at the causal factors involved. In some cases, prediction is warranted; in other cases it is not.

Rules normally have a certain generality. It is possible, by my analysis, to adopt a rule, follow it once, and then discard it, Wittgenstein to the contrary notwithstanding. But normally rules cover a number of cases, and cultural rules usually apply to a number of actors. The situation with plans is quite different. By a plan I mean a conceptual structure that lays out, at least in general terms but often in detail, a course of behavior believed to be instrumental in the attainment of some goal. A plan may be formulated in linguistic symbols, but it need not be; a blueprint is a plan, but not (or at least not chiefly) one that is linguistically formulated. As is true of rules, a plan has no truth value; it may be followed or not, successful or not, but it cannot be true or false. A plan is a plan, whether anybody uses it or not; what is important is that it lays out a course of instrumental action that could be used. A blueprint is still a plan for a building, whether or not the building is ever built. One may plan a campaign without ever carrying it out. It is the instrumental character of a plan that deprives it of truth value.

A rule is normative; a plan may or may not be. If I plan a way of winning at chess, there is nothing normative about that plan; it is simply what I intend to do. I think up a plan for my day's activities, but if I do not follow the plan I will experience no pangs of guilt. On the other hand, when a plan is adopted—particularly when adopted by a group—it becomes normative. Thus a football play is an example of planned behavior to which the whole team is committed, and failure to do one's part as prescribed by the plan is sanctionable. The difference is not in the plan itself but in the commitment to it. A playbook contains many football plays; these are plans, whether used or not. But when a given play is called, the team is committed to execute that plan, and woe to him who fails in his assignment. One sees here again the importance of Fishbein and Ajzen's distinction between attitude and subjective norm.

As with rules, there is a distinction between satisfying a plan and following it. Given any behavior, it is doubtless possible to imagine some plan that is satisfied by that behavior. But as with rules, to follow a plan requires knowing the plan, satisfying the plan, and seeing to it that one's behavior satisfies the plan. This is again a case of matching behavior to a concept, and a plan—when being followed—is prescriptive. Since plans are instrumental for the attainment of goals, one obvious motive for following a plan is the attainment of the goal. But since there are usually alternative plans which would attain the same goal, other factors may enter. They need not; one may devise a plan, never even consider any alternative, and proceed to act on it. This is not a particularly rational form of behavior, but it is one which happens all the time. In those cases that we like to call rational, however, one will consider various alternative plans and choose the "best" one, which presumably means the one which has the highest probability of attaining the goal with the minimum of cost and risk to the actor. It is doubtful that there is often a "best" plan in this sense. Given that there seems to be no limit to the number of possible plans for achieving a given goal, it is usually impossible to say that one plan is the "best" one, particularly since estimates of the probability of success, the cost, and the risk to the actor are all likely to be quite vague. Thus one finds considerable variation in the plans people pursue to attain a given objective, which may have more to do with personal style than with rational calculation.

How can one tell when an actor is following a particular plan? The case is not as simple as that for rules. Plans are often one-shot affairs; once the goal is attained, there may be no reason to seek a similar goal. Obviously, the simplest way to determine what plan people are following is to ask them, and the actors' testimony is always the best evidence in such a case. But it is not infallible; people may disguise their plans and lie about them, often with excellent reason. Further, testimony by the actor may often not be available. Was Oswald planning to kill Connally when he shot Kennedy, or was he planning to kill only the President? Suppose then that one has only the actual conduct of the actor to go on. How would one know if the behavior was planned and what the plan was?

An actual case may serve as a useful example here. Following the break-in at the Watergate Hotel, the Nixon administration embarked on a plan to cover up what had happened. Since we know from the White House tapes that the cover-up was ordered by Nixon himself, there is no real doubt about what happened. But before the release of the crucial tapes, many people already had become convinced that there was a planned cover-up, that Nixon knew about the cover-up, and that he had ordered it. What led them to this conclusion?

When the original arrest of the burglars occurred, few people believed that high-level members of the Nixon administration or campaign were involved. The reason was clearly that the action was stupid to the point of irrationality, and few thought the upper levels of the Nixon elite capable of such stupidity. Hence the attempt to portray the break-in as the action of a few low-level zealots was initially successful. But then evidence began to emerge that was inconsistent with that view. The failure of the government prosecutors to follow up obvious leads in the trial of the burglars, the CIA connections of James McCord, and similar factors led Judge John Sirica to conclude that he was being lied to. The money trail began to lead in unexpected and—on the basis of the administration's story—unaccountable directions. As more and more people became identified as having been involved—people with increasingly high positions in the Nixon elite—and as the increasingly peculiar use of increasingly large sums of money came to light, the question that was repeatedly asked was, who could have ordered this? Who had the power? And as the White House efforts to contain the scandal began to fall apart—the investigation by John Dean turned out not to have been an investigation, Archibald Cox was fired for refusing to be put off, evidence was tampered with—Nixon's behavior was seen as less and less consistent with any plan for exposing what had occurred and more and more consistent with a plan to cover up what had happened. Dean's testimony was probably the crucial event, because not only did Dean reveal for the first time how deeply the upper echelon of the Nixon elite was involved but he also suggested the existence of the taping system. Finally, of course, it was the order by the Supreme Court to Nixon to turn over the tapes, and the conversations recorded on those tapes, which brought Nixon down.

If one looks at this whole process of discovery, it is fairly clear what led people increasingly to suspect Nixon himself. As the nation's chief executive officer it was Nixon's responsibility to see to it that any illegal actions by members of his administration were exposed and punished. The initial assumption (by those who did not know Nixon) was that such was his plan. But two things went wrong: Despite his claims that he was seeking a complete revelation of the truth, Nixon's own behavior did not satisfy that plan, and it did so less and less as time went on. Second, activities of an illegal nature by Nixon's men began to come to light. Nixon held sanctioning power over all these people—they worked for him. No one thought he should, or could, know every detail of what they did, but that he did not know about the handling of millions of dollars of campaign money and about illegal actions by top administration personnel was simply implausible. And that a political leader, whose viability depended upon public trust and support, would permit himself repeatedly to be caught lying (or at least flagrantly in error) about the actions of his own chief subordinates strongly suggested that he had an overriding motive for taking such actions. Well before the release of the final tapes, many people had come to the conclusion that the only motive that could explain Nixon's conduct was his desire to save himself from impeachment and prison.

If we abstract from the details of this sorry episode and focus on its structure, what we see is this. An actor, A, occupied a position that involved the obligation to follow a certain plan of action under a particular set of conditions. Those conditions obtained. Although A was assumed to be following the plan, his behavior did not satisfy the expected plan. Moreover, it became apparent that the actions of other actors subject to A's authority also deviated from the expected norms. All of the deviations were consistent with the hypothesis that A was following a plan sharply at variance with what had been expected of him on the basis of his official position. Moreover, the revelations about both A's behavior and that of his subordinates were detrimental to A in respects which A was known, both from his past record and his official position, to value highly. But the deviant plan could be seen as a means of avoiding the outcome that, on the basis of what was known about A, could be assumed to be for him the worst possible outcome. Therefore, one concluded that A was following the deviant plan, since his behavior satisfied it, the imputed motive was sufficient to account for his following it, and no other explanation seemed plausible.

To assert that an actor A is following a plan, therefore, in the absence of any direct statement to that effect by A and based only on observations of A's behavior, the following seem to be necessary: First, the plan must be such that A could have it; Charlemagne could not have planned to drop an atomic bomb on Beijing. Second, A's behavior must satisfy the plan nearly enough that any deviance can plausibly be attributed to performance error. Third, the plan must be such that A could be expected to believe it instrumental for the attainment of a goal that there is convincing reason to believe A desires. Fourth, there must be reason to believe A has motives for following the plan powerful enough to override any contrary motives and any risks involved in carrying out the plan. It hardly need be said that this is a tall order. Did Stalin plan to conquer Western Europe? Did Mao plan to conquer Taiwan? Did Chamberlain appease Hitler in the hope he would attack Russia rather than France and England? Only hypothetical answers can now be given to any of these questions. But hypothetical answers are better than no answers at all if they succeed in integrating all the known data, providing their hypothetical status is kept in mind.

Explanation

Explanations and predictions of human behavior can be given in terms of rules and plans, but not in terms of rules and plans alone. Rules and plans are conceptual structures that fall under the general heading of beliefs. What must be added to these are goals, desires, intentions—in other words, motives. Rules and plans do not describe regularities in nature. They are not statements of causal relations, although they may involve causal statements as subcomponents. The critical question is always whether the rule or plan will be followed, and that is a question of motivation—of goals, desires, attitudes, intentions, evaluations, and values. Both beliefs and motives, of course, are culturally constructed. Granting that some goals and desires are caused by biological factors, how they will be expressed is always determined by the culture. And many goals and motives are not biologically based but are produced in us by our culture. If the desire for salvation does not now motivate most Americans, that should not prevent our recognizing that it did motivate seventeenth-century English colonists in New England. Fortunately, data concerning beliefs and motives can often be obtained both for contemporary societies and for historical ones—at least, for those historical societies where the archaeological record is supplemented by a documentary record.

Let us look first at public rules. Let A_n designate a partially ordered sequence of actions, S, a type of situation, K, some subset of a society, t, a variable ranging over time, and x, a variable ranging over people. Then an elementary case of a rule will be:

R: (x) (t) (x ε K & x is in S at t then x should perform A_n starting at f(t))

where "f(t)" is some appropriate function of t (e.g., t + n seconds). Clearly R is normative, and does not by itself carry explanatory or predictive power. The crucial question is whether or not R will be followed, that is, whether or not x is committed to following R.

Curiously, not a great deal seems to be known about the nature of commitment.[61] The most comprehensive treatment of the subject is that of Bandura. According to his social learning theory, rule commitment consists in the adoption of the rule as an internal standard, the desire of agents to conform their action to the rule, their evaluation of their own actions in terms of the rule, and their self-reward or self-punishment on the basis of that evaluation.[62] It should be emphasized that, according to this view, agents may be committed to following a rule that they would prefer not to follow, as we saw in the case of prison inmates. The question of why one is committed to following a rule is quite a different question than that of whether or not one is in fact committed to following it.

Commitment alone does not guarantee that the behavior required by the rule will be forthcoming. In the first place, it is clear that commitment admits of degrees, and that the greater the commitment the greater the probability that one will try to follow the rule. But in the second place, it must be possible for the agent to perform the required actions. As Ajzen has emphasized, the agents must believe that they can perform the behavior and must in fact be correct in this belief, at least to a significant extent. It should be borne in mind that the greatest hitters in the history of baseball have never been able to hit safely in even fifty percent of their times at bat over the course of a season, despite their most determined efforts to do so. Commitment can at most produce the attempt to follow the rule. How successful the attempt will be will depend upon the agent's control of the situation. This factor will show itself in the error rate—one minus the probability that x performs the behavior, given that he or she is committed to following the rule. But as Ajzen has shown, agents' perception of their degree of control will also affect their commitment, since one is unlikely to retain commitment to a rule if the performance is impossible, unless the rewards are for trying rather than succeeding.[63] This factor should show up in the strength of the commitment.

The explanation of action by a rule therefore takes something like the following form:

1. R.

2. $x \in K$.

3. x is in S at t.

4. The strength of x's commitment to following R at t is M.

5. P(x tries to perform A_n at f(t)/the strength of x's commitment to following R at t is M) = q.

6. P(x performs A_n at f(t)/ x tries to perform A_n at f(t) & x's commitment to following R at t is M) = p.

7. Therefore P (x succeeds in performing A_n at f(t)) = pq.

8. In fact, x performed A_n at f(t).

This is a version of Railton's DNP type of explanation. Line 7 follows deductively from the preceding statements; line 8 is the addendum stating that the act was in fact performed, although its being performed was only probable.

Whether the explanation should be probabilistic or deterministic is a debatable question, and depends largely on how the theory is formulated. We know that the underlying mechanisms determining human action must be extraordinarily complex. Given the demonstrable effects of beliefs, attitudes, intentions, and commitment, and the fact that no two human beings have identical histories, one would hardly expect to find simple invariable sequences in human conduct. Nevertheless, deterministic processes acting on large numbers of elements can lead to statistical regularities. There is at present no way to decide between the deterministic and the probabilistic theories, and therefore no grounds for assuming either theory to be right or wrong. Put differently, explanations of human action can be formulated either deterministically or probabilistically. If the former, it is necessary to supplement the theory with a probabilistic error theory that is, from the standpoint of the basic theory, wholly *ad hoc*. If the latter, the most that can be deduced is the probability that an action occurs. There is no basis at present for deciding between these formulations. Therefore, in the schemata given here, I shall use the DNP form, but the deterministic alternative remains open.

Before considering the causal issue in more detail, it may be useful to pursue the question of the explanatory schemata for private rules. The private rule might be formulated for an individual x as:

R': $(t)(x$ is in S at t then x should perform A_n at $f(t))$.

On the assumption that x performs R' on multiple occasions, statistical evidence can be amassed to support this explanation.

The causal structure will be:

(1) R'.

(2) x is in S at t.

(3) The strength of x's commitment to following R' at t is M.

(4) P (x tries to perform A_n at $f(t)$/the strength of x's commitment to following R' is M at t) = q.

(5) P (x performs A_n at $f(t)$/x tries to perform A_n at $f(t)$ & x's commitment to following R' at t is M) = p.

(6) Therefore, P (x succeeds in performing A_n at $f(t)$) = pq.

(7) In fact, x performed A_n at $f(t)$.

The case of plans is in some respects more complex both because the structure of plans can be enormously variable and because plans may or may not be normative. Ajzen's theory of planned behavior has been shown to be effective in predicting and explaining very specific acts, but its ability to predict repeated actions over an extended period of time is enhanced by including identity theory variables.[64] Nevertheless, Ajzen's concept of an intention to try can certainly be elaborated to include quite complex plans with various relations among the plan's component parts. The normative aspect could perhaps be dealt with by including the agent among the reference individuals, since it is the agent's commitment to conforming his action to the beliefs of the reference individuals/groups which determines the value of the SN_t variable. How far beyond this it may be desirable to supplement the theory of planned behavior with further variables, such as those from self theory, is an empirical question upon which it would be foolish to speculate, since considerable current research seems to be focused on this issue. In any event, Ajzen's theory has already provided a basis for causal explanations of planned behavior, and one may be reasonably confident that the theory will be improved as time goes on.

These arguments leave a number of major questions unanswered. One which the reader will have noted long since is the following. According to Davidson,[65] Quine,[66] and others, only events can be causes or effects. Yet although I have followed Davidson[67] and Brand[68] in holding that beliefs, desires, and intentions are causes of action, I hold that these are not events but states. But as we saw above, there is no clear way to differentiate events from states or processes, and in any case no particular reason to think that causes must be events. One of course can argue that whatever the status one wishes to assign to states, the onset of a state is certainly an event. Whatever the truth of this claim, it has little relevance to the issue of beliefs and motives. Typically, people have beliefs and motives for an extended period before any action ensues. Thus, for example, consider hunger. If it is possible to date the onset of hunger precisely, it is certainly true that most people do not eat the moment they feel hunger. In fact the intensity of hunger increases with the time since last eating, and the probability that one will eat increases with the intensity of hunger, at least up to a point. One cannot say, therefore, that the onset of hunger causes eating. What is true of hunger is even more obviously true of many other states. People often have both motives and beliefs for long periods of time before they act on them. So even if the onset of these states is an event, it does not cause action—at least if the Humean criteria are adhered to. But what then does determine when actions occur?

The answer is that the time of occurrence is determined by the rule or plan itself. Thus suppose I plan to go to a movie after dinner. There is no physical connection between finishing dinner and going to a movie; the connection exists only because the plan creates it. Yet if the plan is being followed, my action of going to the movie will follow hard upon my finishing dinner. The cause is the plan and my commitment to it; the plan itself specifies the occasion for my acting. The same considerations apply to rules. Typically, a rule specifies that an action is to be performed whenever certain situational conditions are met, or within a certain time after those conditions have been met. Following the rule thus implies acting at the time specified in the rule. There is therefore no real difficulty in states of belief and motivation causing actions at specified times, as long as the beliefs involved are rules or plans.

But are we not now caught in a regress? Adopting a plan or rule is an action. How can states such as desires or intentions and beliefs cause internal actions of this sort to occur at specific times? Here it is well to recall some simple facts about human development. When infants' bladders fill, they experience discomfort, which is relieved by voiding. The action is involuntary and is governed by purely physical processes; when the pressure reaches a physiologically determined threshold, the child voids. In due course, children learn—are taught—not to void whenever they experience bladder pressure but to delay until the proper place and time are reached. How is the influence of the desire delayed? It is delayed not just by the children's learning that one urinates only in the toilet but by their internalizing this rule as a standard by which their behavior is to be governed. The motivation for adopting this rule is parental praise or punishment, and self-praise or punishment. In a relatively short time, children become able to regulate their own voiding by self-generated incentives alone. That is, having learned the rule as a belief and adopted it (i.e., committed themselves to it) the children thereafter seek to match their performance to the rule, evaluate their performance by the rule, and reward or punish themselves according to that evaluation.

The case of pure unmediated desire causing action whenever it reaches a certain threshold is that of the neonate. But socialization involves precisely the sort of internalization of standards and learning to regulate one's self in conformity with these standards that we have just discussed. Among the most important things we learn in socialization are rules for how and when desires are to be satisfied. When one is hungry, one does not at the first pang rush to the kitchen and devour any food in sight. Rather, one reflects on what food one would most enjoy, on when it will be convenient to eat, on where one will go to eat, on whether one will eat alone, or with company, and if the latter, what company, and so forth. In short, one formulates a plan for satisfying the desire, and adopts it. One then carries out the plan, and by doing so makes of eating a more satisfactory experience than it would otherwise have been.

The very humdrum nature of this example makes the point. Becoming human is a process of bringing desires under control, of learning that the onset of a desire or a desire reaching a given threshold is the occasion for decision and planning as to how, when, where, or whether the desire will be satisfied. This is a metarule governing rule and plan formation that is then internalized, thereby conferring upon us a generalized capacity for bringing order out of the chaos of desires. Without such a capacity, not only would rational action be impossible, so would all organized coherent human action.[69]

If the argument of this chapter is correct, rules and plans play an important part in the explanation of many human actions. Plans may be taken as intentions, as construed in Ajzen's theory of planned behavior, although for more elaborate plans that theory will doubtless need to be supplemented. Rules are norms governing action; they are not general laws, nor are they alone causes of action. It is, rather, the commitment of the agent to the rule which provides the motive for the execution of rule-governed action. Both rule-governed and plan-governed actions are causally determined, and can be explained in terms of concepts such as belief, attitude, evaluation, intention, desire, and psychological commitment. It is true that our psychological models for action explanation are less than perfect, but they are good enough and well enough supported by empirical evidence to provide considerable explanatory and predictive power. Whether these models are spelled out in detail in every particular case or simply referred to by singular causal statements, they provide the causal underpinnings for our understanding of human conduct.

Notes

1. Hong-Wen Charng, Jane Allyn Piliavin, and Peter L. Collero, "Role Identity and Reasoned Action in the Prediction of Repeated Behavior," *Social Psychology Quarterly* 51:303–317 (1988). See however Ajzen, *Attitudes*, ch. 3.

2. Joan Safran Ganz, *Rules: A Systematic Study* (The Hague: Mouton, 1971), 17ff. Ganz gives an excellent survey of the properties of rules, upon which I have drawn heavily.

3. Wittgenstein, *Philosophical Investigations*, Part 1, §85.

4. Ganz, *Rules*, 17–19.

5. Ibid., 94ff, 104.

6. Jerrold L. Aronson, *A Realist Philosophy of Science* (New York: St. Martin's Press, 1984), ch. 9.

7. Ganz, *Rules*, 18.

8. Ibid., 26–37. Robert Allen Schwartz, *Preliminary Studies in Rules and Behavior* (University of Pennsylvania dissertation, 1966), 49ff. The satisfying-following terminology is Schwartz's.

9. Ganz, *Rules*, 6.

10. Ibid., 112.

11. Ibid., 114.

12. Ibid., 122–123.

13. Ibid., 105–113.

14. Bandura, *Social Foundations*, 100–104, 209–219.

15. Lila R. Gleitman and Eric Wanner, "Language Acquisition: The State of the State of the Art" in Eric Wanner and Lila R. Gleitman, eds., *Language Acquisition* (Cambridge: Cambridge University Press, 1982), 3–4.

16. Eve V. Clark, "Awareness of Language: Some Evidence from What Children Say and Do" in A. Sinclair, R. J. Jarvella, and W. J. M. Levelt, eds., *The Child's Conception of Language* (Berlin: Springer-Verlag, 1978), 17–43. Carol L. Smith and Helen Tager-Flusberg, "Metalinguistic Awareness and Language Development," *Journal of Experimental Child Psychology* 34:449–468 (1982).

17. Annette Karmiloff-Smith, "From Meta-Processes to Conscious Access: Evidence from Children's Metalinguistic and Repair Data," *Cognition* 23:95–147 (1986), 105.

18. Ibid., 107.

19. Ibid., 108.

20. Ibid., 110.

21. Ibid.

22. See above, 71–72.

23. Eve V. Clark, "Language Change During Language Acquisition," in Michael E. Lamb and Ann L. Brown, eds., *Advances in Developmental Psychology* (Hillsdale, N.J.: Erlbaum, 1982), vol. 2, 173.

24. Ibid., 177.

25. Clark, "Awareness," 35.

26. Clark, "Language," 180. (Emphasis in original)

27. Karmiloff-Smith, "From Meta-Processes," 130–137.

28. Hallowell, personal communication.

29. Bandura, *Social Foundations*, 459–461.

30. Jean Emile Gombert, "Are Young Children's Speech Adaptations Conscious or Automatic? A Short Theoretical Note," *International Journal of Psychology* 22:375–382 (1987).

31. Bandura, *Social Foundations*, 100–101.

32. Goodman, *Fact*, 87–120.

33. Bandura, *Social Foundations*, 100–104, 209–219.

34. Ganz, *Rules*, 66.

35. Wittgenstein, *Philosophical Investigations*, Part 1, §143.

36. Ibid., Part 1, §201. (Emphasis in original)

37. Saul A. Kripke, *Wittgenstein on Rules and Private Language* (Cambridge, Mass.: Harvard University Press, 1982), 9.

38. Ibid.

39. Ibid., ch. 2.

40. Goodman, *Fact*, 74–83.

41. Kripke, *Wittgenstein*, 11.

42. Ibid., 90–92.

43. Wittgenstein, *Philosophical Investigations*, Part 1, §335, 587–600, 646.

44. Kripke, *Wittgenstein*, 41–42.

45. Wittgenstein, *Philosophical Investigations*, Part 2, §xiii.

46. Wilfrid Sellars, "Empiricism and the Philosophy of Mind" in Wilfrid Sellars, *Science, Perception and Reality*, (London: Routledge and Kegan Paul, 1963), 127–196. Paul M. Churchland, *Scientific Realism and the Plasticity of Mind* (Cambridge: Cambridge University Press, 1979); Daniel Dennett, *The Intentional Stance* (Cambridge, Mass.: MIT Press, 1987); William G. Lycan, *Consciousness* (Cambridge, Mass.: MIT Press, 1987). Jay L. Garfield, *Belief in Psychology* (Cambridge, Mass.: MIT Press, 1988).

47. David R. Olson, "On the Origins of Beliefs and Other Intentional States in Children" in Astington et al., *Theories of Mind*, 417.

48. Leslie, "Some Implications" in Ibid., 19–46; Henry M. Wellman, "First Steps in the Child's Theorizing About the Mind" in Ibid., 64–92; Josef Perner, "Developing Semantics for Theories of Mind: From Propositional Attitudes to Mental Representations" in Ibid., 141–172.

49. Olson, Astington, and Harris, "Introduction" in Ibid., 3.

50. See chapter 2, 64–74.

51. Janet W. Astington and Alison Gopnik, "Knowing You've Changed Your Mind: Children's Understanding of Representational Change" in Astington et al., *Theories of Mind*, 201.

52. Henry M. Wellman, "The Origins of Metacognition" in D. L. Forrest-Pressley, G. E. MacKinnon, and T. Gary Waller, eds., *Metacognition, Cognition, and Human Performance* (New York: Academic Press, 1985), vol. 1, 1–31.

53. C. I. Lewis, *An Analysis of Knowledge and Valuation* (La Salle, Ill.: Open Court, 1946), ch. 11.

54. Joseph W. Alba and Lynn Hasher, "Is Memory Schematic?," *Psychological Bulletin* 93:203–231 (1983). Allan Paivio, *Mental Representations: A Dual Coding Approach* (Oxford: Clarendon Press, 1986). Ulric Neisser, "Memory: What are The Important Questions?" and "Snapshots or Benchmarks?" in Ulric Neisser, ed., *Memory Observed* (San Francisco: W. H. Freeman and Co., 1982), 3–19, 43–48. Charles P. Thompson and Thaddeus Cowan, "Flashbulb Memories: A Nicer Interpretation of a Neisser Recollection," *Cognition* 22:199–200 (1986). Ulric Neisser, "Remembering Pearl Harbor: Reply to Thompson and Cowan," *Cognition* 23:285–286 (1986). William K. Estes, *Models of Learning, Memory, and Choice* (New York: Praeger Publishers, 1982), 127–245.

55. James, *Principles of Psychology*, vol. 1, 463.

56. Kripke, *Wittgenstein*, 3–4.

57. Wittgenstein, *Philosophical Investigations*, Part 1, §258.

58. Ibid., Part 1, §243.

59. Ibid., Part 1, §265.

60. Ganz, *Rules*, 77.

61. John R. Hollenbeck and Howard J. Klein, "Goal Commitment and the Goal-Setting Process: Problems, Prospects, and Proposals for Future Research," *Journal of Applied Psychology* 72:212–220 (1987).

62. Bandura, *Social Foundations*, 301, 350–354, 375, 477.

63. The point is not trivial. Calvinists have believed that they had to strive to obey the law even though it is impossible for fallen man to do so.

64. Charng, Piliavin, and Collero, "Role Identity."

65. Davidson, *Essays*, 154–162.

66. Quine, *Roots of Reference*, 6.

67. Davidson, *Essays*, 4–19.

68. Brand, *Intending*, 15–32.

69. Bandura, *Social Foundations*, ch. 8.

Chapter 6

Truth and Reality

This chapter seeks to provide support for Premise (1): There is a real world of which true knowledge is possible, and partial support for Premise (7): Members of one culture can understand members of other cultures, including members of antecedent states of their own culture. I adopt Kripke's theory of truth, of which a brief sketch is presented, and argue in support of several propositions concerning confirmation—particularly that the confirmation of a theory is relative to that of its rivals. I also consider the truth status of the preformation system of physical objects with which we are born and argue that objects are posits to explain our experience. Issues of truth and confirmation lead to a consideration of Quine's Underdetermination Thesis, which I argue is false. They also lead to issues of incommensurability among theories. As Kuhn as pointed out, incommensurability does not imply incomparability. Much of the confusion over this issue is owing to a failure to distinguish translation from interpretation, and once this distinction is drawn, it becomes clear that incommensurability does not imply the sort of relativism which has too often been attributed to it. Against Davidson I argue that the conceptual scheme-content distinction does make sense, although I conclude as he does that theories are comparable. Thus the world views of other cultures can be compared with our own.

I argue for a form of realism in which the existence of a real world is a postulate to explain our experience rather than a presupposition of inquiry. True knowledge of the real world is possible even though complete knowledge of it is not—that is, we are led to postulate the existence of some states of affairs about which many of the propositions we can formulate will be undecidable. Nevertheless, I argue that science will lead to a best theory which is also a true theory, and that our best confirmed theory is our best present estimate of that best theory. Hence we can have "true knowledge"—more strictly, well-confirmed theories that are our best estimate of the true knowledge—about the real world.

Truth

The problem of truth lies at the very heart of any effort to understand the world. If we are never justified in holding a sentence to be true, it is hard to see how we can ever claim to have knowledge of anything. Yet an adequate theory of truth, like the Holy Grail, has eluded even the most determined philosophic quests throughout the history of philosophy. Nevertheless, we have somewhat better reasons to hope for a solution to the problem of truth than for a recovery of the Grail. Tarski's work, and more recently Kripke's, mark major advances toward the development of an adequate theory of truth, and although we do not yet have a satisfactory theory for natural languages, the results achieved are sufficiently impressive to justify optimism concerning future work. While nothing like a general treatment of this subject is possible here, it will be worthwhile to describe briefly some of the major developments that have led to most of the present work.

Tarski's work has long been regarded as the pre-eminent modern theory of truth.[1] The virtues of Tarski's theory are too well known to need any review here. The introduction of the object-language, meta-language distinction and the resulting hierarchy of languages did provide a way of avoiding the semantic paradoxes, and his Convention T seemed to provide a clear and precise, if unexciting, criterion for determining when a statement is true.[2] Nevertheless, there are drawbacks to Tarski's theory which have long disturbed philosophers. Two of these have been particularly noted. First, Tarski's theory of truth is limited to formalized languages only, and is thus inapplicable to natural languages. The reason for this is quite clear. Tarski concluded that within natural languages there was no way to avoid the semantic paradoxes such as the liar, and he therefore restricted his theory to formalized languages where these paradoxes could be avoided.[3] Yet in natural languages, sentences are said to be true or false. Tarski's theory offers us no way to deal with these sentences of natural languages; indeed, Tarski believed that there could be no consistent theory of truth for natural language sentences.

Second, the truth predicate defined by Tarski is specific to a particular language at a particular level of the language hierarchy. Thus instead of having a definition of "true," we have a definition of "$true_n$," where "n" is an index referring to the nth-level language of the hierarchy. But this is not the way we normally talk about truth. It seems at least very odd to say that what we mean by "truth" in the meta-meta-language is different from what we mean by "truth" in the meta-language.[4] These and other problems have led to continuing efforts to develop a theory of truth that can avoid the paradoxes and yet not be subject to the restrictions of Tarski's theory.

The most important breakthrough in this area is Kripke's theory. Like Tarski's, Kripke's theory is based on the fundamental insight that, "We may say that we are entitled to assert (or deny) of any sentence that it is true precisely under the circumstances when we can assert (or deny) the sentence itself."[5] This is of course the insight Tarski sought to capture in Convention T. But Kripke's development of this insight takes a different course than Tarski's. Kripke makes essential use of the notion of "groundedness" which may be informally explicated as follows:

> In general, if a sentence . . . asserts that (all, some, most, etc.) of the sentences of a certain class C are true, its truth value can be ascertained if the truth values of the sentences in the class C are ascertained. If some of these sentences themselves involve the notion of truth, their truth value in turn must be ascertained by looking at *other* sentences, and so on. If ultimately this process terminates in sentences not mentioning the concept of truth, so that the truth value of the original statement can be ascertained, we call the original sentence *grounded*; otherwise, ungrounded.[6]

So a sentence is grounded only if its truth or falsity depends on factors which do not involve the notion of truth.

Suppose we begin with a language that does not contain its own truth predicate $T(x)$, and an interpretation of the language on some non-empty domain D which yields sentences such as, "Snow is white," "Grass is green," and so on. If we then add to this language the truth predicate $T(x)$, we would want it to be the case that "snow is white" is in the extension of $T(x)$ just in case snow is white, and not in the extension of $T(x)$ just in case snow is not white. That is to say, we would want a sentence A, and the sentence "'A' is true," to have the same semantic value. An interpretation of $T(x)$ which meets this requirement, Kripke calls a fixed point.

As Tarski showed, if the interpretation of the language involves the classical two-valued logic, it is not in general possible to find an interpretation of the language which meets the fixed point requirement. This is shown by the existence of the Liar Paradox. Kripke circumvents this obstacle by using Kleene's strong three-valued logic, where the values "true" and "false" have the usual interpretation, and "undefined" serves as a third value applicable to sentences which cannot be shown to be either true or false.[7]

More strictly, let L be a language that does not contain a truth predicate $T(x)$, and D a non-empty domain; let the variables of L range over non-empty subsets of D, and the primitive n-ary predicates of L be interpreted by n-ary relations on D, and let L contain the resources necessary to represent its own syntax. Suppose then that to L we add $T(x)$. An interpretation of $T(x)$ is given by (S_1, S_2), where S_1 is the extension of $T(x)$, S_2 is its antiextension, and $T(x)$ is undefined for elements not in $S_1 \cup S_2$. Let L' (S_1, S_2) be the interpretation of L augmented by $T(x)$ that results from interpreting $T(x)$ by (S_1, S_2). Let $S_1{}^*$ be the set of true sentences of L' (S_1, S_2), and let $S_2{}^*$ be the set of elements of D which are either not sentences of L'(S_1, S_2) or false sentences of L'(S_1, S_2). If the valuation scheme is represented by the function ϕ, then the fixed point requirement may be expressed as $\phi((S_1, S_2)) = (S_1{}^*, S_2{}^*)$, where ϕ is defined on all pairs of disjoint subsets of D.

As Kripke shows, one can define a hierarchy of languages, similar to Tarski's hierarchy, starting with L_0 as L' (Λ, Λ), where Λ is the empty set, and such that, if for any a, we have defined $L_a = $ L' (S_1, S_2), then $L_{a+1} = $ L' $(S_1{}^*, S_2{}^*)$. Suppose now that we introduce the notion of *extends* as follows:

$(S_1!, S_2!)$ *extends* (S_1, S_2) iff $S_1 \subseteq S_1!$ and $S_2 \subseteq S_2!$ (symbolized by $(S_1, S_2) \leq (S_1!, S_2!)$).

Given this notion and the hierarchy of languages, Kripke points out:

> Now a basic property of our valuation rules is the following: ϕ is a monotone (order-preserving) operation on $\leq$: that is, if $(S_1, S_2) \leq (S_1!, S_2!)$, $\phi((S_1, S_2) \leq \phi((S_1!, S_2!))$. In other words, *if $(S_1, S_2) \leq (S_1!, S_2!)$, then any sentence that is true (or false) in L' (S_1, S_2) retains its truth value in L' $(S_1!, S_2!)$.* What this means is that *if the interpretation of $T(x)$ is extended by giving it a definite truth value for cases that were previously undefined, no truth value previously established changes or becomes undefined; at most, certain previously undefined truth values become defined.*[8]

Thus, if in the language hierarchy, there is a L_k in which a sentence A has a defined truth value, A will have that same truth value for every language L_n, k<n for all finite n. But the hierarchy extends to transfinite levels as well. The first transfinite level, L_ω, is L = L $(S_{1\omega}, S_{2\omega})$ where $S_{1\omega}$ is the union of all S_{1a} for all finite a, and $S_{2\omega}$ the union of all S_{2a} for all finite a. We then have the transfinite sequence L_ω, $L_{\omega+1}$, . . . until the next limit ordinal is reached, and so on. As Kripke emphasizes, "Even with the transfinite levels included, it remains true that the extension and the antiextension of T(x) increase with increasing a."[9] Moreover, Kripke proves that in this hierarchy there will exist a minimum fixed point L_σ—that is, an interpreted language L' (S_{1k}, S_{2k}) such that $\phi(S_{1k}, S_{2k}) = (S_{1,k+1}, S_{2,k+1})$. Such a fixed point language contains its own truth predicate.

On the basis of these results, Kripke is able to give a formal definition of groundedness: "Given a sentence A of L, let us define A to be *grounded* if it has a truth value in the smallest fixed point L_σ ; otherwise, *ungrounded*."[10] Thus the intuitive notion discussed above receives a precise formal definition.

The minimum fixed point is by no means the only fixed point; in fact the existence of other fixed points plays an important role in Kripke's theory. Consider for example the following two sentences:

(1) (1) is true.
(2) (2) is false.

(1) is ungrounded, but it is not paradoxical—it does not lead us into contradiction. Since it is ungrounded, it can be assigned a truth value arbitrarily. But now consider:

(3) Either (3) or its negation is true.

(3) can be true or undefined, but it cannot be false, even though it is ungrounded. This fact leads Kripke to define the notion of an intrinsic fixed point—namely, a fixed point is intrinsic "iff it assigns no sentence a truth value conflicting with its truth value at any other fixed point."[11] A sentence has an intrinsic truth value if and only if it has a truth value in an intrinsic fixed point. (3) is an example of such a sentence.[12] (2) on the other hand, is not only ungrounded but paradoxical—indeed, it is a form of the Liar's Paradox. Kripke is now able to define a sentence as "*paradoxical* if it has no truth value in *any* fixed point."[13] Thus the truth value of (2) is always undefined. The Liar does not cease to be paradoxical, but that paradox no longer involves a conflict of truth values because it has no truth value at all.

Kripke's theory of truth has very important advantages over Tarski's. First, it shows that a language may contain its own truth predicate without succumbing to the Liar's Paradox, and it is to my knowledge the most successful attempt to do this. Second, it uses only a single truth predicate instead of the level-specific truth predicates of the Tarski hierarchy. Third, it is applicable to languages containing modal operators and propositional attitudes, although so far as I know these applications have yet to be fully worked out.[14] Although not yet extended to natural languages, it comes closer to doing this than Tarski's theory, and has inspired a great deal of new work directed toward that goal.[15]

Tarski's theory has often been described as a form of the correspondence theory of truth: the truth of a sentence p consists in its corresponding to the facts stated by p. Kripke notes that Convention T must be modified to fit the three valued approach—for example, T could be put: "'P' is true" is true (false) iff p is true (false)[16]—but this modification does not affect the correspondence issue. In fact, Kripke does not discuss this matter, although—since he holds that the groundedness of a sentence depends upon the facts—he may also mean that its truth is so dependent.[17] But I think it does no violence to his theory, and may even represent his own view, to say that the truth or falsity of a grounded sentence depends on the empirical evidence.[18] It may seem at first that this is distinction without a difference, and certainly it is not a difference that affects Kripke's theory. But there is a difference.

Sentences such as "Snow is white" and "Rabbits have four legs" are taken, by Quine and others, to be observational sentences. When are such sentences true or false? We are tempted to say, when we perceive that things are as the sentences assert that they are. But as we saw in Chapter 1, there is reason to believe that human beings are programmed to perceive the world in terms of objects such as rabbits. Such a preformation system may be hardwired, but that of course does not prove that it is true.

There are two dangers which must be avoided here. One is the evolutionist argument, which holds that the object concept is the product of natural selection and that therefore it must be true. The conclusion does not follow. Doubtless we are products of natural selection and so are our perceptual abilities and any cognitive categories we bring to the interpretation of experience. But all that shows is that we are not so maladapted that we have perished. The shark is one of the most successful survivors in nature. That does not prove that the shark's view of the world—whatever that is— is true.

The other argument is the Kantian argument that because "object" is a category we bring to experience, it is a necessary and universal category of any world we *can* know. There is no transcendental deduction here. The fact that we first conceptualize the world of experience in terms of objects does not prove that we cannot subsequently transcend that initial conceptualization. The most successful theory of physics that we have ever had is the quantum theory, and as is well known the wave-particle duality and the uncertainty principle have led to endless debates over what sorts of objects subatomic wavicles really are. Perhaps they are superstrings in a ten- or twenty-six-dimensional space.[19] But whatever they are, they are clearly not objects in the ordinary common sense way of thinking.

It does not follow from this that our ordinary real object statements are false. Rather what does follow is that the character of the world we know by experience is to be explained by theories that postulate the existence of rather bizarre sorts of entities. A rabbit is still a rabbit, whether composed of superstrings or Aristotlean substance. In this sense, Quine and others have been profoundly right to see that alternatives to the common ontology of physical objects were possible. My disagreements with them concern the level at which such a transcending of common sense can take place, not the basic insight that human beings can go beyond their native endowment, although only when they have advanced to the very frontiers of thought.

Observation sentences containing real object terms are themselves hypotheses that posit real objects as explanations of our experience. As we saw above,[20] what seems to be a perceptual judgment about the location of a table in time and space may turn out to be false and have to be rejected. Nor are hallucinations the only cases of this sort. As is well known, we often "see" a table as having a rectangular or circular top, although our actual view is a perspectival one. And we often make mistakes in leaping from our perspectival view to a conclusion about the nature of the object. One may see an oval table as having a round top, or a rhomboid table as rectangular. In such cases, when we find ourselves embarrassed, what we do is to re-examine our actual perceptual experience. That experience may be informed by our concepts, but it is the basis from which we have to start and upon which our further judgments must ultimately rest. If it is made rather than given, it is nevertheless indubitable for us. Purple spades and apparent motions are components of our experience, whether they correspond to real things in the world or not; the problem is to explain them. If the simplest explanation for my seeing a table before me is that there is a real table before me, that should not delude us into thinking that the real table is not a posit to explain my perceptual experience.

Experience itself simply *is*. Whether the experience is an experience of something beyond itself is a theoretical question—it involves theoretical postulates—but experience itself is what has to be explained. Experience is not a matter of nerve stimulations. It may be true, according to our theory, that stimulations of certain nerves cause certain experiences, but we do not experience the nerve stimulations as such. Rather, the theory that nerve stimulations cause those experiences is itself based on other experiences. It is experience that is the basis of our knowledge. Experience is not a pure "given" independent of all conceptualization. But it is nevertheless that from which inquiry starts.

Confirmation

Having a theory of truth does not solve the problem of how one knows when a particular hypothesis or theory is true. That is the issue of confirmation—a subject that has probably exercised philosophers of science more than any other and on which there is vast literature. Fortunately, it is not necessary for our purposes to solve the myriad problems of confirmation, but it is important to emphasize several points about the confirmation process. Although not all hypotheses and theories of science are completely universal, many are, so any adequate approach to confirmation must be able to deal with such cases.

It is elementary that no finite set of singular sentences can establish the truth of a universal statement. This fact leads at once to the conclusion that our hypotheses and theories are underdetermined by experience, since all that experience can yield us is a finite set of singular sentences. This conclusion is surely true, but underdetermination of this sort should not be confused with the Underdetermination Thesis for science espoused by Quine—a thesis to which we will return shortly. What underdetermination in the sense presently before us shows is that certainty is an illusory goal. No matter how much evidence we amass in support of a hypothesis or theory, the possibility will always remain that further evidence will disconfirm the hypothesis or theory. This fact does not imply that the hypothesis or theory is not true; it only shows that we can never be certain that it is true.

In "Two Dogmas," Quine pointed out that no empirical finding can force us to abandon a hypothesis we are determined to hold, and that we can be led to reject a hypothesis even though all the evidence favors it.[21] The first point arises from the fact that testable consequences are not derived from the test hypothesis alone but from the conjunction of the test hypothesis with other auxiliary hypotheses. Hence a negative outcome of the test can be accommodated by rejecting either the test hypothesis or any one of the auxiliary hypotheses. By a sufficiently ingenious adjustment of the auxiliary hypotheses, we can therefore preserve the test hypothesis, come what may. The second point arises from the fact that even though we may have a hypothesis or theory consistent with all the known observational evidence, there may exist a simpler hypothesis or theory (or one preferable on other grounds) that we will adopt in place of our original hypothesis or theory, even though no disconfirming evidence is known. These arguments of Quine's are well known and I believe are fully accepted. It is the consequences of the second argument that I wish to pursue here.

The fact that a hypothesis (theory) consistent with all known evidence can be rejected in favor of an alternative hypothesis (theory) equally consistent with the evidence but superior on some other basis (simplicity, relation to other theories, etc.) shows that the acceptance of a hypothesis (theory) is always relative to the alternatives available. This point has been made by many philosophers in a variety of ways. Thus Kuhn has noted that scientists will not reject a theory, regardless of negative evidence, unless they have a better alternative theory to put in its place.[22] Confirmation therefore always involves a choice among alternative hypotheses, and the confirmation of a given hypothesis is always relative to those alternatives. No matter how great the evidence supporting a given theory, there can be no assurance that a better theory will never be found. Surely in the eighteenth and most of the nineteenth centuries, Newton's theory of mechanics seemed to be so strongly supported that no one thought it would ever be disconfirmed, and no one can say for certain that the same fate does not await Einstein's theory.

Given the relative character of confirmation, Aronson seems to be right in holding that the basic logic of confirmation is the maximum likelihood principle.[23] The argument in favor of the maximum likelihood principle is not simply an abstract argument; in fact, maximum likelihood methods are employed throughout the sciences wherever statistical hypotheses are involved. Moreover, the rationale for its use seems irrefutable. Given a set of known data, what more could one ask of the hypothesis than that it should make that data more probable than does any alternative hypothesis? If one has a choice between two hypotheses, H_1 and H_2, and one has some set of observation statements, O, and if the probability of the members of O on H_1 is greater than their probability on H_2, it is difficult to imagine a situation in which one would consider it reasonable to adopt H_2 instead of H_1. The maximum likelihood principle articulates a criterion that I think any reasonable theory of confirmation must adopt.

Aronson's critique of Salmon's Bayesian theory of confirmation also seems to me to be on the mark.[24] The difficulty of determining the prior probabilities for the hypothesis and for the evidence seem to me to be formidable obstacles to Salmon's approach, and despite the fact that the influence of the initial choices of the priors diminishes with repeated testing, the Bayesian model does not seem to have acquired the support among scientists that the maximum likelihood principle has.

I referred above to two points concerning confirmation that Quine made in "Two Dogmas." The first was that a negative outcome for an experiment does not necessarily force us to abandon the test hypothesis, since auxiliary hypotheses can be changed instead. This point has been used to argue against the possibility of there being any such thing as a crucial experiment. For if Quine's argument holds, it would seem that no experimental or observational outcome could ever force the abandonment of the test hypothesis. However, Aronson has pointed out that this conclusion is too strong. Thus, if H_1 and H_2 are alternative hypotheses, C is a testable consequence, and A is a set of auxiliary hypotheses such that:

(1) H_1 & A then C
(2) H_2 & A then ~C

then whether C or ~C occurs can decide between H_1 and H_2. Of course, for this design to work, the members of A must be logically independent of H_1 and H_2. Furthermore, C and ~C must represent alternatives not only exclusive but one of which must be true (i.e., the angular momenta of silver atoms either vary continuously or discontinuously).[25] But if these conditions are met, it certainly appears that so-called crucial experiments can be performed.

These conditions, however, are not met in the usual case. H_1 and H_2 may be constituent hypotheses of different theories, so that different auxiliary hypotheses are involved in deriving testable consequences from them. In such a case, the requirement that the "As" in (1) and (2) be the same is violated. It is also not always the case that the consequences, C and ~C, are exhaustive as well as exclusive. What Aronson has in mind here is that within the context of the scientific theory being employed, they should be exhaustive. If both were to turn out false, that would imply that something is fundamentally wrong with the whole conceptual framework.

> If angular momentum is a quantity that is neither continuous nor discontinuous, then what kind of a quantity is it? Maybe it would leave us with the perplexity that angular momentum is not really quantifiable at all in the same way natural philosophers in the past such as Galileo, Descartes and Locke treated colours, sounds, smells, etc., as 'secondary qualities' which were not worthy to be classified as real or inherent qualities of things. If so, contemporary physics, classical or quantum, would be left in a quandary.[26]

But it is worth noting that such "impossible" results have happened before.

It seems to me more realistic to recognize that in deriving testable consequences from alternative hypotheses, the sets of auxiliary hypotheses used are very often not identical. The resulting situation is untidy, compared with the neat model represented by (1) and (2), but that does not rule out the possibility of deciding between alternative hypotheses. Suppose for example that H_1 and H_2 are again the test hypotheses, C the testable consequence, and $A_1 \ldots A_n$ the auxiliary hypotheses. Then we might have:

(3) H_1 & A_1 & ... & A_k then C
(4) H_2 & A_2 & ... & A_n then ~C

Here there is some overlap between the two sets of As but also some difference. Suppose to fix ideas they differ only in A_1 and A_n. Then if ~C occurs, we could revise either H_1 or A_1; if C occurs, we could revise either H_2 or A_n. But this does not mean that everything is in the wind: In designing a test of a hypothesis, one does not use auxiliary hypotheses that are less certain than the test hypothesis; to do so would be a mark of poor scientific judgment. The reason that H_1 (or H_2) would in fact be rejected here is that we are uncertain about their truth (why else would we be testing them?), or more strictly, we are less certain of their truth than we are of the truth of the As.

What I suggest happens here is that within the scientific community at any given time, there is a rough but fairly consistent distribution of subjective probabilities over the sentences of the prevailing theories. When one is confronted with an anomalous result, one will doubt first those sentences relevant to the result which have the lowest subjective probabilities. Hence in (3), H_1 has a lower subjective probability than any A and will be rejected if ~C occurs. Such a distribution of subjective probabilities, of course, will vary from one individual to another: Consistency within the scientific community is only approximate. But these probabilities are also subject to change over time, and if experiments involving some particular set of auxiliaries keep yielding peculiar results, they will be questioned (i.e., the subjective probabilities of those auxiliaries will decline). Thus Kuhn has remarked on the fact that paradigm theories are not called into question until there is an accumulation of anomalous results; it is the piling up of inexplicable outcomes that changes the probability distribution.[27]

It would seem, therefore, that decisions can be made between alternative hypotheses even when they do not conform to the neat crucial experiment model proposed by Aronson. What is required is that the test hypothesis should be less certain than the auxiliaries. Of course, one can go wrong here; it may be that one of the auxiliaries is the villain. But if that is the case, the villainy should be discoverable through further experiment. It is also true that resolute believers in Flat Earth can, by sufficiently heroic *ad hoc* gymnastics, preserve their beloved theory, come what may. But the net result for Flat Earthers will be a distribution of subjective probabilities over the sentences of science so at variance with those of others in the scientific community that they find themselves excluded from the field.[28] That such resolute pigheadedness is possible does not mean that the Flat Earth theory cannot be empirically disconfirmed, unless one wants to hold that the distributions of subjective probabilities held by members of the scientific community are not conditioned by empirical evidence—a claim I think no one defends.

What I hope these very brief remarks have brought out is that the underdetermination of scientific theories and hypotheses by experience does not prevent one theory (hypothesis) from being better confirmed than an alternative theory (hypothesis) against which it is being tested. Confirmation as here described is a relative matter; hypotheses H_1 is better confirmed than H_2. We can never be certain that H_1 is true, nor can we be certain that some other hypothesis H^* will not be devised which turns out to be better confirmed than H_1. But none of this prevents us from holding that, given a set of evidence statements, E, one hypothesis is better confirmed by that evidence than an alternative, in the sense that the evidence is more probable on the one hypothesis than on the other. If this much is granted, we can now turn to the more complex issue of underdetermination—Quine's Underdetermination Thesis.

The Underdetermination Thesis[29]

Certainly one of the most powerful attacks on the possibility that there can be a "best" scientific theory, at least in any meaningful sense, is Quine's Underdetermination Thesis. First put forward in a 1975 paper,[30] Quine has subsequently considered some modifications in his views, but his basic position seems to remain that of the original paper. In what follows, I shall deal with the thesis as Quine presented it in 1975.[31]

The Underdetermination Thesis concerns the relationship of scientific theories to the observation sentences that support them. Quine gives no definition of an observation sentence, but he does specify two marks by which they can be identified. First, "witnesses will agree on the spot in . . . assenting to an observation sentence"[32] or in dissenting from it. Second, one can learn the correct application of an observation sentence by ostension, as well as by other methods. Quine gives as an example of such an observation sentence "Lo, a rabbit." Thus, for Quine, sentences containing terms usually understood as real object terms, such as "rabbit" or "ball," may count as observation sentences. Such sentences are clearly not phenomenal reports.[33]

Quine calls these observation sentences "occasion sentences" because their truth or falsity depends upon the occasion of their utterance. "Lo, a rabbit" is true if a rabbit is present, false otherwise. To be scientifically useful, occasion sentences must be transformed into what he calls "standing sentences"—sentences that are true or false independently of the particular occasion on which they are uttered.[34] To so transform them, Quine proposes pairing each occasion sentence to a set of spatio-temporal coordinates, so that "Lo, a rabbit" might become, "There is a rabbit at the point having coordinates p,q,r,s." Such a sentence, if true at all, is always true. We can then form conditional statements that have standing sentences as their antecedents and consequents. It is such conditionals that are actually derivable from scientific theories.[35]

In calling such sentences "observational," Quine does not mean that they are uncontaminated by theory. It is one of Quine's claims that there is no pure given in experience—all experience involves conceptual elements. But he holds that there is a continuum running from the more strictly observational to the more strictly theoretical or conceptual, and what he calls "observational sentences" are at the observational end of this continuum.[36] Scientists regard statements such as, "This litmus paper is blue" as observational statements, despite their containing references to what Quine would term a "theoretical posit."

Quine gives a minimal definition of a theory as a set of logically consistent statements. It is possible, of course, to axiomitize such a theory in many different ways, all of which, being axiomitizations of the same theory, are logically equivalent. Any particular choice of an axiom set can be regarded as a theory formulation, and such a formulation can be treated as a single sentence that is the conjunction of the axioms. A "finite theory formulation" Quine defines as a theory formulation in which the number of axioms is finite.[37]

With these definitions established, Quine poses the following problem: If in some finite theory formulation we were to interchange two of its theoretical (i.e., non-observational) terms such as "electron" and "molecule," would the new theory formulation obtained by making this interchange be equivalent to the theory formulation before the interchange was made? Since the two theory formulations would say quite different things about molecules and electrons, they would not be logically equivalent. Yet it is quite clear that this sort of inequivalence is trivial; all we have done is to switch names while the theory itself is unchanged. The one theory formulation is indeed a mere notional variant of the other. To avoid such trivial inequivalences, Quine extends the notion of equivalence to include any two theory formulations that imply exactly the same observational sentences and are such that there is "a reconstrual of predicates that transforms the one theory into a logical equivalent of the other."[38]

Quine now states the Underdetermination Thesis as follows: "For any one (finite) theory formulation there is another that is empirically equivalent to it but logically incompatible with it, and cannot be rendered logically equivalent to it by any reconstrual of predicates."[39] This statement of the thesis can be construed in two different ways, one stronger than the other. The Weak Form of the Thesis is this: Suppose we have an infinite set of heterogeneous observation sentences and a finite theory formulation, T, from which all the observation sentences in the set are derivable. Then there exists an alternative theory formulation, T', logically incompatible with T and such that it cannot be reconciled with T by any reconstrual of predicates, but from which all the observation sentences in the set are also derivable. For example, suppose that at present we had a particular theory of gravitation, G. Then, if the Underdetermination Thesis is true, there must exist an alternative theory of gravitation, G', that is both logically incompatible and irreconcilable with G but which accounts for precisely the same observation sentences that G accounts for. This claim may or may not be true, but it is not a claim that would particularly upset most scientists. They would simply point out that this is precisely the reason why new observations must be sought that can be used to discriminate between the competing theories.

The Strong Form of the Underdetermination Thesis however is one which will upset scientists and many others. Quine supposes a spatio-temporal coordinate system for the entire universe. Then suppose each observational occasion sentence "expressible in our language"[40] to be paired to each combination of spatio-temporal coordinates so as to form standing sentences. From these we can then generate observational conditionals having one such standing sentence as antecedent and another as consequent. This set of observational conditionals will then constitute, according to Quine, all *possible* observational conditionals. Suppose now a finite theory formulation, T*, that accounts for all of these possible observational conditionals that are true. Then it is the claim of the Strong Form of the Underdetermination Thesis that there must exist an alternative finite theory formulation T! that accounts for just the same observational conditionals as T* but which is logically incompatible with T* and which cannot be reconciled with T* by any reconstrual of predicates.

Suppose that the Strong Form of the Underdetermination Thesis is true. Could we ever tell which of the two finite theory formulations, T* or T!, was true? Quine's answer is that we could not, for they are empirically equivalent theories of the world—they both account for all possible observation sentences. But since the two finite theory formulations are incompatible and irreconcilable, both cannot be true. What would "true" mean in such a situation? What could be said about reality? Would it even make sense to say that reality was knowable? Clearly, the Strong Form of the Underdetermination Thesis poses a fundamental challenge to traditional notions of truth, reality, and knowledge.

But Quine himself points out that the Underdetermination Thesis cannot be defended in so sweeping a form. There are cases where it clearly fails. If the number of observational conditionals is finite, or if all the observational conditionals are embraced in a finite number of universally quantified conditionals, the Thesis does not hold.[41] Quine therefore restricts the Thesis to cases where the number of observational conditionals is infinite and where their heterogeneity is such that the finite theory formulation accounting for them cannot be equivalent to a conjunction of a finite number of universally quantified conditionals.[42]

Yet even these restrictions are not enough. As Quine says

> We might study two incompatible theory formulations, trying in vain to imagine an observation that could decide between them, and we might conclude that they are empirically equivalent; we might conclude this without seeing a reconciling reconstrual of predicates. This we might; but there still could be a reconciling reconstrual of predicates, subtle and complex and forever undiscovered. The thesis of underdetermination, even in my latest tempered version, asserts that our system of the world is bound to have empirically equivalent alternatives that are not reconcilable by reconstrual of predicates however devious. This, for me, is an open question.
>
> Failing that, a last ditch version of the thesis of under-determination would assert merely that our system of the world is bound to have empirically equivalent alternatives which, if we were to discover them, we would see no way of reconciling by reconstrual of predicates. This vague and modest thesis I do believe. For all its modesty and vagueness, moreover, I think it vitally important to one's attitude toward science.[43]

This "last ditch version" of the Underdetermination Thesis seems at first rather tentative. Quine does not claim to have demonstrated its truth, nor indeed that it can be demonstrated, for it is certainly not clear how one could prove that there is no reconstrual of predicates which could transform seemingly incompatible and irreconcilable finite theory formulations into logically equivalent ones. But Quine does give us reasons for believing that this version of the Underdetermination Thesis is true. Scientific theories imply the observational conditionals they explain, but the converse is not true—the observational conditionals do not imply the theories. But it is a fact of logic that alternative theory formulations can imply the same observational conditionals. It therefore seems plausible to say that even in the case of all possible observational conditionals, there can be alternative theory formulations that can imply them. It is the nature of the logical relation between finite theory formulations and observational conditionals which gives the Underdetermination Thesis its plausibility.[44]

This plausibility, however, should not obscure the fact that there are important objections to the Underdetermination Thesis. If the Thesis is to hold, it must be possible to specify precisely what the members of the set of observational conditionals are. As Putnam has noted,

> When Quine speaks of the totality of all *possible observations*, he means the totality of all *true observation sentences*, i.e. of the totality of all *ordered pairs consisting of an observation sentence and a point in space-time at which that observation sentence could have been truly uttered*, whether or not someone was present at that point in space-time to truly utter it. He does not count counterfactual observation sentences . . . and *a fortiori*, he does not count sentences about what the outcomes of various experiments *would have been* if those experiments had been performed.[45]

But such sentences, Putnam argues, should be included. "As long as the theories imply different predictions about what *would* have happened *if* the experiment *had* been performed, then they are inequivalent, as most physicists understand the matter."[46]

Even this correction, however, is not enough, for there is a further problem in specifying the membership of this set. For the Strong Form of the Underdetermination Thesis to hold, it must apply to all possible observational conditionals—"all *possible* observations"[47] as Quine says—treated as a determinate although infinite set like the set of real numbers. But as we saw above, Quine's observation sentences are formulated in terms of "rabbits" and similar object terms which are not reducible to any collection of phenomenal properties. Among the objects that enter into scientific observations are a variety of scientific instruments. It is not news that observations in science are usually made either upon or by the help of instruments; it is also not news that there are constant changes occurring in the instrumentation that scientists use. New instruments are constantly being invented to replace older and less satisfactory ones. These instruments are themselves the results of scientific theories that determine their design and function. There is a constant interplay between scientific instrumentation and scientific theories; new theories lead to new instruments, which produce new observations, which help to generate new theories, and so on. As this process of instrument invention goes on, new terms are coined to refer to these instruments, and very often further terms are invented to refer to what is observed through the use of the instruments. Thus the language of science is continuously changing, just as scientific instruments, and science itself, change continuously. And that, of course, means that the observation sentences of science are also constantly changing. Twenty years ago a physicist tracking a particle would have been talking about the photograph of the tracks in a cloud chamber. Today, he would be discussing the computer constructed image derived from an electronic ionization detector. But when Quine generates his set of all possible observational conditionals by pairing each space-time point with "each observation sentence expressible in our language"[48], he takes "our language" to be unchanging and to be fixed independently of the scientific theories being compared. Thus "our language"—that is, the language spoken at time t—is used to formulate all possible observation sentences at all possible times. This might be a plausible strategy if Quine's observational conditionals were formulated in a phenomenalist vocabulary; it might be possible to argue that a phenomenalist vocabulary could be created that would suffice for the description of any phenomenon we can ever perceive. But this is not the way Quine has described observation sentences. In his description, the language in which observation sentences must be formulated will undergo repeated and unpredictable changes as theories and instrumentation evolve. It follows that no fixed set of observation sentences exists except at a particular time; when time is made variable the membership of the set also becomes variable.[49]

Quine could reply that since, under the Strong Form of the Underdetermination Thesis, all final theories of the world imply the same observation sentences, there could not be a difference in observation sentences among such theories due to instrumentation or anything else. But this puts the cart before the horse, for it assumes we have already reached theories that account for all observation sentences. But how can we know this, unless we already know what the set of all observation sentences is? Without such an antecedent specification of the membership of the set, the Underdetermination Thesis becomes circular. And no such antecedent specification is possible.

One answer to this objection would be to let the phrase "expressible in our language" refer to our language at time t—e.g., L_t. One could then treat time as variable and quantify over all times. Thus one would have the claim that, for every time t, if at t a theory T* accounts for all observation sentences expressible in L_t, then there exists a theory T! which does so as well. But in this formulation there is no final state, no last time. Hence although the empirical equivalence of T* and T! might prevail at t, there is no reason to believe that it would hold with different observation sentences at t+n, or for that matter that either T* or T! would continue to hold. It might indeed be the case that at t+n, there would be different alternative theories that would be empirically equivalent and account for all observation sentences in L_{t+n}, but then the same situation recurs at t+n+1. In other words, this move reduces the Strong Form of the Underdetermination Thesis to the Weak Form, and so renders it relatively harmless.

But if one interprets the quantifier collectively rather than distributively, one would end up with the set of all observation sentences ever held as true, including those that have since been rejected, either owing to errors in the observations themselves or to the use of obsolete instruments. The resulting set of observation sentences—of standing observational conditionals—would not be inconsistent, since observation sentences asserted at different time-space points cannot contradict each other—but it will also not be an acceptable scientific data-base. Better observations should replace inferior ones, not be added to them.

Quine could still argue that his method of characterizing observation sentences as those upon which witnesses will agree and which can be learned by ostension does not depend upon any particular language and does uniquely determine the set. But Quine's own arguments about the indeterminacy of ostension, and particularly about deferred ostension, would contradict such an argument.[50] Agreement of witnesses seems no more helpful as a basis for his position. As we have seen above, hypotheses and conceptualizations play a significant role in perception—hence perception is not wholly independent of language. Witnesses whose sensory receptors are similarly stimulated may use different observation sentences to describe their situations.[51] Moreover, whatever the sensory stimulations received, what will be perceived will depend to a considerable degree upon which stimulations the witnesses attend to.[52] This defense therefore does not seem adequate to support Quine's theory.

This objection—that Quine regards the set of all possible observation sentences as a fixed totality when in fact it is not—leads to a yet more basic problem. In presenting the Underdetermination Thesis, Quine takes it to be a thesis about science. But science is not just a matter of theories and observations; as C. S. Peirce was fond of pointing out, science is not identical with any particular bodies of knowledge. Rather, science is a process of inquiry—a process in which theories are generated to account for observational data, tested by observation and experiment, revised in terms of the results of such tests, retested, rerevised, and so on endlessly.[53] Theories lead to new observations by predicting what observational outcomes should occur if the theories are true. They also tell us how to manipulate natural phenomena to produce the predicted outcomes. In short, theories and observations are involved in a continuing process relation of inquiry, and that process is the heart of science.

Most scientists would have no hesitation in agreeing that, given some fixed body of observational data, alternative accounts can always be invented which will provide explanations of those data. But there is all the difference in the world between the ability of a theory to explain some pre-set body of observational data and its ability to predict accurately new observational phenomena previously unknown. It is the capacity of science to lead to new knowledge that particularly impresses scientists. Even if, for some set of already specified observational sentences, it is possible to create a theory that will give an explanation of them, it does not follow that such a theory can predict with accuracy new observations not hitherto known, or predict other observations that, although previously known, were not part of the set that the theory was created to explain. Scientist have always seen the acid test of a theory as its predictive power—its capacity to predict new observational data—or to account for observations that, even if previously known, were not considered relevant when the theory was formulated. Thus the precession of Mercury's orbit had been known long before Einstein developed relativity theory, but neither Einstein nor anyone else thought it relevant when relativity theory was created, and Einstein was surprised to find that his theory could account for it.[54]

If this characterization of science is accepted, then the Strong Form of the Underdetermination Thesis does not properly apply to science at all. The state that Quine envisages is one in which all possible observation sentences are explained—a state in which science, viewed as a process of inquiry, has been completed. The alternative theories described by Quine cannot be subjected to observational or experimental test if all observational and experimental outcomes are already explained; there is nothing new left to predict, no hitherto unexplained phenomena to be accounted for, no new discovery left to be made. This is not a case to which the process of scientific inquiry is applicable; it is a case of post-scientific knowledge in which there is nothing left to do except generate alternative theories to account for a fixed set of completed observations. This is of course exactly the sort of situation in which one would expect numerous alternative and competing theories to proliferate because any possibility of testing which of them is correct has been eliminated by fiat.

As we have already seen, given a situation in which there is a fixed body of observational data, it is no surprise that alternative theories can be created which are able to explain those data equally well. It may even be that many of these alternative theories are logically incompatible with each other and that they are pairwise irreconcilable by reconstrual of predicates.

But from the equivalence of these theories in explaining the fixed set of observational data, it does not follow that they will also be equivalent when it comes to predicting new and hitherto unknown phenomena or in accounting for observations whose relevance had not been previously detected. Hence the Underdetermination Thesis in its Weak Form is not a claim that will disturb scientists; it would simply indicate to them what they already knew, that new observational data must be found to permit a decision between the alternative theories. It is exactly this possibility of such a decision through further inquiry that is forbidden by the Strong Form of the Underdetermination Thesis. There can be no new observational data where all *possible* observations are already explained by all of the competing theories. But this attempt to terminate inquiry by fiat is illegitimate; it supposes the completion of a process of inquiry that is in fact indefinitely extended, so that no new observational phenomena can be found, it supposes that the set of all possible observation sentences is definable in terms of a given language at a particular time, despite the fact that the language itself is constantly changing as a result of scientific inquiry, and it supposes that once a sentence becomes a member of that set, it always remains a member of that set. Since none of these claims are justifiable, I suggest that the Underdetermination Thesis in its Strong Form must be rejected.

If the arguments presented above are sound, Quine has not shown that inquiry will not lead to a "best" theory. But what would such a "best" theory be? As C. S. Peirce pointed out over a century ago,[55] such a theory can be defined as one which, having emerged at some point in the process of scientific inquiry, will ever after be affirmed. This way of putting the matter involves no reference to any completed totality of observation sentences or any state of post-scientific knowledge. It does appear to assume that the process of inquiry will go on indefinitely—an assumption to which we will return—and it defines the best theory, if any, as that which will always meet the tests that arise in the course of inquiry. Moreover, such a definition fits well with the concept of confirmation discussed above. Confirmation is a process of testing a theory against alternative theories, and that theory is the better confirmed that makes all the known evidence more probable than do any of its rivals. The best theory may be defined, then, as that theory that always beats all challengers. This is simply a definition of the best theory; we have not shown that there actually is or will be a best theory, but if the Underdetermination Thesis is rejected, there is no reason to believe that a best theory is impossible. Of course, we could never know that a given theory was the best theory, since further tests would always be possible in the future. If we could know that our present theory was the best, we could have certain knowledge, and certainty is what we shall never have.

But the point is that the concept of a best theory can be defined without involving a state of post-scientific knowledge.

Incommensurable Theories

The argument thus far assumes that any two theories concerning the same subject matter are comparable. But relativists have challenged this assumption by arguing that there are "incommensurable" systems of belief. If that were so, it would be theoretically possible for there to be different but competing theories formulated in those systems which could never be tested against each other, and therefore among which no decision could be reached.

"Relativism" can mean a number of different things, and it is important to be clear just what the issue is. The question posed here does not involve the standard of truth; rather, the question is whether or not there are theories that cannot be tested against the usual scientific standard of truth because they cannot be compared to other theories. Much of the current fad of this sort of relativism stems from Thomas Kuhn's immensely popular book, *The Structure of Scientific Revolutions*. Kuhn did describe scientific theories before and after revolutions as being incommensurable, but if his later clarifications of his position had received the same attention as his earlier work, less radical conclusions might have been drawn from it. As Kuhn himself has remarked, "Most or all discussions of incommensurability have depended upon the literally correct but regularly over-interpreted assumption that, if two theories are incommensurable, they must be stated in mutually untranslatable languages."[56] A great deal here depends upon just what "translation" is taken to mean. As Kuhn notes,

> Translation is something done by a person who knows two languages. . . . The translation consists exclusively of words and phrases that replace (not necessarily one-for-one) words and phrases in the original. Glosses and translator's prefaces are not part of the translation, and a perfect translation would have no need for them.[57]

Obviously, this is an extraordinarily narrow definition of translation—one which no professional translator would accept. It comes close to seeing the two languages as notational variants of each other, as if Morse code were a translation of English. But as Kuhn stresses, this definition "is not mine."[58]

Translation so conceived must be distinguished from interpretation—a process in which the scholar may initially command only a single language and be faced with the problem of making sense of a text or language that he does not understand. "Quine's 'radical translator' is in fact an interpreter,"[59] and Kuhn attributes much of the obscurity of the recent debate over translation to Quine's failure to distinguish translation from interpretation. The interpreter does not simply substitute equivalent terms; if he succeeds, "What he or she has in the first instance done is learn a new language"[60] This is not the same as translating from one language into another.

Of course, the distinctions drawn here are polemical distinctions; no actual translator would accept this Morse code view of translation, and all would insist that the process of translation always involves interpretation. Nevertheless, for polemical purposes, the distinctions are useful because they enable Kuhn to articulate his view. Discussing phlogiston chemistry and Newtonian mechanics, Kuhn points out that some terms of these theories must be learned together as interconnected systems, and that their meanings in those theories cannot be simply equated with terms in current chemistry or physics. Some, like "phlogiston" have vanished from the scientific language; others, like "principle," have quite different meanings now than they had in the eighteenth century; still others, like "element," remain in use but with altered senses.[61] These terms refer to parts of an interconnected set of concepts in a now discarded scientific theory, and can only be understood in terms of that system as a whole. Obviously they cannot be incorporated into present scientific theories since the theory in terms of which they are defined is defunct.

This sort of "local holism" is what Kuhn means by "local incommensurability."[62] But he stresses that it is not confined to cases such as phlogiston. Word learning involves the use of contrast as well as similarity; to learn the reference of "geese" requires learning the reference of "swan" too, so words are generally learned in interrelated systems. But it is not reference alone that creates the problem; indeed, Kuhn stresses that much of the confusion that has arisen in these discussions has been owing to the determination of philosophers to stick to extensional languages. Kuhn puts his point as follows:

> Imagine, for a moment, that for each individual a referring term is a node in a lexical network from which radiate labels for the criteria that he or she uses in identifying the referents of the nodal term. Those criteria will tie some terms together and distance them from others, thus building a multi-dimensional structure within the lexicon. That structure mirrors aspects of the structure of the world which the lexicon can be used to describe, and it simultaneously limits the phenomena that can be described with the lexicon's aid.[63]

Kuhn holds that the reciprocal relations among these terms are implicated in their meanings, so that "None of them, taken by itself, has an independently specifiable meaning."[64]

But this structure, characteristic of a particular language, will usually not match exactly any lexical structure in another language. Hence it will be impossible to say in one language exactly what is said in another. But none of this implies that the languages are incomparable or mutually unintelligible.

> Translation is, of course, only the first resort of those who seek comprehension. Communication can be established in its absence. But where translation is not feasible, the very different processes of interpretation and language acquisition are required. These processes are not arcane. Historians, anthropologists, and perhaps small children engage in them every day. But they are not well understood, and their comprehension is likely to require the attention of a wider philosophic circle than the one currently engaged with them.[65]

To talk of incommensurability is not therefore to say systems or languages are incomparable or mutually unintelligible.

Davidson has also attacked the problem of interpretation—particularly of "radical interpretation," meaning the interpretation of expressions in a completely unknown tongue.[66] His approach has been to argue that a theory of radical interpretation can be built on the basis of Tarski's theory of truth. To do this, Davidson inverts Tarski's procedure; whereas Tarski assumed meaning (translation) in order to define truth, Davidson assumes truth in order to define, if not meaning, at least the knowledge necessary for interpretation. Thus consider a Tarski-type sentence (T-sentence) such as,

(1) 's' is true iff p,

where 's' is a structural description of a sentence s in the object language and 'p' is a translation of s. If we assume an understanding of "true," then (1) becomes the basis for a theory that, for any sentence in a language L, tells us the conditions under which that sentence is true. As Davidson remarks

> The definition works by giving necessary and sufficient conditions for the truth of every sentence, and to give truth conditions is a way of giving the meaning of a sentence. To know the semantic concept of truth for a language is to know what it is

for a sentence—any sentence—to be true, and this amounts, in one good sense we can give to the phrase, to understanding the language.[67]

To carry this out, Davidson replaces the requirement that p translate s by the requirement that p and s be materially equivalent.[68] "True" is then given an empirical interpretation as "held for true by speakers of L."[69] The sentences are then relativized to speakers and times in order to deal with demonstratives.[70] The result should be a theory covering all sentences of L held for true by speakers at given times and correlating them to the conditions under which they are held for true. Given the holistic character of the theory, it should then, Davidson believes, be possible to arrive at interpretations for particular sentential elements such as words.[71]

It is this requirement that the theory apply to all true sentences of the language that provides the protection against sentences such as:

(2) "Snow is white" is true iff grass is green.

Although "Snow is white" and "Grass is green" are materially equivalent, the fact that the theory also applies to "This is snow" and "This is white" Davidson claims will prevent the adoption of (2).[72] Such an approach can clearly be applied to an alien tongue provided we can identify when speakers of that tongue hold sentences for true.

Davidson's program has been the most discussed theory of radical interpretation in the recent philosophical literature. As Davidson is the first to admit, the program is as yet incomplete, although he believes substantial progress has been made.[73] Yet it is clear that Davidson has not provided a fully adequate formulation of a theory of interpretation.[74] Davidson himself comments in his later paper

> Even if everything I have said in defence of my formulation of what suffices for interpretation is right, it remains the case that nothing strictly constitutes a theory of meaning. A theory of truth, no matter how well selected, is not a theory of meaning. . . . [75]

Moreover, Davidson regards the interpretations yielded by the theory as at best underdetermined by the data, so that different interpretations apply equally to the same body of evidence.[76]

The process of interpretation is one in which an inquirer, confronted by utterances that are unfamiliar, seeks to explain what those phenomena mean. The fact that a language L_1 does not contain a string s_1 that is an exact equivalent for a sting s_2 of language L_2 shows that a translation (in the narrow sense used above) is impossible, but it does not show that one cannot explain in L_1 what s_2 means. An interpretation is a theory about the meaning of something; it does not necessarily produce an equivalent utterance that constitutes a translation. A given taxonomy in L_1 may not match any taxonomy in L_2; nevertheless, it may be possible to explain in L_1 what the taxonomy in L_2 is, what criteria it employs, and how and for what it is used. Obviously, interpretation depends on the resources available in the languages in question, but where those resources are rich, there is no reason to think that interpretation—even radical interpretation—is impossible.

As we have seen, meanings are conceptual cores, and, given the evidence supporting the existence of concepts as mental entities, they may be taken to be real. For unfamiliar utterances, if they are meaningful to their authors, there is a fact of the matter as to what they mean. We also know that human beings, by virtue of their native endowment, experience the world as a world of physical objects enduring in time and space. Ostension does therefore ground us in a shared world, not necessarily because the world is that way, but because being human we experience it that way. Similarly, we know that, by virtue of our biological nature, there are processes and actions common to all human beings. Predicates such as color terms or temperature terms—predicates referring to observable features—can be identified by the usual means of comparison and contrast, and functional predicates of observable actions similarly. These facts provide a basis from which to start in developing interpretative hypotheses. Clearly, these are empirical hypotheses that must be confirmed, but the general procedure lies within the scope of the hypothetical-deductive-inductive method of inquiry. The evidence of course will be behavior and linguistic usage, including what statements are held for true, once we know how to tell which statements these are. Thus Davidson's theory provides an important component of a theory of interpretation which helps us to extend our grasp of the alien tongue beyond words and sentences interpretable through simple ostension.

Part of what is appealing about Davidson's program is that it seems so obvious what the meaning of "Snow is white" must be when one can ostensively indicate the state of affairs to which it refers. But one can do this by ostension without Davidson's program. And indeed Davidson's program will not work at all unless one can do this. What Davidson's theory gives us in radical interpretation is a T-sentence for every sentence in the alien tongue without telling us what any one of these sentences means. It does not help us to know that "This is snow" is true iff this is snow unless we know what "this" and "snow" refer to, and nothing in the T-sentence alone, or all the T-sentences together, tells us that. The only way we can know what they refer to in these circumstances is by having them ostensively defined.

Davidson would no doubt reply that Tarski's semantic definition of truth is based on satisfaction and so requires that we know what sequences satisfy our sentences, including sentences such as, "This is snow." But in giving "true" the empirical interpretation "held for true by a speaker of L" in a situation where our only purchase on L is our ability to tell which ununderstood strings speakers hold for true, we sacrifice our knowledge of what the sentences are true of, unless that knowledge is added by ostension. Thus at the level of sentences about perceptibles, Davidson's program adds little to what we can do without it.

Where Davidson's program does add power is in cases such as Kuhn's example of phlogiston. Knowing that statements about phlogiston are held for true by speakers and refer to states of affairs believed to exist by the speakers is a vital step in coming to grasp the systems of interrelated terms which constitute the theory. As Kuhn points out, this sort of learning of systems of interrelated terms is typical of language learning generally. The young child learning taxonomies for colors or animals starts by taking the usage of the adult as its standard and adjusts criteria until it can match adult usage. So in interpreting an alien tongue, knowing what is held for true, particularly in cases where the referent is wholly or partially imperceptible by us, forces us to hypothesize systems of interrelated meanings and referents which will enable us to interpret as true those sentences that the native speakers hold for true.

My objection to Davidson's theory is not that it fails to explain the meaning of alien utterances, although Davidson himself admits that his theory does not issue in a theory of meaning, but that his theory does not utilize all the resources we have for providing interpretations. What we now know about human cognition and human culture provides bases for interpreting alien utterances that give greater access to the alien meanings than Davidson allows. Further, it is not clear how by Davidson's theory we ever come to know what the alien speakers hold for true, whereas if we can start with the certainty that they do hold certain kinds of beliefs (e.g., about physical objects) that will be true for them, it is much easier to see how we can acquire this crucial knowledge. Davidson's approach then becomes an important supplement that helps us to extend our interpretive hypotheses further.

Indeed, it is not at all clear that such an interpretive theory about an alien language is underdetermined in any sense except that in which all empirical theories are, namely, that it cannot be certain but must always remain open to correction. Specifically, there is no reason to see Quinean underdetermination in this case. The alien language provides an infinite set of strings against which to test our understanding. Given the initial interpretations based on human commonalities, we can extend our knowledge as we learn which strings are held for true, which are held for grammatical, which are held to refer to observables, which are held for true on the basis of others, and so forth. There is nothing in this picture to show that an accurate understanding of the alien language cannot be attained. Interpretive theories are no different than other theories that seek truth about matters of fact.

Real translation—translation as actually practiced—presupposes interpretation.[77] To translate from one language to another, one must know both. If one rejects as unrealistic the Morse code model of translation, one has to deal with the fact that some relational structures of the source language will not be isomorphic to those of the target language. This is why translators insist that translation is at least in part an interpretive process. It is often not possible simultaneously to preserve in translation the "propositional meaning" (on the basis of which the sentence is true or false), the "expressive meaning" (the expressions of feeling and attitude of the speaker), and the "evoked meaning" (arising from dialect or register variation); so the translator must make compromises among these.[78] There are well-known grammatical differences between languages—such as pronominal systems that in some languages convey deference or familiarity they do not convey in others[79]—and many problems in matching thematic structure. As Baker notes, "Certain features of syntactic structure such as restrictions on word order, the principle of end-weight, and the natural phraseology of the target language often mean that the thematic organization of the source text has to be abandoned."[80] The most that a professional translator will claim for a translation of an utterance is that the meaning of the translated text approximates that of the text being translated; the perfect translation is an illusory goal.[81]

But what follows from these facts about translation is not incomparability or unintelligibility between languages. It is quite one thing to say that a string in the source language has the same meaning as a string in the target language; it is quite another to explain in the target language what the string in the source language means. This may very well involve explaining in detail what the associations of the elements in the original string are and how they differ from comparable ones in the target language—a statement about that string, not a statement that is equivalent to that string. It may also involve borrowing terms from the source language and creating the concept to which they refer by explaining the similarities, contrasts, and causal relations that underly those concepts. This is as Kuhn notes a process of language learning—indeed, of concept learning; that this can be done is proven by the fact that speakers of the source language also had to learn the term and/or concept in the just this way. After all, how did Priestley learn the phlogiston theory, if not by methods of this sort? The lack of equivalence between terms of the source and target languages does not show that the target language cannot be employed as a metalanguage to explain the reference and meaning of the terms in the source language. Interpreting is not identical with translating.

There is no ground for saying that two theories that are "incommensurable"—that is, which contain systems of interrelated terms that cannot be perfectly mapped into each other—are mutually unintelligible or incomparable. The Einsteinian Revolution in physics was surely a scientific revolution if ever there was one, and Kuhn has shown that terms such as "mass" have different meanings in Einsteinian and Newtonian physics. But it is also quite clear that these theories were, and are, compared; that from them incompatible predictions concerning empirical phenomena were derived, such as the behavior of light in the gravitational field of the sun; and that Einsteinian physics supplanted Newtonian physics primarily on the basis of its superiority in predicting and explaining certain empirical phenomena. None of this calls into question Kuhn's contention that other factors were also involved and that something like a conversion experience or a gestalt switch occurred for scientists as they transferred allegiance from one theory to the other. But Kuhn has never suggested, so far as I know, that adherents of one theory did not understand the other; surely Einstein understood Newton's theory, even though he rejected it. There is no ground for holding that different theories cannot be tested against each other and a decision between them reached, given that there is an agreed-upon standard of truth. A true relativist would object that this final qualification begs the question; it does not beg the question raised here, but it does beg the question of the relativity of truth standards. That, however, is another question, to which we will return below.

Davidson has attacked the claim that there can be incommensurable conceptual schemes, and I would like to consider his argument in some detail because his rejection of the conceptual scheme–content distinction seems to me a mistake. Davidson takes a conceptual scheme to be identical with a language, and further holds that intertranslatable languages have the same conceptual scheme.[82] Thus, translatability is for him a criterion for commensurability. He then points out that talk of relativity in physics (e.g., relative position) makes sense only in terms of a basic coordinate system or reference point, and asks what such a reference point would be for conceptual schemes. His answer is that the reference point used by relativists is empirical content:

> The idea is then that something is a language, and associated
> with a conceptual scheme, whether we can translate it or not, if
> it stands in a certain relation (predicting, organizing, facing or
> fitting) to experience (nature, reality, sensory promptings). The
> problem is to say what the relation is, and to be clearer about
> the entities related.[83]

The relations proposed by the relativists, he argues, come down to organizing or fitting, and the entities the conceptual scheme organizes or fits to reality or experience. Davidson then examines whether or not conceptual schemes, so understood, can be either totally or partially incommensurable.

Against the possibility of total incommensurability, Davidson argues that for a scheme to organize something, that thing must consist of individuated parts. Whether it is reality or experience that is being organized, it must in either case be individuated; if we are to know whether another conceptual scheme individuates either of those in a way different from our own, we must have some basis in shared extensions against which the differences can be marked. If there were no such basis, we could not tell that the conceptual scheme was a conceptual scheme or a language.[84] Since for Davidson individuation is done by a language, to say we know how another conceptual scheme individuates the world is to say we can translate that language, which contradicts the claim of incommensurability. Fitting as a relation of conceptual schemes to empirical content, Davidson argues, is a matter of reality or experience providing evidence for sentences and theories.[85] But Davidson argues that "the notion of fitting the totality of experience, like the notions of fitting the facts, or being true to the facts, adds nothing intelligible to the simple concept of being true."[86] Following Tarski, Davidson says, "The sentence 'My skin is warm' is true if and only if my skin is warm. Here there is no reference to a fact, a world, an experience, or a piece of evidence"; but in this case, "The criterion of a conceptual scheme different from our own now becomes: largely true but not translatable."[87] But, Davidson argues, this is unintelligible since Tarski's Convention T requires that in "'s' is true iff p," "p" be either in English or translatable into English. We could not make sense of a sentence being true but not translatable. Davidson therefore rejects the idea of a totally incommensurable conceptual scheme; the idea itself he thinks is incoherent.

What of partial incommensurability? Like Quine, Davidson holds that we can know that people hold a sentence true without knowing what they mean by the sentence or what belief it represents.[88] But, Davidson argues,

What matters is this: if all we know is what sentences a speaker holds true, and we cannot assume that his language is our own, then we cannot take even a first step toward interpretation without knowing or assuming a great deal about the speaker's beliefs. Since knowledge of beliefs comes only with the ability to interpret words, the only possibility at the start is to assume general agreement on beliefs.[89]

We have as it were one equation in two unknowns—concepts and beliefs; to solve for one we must assume the other. Hence, "when others think differently from us, no general principle, or appeal to evidence, can force us to decide that the difference lies in our beliefs rather than in our concepts."[90] Thus even with only partial incommensurability, we could not tell when another's beliefs were different from ours. Hence Davidson concludes that the dualism of scheme and content is unintelligible, and therefore so is the notion of incommensurable schemes.

There are a number of points on which I must disagree with this analysis. First, conceptual schemes are not identical with families of inter-translatable languages. As we have seen, a language can express a conceptual scheme, although it may do so incompletely. Moreover, there can be multiple conceptual schemes in one language. Those scientific systems for which Kuhn has claimed incommensurability are all stateable in English. Whorfian claims notwithstanding, a language is not the same as a conceptual scheme.

Second, the individuation of the experienced world into objects is not done by language; it is done by cognitive mechanisms that are apparently innate. There is therefore an experienced world to be organized that is common across cultures. This individuated world of objects forms a basis against which other differences in organizing and classification can be discerned.

Third, Davidson's reading of Tarski is a bit swift. Davidson's assertion here rests on his argument in an earlier article where, following Tarski, he maintains that the satisfaction of the schema "x loves y" consists in having a function f that assigns to x those things that are lovers of those things that f assigns to y. Davidson says

Thus "Dolores loves Dagmar" would be satisfied by Dolores and Dagmar (in that order), provided Dolores loved Dagmar. I suppose Dolores and Dagmar (in that order) is not a fact either—the fact that verifies "Dolores loves Dagmar" should somehow include the loving. This "somehow" has always been the nemesis of theories of truth based on facts.[91]

Thus Davidson believes Tarski's method of defining truth by satisfaction allows "truth" to express a relation between language and the world without requiring any "facts" or other intermediaries.

The problem with this is that, as Davidson is well aware, the trick works by separating "true" from "true of." Thus Davidson explicates "satisfies" by "a function satisfies an unstructured n-place predicate with variables in its n places if the predicate is *true of* the entities (in order) that the function assigns to those variables."[92] But what does this mean? Davidson holds truth to be a relation between language and the world. Assigning entities in the world as values of the variables of the linguistic schema is such a relation, but not one which alone yields truth; the predicates must in addition be *true of* the entities assigned. This cannot be explicated by saying that "loves" is *true of* Dolores and Dagmar (in that order) only if the sentence "Dolores loves Dagmar" is true without abandoning the attempt to define "true" in terms of "true of."

What then makes the predicate *true of* this couple? The predicate "loves" is a linguistic entity; love is an emotional relation between people in the world. What "true of" does here is to say that the entities designated by the variables stand in the peculiar emotional relation referred to by the predicate. It is the existence of that non-linguistic relation in the world among those entities that makes the predicate *true of* them. Once that is established, it is clearly no great step to defining "truth" in terms of "true of." But what this comes down to is saying that the linguistic expression, "Dolores loves Dagmar," is true if and only if Dolores stands in the particular non-linguistic emotional relation of loving to Dagmar. Whether one wants to call the right side of the biconditional a "fact" or not is perhaps a matter of definition, but it is clearly what I would call a "state of affairs." That state of affairs must obtain for the sentence to be true. Or, better, the sentence being true shows that that state of affairs really obtains. How we know that the sentence is true is a matter of what experiences we have which confirm the sentence.

Davidson would object that under this construction a sentence would refer to a state of affairs, and that, "There are very strong reasons, as Frege pointed out, for supposing that if sentences, when standing alone or in truth-functional contexts, name anything, then all true sentences name the same thing."[93] I would not agree that sentences "name" although I believe that they refer to states of affairs. But the basic problem is that Frege's famous argument depends upon the principle that logically equivalent sentences designate the same thing. This principle is manifestly false. "All men are mortal" and "The planets move in elliptical orbits" are alike in truth-value, but they clearly refer to quite different states of affairs. The problems involved here are enormously complex and lie far beyond the scope of this work, but their difficulty does not justify adopting a principle that leads to a raft of absurd conclusions.[94]

Partial incommensurability, as Davidson construes it, comes down to the case in which we know that the speaker of another language holds certain sentences to be true but we know neither what he believes nor what he means. This amounts to Quine's case of radical translation. In order to develop any translation at all, Davidson holds, we must assume some foundation in agreement of beliefs, and work from there to expand the basis of shared language. Disagreement can then be attributed either to differences in belief or to differences in meaning, "but when others think differently from us, no general principle, or appeal to evidence, can force us to decide that the difference lies in our beliefs rather than in our concepts."[95]

Here again the fact that we know human beings individuate the world into objects and that linguistic terms for such objects are learned by ostension provides an entree into the linguistic system which is not arbitrary. Of course, we may make errors about which terms apply to what things, but these sorts of errors can be eliminated by multiplying examples. Where we find that speakers of another tongue have extensions for their terms that do not correspond to those for English terms, we are clearly dealing with an alien classification scheme to be mastered by trying to discover the basis for the taxonomy. Thus a native group may classify its local flora in ways quite different from any we have previously experienced. As we begin to learn the syntax, so that we can produce sentences involving relations among terms, we can vary terms in a context or contexts while holding a term fixed, and so develop an understanding of what is believed about what. Thus if "sarit" refers to one type of seed pod and "sorda" to another, if "sarit" pods are eaten while "sorda" pods are not, and if pretending to eat a "sorda" pod elicits a negative response from natives, we shall not be far off in concluding that they believe "sarit" to be food and "sorda" not, as least for humans. Why this distinction is made will be a problem to be solved, but that it is made is clear. In short, Quine's hypothetical case of radical translation creates the problem it does by underestimating what is shared by humans in their cognition of the world. There is a basis here upon which to build, step by step, an interpretation of others' language and an understanding of their conceptual scheme.

The conceptual scheme–empirical content distinction does make sense. The problems with it are generated by identifying conceptual schemes with languages and underestimating the amount of common ground shared by humans. There can be multiple conceptual schemes in a given language, and different languages can express the same conceptual scheme. Where two conceptual schemes or languages have taxonomies that are not co-extensional, one cannot translate from one to the other by substituting, for a term of one, a term of the other with the same extension. But as we saw above, that does not mean that one cannot correctly interpret in one language what is being said in the other.

That different cultures have different systems of belief is simply a fact, to which a mountain of anthropological data attests. But it is also a fact that we can understand other cultures and their beliefs. Anything one human being can learn, another of comparable intelligence can also learn. It may be that, should we ever contact intelligent life forms from another star system—life forms with different senses, different cognitive processes, different emotions—we may find ourselves faced with a conceptual scheme of which we cannot make any sense. But it seems safe to say that such a situation will not arise among human beings here on Earth. Cultural differences exist and have existed, but if we have adequate access to members of those cultures, we can learn to understand their language, their world view, and their culture.

Relativism therefore does not pose a problem for the position taken here. We can understand, or learn to understand, alternative theories even when couched in different conceptual schemes from our own. These alternatives may then become competitors among which a decision must be made by further empirical test and observation. Relativism does not resurrect the Underdetermination Thesis.

Realism and the Best Theory

But defining the notion of a "best" theory is not enough; what grounds are there for believing that there is, or can be, a "best" theory? Granted that Quine's proof to the contrary fails, what reason is there to believe that the process of inquiry will lead to a theory that will ever after be affirmed? Why should we not yield to what has been called "the pessimistic induction"—that since every past theory has proven false, every future theory will also prove false?[96] Surely the contrary claim smacks of the traditional view of science as "progressive."

The issue of whether or not there is progress in science has been hotly debated since Kuhn published his book on scientific revolutions in 1962. The old model of the growth of science, according to which step by step the false statements of science are overturned to be replaced by ever more true ones, thus producing a type of smooth asymptotic approach to the true theory, was shown by Kuhn to be inconsistent with what actually happens in scientific revolutions. As he demonstrated, the new theories that emerge victorious from scientific revolutions are radically different from their predecessors, not purified versions of them. Kuhn's theory was explicitly evolutionary. He saw new paradigm theories as created to resolve accumulating anomalies that had been generated in the course of normal research and that the previous paradigm theory had been unable to explain. Kuhn particularly stressed the fact that the process of evolution in science, like that in biology, has no goal (such as the truth) but is essentially directionless. Thus in the Kuhnian view, the evolution of science is a process that alternates between periods of relatively stable growth (normal science) and periods of radical change (revolutionary science) without end or final cause, and without the later stages of the process being in any sense "truer" than the earlier ones.

There are two problems with this description of the history of science which are particularly troubling. The first is Kuhn's description of the process of change in scientific thought. The problem is brought out most clearly when one contrasts the history of science with the history of theology. In theology as in science, it is possible to identify paradigmatic theories (Calvinism, for example), periods of "normal research" (e.g., the elaboration of Edwardsean theology in the century after Edwards), and periods of "revolution" (e.g., the Reformation). But what one finds in theology, but not in science, is an endless proliferation of competing and incompatible theories, each claiming to be true. Thus the history of Calvinism in America is a history of one schism after another, the result being a large number of sectarian and denominational groups that hold incompatible doctrines. This is indeed fortuitous variation without natural selection. But this is not what one finds in science. As Kuhn showed, when a new paradigm theory emerges, the scientific community eventually reunites under its banner and a new era of normal research begins. The scientific community does not divide into proliferating "schools" each with its own pet paradigm. The reason for this, according to Kuhn, lies in the peculiar characteristics of the scientific community. But Kuhn has never been able to explain what those peculiar characteristics of the scientific community are, so the fact that such unity is always reestablished remains a mystery.

Quine is also well aware of this problem. If Quine's Underdetermination Thesis were true, what one would expect to find in the history of science is precisely what one finds in the history of theology—a constant proliferation of empirically equivalent but incompatible and irreconcilable theories—an evolution characterized by ever-diverging and exclusive research traditions. Since this is not at all what the history of science shows, Quine seeks to account for that as follows:

> Terminology aside, what wants recognizing is that a physical theory of radically different form from ours, with nothing even recognizably similar to our quantification or objective refer-

ence, might still be empirically equivalent to ours, in the sense of predicting the same episodes of sensory bombardment on the strength of the same past episodes. Once this is recognized, the scientific achievement of our culture becomes in a way more impressive than ever. For, in the midst of all this formless freedom for variation, our science has developed in such a way as to maintain always a manageably narrow spectrum of visible alternatives among which to choose when need arises to revise a theory. It is this narrowing of sights, or tunnel vision, that has made for the continuity of science, through the vicissitudes of refutation and correction. And it is this also that has fostered the illusion of there being only one solution to the riddle of the universe.[97]

What, "in the midst of all this formless freedom for variation," accounts for the continuity of science? Quine's answer is that our culture somehow induces "tunnel vision" or a "narrowing of sights." Somehow, but how? Quine does not explain this process; he merely describes it. Nor is this sort of "tunnel vision" unique to science. Anthropologists and historians have long since noted that cultures involve particular theoretical orientations toward the world, which play an important part in determining their development through time; under the right conditions such a theoretical orientation may achieve a steady state that can persist across a number of generations.[98] However, such theoretical orientations do not normally lead to greater power over nature or adequacy of prediction in the long run, although they may do so in the short run. On the contrary, the common outcome of such "tunnel vision" has been fairly rapid failure after a brief period of success. Conditions change; what had been adaptive ceases to be so; new problems arise with which the theoretical orientation cannot cope; cultural crises result.

Quine's "narrowing of sights" is similar to a process that Kuhn describes within science itself. Once a new paradigm has been adopted by the scientific community, it serves to define the problems, methods, instrumentation, and goals of the community and inaugurates a new period of normal research. But as Kuhn stresses, it is characteristic of normal research that, however progressive it may appear to those involved in it, it sooner or later generates those anomalies that lead to the breakdown of its own paradigm and so produces crisis and revolution.[99] The revolution ends one tradition of normal research and inaugurates a different one; after the revolution we are in a different "tunnel."[100] Thus, while what Quine calls a "narrowing of sights" may in some sense describe the course of science between revolutions, it does not help us to understand why the scientific community reforms behind a new paradigm after the revolution. If the growth of science is a Darwinian process of evolution, as Kuhn suggests, what is the selective factor that kills off the variants? Neither Quine nor Kuhn provide us with an answer to this problem.

The second problem is that whatever one may hold about the process of change in scientific theories, Kuhn has never denied that in science there is progress of a sort; our scientific theories of today have vastly more *power*, understood as the ability to control and manipulate nature, and far greater *adequacy*, understood as the ability to predict and explain our experience, than did those that preceded them. The course of scientific development may not be "progressive" in the pre-Kuhnian sense, but it is incontestable that, as science has developed, it has dramatically expanded our power over nature. Indeed, the most remarkable characteristic of science is the degree to which it has expanded in power and adequacy over time. Moreover, no such advance in power and adequacy is to be observed in some other areas of thought such as theology. Despite the fact that religion, and therefore some form of theology, appears to long predate even the introduction of writing, I doubt that many today would claim theology has greater power or adequacy than it has had in earlier periods of human history.

That science has followed a narrow course of development rather than fragmenting into multiple conflicting schools, and that science has shown a quite steady increase in power and adequacy over the course of its development are facts about science which I believe no one contests. Neither Kuhn's theory nor Quine's offers any acceptable explanation of these facts. How then are they to be explained?

As a theory to account for these features of science, let us suppose the following:

(1) There exists a reality having a definite structure, major portions of which are relatively constant over time.

(2) We interact with that reality (of which we are a part) in ways that produce experienced effects in us.[101]

Suppose that we seek to investigate that reality by using those methods that have thus far served us so well in science; what sort of knowledge would we need to obtain to be able to explain, predict, and control that reality and its interrelations and interactions with us? I think few would doubt that we would be most successful in achieving these objectives if we could create a theoretical model that gave us a complete and accurate picture of the nature and structure of that reality. A model of this sort would provide us with a comprehensive knowledge of reality and of the experiences of the real that we can expect or induce. This is of course the correspondence theory of truth, which has generally been associated with philosophical Realism. Let us call such a world theory that is true in the correspondence theory sense of "true" the theory T_c.

Would the Best Theory, as previously defined, be identical with T_c? It would not. Recall that our reality is a hypothesis to account for such phenomena as the success of science. It would certainly make little sense to hypothesize for this purpose the existence of domains of reality which would be irrelevant to human experience and which could therefore never be known. But our hypothesized reality will nevertheless involve states and events of which our experience will necessarily be incomplete. Thus consider the following statement:

(3) There is a planet in the Andromeda galaxy on which roses grow.

I think it is safe to say that we will never be able to verify or falsify this statement. Yet according to our present astronomical theory, the Andromeda galaxy is a real galaxy; either some stars in that galaxy have planets or no stars in that galaxy have planets. In the latter case, (3) is false; in the former, either there is a planet on which roses grow or there is not. Hence (3) is either true or false, but undecidable.

The truth or falsity of (3) is not the result of having assumed bivalence as a premise. Indeed, the theory of truth presented above is not based on classical logic and does not involve bivalence. The hypothesis of the existence of a definite reality arises here within a theory accounting for certain aspects of our experience. It is a consequence of that hypothesis that aspects of that reality exist which are matters of fact but about which, given our temporal, spatial, and other relations to those facts, we will never know more than that they must exist or have existed. Bivalence holds here, not with respect to all statements, but with respect to all statements referring to a reality that we postulate to be determinate. This is not a gratuitous metaphysical assumption; it is a consequence of the reality hypotheses, themselves empirically warranted, and scientific theories, such as those of astronomy, also empirically warranted. The fact that (3) has a determinate truth value, although we can never know what it is, is a consequence of our theory, not a presupposition of our theory.

What then is the truth status of the Best Theory? We have seen that the Best Theory cannot be identical to T_c—the perfect correspondence theory. Can it still be true? Certainly it can. The Best Theory will not be an absolutely complete description of every detail of the real, since there will be sentences whose truth values we will never discover. Thus the iron atoms in my blood must have been produced in a supernova, or some number of supernovas, but it is quite inconceivable that we shall ever know which supernovas these were. But an incomplete theory is not a false theory. There is no contradiction between knowing some things truly about a subject and not knowing everything about that subject. We can know what we have sufficient evidence for. Given adequate evidence we can confirm or disconfirm our theories—that is, show that one is superior to another. That is all that the notion of the Best Theory requires.

But does not the notion of a Best Theory contradict Kuhn's account of the development of scientific theories? I think not. The view of science that Kuhn attacked was the model of a smooth asymptotic approach to the truth—a view according to which each scientific theory is a closer approximation to the truth than its predecessor, so that although we may never actually attain the truth, still the truth serves as the limit to which our series of theories converges. This was of course a view based on the analogy to mathematical convergence and it was never more than metaphoric; no one ever provided a measure of distance in terms of which this notion of convergence could be defined. Kuhn has shown that this classical view will not do.[102] However, it is also true that as scientific inquiry proceeds through time, our scientific theories do become more powerful and more adequate. One can therefore still speak of scientific progress, meaning that scientific theories acquire increasing power and adequacy as the process of inquiry continues. Yet as Kuhn has shown, the sequence of theories characterized by this increase in power and adequacy does not show any apparent progression toward a final form or limit. Indeed, the theories produced by successive scientific revolutions are radically unlike each other.

Whatever reality there may be must therefore be complex enough so that various conceptualizations of it are possible depending upon how we approach it, what hypotheses we apply to it, and what experiences we have of it. It is in fact not hard to cite examples where just this sort of process has occurred. The history of astronomy provides an excellent case in point. Despite the earlier writings of the Pythagoreans,[103] the point at which one can probably first speak of an astronomical theory is with the work of Eudoxus in the fourth century B.C., in which the doctrine of the homocentric spheres was systematically developed. The theory was further refined by Kalippus and became the basis of Aristotle's astronomy.[104] One has here the basic idea of a stationary Earth at the center of the universe, and surrounding the Earth a series of concentric spheres with the planets and stars so attached to those spheres that their observed motion are accounted for by the rotations of the spheres. The outstanding anomaly facing this theory was the variation in the brightness of the planets, and it was probably this that led Apollonius in the third century B.C. to propose eccentric orbits and Aristarchus of Salmos a bit later to propose the first known heliocentric theory.[105] Thus the line of development from Eudoxus to Aristarchus, while hardly an asymptotic approach to the modern theory, shows a clear progression in that direction. But this line of development was not pursued; instead, the epicyclic theory developed by Appolonius of Perge, Hipparchus, and Ptolemy became the reigning paradigm in large part because of its ability to explain the stations and retrogressions of the planets.[106] For over one thousand years, the Ptolemaic theory was the accepted theory in Europe, despite the fact that as normal research elaborated this theory, even its adherents ceased to believe that it corresponded to physical reality. Not until Copernicus published in 1543 was the heliocentric theory revived, and not until Kepler's work appeared did the superiority of the heliocentric theory really become clear.

Compared to many other physical phenomena, the motions of the six interior planets and the moon are not very complex—at least until the problem of interactions among the planets is introduced, which was well after Kepler's time. Yet look how wayward was the course astronomical theory followed in creating an accurate model of this system. There is clearly no smooth approach to the truth in the manner called for by the asymptotic approximation theory. But what is clear is that with a constantly increasing body of observational knowledge—especially that created by Brahe—the correct theory did eventually emerge, despite the wayward course of development. To say that scientific investigation will lead to a "best" theory, it is not necessary to hold that there will be any sort of "smooth" convergence to a limit. All that is necessary, as Peirce noted, is to say that a theory will emerge that will ever after be affirmed.

But is the notion of a Best Theory a tenable notion? Certainly it seems to involve a radical idealization, namely, an infinite process of inquiry. Clearly that idealization does not fit the facts. The world will end someday, and the human race will die out—probably long before the world ends. But an ideal definition does not require that the actual process of inquiry be infinite; what it requires is that if the process of inquiry were indefinitely extended it would yield a Best Theory. Why should one believe that? We drew the contrast above between the development of theology and that of science. The development of theology does resemble the sort of evolutionary process described by Kuhn, without any principle of selection. Hence one gets proliferating theories, and the proliferation is unchecked. But in the case of science, however one wants to account for the emergence of new theories, the critical point is that the old theories die out—there is a selective principle at work.

What is that selective principle? Kuhn's attempt to find it in the social structure of the scientific community and Quine's notion of tunnel vision have not worked. What then is the selective factor? The obvious answer is the real world. If scientific theories do attempt to describe the nature of at least some portion of the real, then it is reasonable to hold that some theories do that better than others, and that those theories that do it best confer on their adherents greater power and adequacy than do others. Given that the goal of scientists is to develop true theories about reality (and that is a factual statement well supported by evidence), those theories that explain the most and confer the greatest power and adequacy are preferred to others. Thus this theory does explain why the course of development of science should be so different from the course of development of other theoretical fields like theology (on the assumption, obviously, that either God is not real or that statements about God are undecidable). As Hilary Putnam (in one of his incarnations) has remarked, "The positive argument for realism is that it is the only philosophy that doesn't make the success of science a miracle."[107]

It will be objected that since all theories are stronger than their empirical components (i.e., the observation sentences of the theory), two different theories may have the same observational component, and that therefore there can be no single Best Theory. This is, of course, the objection of the Underdetermination Thesis, and the answer to it has already been given in part, namely, the fact that two incompatible theories explain the same set of observations does not imply that they will be equally successful in predicting new observations or explaining other observations not in the set. Hence as long as the process of inquiry continues, it will be possible to decide among different theories on the basis of the new observations they predict.

But one may now go further. Our theories purport to describe the real. On the basis of our earlier assertions (1) and (2), theories that differ in their theoretical posits give us different pictures of the real, and to the degree that they are incompatible, those pictures are incompatible. That is, if (1) and (2) are correct, the non-observational portions of our theories are not simply arbitrary devices for manipulating the observational component, but are hypotheses about how the world really is. It seems clear that a theory correctly describing the actual nature of some portion of the real will provide a far better basis for predicting new features of its behavior than a theory that does not. Indeed, if our theory about a given segment of reality is true, we should be able to predict its behavior accurately. But to the degree that the alternative theories are incompatible with the true theory, they give incompatible and false descriptions of that segment of reality. This should mean that they will be less successful in predicting what our experience of that reality will be. There is thus reason to believe that if the process of inquiry were to be indefinitely extended, a Best Theory would emerge.

If this argument is accepted, then it follows that our best confirmed theory at a given time is our best estimate at that time of the Best Theory, or the true theory. As we saw, our best-confirmed theory at a given time can be horrendously wrong; it may even be less accurate than a theory previously held and rejected. There is no smooth convergence. But if the process of inquiry continues, we are justified in believing that eventually a Best Theory will be found. We can never be justified in claiming that our current best confirmed theory is true, since further investigation may reveal errors in it, but we can also not be sure that our current theory is not true. Recognizing the fallibility of our knowledge, nevertheless the best estimate we can now make of the truth is our present best-confirmed theory.

I have argued above that the basis from which inquiry starts is experience. It is not claimed that experience is a pure "given"; we have seen evidence to the contrary. Nor does it make any sense to say that experience is "true" or "false." Experience just is; theory laden or not, it is the basis from which we start. The problem is to explain it. What experience is is expressed in perceptual judgments. As has been noted, perceptual judgments are not all of a kind. "There is a table there" is a perceptual judgment, but since it is also a real-object statement, it can be false. "I see a table there" is a statement about what I see, and whether there really is a table there or not, if I saw one then the report of what I saw is right—it accurately reports my experience. If the table was an illusion, I had an experience of an illusory table; the difference is in the nature of the object I experienced, not in the experience itself. Of course a perceptual judgment can be wrong if I lied about my experience, but it is very hard to see how it can be wrong if it is a sincere description of what my experience was at a given moment. Perceptual judgments describe our experience, whether of purple spades or searing pain.

The objective of inquiry is the explanation of experience. If experience simply is, it is not at all clear what it is, or why it has the characteristics that it does. This means, of course, that we seek to explain experience as it is described in our perceptual judgments: These statements give us a verbal formulation of what our experience is. And to explain our experience is to develop causal theories to explain what we experience and why. The theory of physical objects gives a causal explanation for many of our experiences; we see a table at a given time and place because there is a table at that time and place and we are so situated that we can observe it. It makes no difference here whether our proclivity to see physical objects is due to a preformation system or not. At this level, the postulation of physical objects does explain our experience and that is the relevant point.

If a theory is better confirmed that any rival theory, it is the best explanation we have of some portion of our experience. As applied to a theory, confirmation is a holistic property, and applies to the entire theory. If the theory contains statements asserting the existence of certain entities, then the confirmation of the theory is also a confirmation of those assertions. Quantum theory says that there are neutrinos, and quantum theory is well confirmed; therefore, the claim that there are neutrinos is well confirmed.

If a theory is true, then whatever is said to exist in that theory is real. The description of the world, or a particular part of the world, given by a true theory is a description of the world as it really is. Reality in other words is what is postulated to exist in a true theory. I am not here assuming a pre-existing reality as a premise; rather, I am defining reality as what is postulated to exist in a true theory. It might be objected that this position compromises the independence of the real—that is, makes the real depend on what we think. This is not so. If our true theory holds that the real is independent of our knowledge about it, then since the real is what the true theory says it is, reality is indeed independent of what we think about it. Unless the true theory should hold that the human mind creates reality by thinking about it—a possibility which today seems remote—nothing in this theory compromises the independence of the real.

The postulation of a real world is an essential part of our theory to explain our experience and its characteristics. And one striking feature of our experience is the behavior of science itself. It is certainly one of the most remarkable characteristics of the scientific enterprise that over time it has produced theories of steadily increasing power and adequacy, and that instead of fragmenting into different schools or sects devoted to different but incompatible theories, the scientific community has repeatedly united behind new paradigms. To account for these characteristics of science it seems necessary to postulate a reality the nature of which is partially but increasingly revealed by scientific inquiry. It is the existence of that reality and the behavior of scientists toward it which accounts for these characteristics of science, and which justifies our belief that, should inquiry go on indefinitely, a Best Theory would be found.

But is it not circular to use such an empirical theory to explain science? Probably, but the circularity is not vicious. I do not seek to justify science; I can imagine no justification of science beyond what science itself provides. My endeavor is to explain why science, as a form of human thought and action, has the characteristics it does. I postulate a definite reality because scientific theories postulate the existence of such a reality and because I can think of no other way of explaining certain major features of the development of science. If this is realism, it is a realism generated within the empirical investigation itself, not one taken as a metaphysical presupposition of science. It is science that tells us what is real. The real is what is said to exist in a true theory. And this seems to me an eminently sensible position toward truth and reality. What else could one mean by saying that there really are electrons than that electrons are postulated to exist in the best confirmed theory of physics that we have?

Notes

1. Alfred Tarski, "The Concept of Truth in Formalized Languages," *Logic, Semantics, Metamathematics* (Oxford: Clarendon Press, 1956), 152–278.

2. Ibid., 187–188.

3. Ibid., 162–165.

4. Saul Kripke, "Outline of a Theory of Truth," *Journal of Philosophy* 72:690–716 (1975), 695.

5. Ibid., 701.

6. Ibid., 693–694. (Emphasis in original)

7. Ibid., 700. Michael Kremer, "Kripke and the Logic of Truth" *Journal of Philosophical Logic* 17:225–278 (1988), 230. Stephen Cole Kleene, *Introduction to Metamathematics* (New York: D. Van Nostrand Co., 1952), 332–340.

8. Kripke, "Outline," 703. (Emphasis in original)

9. Ibid., 704.

10. Ibid., 706. (Emphasis in original)

11. Ibid., 709.

12. Ibid.

13. Ibid., 708. (Emphasis in original)

14. Ibid., 713–714.

15. On Kripke's theory, see also Melvin Fitting, "Notes on the Mathematical Aspects of Kripke's Theory of Truth," *Notre Dame Journal of Formal Logic* 27:75–88 (1986). Albert Visser, "Semantics and the Liar Paradox" in D. Gabbay and F. Guenthner, eds., *Handbook of Philosophical Logic*, vol. 4 (Dordrecht: D. Reidel Co., 1989), 617–706. For more critical views of Kripke's theory, see Anil Gupta, "Truth and Paradox," *Journal of Philosophical Logic* 11:1–60 (1982), R. M. Martin, *Pragmatics, Truth, and Language* (Dordrecht: D. Reidel Publishing Co., 1979), ch. 13. See also the important new work by Vann McGee, *Truth, Vagueness, and Paradox* (Indianapolis, Ind.: Hackett Publishing Co., 1991).

16. Kripke, "Outline," 714–715.

17. Ibid., 692, 694.

18. Ibid., 690.

19. Stephen W. Hawking, *A Brief History of Time* (New York: Bantam Books, 1988), 162.

20. See above, 50–54.

21. Quine, "Two Dogmas," sec. 6.

22. Thomas S. Kuhn, *The Structure of Scientific Revolutions* (Chicago: University of Chicago Press, 1970), ch. 8.

23. Aronson, *Realist Philosophy*, 142.

24. Ibid., 139–142.

25. Ibid., 143–150.

26. Ibid., 145.

27. Kuhn, *Scientific Revolutions,* chs. 7, 8. Such a view in terms of the distribution of subjective probabilities seems close to Quine's argument in "Two Dogmas," sec. 6.

28. Kuhn, *Scientific Revolutions,*, 159.

29. The argument of this section, and part of the argument in the section after the next, are drawn from my article, "The Underdetermination Thesis" in Robert W. Burch and Herman J. Saatkamp, Jr., eds., *Frontiers in American Philosophy* (College Station: Texas A&M University Press, 1992), 157–165.

30. W. V. Quine, "On Empirically Equivalent Systems of the World," *Erkenntnis* 9:313–328 (1975).

31. In the 1975 paper, Quine was clearly worried about the implications of the Underdetermination Thesis for the notion of truth. At that point, he adopted what he later called a "sectarian" view—that one should pursue whatever theory one does in fact hold and treat the empirically equivalent but incompatible and irreconcilable alternatives as false. Later, Quine suggested that the problem could be solved by adopting what he called an "ecumenical" position, treating the incompatible theories as independent and therefore compatible ways of describing the world. Thus, to use the example of the interchange of "electron" and "molecule" cited above, one could rename these concepts in one of the theories as "quelectrons" and "qumolecules," and then threat the two theories as we treat wave and particle theories—as simply different ways of describing the world. The two can then be combined as two "lobes" of a single consistent theory, and "we can simultaneously reckon as factual whatever is asserted in either." [Quine, "Reply to Gib-

son," 156.] But by 1986 Quine recognized that the ecumenical position had an undesirable consequence. What happens when the theories constituting one "lobe" contain alien terms not included in the other?

> The sentences containing them constitute a gratuitous annex to the original theory, since the whole combination is still empirically equivalent to the original. It is as if some scientifically undigested terms of metaphysics or religion, say 'essence' or 'grace' or 'Nirvana', were admitted into science along with their pertinent doctrine, and tolerated on the ground merely that they contravened no observation. It would be an abandonment of the scientist's quest for economy and of the empiricist's standard of meaningfulness. [Ibid., 157].

Quine has therefore rejected the ecumenical position and returned to the original sectarian position of the 1975 paper. See Quine, *Theories and Things*, 29–30. Quine, "Reply to Gibson," 155–157.

32. Quine, "Systems of the World," 315.

33. Ibid., 316.

34. Ibid., 316–317.

35. Ibid., 317.

36. Quine, "Two Dogmas," 42–44.

37. Quine, "Systems of the World," 318.

38. Ibid., 320.

39. Ibid., 322.

40. Ibid., 316–317.

41. Ibid., 323.

42. Ibid., 324.

43. Ibid., 326–327.

44. Ibid., 313.

45. Putnam, *Mind*, 180. (Emphasis in original)

46. Ibid., 181. (Emphasis in original)

47. Quine, "Reasons for Indeterminacy," 179. (Emphasis in original)

48. Quine, "Systems of the World," 316–317.

49. Murphey, "The Underdetermination Thesis." Murray G. Murphey, "From Positivism to Negativism to Common Sense," paper delivered at Philosophy

and American Culture Conference, California State University, Fullerton, March 10, 1990. A very similar objection to Quine's definition of the set of observation sentences has recently been made by Larry Laudan and Jarrett Leplin, "Empirical Equivalence and Underdetermination," *Journal of Philosophy* 88:449–472 (1991). However, the principle thrust of their argument is to challenge the whole notion of empirical equivalence, on the ground that the derivation of testable consequences involves the use of auxiliary hypotheses not themselves part of the theory being tested, so that two theories empirically equivalent in Quine's sense may be evidentially supported by different empirical statements. Moreover, they argue that there are "modes of nonconsequential empirical support in science" (Ibid., 464) which theorists such as Quine, Hempel, and Popper have neglected, so that, "Theories with exactly the same evidential consequences may admit of differing degrees of empirical support" (Ibid.,465). Thus, empirical equivalence, even if it could be established, would not imply underdetermination.

The Laudan and Leplin argument regarding auxiliary hypotheses certainly poses a problem for the Weak Form of the Underdetermination Thesis. But it does not affect the Strong Form, since by Quine's definition of the Final Theory it is a total theory of the world. Any auxiliary hypothesis used in the derivation of consequences which is not part of this theory and which itself has empirical consequences would therefore have to be inconsistent with the Final Theory, and could not be legitimately conjoined with it. Similarly, since by hypothesis all Quine's alternative Final Theories explain all observation sentences, one could not find an observation sentence that supports one but not the other. That such completely non-consequential modes of reasoning as analogy may be evidentially probative is true, as they emphasize, if one looks at the reasoning by which certain scientists have been led to formulate theories that have turned out to be confirmed. But this seems rather treacherous ground. No doubt the plausibility of the caloric theory of heat owed a good deal to its analogy to such Newtonian-type theories as the one fluid theory of electricity, but it is not clear that one would want to take this as a case of evidentially probative support. The issue is obviously one which will require considerably more analysis.

50. Quine, "Ontological Relativity," 40.

51. Bruner, *Beyond the Information Given*, Part 1; Arnold Lewis Glass, Keith James Holyoak, and John Lester Santa, *Cognition* (Reading, Mass.: Addison-Wesley, 1979), chs. 2, 3.

52. See Chapter 1.

53. Charles S. Peirce, *The Collected Papers of Charles Sanders Peirce*, vols. 1–6, ed. Charles Hartshorne and Paul Weiss; vols. 7–8, ed. Arthur Burks (Cambridge, Mass.: Harvard University Press, 1931–1958), 1.233ff., 5.311.

54. Philipp Frank, *Einstein: His Life and Times* (London: Jonathan Cape, 1953), 133–134, 164–165.

55. Peirce, *Collected Papers,* 5.311, 7.327, 8.12.

56. Thomas Kuhn, "Commensurability, Comparability, Communicability" in Peter D. Asquith and Thomas Nickles, eds., *PSA 1982* (East Lansing, Mich.: Philosophy of Science Association, 1983), vol. 2, 669–670.

57. Ibid., 672.

58. Ibid.

59. Ibid.

60. Ibid., 673.

61. Ibid., 676.

62. Ibid., 682.

63. Ibid., 682–683.

64. Thomas S. Kuhn, "Response to Commentaries" in Asquith and Nickles, *PSA*, 714.

65. Kuhn, "Commensurability," 683.

66. Donald Davidson, *Inquiries into Truth and Interpretation* (Oxford: Clarendon Press, 1984), 125–140.

67. Ibid., 24.

68. Ibid., 134.

69. Ibid., 135.

70. Ibid., 33–35.

71. Ibid., 25, 139.

72. Ibid., 25–26.

73. Ibid., 132, 171–179.

74. Ibid., 172.

75. Ibid., 178–179.

76. Ibid., 139.

77. Roger T. Bell, *Translation and Translating: Theory and Practice* (London: Longmans, 1991), ch. 1.

78. Mona Baker, *In Other Words* (London: Routledge, 1992), 13–17.

79. Ibid., 96.

80. Ibid., 172.

81. John Biguenet and Rainer Schulte, eds., *The Craft of Translation* (Chicago: University of Chicago Press, 1989), vii.

82. Donald Davidson, "On the Very Idea of a Conceptual Scheme" in Jack W. Meiland and Michael Krausz, eds., *Relativism: Cognitive and Moral* (Notre Dame, Ind.: University of Notre Dame Press, 1982), 67.

83. Ibid., 74.

84. Ibid.

85. Ibid., 75.

86. Ibid., 75–76.

87. Ibid., 76.

88. Ibid., 77.

89. Ibid., 78.

90. Ibid., 79.

91. Davidson, *Inquiries*, 48.

92. Ibid., 47. (Emphasis in original)

93. Ibid., 39–40.

94. John Wallace, "Propositional Attitudes and Identity," *Journal of Philosophy* 66:145–152 (1969).

95. Davidson, "On the Very Idea," 79.

96. W. H. Newton-Smith, *The Rationality of Science* (Boston: Routledge and Kegan Paul, 1981), 183–184.

97. Quine, "Nature of Natural Knowledge," 81.

98. Anthony F. C. Wallace, "Revitalization Movements," *American Anthropologist* 58:264–281 (1956).

99. Kuhn, *Scientific Revolutions*, ch. 3.

100. Ibid., ch. 10.

101. Murphey, "Underdetermination Thesis."

102. Kuhn, *Scientific Revolutions*, chs. 12, 13.

103. J. L. E. Dreyer, *A History of Astronomy from Thales to Kepler* (New York: Dover Press, 1953), ch. 2.

104. Ibid., 102, 103–107, ch. 5.

105. Ibid., ch. 6.

106. Ibid., ch. 7.

107. Hilary Putnam, quoted in Aronson, *Realist Philosophy*, 206. Putnam's position has changed over time, and I am not certain he would still make this claim. At one time, I thought that my position was somewhat similar to what he has called "internal realism." After reading his latest book, I think I was probably mistaken. See Hilary Putnam, *The Many Faces of Realism* (LaSalle, Ill.: Open Court, 1989).

Chapter 7

Knowledge of the Past

The purpose of this chapter is to establish Premises (5) through (7)—namely, (5): There exists a past in which human beings lived and acted; (6): We can have some accurate knowledge of that past; and (7): Members of one culture can understand members of other cultures, including members of antecedent states of their own culture. In support of (5), I argue that the existence of the past itself, as well as of the entities and events in the past, is a theoretical construct to account for presently existing data. From an epistemological point of view, past actors are theoretical constructs; ontologically, they are real entities if the theory in which their existence is postulated is true. My position is therefore a realist position with respect to the past, in the sense described in Chapter 6.

Access to past societies and cultures involves the analysis of present objects viewed as evidence of the past. I return again to the questions of hermeneutics, interpretation, and translation, and argue that given adequate sources, we can develop highly probable theories about what texts written in the past meant to their authors and readers. Thus as Premises (6) and (7) hold, we can have accurate knowledge about actors of the past, whether they come from different cultures or from earlier stages of our own. The explanation of past events requires not only a knowledge of physical, biological, and psychological universals but also a knowledge of the specific cultures in which the events occurred. Rules, plans, beliefs, and desires are all culturally variable, and explanations involving such factors will usually be culturally specific. Such explanations, however, are causal explanations in the sense discussed in Chapters 3, 4, and 5.

I then deal with various objections to this point of view, particularly with the objections usually labelled "narrativist." As an examination of the views of White, Mink, and McCullagh shows, narrative is not a form of explanation. While most history is written in narrative form, its explanatory power depends upon the causal model it contains. Narratives can be used to present causal explanations of the sort previously discussed, but they are not themselves explanations. Finally I discuss the problem of the confirmation of historical theories.

The Past and Its Contents

It is customary to refer to the study of the past as "history." Unfortunately, this term has multiple meanings that are not entirely consistent. "History" often means (1) what happened in the past—the *res gestae*; (2) our knowledge about what happened in the past; (3) what is written by people called "historians," a term not limited to the members of academic departments of "History" but which includes a rather motley mix of people who, for one reason or another, seek to write about the past. Because of the ambiguity of this term, I shall use it in the second sense, and I shall use the term "historian" to refer to any scholar who seeks knowledge of the past, whatever the academic affiliation of such a person.

But what precisely is the subject of this study? It has commonly been said that the past itself cannot be observed; as Louis Mink remarked, "The past isn't *there*."[1] That being the case, it does seem clear that no evidence concerning the past can itself be past. Since the future is also beyond our powers of observation, it follows that all evidence regarding the past must be present. Insofar as our knowledge of the past has an empirical foundation, the evidence—the physical objects we observe, the sounds we hear, that constitute that evidence—must be available to our senses now. Nothing can serve as evidence for the past but what exists now.[2]

Yet even this way of putting the matter involves an assumption for which we have as yet no warrant that there is a past for which present objects can be evidence. How do we know that there is a past, or, more strictly, was a past? We know something of our own past by our memories, which, as we have already discussed, we treat as *prima facie* credible. But what about the deep past—the past before we existed, before our parents or grandparents? How do we know that there was any such past? When did it begin? The question may seem absurd, but reflection upon the variety of answers that have been given to it shows that it is not. Some have believed

God created the world in 4004 B.C.—a perfectly sane belief, given certain assumptions. Others have thought the world eternal. Our view that the universe itself, and time with it, came into existence about fifteen to twenty billion years ago is a very modern view indeed, undreamt of until this century. And our present view of the human past was revolutionary when Darwin first proposed it in 1871 (really in 1859, although he avoided the question of human origins at that time[3]). It should be very sobering indeed to reflect that until Darwin, no one had dreamt of an origin of mankind of the sort he proposed, despite the fact that every culture has had some sort of origin myth. And even today, we still do not have a clear picture of the evolution of homo sapiens; there are still arguments among the experts as to just when homo sapiens appeared on earth and just what his ancestry was. Therefore, the question of the nature and extent of the past is a very real question requiring an answer.

Our current theories of the origin and duration of the universe are based upon physical theories and evidence available to our senses now. It was the discovery by Hubble that the light of most galaxies visible to us is red-shifted which led to the theory of the Big Bang—that is, the Big Bang theory is postulated to explain such phenomena as the observed red shift. The whole complex theory of the origin of the universe is designed to explain observations we make now. So too the theory of evolution, and in particular of the evolution of homo sapiens, rests upon a variety of evidence available to us now. The deep past—physical, biological, and human—is a postulate to account for present phenomena. What else, after all, could it be? Science fiction to the contrary notwithstanding, we cannot travel back in time; we cannot go back and interview Lucy. From an epistemological point of view, the whole past is a construct born of a theory to account for peculiarities of the world as we now find it.

The fact that from an epistemological point of view the past has this postulational character does not impugn the reality of the past. The question of the ontological status of the past is a different question than the question of its epistemological status. If our theory of the Big Bang is true, the Big Bang really occurred; if our theory of evolution is true, our ancestors really were some type of large ground ape of African origin. The situation is no different with respect to any postulated persons or events in the past. The entities and events postulated to exist in true theories are real, and this is the only sense in which one can talk about the reality of the past.

The data upon which our theories of the past rest are observations made of people or objects that exist now. When we ask other people to tell us what they remember about the past, it is their present statements that are data for us; so too, when we rely on our own memories for information about the past, it is our present memories that we use. Archaeologists and material culturalists build theories on the basis of physical objects—ceramics, bones, furniture, houses—that we can see now. "Documents" are simply physical objects upon which there are inscriptions that we interpret as writings; obviously, we cannot "read" a document we cannot now see. It is often said that we use observations, or testimony, made by people from the past, as for example, much of what we know about early Greek philosophers is derived from what Aristotle said about them. But how do we know what Aristotle said about them? Obviously, not by asking Aristotle! We know because these statements occur in documents we have now that we believe were written by Aristotle (more exactly, copied from documents by Aristotle). But that Aristotle ever existed is part of our theory to account for the existence and character of these documents we have now. If our theory about Aristotle is wrong, then we have no testimony of Aristotle's about early Greek philosophers. In every case, the observational base for our knowledge of the past is observations of presently existing objects.

When we treat a presently existing object as a letter by Thomas Jefferson or a sermon by Jonathan Edwards or a painting by Charles Peale, we have classified the object, and our classification constitutes a classificatory hypothesis that is subject to test. A letter by Thomas Jefferson cannot have been written on paper made with Esparto grass, and a sermon by Jonathan Edwards cannot be written in ink containing aniline dye. As the well-known case of the Vinland Map should make clear, such classificatory hypothesis do sometimes turn out to be false. The whole of what has traditionally been called "external criticism" of the "document" is in fact a set of methods for testing the classificatory hypotheses that determine what an object can be evidence for.[4] These hypotheses involve stipulations of who produced the object, where, when, why, and what has happened to it since its original creation. As the case of the Vinland Map shows, these methods have now become extremely sophisticated and provide very powerful tools for establishing the evidential base for the study of the past.

The theories of the human past generated to account for such evidence postulate the existence of a wide variety of entities, ranging from social institutions to natural phenomena such as storms or droughts. Chiefly and fundamentally, however, most of the constructs postulated in these theories are persons and their behavior. It is the people who existed and the actions they took that usually serve to explain the data that we have. This means that the epistemological status of past persons is not essentially different from the epistemological status of subatomic particles such as quarks. They are real people if the theory postulating them is true; if it is false, there are no such people (or if you like, there never were such people). Did Napoleon exist? If we say yes, it is because assuming that Napoleon existed explains an enormous amount of present data far better than any alternative theory we have been able to construct. Did Jesus exist? Probably. At least the assumption that there was such a person accounts for a wide range of data that are very difficult to explain in any other way. Did Achilles exist? Probably not. Probably Achilles is an imaginary figure created by Homer, although the legend may well be based on the deeds of some actual person or persons. Thus the persons, objects, and events of the past are postulates that are created to account for present data. No human now alive ever saw Napoleon or Jesus or Achilles. If we believe they existed, we do so because postulating their existence gives us the best available explanation of the data we now have.

Several objections have been raised to this thesis about our knowledge of the past. First, it has seemed to some that such a claim undermines the reality of historical entities.[5] This is not true. The objection arises from a confusion of epistemological issues with ontological ones. It no more follows from the claim that the epistemological status of past entities is that of constructs that they are not ontologically real than it follows that electrons are not ontological real because they have the epistemological status of theoretical constructs. What is postulated to exist in a true theory is real, so if our theory of the past is true, the entities whose existence it postulates are real.

The second objection is that if past entities are theoretical constructs, then the past of Michael Gorbachev must be a theoretical construct, whereas the present Michael Gorbachev is a real object. But this, it is said, is incoherent; Gorbachev cannot be different things at different times.[6] This objection rests upon the doctrine of epistemological realism that I have argued throughout to be false. Present real objects—including those we now perceive—are posits to account for our sensory experience. On this point, I believe Quine is quite right. We posit the existence of objects to account for what we experience, and when our experience ceases to justify such a posit, we abandon it. There is therefore no discontinuity between the epistemological status of present and past objects or processes. Gorbachev's identity is not in jeopardy.

A third objection is that this position draws a distinction without a difference. If all real objects are posits—constructs—then saying that historical entities are constructs like quarks is saying no more than that they are real objects. But there is a difference. We normally contrast quarks and tables on the ground that quarks are unobservable entities and their existence must be postulated, whereas tables are directly observable. The view that tables are posits does not abolish this distinction; the difference between what is perceptible and what is not remains as clear on this as on any other theory. The reason for classing historical entities and events with quarks and not with tables is that historical entities and events, like quarks, are not observables. One cannot perceive the objects or events of the past.

Furthermore, historical constructs are unobservable *in principle* just as quarks are. Despite science fiction accounts of time travel, we know that travelling backward in time violates basic laws of nature. Therefore the evidence for the existence of historical objects and events must be indirect; like quarks, they are postulated as constructs in theories that must be confirmed against present data. From an epistemological point of view, therefore, entities and events of the past are theoretical constructs like quarks, not perceptible entities like tables.

The fact that we have memories of perceptual experiences of past entities and events does not alter this situation. In the first place, we have memories of very little of what we postulate to have existed in the past; no man now alive remembers meeting Jesus or Napoleon or Achilles. But in the second place, a memory of a perceptual experience is not the same as a perceptual experience. Our present memories of such experiences, or the present memories of others now alive, may be used as evidence to support the postulate that certain entities or events once obtained, but they are not themselves perceptual experiences. We may have good reasons to believe these accounts, and in the case of our own memories to grant them *prima facie* credibility, but they remain indirect evidence for the existence of past realities, not perceptual evidence. Thus it remains true that in postulating the existence of objects and events in the past, and indeed of the past itself, we are postulating the real existence of things that are in principle unobservable by us today. Such entities and events are clearly theoretical constructs.

The fourth objection is that, whatever the status of the Underdetermination Thesis with respect to physics, it must be true with respect to theories regarding the past because the amount of data regarding the past is finite—hence, there can be no indefinitely extended process of inquiry concerning the past. But this objection is mistaken. No doubt there are a finite number of objects in the world—even of subatomic particles. So while it is true that we are constantly finding new objects that serve as evidence about the past, the total number of such objects must surely be finite. But this does not prove that the total number of observations, or observation sentences, is finite. What is true is that we are constantly finding not only new data but also new ways to extract information from objects that we have long known to exist, and so of deriving new observations for use in testing theories about the past. There is no reason to believe that this process will end. No doubt at any given point in the process, there will be a finite number of observation sentences known, and so it will be possible to generate alternative theories that also account for all of them. But there will always be new observation sentences that can be generated and used to discriminate among those theories. There is no more reason to hold that the Strong Form of the Underdetermination Thesis applies to the study of the past than to the study of physics.

Given that theories of the past postulate the existence of persons, they also clearly postulate various relations and interactions among those persons. This is hardly surprising; physical theories postulate not only quarks but relations among them. In the study of the past, this often leads to inferences concerning the existence of persons and events for which we have no explicit evidence. Thus there is substantial ground for believing that the Teacher of Righteousness existed.[7] If so, he must have been born at a specific place and time and have had parents. We have in this case no evidence at all concerning his parentage or birth, but from the fact he was a man we can infer that his parents existed and that he was born as all other humans are. Similarly, we know that there were large numbers of American Indians in North and South America before the coming of the Europeans. How many there were is a much debated issue, with estimates varying widely among competent authorities, but that a large number were here is supported by both direct evidence and by inference from the number that the Europeans found here and the estimated death rates owing to the introduction of European diseases.[8] In such cases our knowledge is incomplete, but not false. There is no contradiction between our knowing some things truly about a subject while not knowing some other things.

To say that the Teacher of Righteousness was human is to attribute to him the properties generic to human beings. But one must be very careful regarding what one takes to be generic properties. That all human beings are born of human parents is a biological universal regarding human beings upon which inferences can be securely based. The problem arises when concepts such as "human nature" are introduced which involve psychological as well as biological characteristics. No one doubts that there are psychological as well as biological universals—the ability to learn, for example. But as anthropologists have pointed out, the human personality is in part culturally constituted. While it may be true that motivational processes are universal, particular motives and their relations often are not. Culture is necessary, not only to human survival, but also to the formation of the human being as a person. One cannot therefore discuss "human nature" as a changeless universal type, the same in all places and at all times. Culture and personality are not independent. This fact requires that any theory of human beings in the past must also be a theory of their culture.[9]

Culture

Although the anthropological term "culture" has its roots in the German word "Kultur" and the nineteenth-century British use of "culture" to refer to the degree of intellectual and moral cultivation attained by an individual or society, the modern use of the term dates from Boas, who was the first to speak of different societies having different "cultures."[10] Since Boas, there has been a general consensus that the term should be used to refer to habits, beliefs, goals, institutions that are acquired by learning rather than being genetically transmitted. Within this general consensus, however, there has been a wide variety of specific definitions of culture, ranging from the superorganicism of the early Kroeber to the materialism of Harris.[11] These disagreements have reflected the differential importance of certain issues—the necessity of distinguishing cultural differences from racial differences, the fact that cultures are learned, the fact cultures are shared, the recognition that quite different cultures may provide equally valuable "forms of life," and so on. Many of the disagreements accordingly are more matters of emphasis than of substantive argument, but some also involve quite fundamental issues.

I doubt that it is possible to give a one sentence definition of the term "culture" without resorting to constructions too convoluted to be useful. But I think it is quite possible to explain what "culture" means in a somewhat more discursive fashion. As I shall use the term here, it may be explicated as follows. First, it is usually said that culture is learned. This emphasis on learning is not misplaced, but the great stress on it is partly due to the desire to distinguish what is cultural from what is genetically determined. At the same time, many anthropologists include in the culture the material objects made or used by the society; obviously, material objects are not learned. We may learn how to make them or how to use them, but we do not learn them. Therefore, if one wishes to include the material objects made and/or used by the society as part of the culture, one must modify the claim that culture is learned; the behavioral and ideological elements of culture are learned, but the material objects whose use or construction is learned by members of the society are also part of the culture—what is called the "material culture."

Second, culture is often asserted to consist of norms or standards for such activities as perceiving, believing, and doing.[12] Certainly such standards are part of the culture. But the culture is hardly an unordered collection of such norms; there are systematic relations among norms, and those relations are not themselves always normative. To the extent that culture is systematic—and I think most anthropologists agree that it is, at least to some degree—it cannot be a purely normative phenomenon.

Third, it is commonly asserted that culture is shared. But it is very difficult to find agreement on the nature of this sharing. Certainly the emphasis on sharing is necessary to exclude purely idiosyncratic elements; culture is not the sum set of all the behaviors of all its members. On the other hand, different groups within the society differ in belief, action, norms, and other factors, so that it is false to say every member of the society has the same cultural elements organized in the same way. Goodenough's concept of "specialties" is one attempt to deal with this problem,[13] but I have in mind a more general phenomenon.

Consider a social position—that is, a property the possession of which by some subset of members of the society causes those members to be accorded certain distinctive rights and duties, and to be expected to perform in distinctive ways. Thus, for example, *physician* is such a social position in our culture. I would remark first that a social position is a property, not a set. A social position is not changed by the addition or deletion to the society of particular individuals having that property, whereas the identity of a set is changed with every change of a member. Second, such a position bears complex relations to other positions—for example, to patients, nurses, hospital administrators—and to the society at large. Each expects of doctors somewhat different things; some positions have sanctioning power with respect to doctors, whereas others do not. The characteristic pattern of action expected of doctors is of course the role of the doctor, but the different aspects of that role are related to the roles played by occupants of other positions. Obviously, one has here an extraordinarily complex structure involving multiple expectations, beliefs, norms, and so forth. What is shared may in some cases be confined to very small groups; some specialists have bodies of knowledge so abstruse that none but the few in that specialty actually share that knowledge. And the total system of relations which links these many positions may not be known to any one member of the society. Indeed, if one thinks of the thousands of positions and roles in contemporary American society, and of the extraordinary complexity of the interrelations among them, I think it is quite obvious that no one person now knows the entire system. Of course, that does not mean the system is unknowable, but that a model adequate to describe it has yet to be constructed.

It will be objected here that I have run together culture and social structure. Quite so. But the Parsonian distinction has never seemed to me a plausible one. One cannot usefully talk about a position or a role without talking about norms, beliefs, expectations, and behavior. I cannot see that there is anything gained by tearing asunder what human life has joined together, even for so-called "analytical" purposes.[14]

Those actions, beliefs, norms, expectations, and so on, that are not only learned but learned as characteristic either of members of the society as a whole, or of positions and other properties recognized as socially significant within the society, are clearly part of the culture. So is the material culture, not only of the society as a whole, but of the various recognized groups within it. And so too is the relational structure that joins these elements together. Of course, those relations may include conflict as well as smoothly integrated complementarity, but no one any longer thinks that cultures are perfectly integrated wholes. Nevertheless, the components do have systematic interrelations, and those interrelations are essential parts of the culture.

Language is of course a part of the culture of a society. As Goodenough pointed out, a society may have multiple languages, but linguistic communication among the members is essential. Goodenough's explanation of how language is shared—that we attribute linguistic norms to each other—seems to me correct, as does his point that individual ideolects vary, so that "the" language is the central tendency of a distribution of ideolects.[15] But I do not see how this model of language, with its great virtue of avoiding reified notions of meaning, can be carried over to culture as a whole, given the enormous variations in norms, beliefs, and other aspects of culture among different groups. Nor does it seem to me possible to deal with the relational system connecting different groups and properties in this way.

I have spoken above of personality as partially formed by culture. It should be obvious that the internalization in a person of standards, beliefs, expectations, goals, etc., represents a change in the personality of that individual, on just about any theory of personality currently in use. The particular versions of these elements adopted by an individual and the peculiar organization of them within the individual's psychological system will interact with the person's genetic endowment to produce a distinctive personality, but elements of the culture are a part of that structure. One cannot therefore consider personality as wholly distinct from culture; they are not the same, but each involves some components of the other.

Texts

It is obvious enough that in studying a contemporary society, we must gain access to its language, and we have already discussed the question of whether or not such interpretations are possible. But consider the case of a past society, all of whose members are long since dead and whose language and culture have died with them. How do we know that such a society ever existed? We can know that to the extent that we have evidence for it, where the evidence, as we have seen, must consist of present objects.

Consider first the class of objects we call "documents"—those upon which there is inscription constituting writing. How do we know a given inscription is writing? It is usually not difficult to distinguish such an inscription from a marking due to natural causes. The reason is, rather obviously, that the people whose writing it is or was would also have had to make this distinction, and therefore in writing humans do not use forms that could be easily mistaken for naturally occurring forms. Discriminating writing from decorative motifs is a much more difficult problem, since glyphic systems—for example, Mayan glyphs—might conceivably be mere decorations. But Spanish explorers were aware from the first contact that the glyphs were a system of writing, and made efforts to translate them.[16]

Even when we are reasonably certain that the inscription before us is writing, it does not follow that we can interpret it. Minoan Linear A, Harappan, and Elamite are all examples of systems of writing which we cannot translate. The study of such systems can yield considerable information about the language without knowing what it means. Ventris knew that Minoan Linear B was an inflected language before he knew what that language was;[17] scholars of Mayan knew that it was a mixed logographic and syllabic system even before great progress had been made in deciphering it.[18] But formal properties of this sort do not suffice to crack the code. Such systems have the general character of uninterpreted formal systems; any number of models are possible. To get beyond this point, there must be semantic clues.

In natural languages, the semantic clues are given by ostension. In languages of the dead, that type of clue is not always available. Sometimes pictographic systems involve recognizable images of identifiable entities that may in fact refer to those entities, but they may also be symbolic or operate on the rebus principle. One cannot therefore assume that a pictograph refers to the object it depicts. To enter the charmed circle of such a language, there has to be some text that provides a translation of some part of the language into a language we already know. The case of the Rosetta Stone is doubtless the most famous example of this. Understanding of the hieroglyphs was entirely lost before the discovery of this bilingual inscription. Even then the task of translation was formidable, given the radical differences in the nature of the two writing systems, and Champollion's achievement in doing it was very great.[19] But without the Rosetta Stone (or some similar bilingual text) it could not have been done at all. Thus we often find ourselves having to gain access to a dead language through intermediaries, as Champollion did through the Greek inscription, but there is no other way.[20]

Counterclaims to this assertion have been made, but they are not convincing. Ventris's success is not really a countercase; Ventris did not discover how to read a dead language; he discovered that Minoan Linear B was Greek written in a different notation. In this case, it was the isomorphism between Linear B and Greek that was the key, but the point is that Ventris already knew Greek. Efforts by Fairservis to provide a translation of Harappan are far more questionable. While it is generally agreed that Harappan is some very early form of Dravidian language, there are a number of different Dravidian languages, and comparisons across three thousand years are, to put it mildly, chancy. Although Fairservis can make a case for many of his readings, other Harappan scholars are not convinced, and some believe that we will never have an answer unless a bilingual text is found. The problem is made particularly severe by the very small number of Harappan texts in existence and the improbability that that number will be greatly increased.[21]

Most texts with which we work are of course in known languages, and the problems of interpretation are more subtle. It has been claimed, in fact, that the original meaning of such a text cannot be recovered, and even that it is pointless to try to recover the meaning. Perhaps Ricoeur is as clear on this matter as any of its proponents.

> Mediation by the text, that is, by expressions fixed in writing but also by all the documents and monuments which have a fundamental feature in common with writing, is connected with the use of explication on the scale of the transmission of historical tradition. This common feature, which constitutes the text as a text, is that the meaning contained therein is rendered *autonomous* with respect to the intention of the author, the initial situation of discourse and the original addressee. Intention, situation, and original addressee constitute the *Sitz-im-Leben* [site-in-life] of the text. The possibility of multiple interpretations is opened up by a text which is thus freed from its *Sitz-im-Leben*. Beyond the polysemy of words in a conversation is the polysemy of a text which invites multiple readings. This is the moment of interpretation in the technical sense of *textual exegesis*. It is also the moment of the hermeneutical circle between the understanding initiated by the reader and the proposals of meaning offered by the text. The most fundamental condition of the hermeneutical circle lies in the structure of pre-understanding which relates all explication to the understanding which precedes and supports it.[22]

The claims here require some examination. A *text* for Ricoeur is "any discourse fixed by writing."[23] Discourse itself is described as having four key characteristics: (1) It takes place at a specific time and place; (2) it has a speaker; (3) it "refers to a world which it claims to describe, express, or represent"; and (4) it is addressed to someone.[24] The "fixation" of discourse in writing alters these characteristics, however. First, once a discourse is written down, it acquires a permanence that transcends the time and place of its composition. The text is an object that endures rather than an event that vanishes with the performance. Second, the text becomes independent of the author; the author may not even be known. The meaning of the text is therefore independent of the intention of the author in writing it; it means whatever it means, regardless of what the author intended it to mean. Finally, whereas discourse has a specific intended auditor (or multiple auditors), the text is addressed to anyone who can read, and therefore has no specific audience.

What is curious about these claims is that they hold true (if at all) only of a peculiar use of texts—what might be described as a "literary" use. Perhaps the *Iliad* can be treated this way—perhaps, but not obviously. Certainly these claims do not hold of a text used as historical evidence. Consider a letter written by Roosevelt to Churchill. The questions an historian will ask of this text are, what meaning did Roosevelt intend to convey in writing what he did? And what did Churchill think the letter meant?— both in the literal sense of linguistic meaning and in the sense of what Roosevelt intended. One could of course use the letter for other purposes—as a model of style, or evidence for historical linguistics, or various other things. But what an historian will ask is precisely what the author was up to and what the reader thought he was up to. That the letter is written and not spoken is fortunate for us, since it means we have it, but we use it just as though it was "discourse."

Furthermore, the claims Ricoeur makes about reference are odd. Spoken discourse need not be about anything in the immediate situation; how do you point to electrons, or god, or democracy? But certainly one of the first things a scholar tries to do with a text being used as evidence of the past is to determine as fully as possible what the historical "context" of the document was—when written, where, by whom, to whom, about what? Perhaps it is true that in reading the *Iliad* we really don't care if Troy ever existed. But Schliemann did, and so have many others. What Ricoeur seems to be describing here is a particular use of documents in which they are read ahistorically for the "cultivation" of the mind. Even in this peculiar usage, I very much doubt that Ricoeur's claims hold, but certainly they are false about documents used as evidence of the past.

It should also be noted that Ricoeur seems to think it is because writing "fixes" discourse—that is, embodies it in an enduring object—that the other characteristics also hold of the text. But discourse can be "fixed" by tape recordings just as well as writing. Consider the Nixon tapes: Did the fact that those tapes "fixed" certain discourses divorce them from the participants in those conversations or the situation in which they took place or what they referred to? Obviously not. And now with television and videotape we have discourses that will endure for a long time, together with visual evidence concerning the participants. The stress given to writing and reading by Ricoeur not only ignores the modern technology of communication, but it attributes to "fixation" consequences that simply do not follow.

But there is more to this passage of Ricoeur's. In the comment about "pre-understanding" the echoes of Heidegger and Gadamer are quite clear. That we are creatures who live in time, that we inherit a cultural tradition, and that we approach the interpretation of texts, and everything else, with certain ideas already in mind, no one denies. But so what? The same claims hold with respect to all knowledge, in physics as well as history. Why is it held that this poses a more critical problem in the human sciences than in the physical sciences? The answer seems to be that in physical science the object of study, the thing observed, is a natural phenomenon, whereas in the human sciences it is an object having a meaning— a text. But to "interpret" a text requires more than simply a knowledge of a language. According to Ricoeur, words are polysemic; one only achieves a determinate message where words are fixed in a context, linguistic and social. Therefore the meaning of the message cannot be determined apart from the context. But the context—at least the linguistic context—is determined by the constituent words. One has here a part–whole relation in which the understanding of the part depends upon the understanding of the whole, and the understanding of the whole depends upon the understanding of the part. One has, in other words, the hermeneutic circle.[25]

We have touched on some of these issues before, but they must now be dealt with in more detail. Let us take the word "text" to refer to a document of some sort. What one actually confronts is physical marks on a surface of an object. Even to say that these marks are writing is to make a classificatory hypothesis, based on their similarity to other markings of which we have prior experience. Thus we classify as writing certain Harappan glyphs, although we do not know what they mean. But if the marks correspond sufficiently closely to the markings which constitute the written form of a language we know, we take them to be written words of that language, and attribute to them meaning and reference. This entire process is obviously hypothetical; we can be wrong. The markings may turn out to be something else altogether—a decorative motif, for example. But if the hypothesis fits the data—the physical marks—we accept it as correct.

It needs to be emphasized that meaning and reference are attributed to the markings—that is, to the text. The text itself is simply a physical object—a set of inscriptions or figures. This is of course a corollary from the generally accepted fact that linguistic signs—verbal or written—are arbitrary. They have meaning because we attribute meaning to them. To say that these meanings are shared is to say that members of a particular group attribute the same meanings to the text, and that they expect each other to attribute those meanings to that text. A text therefore has a meaning for a group; it is entirely possible that the same text (i.e., physical markings) might have a different meaning to different groups, as is true of certain ciphers.

To say that members of a group attribute a meaning to a text is to say at least that the norms of the language shared by the group are such that the text has that meaning. But it may be, and usually is, the case that more than one meaning or reference can be attributed to the text consistent with those norms. Thus Nunberg's example of "Hearst bought a newspaper," or Chomsky's "Flying planes can be dangerous," are examples of linguistic units to which multiple meanings can be attributed consistent with the norms of English. Selecting the right meaning therefore depends on picking out one from among the possible meanings allowed by the language. But what is meant here by "the right meaning"?

Any meaning is somebody's meaning. Putnam to the contrary notwithstanding, meanings are in the head[26]—somebody's head. Any text has at least one author; it can have more than one, but it cannot have less. It is a true causal statement that a text is created by a person (or by a computer programmed by a person). It does not follow that a text has meaning; the author may have been word doodling or practicing penmanship, and although the individual words may be meaningful, the combinations of words may not. Nor does it follow that where the text has a meaning, it is the meaning intended by the author. We have all had the experience of making an utterance or writing a text for the purpose of expressing a particular intended meaning, and subsequently realizing that what we said/wrote did not at all express what we had intended to express. But on the assumption that the author is linguistically competent, one should accept the hypothesis that the utterance/text expresses the author's intended meaning unless there is evidence to the contrary. That, after all, is what one means by saying that the author is linguistically competent. Hence one may assume (barring contrary evidence) that one meaning of the text is the author's intended meaning.

But the author's intended meaning is not the only meaning that text can have. Most texts are addressed to some audience, whether it is a specific reader intended by the author (as in the case of a letter) or a larger and only generally defined group (as in the case of a political tract). What the reader/hearer thinks the text/utterance meant may not be what the author intended. And different readers/hearers may attribute different meanings to the text/utterance. Thus, there may be a plethora of different meanings attributed to a particular text, all of which are consistent with the norms of the language. Which one is the right meaning?

The answer to that question obviously depends on what meaning we want. If the text is used as historical evidence, it can be evidence concerning the authors or concerning some or all of their readers. For example, in studying the Roosevelt-Churchill correspondence, one wants to know first, what did the writer mean by what he wrote? And second, what did the recipient think the letter meant? Both questions are legitimate; both are important; but they are not the same. Similarly, in studying the Millerites, one will want to know what meaning they attributed to certain portions of the Bible; one will not care (unless one is a Millerite) what the original authors of those Biblical texts intended those passages to mean. As this should make clear, the meaning we are interested in may be the meaning that any person of interest to us attributes to the text. It does not matter whether that person is a contemporary of the author or lived two thousand years later. The question is not, what is *the* meaning, but rather what did the text mean to x, where x can be anyone, author or reader, living or dead, to whom the text has had a meaning.

But can such a meaning be determined? Can we find out what the author or the reader meant by the text? Besides the actual words of the text, the chief clue we have to work from here is the context in which the text was produced or read. One part of this context is, as we have seen, linguistic—that is, the larger text (if there is one) of which the given text is a part. But linguistic norms alone do not necessarily yield a unique meaning. As Hirsch notes, "This is true even of the simplest declarative sentence like "My car ran out of gas" (did my Pullman dash from a cloud of Argon?)."[27] When we interpret a text, we begin with certain hypotheses about the kind of text it is. Hirsch refers to these as hypotheses about "genre"—about the kind of text we are dealing with.[28] If it has the visual appearance of a sonnet, we expect a sonnet; if it is an article in the *Journal of Mathematical Psychology*, we expect a technical article on psychology. These hypotheses of course may be wrong; the sonnet may be prose sliced to look like a sonnet, and the article may be a short story. Indeed, the text may not belong to any genre with which we are familiar, and we may have to discover what its genre is. But the role of hypotheses, as "sets" or a readiness to "see" the object as being of a particular sort is not fundamentally different from those of Bruner's subjects who "saw" purple spades and hearts. Experience gives rise to hypotheses about future experience, of texts and playing cards as of cabbages and kings. Since these hypotheses can be wrong, and often are, there is nothing circular about this process.

One has also to look at the socio-cultural context. Here there is an important error in Ricoeur's view which needs to be noted.[29] Part of the context of a text or utterance (in general, of a locutionary act) is provided by the illocutionary and perlocutionary acts performed in and by the utterance. As Austin pointed out, the performance of these acts requires that the locution be advanced "with a certain sense and with a certain reference,"[30] although not necessarily just one. It is true, as Ricoeur says, that an illocutionary force indicator may be included in the locution (e.g., "I promise I'll always love you," instead of "I'll always love you"). But including the force indicator in the locution does not make the illocutionary act part of the locutionary act. Uttering "I promise I'll always love you" does not constitute the illocutionary act of promising, any more than standing on the street corner and crying, "I sentence Richard Nixon to twenty years at hard labor," constitutes sentencing. The felicity conditions for the illocutionary act must be met; the locutionary act must be performed in the right situation and in the right way. The illocutionary and perlocutionary forces of locutions are never part of the meaning of the locution; they are part of the context that helps to determine which among the linguistically possible meanings is operative.

More generally, to determine the context of an utterance or text, one needs to know who wrote (said) it, where, when, why, under what conditions, etc., (and who read/heard it, where, when, why, under what conditions, etc.). These factors, which are external to the text itself and to its meaning and reference, provide the evidence necessary to determine which of the linguistically possible meanings is operative in a particular case. Thus, Hartshorne and Weiss prefaced one volume of the Peirce papers with a quote from Peirce which appeared to be a judgment that his philosophic system lacked coherence and completeness. When that statement is put back into its context in the lecture from which it was taken, and when that whole is considered in terms of Peirce's financial position, age, the audience addressed, and so on, it becomes quickly apparent that this was an appeal for money, not a philosophic judgement.[31]

Hirsch's great contribution to the argument over interpretation has been to insist that the text does not contain its own meaning, that all meaning is someone's meaning, and that if an interpretation is to have "validity," to have greater or less probability of being correct than some other interpretation, then there has to be a particular someone whose meaning is taken as the standard. For Hirsch in his earlier work, this is the author. But as Meiland has pointed out, and Hirsch subsequently agreed,[32] it need not be the author; any person's meaning can serve as the standard.

However, I would put the matter somewhat differently. I would argue that we start from a text (meaning the physical object) and develop hypotheses concerning what that text meant to x, where x can be the author(s) or reader(s), contemporary or not. The meaning attributed by x is then what we want to know, and we search for the hypothesis concerning x's meaning that is more probable than any other, given both the internal and the external evidence. As Hirsch says, this does not give us certain knowledge, but it gives us the only kind of knowledge we can have—a theory better confirmed than any alternative. Of course, in dealing with historical documents it can be the case that our evidence is so limited that no unambiguous reading can be attained, but this is a general problem about the limitation imposed on knowledge by inadequate data. It involves no special indeterminacy of interpretation.

Hirsch's examination of the process of testing hypotheses about the meaning of texts seems to me sound, and—assuming adequate data—shows that the alleged circularity of the hermeneutic circle does not hold.[33] Testing a hypothesis about the meaning of a particular document is not simply a question of developing a hypothesis from the data of the text and then using that hypothesis to explain the very data from which it was derived. Bringing evidence to bear on the problem from outside the text itself, whether it is linguistic evidence about how a writer employs a word in other writings, or situational evidence about the speech act being performed, or whatever, breaks the circularity. Hirsch, of course, considered only the problem of determining the author's intended meaning, but the same methods he advances can be used to get that of the reader/hearer, together with other data such as the actions taken or responses made by the reader/hearer as a result of his experience of the text/utterance. Thus the processes of textual interpretation lie within the methodological scope of the hypothetico-deductive-inductive method;[34] they do not call for some arcane or intuitive type of "understanding." The human sciences are sciences in the same sense as all the other sciences.

Culture and Explanation

The primary task in the study of any society is the delineation of the culture and the environment. The term "culture" has already been discussed. By the "environment" of the society I mean the physical, biological, and social environment in which the society exists. Such factors as climate, topography, natural resources, flora and fauna, and diseases that may have an influence on the society of interest are all aspects of the environment. The environment so conceived is clearly the environment as described by the investigator, whether members of the society of interest are aware of those factors or not. Thus, prior to the European invasion of America, fossil fuels like coal and oil were part of the environment, although the native inhabitants either did not know of them or saw no significance in them. Nevertheless, their presence was to prove important for the future of the area, and a knowledge of them helps to define what will be the potentialities of a society in that environment. But this environment is quite different from what Hallowell called "the behavioral environment," which is the environment as conceived by the members of the society. The behavioral environment is part of the culture; it is what members of the society believe about the real environment. Much of the fate of the society in question will depend upon the interplay between the behavioral environment and the real environment, for it is the behavioral environment on the basis of which action is planned, but the real environment that largely determines what the outcomes of the action will be.[35]

But why is the study of the culture and the environment the "primary" task in the study of a society? First, because to understand what members of a society do requires understanding these basic factors. Second, because the fate of the society—the changes that will occur and the responses of the society to those changes—depend upon these factors. And third, because these factors provide the context within which individual action must be understood. That the first reason is true is fairly obvious. Insofar as the actions taken are determined by the culture, they must be explained in terms of the culture. Rule-governed behavior is a simple example. What I have called "cultural rules" above—rules that are followed by significant numbers of people in the society or that are institutionalized in the society—are part of the culture. English grammar, the driving code, rules of etiquette—these are all part of American culture, and to explain people's speech or their driving or their manner of greeting a friend by such rules is to explain them by their culture. Indeed, an enormous amount of what most people do every day is explicable in terms of their culture. But the explanatory role of the culture goes far beyond rule-governed behavior. To plan an action is to plan it in terms of what one believes the situation is, of what one believes one's own powers and abilities are, and of what one believes reference individuals or groups in one's society will approve or disapprove. These factors are largely determined by the culture. Individuals, of course, may deviate from their culture's way of conceptualizing themselves or their situation or others's beliefs about them, but in the usual case they draw upon the stock of concepts and beliefs provided by their culture and do not deviate very far from these. Thus by far the greater part of our ordinary daily actions are explicable, either wholly or in part, by our culture.

Second, given that it is the culture that enables a society to deal adaptively (or maladaptively) with its environment, surely the fate of the society will depend on the environment and the culture. The Indians of America had developed an adequate culture for dealing with their environment, until the Europeans invaded. Not only could most Indians not deal with the new social environment created by that invasion, they were totally unable to cope with the change in the biological environment created by the importation of European diseases. The result, as we all know, was catastrophic for the Indian societies throughout the Americas.[36] Hundreds of similar examples could be cited, ranging from the demise of the Norse settlements in Greenland owing to climatic change[37] to the disasters which befell China during the nineteenth century.

Third, individual action is always action within a cultural context, and it cannot be understood without taking that context into account. Much traditional history has focused on the actions of leaders and elites. Leadership is a relation between an individual or group who serves as leader and the population who are the followers. That relation varies dramatically from one culture to another. It is impossible to imagine Hitler achieving the power he did in the way he did had he made his career in England. Stalin would have been a miserable failure as an American politician, and Ronald Reagan would not have survived a week in the Soviet political system. Examples are easily multiplied. There are different kinds of political systems, and leaders who can function well in one type of system need not do so in another. Moreover, even within one type, there are radical variations. What makes a leader charismatic for a society at one time will not necessarily work in that society when it has developed a different culture. George Washington was a charismatic leader for the American people in the late eighteenth century; one doubts that he could be so for the American people today.

But the point goes far beyond questions of leadership. Consider the difference in daily activities between the average American adult woman and the average Saudi adult woman, and contrast both with the daily activities of the average adult Iroquois woman in 1600. Even with age, marital status, family size and composition, class, and health held constant, the differences would clearly be enormous. These are cultural differences due to the differences in beliefs—especially religious beliefs, the economies, family and sex roles, technology, etc., all parts of the culture. For the culture is also part of the environment of the individual; to be raised in a Christian society is to be raised in a Christian environment. Further, the personality system of the individual contains internalized norms and beliefs of the culture. Whether one's primary goal in life is salvation, glory, or wealth will depend to a considerable extent upon the culture into which one is socialized.

Culture plays an explanatory role in our understanding of both social and individual action. That seems so obvious that I hope readers are long since convinced, even if they were not at the beginning. It follows that what serves as an explanation for action in one culture may not do so in another. Since cultures vary from society to society, so do the rules governing behavior, the beliefs and motives and norms that determine action and guide plans. Praying may be one thing among Boston Unitarians of the early nineteenth century and quite a different thing among Shi'ite Muslims. This of course is not to deny that there are human universals—physical, biological, or psychological, and even cultural. But it is to emphasize that such universals are very rarely enough to explain human action. Humans learn, and what they learn affects what they do. Since they learn different things in different cultures, they do different things in different cultures, even though the laws of learning are culturally invariant. An understanding of human action is generally culture specific.

The "understanding" we have been talking about here is causal explanation. What one wants to know when one studies another society, or one's own, is why people do what they do. That is a causal question, and the answer to it must be a causal answer. Such explanation of course involves a description of the beliefs, the motives, and the norms of the people, and that in turn requires a description of the culture. But these factors must be combined to form an explanation, and, as we have seen, this involves the use of causal models. It is not necessary that such explanations be given in the form of covering law explanations or that they exhibit the causal processes upon which they are based. But if they really are causal explanations, they must refer to those causal relations, and provide information about the underlying ideal explanatory text.

That in fact this is what serious students of the past actually do should be obvious to anyone familiar with recent work in the field. However, it may be useful to cite two recent examples that have won considerable attention. Greene[38] has recently published a book concerned with the development—the course of change—that took place in England's overseas colonies during the seventeenth and eighteenth centuries. It should be noted that although Greene deals only with English colonial regions, there are a significant number of them—Ireland, New England, the Chesapeake, the Middle Atlantic, the lower South, Jamaica, the Leeward islands, and Barbados. What Greene argues is that in all but one (or possibly two—the island of Nevis he considers deviant from the general pattern of the Leewards) the same model of development applies.

The initial condition is the state of English culture at the time of colonization, which Greene argues was much more commercial, market oriented, mobile, and individualistic than has traditionally been thought. The settlers in all but one colonial area came seeking economic advantages for themselves, carrying the acquisitive individualism of Old England with them across the sea. Out of the interaction of this cultural inheritance with the specific conditions the settlers found upon arrival—conditions that varied from one colonial area to another, but that all involved entrance into a wilderness and/or an area with a hostile native population—there resulted a much simplified form of English culture, lacking the institutions, stratifications, and order of the homeland. With explosive population growth and economic success, the colonial regions then developed a more elaborate society and culture, created institutions and relationships that differentiated and organized their growing societies, and became going concerns. Having thus achieved some stability, considerable prosperity, and rapid growth, they sought increasingly to replicate in themselves the social and cultural order of Old England. Although the result was a highly cre-olized version of Old England, the colonial regions became more alike as they pursued their common goal, rather than less alike.

The deviant case is of course New England, where the Puritan settlers arrived committed to a utopian plan for a Puritan "city on a hill." Thus from the beginning the New Englanders differed in plan and motive and they succeeded in creating an ordered society on their own plan with a rapidity not seen in any other area. But Greene agrees with other historians that the Puritan New Israel failed, largely due to the explosive and unforseen population growth, economic success for which their plan did not allow, and the continuing influence of Old England, exercised in a vari-ety of ways. Thus New England fits what he calls the Declension Model; the Puritan community of the 1630s gave way to a society that by the latter half of the eighteenth century had become very much like the other colonial areas.

I am not concerned here with whether Greene's theory is right or wrong but with its structure. No brief summary can do justice to this work, but I hope what has been said is sufficient to make clear certain points. First of all, Greene deals not with one colonial region but eight. He is seek-ing to establish that a certain causal process took place in all England's colonies, not just one. This is thus a theory that has considerable generality. He does not deal with all colonies—he does not discuss those of France or Spain or Portugal, nor is it clear that he would expect the same causal model to apply in the colonies of those nations since the initial condi-tions—the homeland cultures—were different. But clearly the fact that seven of the eight English-colonized regions show the same process of development—and the eighth is not, in his view, as different as some have claimed—shows that he is describing a generalizable pattern, not a unique or peculiar development.

Furthermore, the causal factors that Greene specifies are many and quite diverse in kind. There is the natural environment into which the set-tlers moved, especially the disease-related features of the environment. Another factor is the goals, aspirations, and beliefs of the colonists—cul-tural factors that brought them to the colonies to begin with and largely determined their behavior once they were there. A third factor is the consequences of their actions in implementing their plans and values—rapid demographic growth, rising economic prosperity, geographic mobility, urban growth, settlement patterns, and so on. Still another factor is the colonists' commitment to, and desire to follow, the normative patterns of the mother country, and to reproduce these in their own settlements. Here one sees the blending of natural, physical, social, and cultural factors that one would expect to find in any attempt to construct an explanation of large scale socio-cultural change.

Even in Greene's deviant case—New England—factors of the same sort are the determinants. The Puritans came to New England committed to establishing a particular type of socio-cultural order—to following a particular plan. Greene does not have to prove this because a generation of scholars since Perry Miller have already done so. The Puritans' early success in achieving this goal may have been overestimated, as Greene thinks, but that they came close to achieving it is generally agreed. The problem has been to explain why they failed in the long run, given their early success. That population growth and economic development were key causes of this failure is clearly true, particularly since neither accorded with the expectations of the original Puritan plan (they did expect prosperity, but not the kind of economic development that actually occurred). So was the influence of Old England, especially after the Restoration, and so was the fact that, besides being Puritans, these people were English and held many of the same values as the other colonists in other regions.

In short, this is a historical work that propounds a theory about the development of the British colonies in the Western hemisphere and Ireland over a period of roughly two hundred years. It is a causal theory, integrating natural, physical, psychological, and socio-cultural factors to provide an explanation of what took place. The theory has generality within a given region of time and space. It is implicit in the theory that, were it possible to replicate the exact socio-cultural, psychological, biological, and physical conditions in a different spatio-temporal region, the same process would be observed, but since such a replication is improbable to the point of impossibility, Greene does not bother to make such a claim. Nevertheless, this is a causal theory in the sense discussed above, and an excellent example of the best of the new history.

It is worth pointing out that Greene's account is not narrative history. The resurgence of narrativism in recent years among philosophers of history owes more to literary fashions and fads than it does to what is actually happening in the historical trade. Particularly in areas such as social, economic, political and demographic history, the narrative is being displaced by analyses of causal processes. This is hardly surprising. As our understanding of causal relations in human society and culture increases, there is less and less need to rely on the arts of the novelist to persuade the reader that the historians know what they are talking about.

David Fischer's massive volume,[39] the first in a projected series of at least six, deals with much the same time period and many of the same settlements—New England, the Chesapeake, the Mid-Atlantic, and those areas settled on the North American continent by the Scotch-Irish. But Fischer's account differs sharply from Greene's. Whereas Greene believes all English colonists brought with them to the colonies essentially the same English culture, Fischer holds that England itself had radically different regional subcultures. Fischer further argues that the colonists who settled each of the four areas with which he deals came from four different regions of Britain, and so brought with them quite different versions of English culture. It was the importation of these different regional cultures that explains the marked cultural differences among the colonial regions, defined as the areas settled by immigrants from the culturally distinct regions of the British Isles. Thus Fischer's theory is a kind of diffusionist model, where the diffusion of British subcultures to America is the result of the migration of culture carriers from the old country to the new.

In his second volume, soon to be published, Fischer uses the same method in dealing with the importation of African culture into America, first seeking to determine the African sources of the imported slaves and the regional cultures in Africa from which they came, and then to specify where they settled in America. It is Fischer's contention that the importation of slaves to the American South was highly selective, and that as a result different African cultures came to prevail in different regions of the South.

The first two volumes of Fischer's series, despite their awesome size, are really only a setting of the initial conditions for the analysis of group interactions and change with which Fischer intends to deal in later volumes. But even in these initial works, there is clearly a causal theory of culture transfer underlying the whole argument. If Fischer is right about the existence and nature of the regional subcultures in Britain and about the settlement patterns of immigrants from these regions in the New World, then many of the characteristics of the colonial cultures are explained by a simple model of culture transfer. The objective is clearly to understand the colonial cultures, but understanding here means showing why they had the characteristics they had. This is a causal question, and Fischer's answer to it is a causal answer.

It is an intriguing aspect of the two works, which appeared at approximately the same time, that the theories they propose contradict each other. The most dramatic contradiction concerns the state of seventeenth-century

British culture. Fischer holds that it was far less unified and much more divided into geographically distinct regional subcultures than has customarily been thought. Greene holds that, at least with respect to those cultural characteristics influencing colonial culture, British culture can be treated as a unified whole, except with respect to religion. It should be emphasized that these are major differences in the theories proposed, *and* that they are differences that can—and will—be settled by empirical research. These are not matters of the scholars's values somehow distorting their vision, of "prejudice" or "alternative and incommensurable interpretations." They are matters of evidence and of testing contradictory theories against that evidence.

The position for which I have argued here is that the study of the past is an empirical study, the evidential base for which is presently existing data, both documentary and artifactual. The past itself, and those entities, events, relationships, and so on that we believe to have existed in the past, are postulates to account for the evidential base. From an epistemological point of view, these postulated entities are theoretical constructs functioning like those in physical theories. Thus our method of studying the past is the hypothetico-deductive method, and theories about the past are not different in kind from those in other areas of science. Whether or not these postulated entities are real is an ontological question, not an epistemological one. They are real if our theory is true, and truth is attainable in the study of the past, given adequate evidence, just as it is in other fields. Our present theory may or may not be true, and even if not true may contain subtheories that are true. But whether they are true or not, our best confirmed present theory is our best estimate of what the truth is.

Theories of this sort about the past seek to attain an understanding of what happened and why it happened. They are causal theories, regardless of the style in which they are formulated. Scholarly works about the past do in fact seek to explain why what happened did happen, and to whom, and where, when, and how it did. Any examination of historical studies will show that the authors do seek to provide such explanations, and the norms of the trade demand that serious works should do so. As we have seen, such explanations involve the use of various sorts of elements, ranging from universal laws to cultural rules, and may be formulated in singular causal statements that convey information about the underlying ideal explanatory text. But when a scholar asserts that historical actors did what they did because they had certain beliefs and motives, a causal explanation is being advanced, whether implicitly or explicitly.

The position taken here, I presume, will be met with various objections, and I would like to consider a number of these. One that is sure to be advanced is the claim that the past cannot be known as it really was, and that our theories about the past must therefore be incomplete and inaccurate. The problem with this objection is that it assumes the truth of Metaphysical Realism and therefore that there is something called the past that is somehow given. The epistemological problem then becomes how we can know this mysterious past. But this leaves us with the same sort of epistemological gap that classic realist theories have faced—namely, how do we know our ideas correspond to this mind independent reality? The fact that this question is obviously unanswerable shows that the question has been wrongly posed.

If instead of assuming the past as a given, we ask why we should think there is a past, the answer is clearly that we think so because we have evidence for its existence. This comes to down saying that the existence of the past and its contents are postulated to account for the evidence we have. Then the question of the reality of the past and its "contents" becomes the question of whether or not the theory in which we postulate their existence is true. As we saw in Chapter 6, there is no reason to deny that such a theory may be true, or that, however imperfect our present theory may be, a true theory may be attained in the long run. We can never know with certainty that we have attained a true theory, since further investigations may always reveal shortcomings in what we believe, but this is true of all human knowledge—certainty, we shall never have.

Narrativism

Since the 1960s, there has been a resurgence of the view that studies of the past must be in narrative form, and that in some fashion narrative represents a "form of explanation." Now, it is certainly an empirical fact that many studies of past persons and events are written in narrative form. The question is whether or not this fact has any significance with respect to the sort of explanations that they offer. It should be obvious that it need not be significant. A narrative typically involves some temporal ordering of a series of events, conditions, and persons. Temporal ordering in itself is a relevant fact about what happens but it is not explanatory; that Julius Caesar died before World War I does not establish any explanatory relation between these events. In fact, mere temporal ordering is not even sufficient to create what is usually called a narrative. The question then becomes, what more is involved in narrative beyond mere temporal ordering, and is the resulting narrative explanatory?

The most prominent advocate of narrative as explanatory is White, whose writings have been very influential. Although White's writings on this subject are numerous, the most complete statement of his views is in

Metahistory,[40] and it will be worthwhile to look at his position in some detail. White describes the process of "conceptualization in the historical work" as having five "levels"—chronicle, story, mode of emplotment, mode of argument, and mode of ideological implication.[41] But these "levels" rest on a prior process of "prefiguration" of the "historical field." It will be well to have White's own statement as to what this involves:

> Historical accounts purport to be verbal models, or icons, of specific segments of the historical process. But such models are needed because the documentary record does not figure forth an unambiguous image of the structure of events attested in them. In order to figure "what *really* happened" in the past, therefore, the historian must first *pre*figure as a possible object of knowledge the whole set of events reported in the documents. This prefigurative act is *poetic* inasmuch as it is precognitive and precritical in the economy of the historian's own consciousness. It is also poetic insofar as it is constitutive of the structure that will subsequently be imaged in the verbal model offered by the historian as a representation and explanation of "what *really* happened" in the past. But it is constitutive not only of a domain which the historian can treat as a possible object of (mental) perception. It is also constitutive of the *concepts* he will use *to identify the objects* that inhabit that domain and *to characterize the kinds of relationships* they can sustain with one another. In the poetic act which precedes the formal analysis of the field, the historian both creates his object of analysis and predetermines the modality of the conceptual strategies he will use to explain it.
>
> But the number of possible explanatory strategies is not infinite. There are, in fact, four principal types, which correspond to the four principal tropes of poetic language.[42]

The tropes referred to are Metaphor, Metonymy, Synecdoche, and Irony. Of these, White says,

> We consider the three tropes thus far discussed [Metaphor, Metonymy, and Synecdoche] as paradigms, provided by language itself, of the operations by which consciousness can prefigure areas of experience that are cognitively problematic in order subsequently to submit them to analysis and explanation. That is to say, in linguistic usage itself, thought is provided with possible alternative paradigms of explanation. Metaphor is rep-

resentational in the way that Formism can be seen to be. Metonymy is reductive in a Mechanistic manner, while Synecdoche is integrative in the way that Organicism is. Metaphor sanctions the prefiguration of the world of experience in object-object terms, Metonymy in part-part terms, and Synecdoche in object-whole terms. Each trope also promotes cultivation of a unique linguistic protocol. These linguistic protocols can be called the languages of identity (Metaphor), extrinsicality (Metonymy), and intrinsicality (Synecdoche).

Against these three tropes, which I characterize as "naive" (since they can be deployed only in the belief in language's capacity to grasp the nature of things in figurative terms), the trope of Irony stands as a "sentimental" (in Schiller's sense of "self-conscious") counterpart. It has been suggested that Irony is essentially dialectical, inasmuch as it represents a self-conscious use of Metaphor in the interests of verbal self-negation. The basic figurative tactic of Irony is catachresis (literally "misuse"), the manifestly absurd Metaphor designed to inspire Ironic second thoughts about the nature of the thing characterized or the inadequacy of the characterization itself. . . .

The trope of Irony, then, provides a linguistic paradigm of a mode of thought which is radically self-critical with respect not only to a given characterization of the world of experience but also to the very effort to capture adequately the truth of things in language. It is, in short, a model of the linguistic protocol in which skepticism in thought and relativism in ethics are conventionally expressed.[43]

White's claim is that *before* historical investigation itself begins, there is a prior stage in which, from the evidence used, the historian develops an imaginative (poetic) construct containing the entities of the "historical field" and their relations. This process is said to be "precognitive" and to be based upon linguistic paradigms (the tropes), which determine the way the historical field will be structured. It is then linguistic forms—the "four basic tropes for the analysis of poetic, or figurative, language"[44]—that determine how the historical field is populated. Once this has been done, *then* according to White the cognitive process begins, with the organization of "the elements in the historical field" into a "chronicle," meaning a temporal ordering of the events to be dealt with. The chronicle is then converted into a "story" "by the characterization of some events in the chronicle in terms of inaugural motifs, of others in terms of terminating motifs, and of yet others in terms of transitional motifs."[45] That is to say, the temporal series of the chronicle is organized into a story having a beginning, a middle, and an end. But what kind of story? White indicates that "Providing the 'meaning' of a story by identifying the *kind of story* that has been told is called explanation by emplotment."[46]

There are for White four kinds of emplotment: Romance, Tragedy, Comedy, and Satire.[47] These are "archetypal"[48] story forms, and the historical narrative or story will be of one of these four types. The choice of a plot type, White thinks, carries "explanatory affect,"[49] presumably because it assimilates the narrative to a form the reader already knows. But emplotment alone does not provide a complete explanation; there are further "levels" at which one "may seek to explicate 'the point of it all' or 'what it all adds up to' in the end."[50] "Formist" explanation, in White's terminology, is "complete when a given set of objects has been properly identified, its class, generic, and specific attributes assigned, and labels attesting to its particularity attached to it. . . . When the historian has established the uniqueness of the particular objects in the field or the variety of the types of phenomena which the fields manifests, he has provided a Formist explanation of the field as such."[51] "Organicist" explanation rests on

> a metaphysical commitment to the paradigm of the microcosmic-macrocosmic relationship; and the Organicist historian will tend to be governed by the desire to see individual entities as components of processes which aggregate into wholes that are greater than, or qualitatively different from, the sum of their parts.[52]

"Mechanist" explanations are causal explanations and involve the search for and use of causal laws; thus covering law explanations and causal process explanations fall under this rubric.[53] "Contextualist" explanation rests on the claim that "'what happened' in the field can be accounted for by the specification of the functional interrelationships existing among the agents and agencies occupying the field at a given time."[54]

The final "level" of explanation for White is ideological, by which he means the ethical implications of the narrative for "the present world of social praxis."[55] According to White, "The very claim to have distinguished a past from a present world of social thought and praxis, and to have determined the formal coherence of that past world, *implies* a conception of the form that knowledge of the present world also must take, insofar as it is *continuous* with that past world."[56] The four ideological positions he terms Anarchism, Conservatism, Radicalism, and Liberalism.[57] The role of these ideological positions is explained thus:

Radicals share with Liberals a belief in the possibility of study-ing history "rationally" and "scientifically," but they have differ-ent conceptions of what a rational and scientific historiography might consist of. The former seeks the laws of historical struc-tures and processes, the latter the general trends or main drift of development. Like Radicals and Liberals, Conservatives and Anarchists believe, in conformity with a general nineteenth-century conviction, that the "meaning" of history can be dis-covered and presented in conceptual schemata that are cogni-tively responsible and not simply authoritarian. But their conception of a distinctively *historical* knowledge requires a faith in "intuition" as the ground on which a putative "science" of history might be constructed. The Anarchist is inclined toward the essentially empathetic techniques of Romanticism in his historical accounts, while the Conservative is inclined to *integrate* his several intuitions of the objects in the historical field into a comprehensive Organicist account of the whole process.[58]

As this suggests, the various forms of emplotment, argument, and ideology are not wholly independent. White holds that there are "elective affinities" among them, such that usually (but not necessarily) Romantic plot goes with Formist argument and Anarchist ideology, Tragic with Mech-anistic and Radical, Comic with Organicist and Conservative, and Satirical with Contextualist and Liberal. Such combinations constitute what White calls the historian's "style."[59]

What is one to make of all this? Whatever the ingenuity of White's scheme, it is objectionable on a number of counts. First, and probably most obviously, history as White conceives it cannot be true. On this point, it will be well to let White speak for himself. Speaking of those historians he regards as models, White says

Their status as possible models of historical representation or conceptualization does not depend upon the nature of the "data" they used to support their generalizations or the theories they invoked to explain them; it depends rather upon the con-sistency, coherence, and the illuminative power of their respec-tive visions of the historical field. This is why they cannot be "refuted," or their generalizations "disconfirmed," either by appeal to new data that might be turned up in subsequent research or by the elaboration of a new theory for interpreting the sets of events that comprise their objects of representation and analysis. Their status as models of historical narration and conceptualization depends, ultimately, on the preconceptual and specifically poetic nature of their perspectives on history and its processes.[60]

The study of the past, as conceived by White, is a poetic, imaginative enterprise for the results of which no truth claims can be advanced. But as a description of what historians do, and of what they say they do, this is patently false. Historians do claim truth for their accounts. White's account therefore is inconsistent with the central objective of the study of the past as it is actually practiced by historians.

What has led White to so bizarre a thesis? I am not interested in the writers who have influenced him (although influences are readily apparent and freely acknowledged), but in the underlying ideas that support this set of claims. And the trouble begins, not surprisingly, at the beginning, with the notion of "prefiguration." In White's view, the historian imaginatively constructs the historical field *before* the cognitive work of historical study begins. This is simply a rather novel version of the thesis of the classical historiography that the historian first establishes what the facts are and *then* proceeds to develop his "interpretation" by selecting among and ordering those facts.[61] Once this position is taken, the historian faces the demand that he justify his selection and ordering of the pre-existing facts, and as a number of writers such as Beard and Becker have pointed out, no criteria can be provided for doing this that are not subjective or at least value-laden. The result is that truth claims for works so generated cannot be made.

But what this shows is that the classical historiography is wrong. Past entities, actions, and events are not just poetically imagined; they are postulated as parts of a theory accounting for the evidence. That Richard III of England existed, that he was killed on Bosworth Field in 1485—these postulates, from an epistemological point of view, are part of our theory accounting for presently existing objects, taken as evidence. Fact and theory are no more separable in the study of the past than subatomic particles are separable from the physical theory which posits their existence. Historical theories can be confirmed or refuted because they do or do not best explain the evidence.

Once one recognizes the basic error in White's theory, much of the rationale for it goes by the board. One could still hold that White has some interesting things to say about the kinds of narratives historians write. White's case studies of Michelet, Ranke, Tocqueville, and Burkhardt could be taken as giving some credence to that claim. But if some historians can be found who fit the mold, others can be found who do not. How would one classify Miller's *New England Mind: The Seventeenth Century* or Wood-ward's *Origins of the New South?* The examples can be proliferated easily enough. And once one is clear that poetic prefiguration is a myth, the appeal of White's linguistic and literary approach is largely lost. Why should one think that all narratives fit "archetypal" patterns derived from literature? Is there no distinction to be drawn between a historical study and a historical novel? Do historians really choose a plot type to impose upon their data? And is all historical work necessarily ideological? As factual statements about what all (or most) historians do, these claims are false. That one can find ideologically biased historians is surely true; that proves nothing about the trade as a whole.

White's work represents one of the more extreme versions of the narrativism now in circulation. A far more deeply considered version is to be found in the writings of Louis Mink. A philosopher of distinction, Mink was one of the leaders of the revolt against the application of Hempel's covering law theory to history, and against positivism generally. It is certainly not surprising that a thinker with a strong interest in aesthetics should have opposed positivism, but what seems to have led Mink to his views on history was the conviction that Hempel's paradigm simply could not be made to fit what historians do. Mink sought to go behind the claims that this or that type of explanation is primary to ask on what sort of understanding knowledge is based.

Mink's answer was "comprehension":

> The fact to which any theory of knowledge must return is the simple fact that experiences come to us *seriatim* in time and yet must be capable of being held together in an image of the manifold of events. The steps of a proof, the actions of a narrative, the notes of a melody, and even the words of a sentence are experienced one after the other, but must be considered in a single mental act before they even constitute data for significant discourse. Such an act, which may be called "comprehension," differs from both judgment and inference and is in fact presupposed by both.[62]

Citing both Descartes and Plato to support this claim, Mink says "It is at least notable that they agree in regarding comprehension as a kind of *totum simul*, the grouping in a single act as a totality of what the discursive intellect otherwise can review only *seriatim*."[63] Now this is not exactly a new idea: Kant said it, Royce developed it, others have used it, so the notion has a respectable pedigree. But Mink goes on to specify three kinds of comprehension—theoretical (the relation of theory to its instances), categorical (the relation of categories to their members), and configurational (the holding together of a number of particular elements in some sort of unity).[64] Comprehension is not knowledge, but "as the human activity by which elements of knowledge are converted into *understanding*, it is the synoptic vision without which (even though transiently and partially attained) we might forever pass in review our shards of knowledge as in some nightmare quiz show where nothing relates "fact" to "fact" except the fragmented identities of the participants and the mounting total of the score."[65]

As one might guess, narrative emerges as a type of configurational comprehension:

> Why do stories bear repeating? In some cases, no doubt, because of the pleasure they give, in others because of the meaning they bear. But in any case, if the theory of comprehension is right, because they aim at producing and strengthening the act of understanding in which actions and events, although represented as occurring in the order of time, can be surveyed as it were in a single glance as bound together in an order of significance, a representation of the *totum simul* which we can never more than partially achieve. This outcome must seem either a truism or a paradox: in the understanding of a narrative the thought of temporal succession as such vanishes—or perhaps, one might say, remains like the smile of the Cheshire Cat.[66]

It is just because the narrative permits one to see the temporal sequence of events as a unity that it functions as a cognitive instrument in permitting us to understand what happened. The narrative is a whole; it cannot be paraphrased[67] nor does it lead to results that can be separated out from the narrative itself.[68]

But can narrative history be true? Mink struggled long and hard with this problem without coming to a conclusion. As he recognized, the narrative does not correspond to life.[69] Furthermore, narratives do not aggregate; adding one narrative to another does not produce a more complete narrative, but just two conjoined narratives.[70] But the problem goes deeper.

> So narrative form in history, as in fiction, is an artifice, the product of individual imagination. Yet at the same time it is accepted as claiming truth—that is, as representing a real ensemble of interrelationships in past actuality. Nor can we say that narrative form is like a hypothesis in science, which is the

product of individual imagination but once suggested leads to research that can confirm or disconfirm it. The crucial difference is that the narrative combination of relations is simply not subject to confirmation or disconfirmation, as any one of them taken separately might be. So we have a second dilemma about historical narrative: as historical it claims to represent, through its form, part of the real complexity of the past, but as narrative it is a product of imaginative construction, which cannot defend its claim to truth by any accepted procedure of argument or authentication.[71]

Mink's solution, insofar as he had one, was a flirtation with the idea of abandoning the notion of history as a representation of a single determinate past.[72] But this, as Mink noted, means that "narrative history and narrative fiction move closer together than common sense could well accept."[73] But there he left the issue, without apparently being able to get further with it before his death.

Can historical narratives be true? White thinks they cannot, and thereby abandons what most historians regard as their primary goal. Mink thought there had to be some sense in which they are true, but he never succeeded in saying what that sense is. More recently, McCullagh has argued that indeed historical narratives are true. His claim is that historians's narratives are true when they provide "a fair overall representation of the central subject of their narratives."[74] This claim is unpacked in terms of a set of criteria for "fair representation." McCullagh says "for an historical narrative to provide a true account of its central subject, all the descriptions of the subject which it contains must be true."[75] This amounts to the demand that the separate descriptive sentences of the narrative be true—a demand which rejects any sort of holistic view of truth. But even if this requirement is met, it is not sufficient, for the individual sentences could be true, McCullagh thinks, and yet the narrative be misleading.[76] Three further criteria are therefore asserted to be necessary. First, "a fair representation of the fortunes of a central subject is one in which all major changes to its characteristic properties and relations are described."[77] By "characteristic properties and relations," McCullagh means those the historian regards as essential or as at least the most important properties and relations of the subject. But how do we know that all the important properties and relations are described? Although McCullagh is an epistemological realist, he admits that the subject as described cannot be compared to the subject *an sich*. "The comparison is made, then, not with the subject itself but with what is known of it, it being assumed that the subject really had the properties believed true of it on the basis of the available evidence."[78] Second, the narrative must not be "misleading" "It must not imply any facts about the subject which are false."[79] There are two ways in which a narrative could be misleading. One is by omitting some feature of the subject that the reader would justifiably expect to be mentioned if it were present, thus falsely suggesting its absence. Thus a biography that never mentioned a man's marriage would suggest to most readers that the subject never married, whether he did or not. The second way is by describing the subject in terms that, although accurate, may have connotations that are not appropriate. McCullagh cites Skinner's example that stressing the concern of radical English political thinkers in the seventeenth century for extending the franchise may suggest to the modern reader that these people were advocates of modern liberal democracy.[80] Third, McCullagh requires that "a narrative be written with a fairly uniform degree of detail"; This requirement really means two things: that "once the level [of generality] of the central subject has been decided, it should be sustained throughout the narrative,"[81] and "at whatever level of generality it is being written, the narrative should maintain the same degree of detail."[82] If these three criteria are met, McCullagh claims, "then the narrative will indeed be true as a whole of the subject it describes."[83]

Nevertheless, McCullagh is a bit worried about the use of the word "true" here:

> Are we justified in calling a fair representation "true"? There is admittedly some reason to doubt that the word "true" is being used correctly here, though I think its application in this case is justified. Strictly speaking, a sentence is true if it correctly represents part of reality. But we can usefully distinguish a true sentence and a fair, or true, description. The sentence "John's dog has two legs, one eye and a bushy tail" may be true; but it hardly provides a fair or true description of John's dog. It omits equally prominent features, such as its mouth, nose, and ears; it gives the misleading impression that the dog does not have four legs and two eyes; and it refers to the bushiness of its tail but says nothing about the rest of its coat. It is a true sentence, but not a true description of the dog. To use the word "true" in the latter sense is to mean "reliable" or "trustworthy." This is an old sense of the word, as in "a good man and true," which seems quite appropriate here. If it is appropriate here, then it is equally appropriate in describing historical narratives which satisfy the three conditions set out above. They give true, that is reliable, impressions of the fortunes of their central subject.[84]

McCullagh is quite right to be worried, for in fact his whole argument begs the question. To see this, consider a history of the Great Depression in the United States. What will be the "major changes to its [the United States economy] characteristic properties and relations" will depend on what theory of the nature and causes of the Great Depression one advances. Milton Friedman, John Galbraith, and Peter Temin each view the Depression in different terms, and disagree over such matters as what caused what. To say that historians must present a "fair representation" of the properties and relations of their subject which they view as important is to say very little indeed; the question is whether or not those properties and relation are in fact important. But what is the criterion for deciding that question? Since the importance of the properties and relations depends upon their role in the theory advanced, the criterion is obviously one for deciding among theories. But McCullagh has no such criterion, nor does his epistemological realist view permit the development of one.

McCullagh's notion of narrative "truth" may seem analogous to Goodman and Elgin's notion of "rightness,"[85] but the analogy is not helpful. Aside from the vagueness of Goodman and Elgin's notion, the essential point is that historical accounts are supposed to be both true and explanatory. "Rightness" in this case must therefore include the choice of those properties necessary for the explanation of the data in question and an accurate description of those properties for the particular case. But, as noted, McCullagh has no criterion for picking out which properties are relevant for causal explanation. Rather, his notion of "truth" seems to be one of a fair "sampling" of properties of the actual subject. But, leaving aside the issue of how one samples properties, the point of the account is not simply to depict the central subject in all its glory but to account for its behavior. And neither explanation of its behavior nor fair sampling of its properties has any intrinsic relation to narrative. A description is not a narrative. Neither is an causal explanation. What then does narrative add?

Narrative is not a distinctive explanatory form. A causal theory can be stated in narrative form, and most historical narratives are implicitly if not explicitly causal accounts. The truth of a narrative is no more and no less than the truth of the causal theory it expresses. It is quite clear that such causal theories can be confirmed or disconfirmed on the basis of evidence, given that the evidence is adequate. But whether the explanatory theory is stated in narrative form or in some other form is irrelevant to the truth of the theory. There is no distinctive truth condition for narratives, as is demonstrated by the inability of any of the narrativists to provide any.

It is not very surprising that so much historical scholarship takes the narrative form. Historical works generally deal with temporal sequences, and narrative offers a simple—seductively simple—way of conveying temporal series. The central portion of a narrative usually involves as well a causal sequence, and since causal chains are often temporally ordered, narrative can be used to formulate such a causal theory. But it should be emphasized that narrative is also a rhetorical device, and that it is used in ordinary speech to convey information in a form which is "tellable," that is, that holds the audience's attention.[86] Nineteenth- and many twentieth-century historians have addressed themselves to audiences beyond the academy, and have therefore been responding to incentives to make their accounts "tellable" to laymen. The turn away from narrative history is a relatively recent phenomenon that has more to do with professionalization, a changed perception of the audience available, and the influence of the social sciences than with a change in philosophic perspectives. Historians have always seen it as their task to give accounts that explain what happened and why, and that are true.

It should be emphasized that these remarks concerning narrative history are not intended to be prescriptive. The point is not what historians should do but what they do do. Most of them write narratives, but most also seek to give true accounts of their subjects and to provide causal explanations of what occurred. There clearly is no reason why a narrative mode of presentation should not be used in writing about the past, but it is important to recognize that narrative form *per se* has nothing to do with the truth of the account or with its explanatory power. The confusion that has arisen over these points has been largely due to the reaction against Hempel's covering law model, which many historians and philosophers saw as a polemical attempt to force history to fit the Procrustean bed of physics. But the inadequacy of Hempel's theory hardly justifies the mystification of White's theory. History is a social science that seeks to describe what happened and to explain why it happened. The particular style in which particular historians may choose to present their results is irrelevant to the truth or explanatory power of their findings.

Confirmation

What poses a problem, and a serious one, for the position taken here is the difficulty of confirming theories about the past. If, as I have argued, our knowledge of the past is a theoretical construction developed to explain present data, then the critical issue is whether or not these theories can be confirmed or disconfirmed. I think it is clear that theories in contemporary social science—theories that deal with the same categories of human culture and human action as theories about the past—do admit of confirmation or disconfirmation. The question is whether or not the methods that apply in the social sciences also apply in the historical sciences. The answer to that question is less clear than one would like.

To pose the problem, consider a large past population N of n members, constituting a society that we wish to study. If this were a contemporary population, the approach would be fairly obvious; draw a probability sample, K, of k members from the population and obtain the necessary data from those k members by the usual data collection methods used in social science. But where the population is past, access to its members can only be through artifacts (documentary or other) that remain to us. Although there are exceptional cases, the general situation is that the subset of k members of the population to which we can gain access in this way is not a probability sample of the population of n members. Since statistical methods of analysis and of hypothesis testing assume probability samples, this fact makes the application of such methods to the historical case at least dubious.

There are really two different points that must be distinguished. First, given our set, K, of k members to whom there can be access, standard statistical methods are adequate to obtain probability samples from K. We can accordingly (if the data are adequate) make generalizations about the set K of accessible members of the past population. But second, we cannot generalize from the set K to the original population N, since the set K is not a probability sample from the original population.

It is sometimes the case that which members of the original population, N, are accessible through existing data is determined by deliberate human action. Sometimes data are destroyed precisely for the purpose of making it impossible for later scholars to learn about a given person or group. But this is a rare situation; much more common is the case where the survival of artifacts is the result of a large number of independent factors—war, flood, fire, decay, and so on. If the operation of these factors were known to be random, it would be possible to construct a probability model of the survival process, but we do not at present know enough about how these factors operate to justify assumptions for such a model. Still, if the process is not random, it certainly involves large elements of chance. It is therefore not an unreasonable approach to try to determine as best we can what biases the data contain and to correct against these biases. Even so, one is only hypothetically justified in using standard statistical hypothesis testing and estimation methods to test a hypothesis regarding N. The best we seem able to do at present is to develop theories that integrate as much of the existing data as possible.

Given this situation, it is particularly important to combine types of data which have different and offsetting biases. Documents require literacy, which is even now not universal. Much artifactual data is drawn from social strata in which literacy is apt to be low. Court records, city directories, census returns, church records, ceramics, tools, furniture, houses, bones—each of these types of data involves characteristic biases. A theory that can integrate a wide range of data types therefore has a better claim than one that is based on only one type of data. There is no formalized hypothesis-testing procedure here, no algorithm by which one can compute the probability of being in error by a given amount, but such methods could be developed if creative statisticians are willing to make the attempt.

A second problem of confirmation arises from the incompleteness of the data available concerning members of past populations. The standard data collection instruments used in the social sciences—the interview schedule and the questionnaire—involve the presentation to the subject of certain stimuli and the recording the subject's responses. Ideally, for every subject a complete set of responses can be generated, so that comparable data are available for all subjects. Observation schedules differ in that the investigator does not present the stimuli to the subject but records the responses made by the subject to stimuli that are observed by the investigator. But in the historical case, such methods are of dubious utility. One cannot present stimuli to the dead, nor can one observe (usually) the stimuli to which they were responding. Oral histories do approximate the case of the interview or questionnaire, but the approximation is not as close as one might think. Ask a man his opinion about the present president of the United States, and you have a good chance of getting a reply that is an accurate indicator of his attitude (if he has one and knows who the President is). Ask him what his opinion of Jack Kennedy was in 1963, and the chance of getting an answer that is an accurate indicator is slight; he may not remember, he may remember all too well and lie about it, or his memory may be so colored by subsequent events that what he thinks he remembers bears little relation to what he actually thought in 1963.

When one gets access to a member of a past population through an artifactual trace—say, for example, a letter—one usually does not know what stimuli evoked the content of the letter. The failure of the writer to mention a given subject therefore does not imply ignorance of the subject or lack of concern about it; it may simply not have been a relevant matter to discuss in this letter to this person. In contemporary social science, non-response in interviews or questionnaires has a well-understood interpretation; a person who cannot or will not answer a question others answer, or who is not available for questioning when others are, is clearly in some respect deviant and must be treated as a problem case. But in the historical case, unless by some chance the data were created in a uniform format, the content of the artifactual traces will vary radically from individual to individual. Non-response—the failure of subject A to discuss topic X although subject B does discuss it—may be purely a chance matter, depending upon the specific stimuli to which A and B responded. It is therefore not clear how to interpret the extremely fragmentary character of historical data. Attempts to construct probability models of how these data might have been generated—for example, stimulus sampling models—have been unsuccessful, and no other systematic approach to the problem has been proposed. What makes the issue particularly important is that many measurement models used in contemporary social science assume complete, or relatively complete, response sets from all respondents. Usually nothing resembling a complete response set can be obtained for a historical subject, and different subjects yield response sets incomplete in different ways. Since we do not know how to interpret this sort of incompleteness, the problem of using such measurement models remains unsolved.

The only real hope of dealing with missing data is either to find the missing data or to find other data from which the missing data can be inferred. Of course, the success of attempts to do the latter depends upon establishing theoretical linkages between types of data, such that from one type certain characteristics of the other can be inferred. Thus we wish to know the incomes of members of an 1820 population in the United States. In general, such information does not exist. Therefore, attempts have been made to infer income from occupation, concerning which data does exist, on the theoretical assumption that occupation and income are highly correlated. In fact, in the 1820s, they are not highly correlated, so the attempt fails.[87] This simple example makes two important points. First, correlations that hold in contemporary American society do not necessarily hold in the past; such a theoretical claim must be confirmed on the past population before it can be used as a basis for inference. Second, only by establishing confirmed theoretical linkages can such inferences about missing data be made.

Historians often profess an unreconstructed empiricism and scorn theory. This is a mistake: Given the fragmentary character of historical data, historians have a greater need for theory than sociologists or economists. It is only by elaborating theories that disparate types of data can be integrated, missing data inferred, and a reasonably comprehensive picture of a past society generated. This point should be fairly obvious upon reflection by anyone who has done historical research. Less obvious perhaps is the fact that all historical knowledge is a theoretical construction to account for present evidence. Hence, if we are to claim truth for our knowledge of the past, it is vitally important that our methods of confirming or disconfirming historical theories be significantly improved. This is the problem upon which historical methodologists should be concentrating their fire.[88]

Notes

1. Louis O. Mink, *Historical Understanding*. Brian Fay, Eugene O. Golob, and Richard T. Vann, eds., (Ithaca, N.Y.: Cornell University Press, 1987), 93. (Emphasis in original)

2. Murray G. Murphey, *Our Knowledge of the Historical Past* (Indianapolis: Bobbs-Merrill, 1973), ch. 1.

3. Charles Darwin, *On The Origin of Species* (London: John Murray, 1859); *The Descent of Man* (London: John Murray, 1871), 2 vols.

4. Murphey, *Our Knowledge*, ch. 2.

5. P. H. Nowell-Smith, "The Constructionist Theory of History," *History and Theory Beiheft 16, The Constitution of the Historical Past* (Middletown: Wesleyan University Press, 1977), 15–19.

6. Ibid., 11–13.

7. John M. Allegro, *The Dead Sea Scrolls and the Christian Myth* (New York: Prometheus Books, 1984).

8. William Cronon, *Changes in the Land* (New York: Hill and Wang, 1983), 85–90.

9. Hallowell, *Culture and Experience*, chs. 1, 4. Geertz, *Interpretation of Cultures*, ch. 2.

10. George W. Stocking, Jr. "Franz Boas and the Culture Concept in Historical Perspective," *American Anthropologist* 68:867–882 (1966).

11. A. L. Kroeber, "The Superorganic," *American Anthropologist* 19:163–213 (1917). Marvin Harris, *Cultural Materialism* (New York: Random House, 1979).

12. Ward H. Goodenough, *Culture, Language, and Society* (Menlo Park, Calif.: Benjamin/Cummings Publishing Co., 1981), ch. 4.

13. Ibid., 107.

14. Talcott Parsons and Edward A. Shils, *Toward a General Theory of Action* (New York: Academic Press, 1951), Part 1, ch. 1.

15. Goodenough, *Culture*, ch. 3.

16. S. D. Houston, *Maya Glyphs* (Berkeley and Los Angeles: University of California Press, 1989), 8.

17. John Chadwick, *The Decipherment of Linear B* (Cambridge: Cambridge University Press, 1967), 55ff. Florian Coulmas, *Writing Systems of the World* (Oxford: Basil Blackwell, 1989), 220.

18. Houston, *Maya Glyphs*, 25.

19. Sir E. A. Wallis Budge, *The Rosetta Stone in the British Museum*. (New York: AMS Press, 1976).

20. Coulmas, *Writing Systems*, 214.

21. Walter A. Fairservis, Jr., "The Script of the Indus Valley Civilization," *Scientific American* 248:58–66 (1983). Old Persian was deciphered without a bilingual text, but this was possible only because the writing system was very simple and because it could be related to other well-known languages—notably, Greek and Sanskrit. Coulmas, *Writing Systems*, 217–218.

22. Paul Ricoeur, *Hermeneutics and the Human Sciences* (New York: Cambridge University Press, 1989). 108. (Emphasis in original)

23. Ibid., 145.

24. Ibid., 133, 198.

25. Ibid., 44, 57, 175, 178, 271.

26. Hilary Putnam, *Reason, Truth and History* (Cambridge: Cambridge University Press, 1990), 19.

27. E. D. Hirsch, Jr., *Validity in Interpretation* (New Haven, Conn.: Yale University Press, 1967), 225.

28. Ibid., 72–82.

29. Ricoeur, *Hermeneutics*, 134–135.

30. John L. Austin, *How to Do Things with Words* (Cambridge, Mass.: Harvard University Press, 1975), 94.

31. Murray G. Murphey, *The Development of Peirce's Philosophy* (Cambridge, Mass.: Harvard University Press, 1961), 1, note 1.

32. Jack W. Meiland, "Interpretation as a Cognitive Discipline," *Philosophy and Literature* 2:23–45 (1978). E. D. Hirsch, Jr., *The Aims of Interpretation* (Chicago: University of Chicago Press, 1976), 79.

33. Hirsch, *Validity*, ch. 5.

34. Ibid., 261ff.

35. Hallowell, *Culture and Experience*, ch. 4.

36. Cronon, *Changes*, ch. 5.

37. Thomas H. McGovern, "Cows, Harp Seals, and Churchbells: Adaptation and Extinction in Norse Greenland," *Human Ecology* 8:245–275 (1980).

38. Jack P. Greene, *Pursuits of Happiness* (Chapel Hill: University of North Carolina Press, 1988).

39. David Hackett Fischer, *Albion's Seed* (New York: Oxford University Press, 1989).

40. Hayden White. *Metahistory* (Baltimore: Johns Hopkins University Press, 1973).

41. Ibid., 5.

42. Ibid., 30–31. (Emphasis in original)

43. Ibid., 36–38.

44. Ibid., 31.

45. Ibid., 5.

46. Ibid., 7. (Emphasis in original)

47. Ibid.

48. Ibid., 8.

49. Ibid., x.

50. Ibid., 11.

51. Ibid., 14.

52. Ibid., 15.

53. Ibid., 17.

54. Ibid., 18.

55. Ibid., 22.

56. Ibid., 21. (Emphasis in original)

57. Ibid., 22.

58. Ibid., 26. (Emphasis in original)

59. Ibid., 29

60. Ibid., 4.

61. Murphey, *Our Knowledge*, ch. 2.

62. Mink, *Historical Understanding*, 36.

63. Ibid., 37.

64. Ibid., 51–53.

65. Ibid., 55. (Emphasis in original)

66. Ibid., 56.

67. Ibid., 172

68. Ibid., 78–79.

69. Ibid., 186.

70. Ibid., 195–196.

71. Ibid., 199.

72. Ibid., 202.

73. Ibid., 203.

74. C. Behan McCullagh, "The Truth of Historical Narratives," *History and Theory*, Beiheft 26, *The Representation of Historical Events* (Middletown: Wesleyan University Press, 1987), 30–46, 31.

75. Ibid., 33.

76. Ibid., 34.

77. Ibid., 35.

78. Ibid., 34.

79. Ibid., 37.

80. Ibid.

81. Ibid., 38.

82. Ibid., 38–39.

83. Ibid., 39.

84. Ibid., 40.

85. Nelson Goodman and Catherine Z. Elgin, *Reconceptions in Philosophy and Other Arts and Sciences* (Indianapolis, Ind.: Hackett Publishing Co., 1988), 155–159.

86. Mary Louise Pratt, *Toward a Speech Act Theory of Literary Discourse* (Bloomington: University of Indiana Press, 1977), 136–147.

87. Stuart Blumin, "Mobility in a Nineteenth-Century American City: Philadelphia, 1820–1860," Ph.D. diss., University of Pennsylvania, 1968.

88. Murphey, *Our Knowledge*, chs. 5, 6.

Chapter 8

Conclusion

This final chapter attempts to summarize what our investigation has shown about the premises underlying historical study. But before doing this, there are two questions whose consideration has been systematically postponed in the preceding chapters and which must now be dealt with— anti-realism and the relativity of truth. It is to these issues that we turn first.

Anti-Realism

Anti-realism is less a position than a collection of positions that have in common only their opposition to realism. As Heil remarks, "Anti-realisms are at least as abundant as anti-realists."[1] However, since there are many different forms of realism,[2] to each of which there is opposed some form of anti-realism, any attempt to cover the entire realist–anti-realist debate would require a volume larger than this one. Therefore discussion will be limited to two anti-realist positions that have a particular relevance to the position I have advanced. These two positions are those of Van Fraassen and of Dummett.

Van Fraassen's anti-realism is an extreme form of empiricism, one which denies truth to any statement that goes beyond what is observable by us: "To accept a theory is (for us) to believe that it is empirically adequate—that what the theory says *about what is observable* (by us) is true," but that what the theory says about things not observable by us is not true.[3] More fully, Van Fraassen states his position as follows:

307

To present a theory is to specify a family of structures, its *models*, and secondly, to specify certain parts of these models (the *empirical substructures*) as candidates for the direct representation of observable phenomena. The structures which can be described in experimental and measurement reports we can call *appearances*: the theory is empirically adequate if it has some model such that all appearances are isomorphic to empirical substructures of that model.[4]

Science attempts to describe those regularities in nature observable by us, and only the portion of a scientific theory that describes observables is true; the remainder of the scientific theory is simply a device useful for "formulation of the questions to be answered in a systematic and compendious fashion, *and* as a guiding factor in the design of experiments to answer those questions."[5] That is, that portion of scientific theories that goes beyond "appearances" has only an instrumental function in contributing to experimental design.

It should be observed that much depends here upon just what Van Fraassen takes to be observable. His criteria of observability are very stringent. Thus he holds that the moons of Jupiter are observable, not because we can see them through a telescope, but "since astronauts will no doubt be able to see them as well from close up."[6] On the other hand, microparticles are not observable, since although we can see the trails made by the particles in a cloud chamber, we cannot see the particles themselves.[7] The crucial point is put as follows:

The human organism is, from the point of view of physics, a certain kind of measuring apparatus. As such it has certain inherent limitations—which will be described in detail in the final physics and biology. It is these limitations to which the "able" in "observable" refers—our limitations, *qua* human beings.[8]

It is important to realize just how stringent this criterion is. Whatever cannot be observed by us with our unaided five senses is excluded. The moons of Jupiter are observable only because it is now technically possible to place human observers where they could observe the moons with the naked eye. It is not clear that the more distant stellar objects meet this criterion since there is no chance we shall ever be able to reach the stars. All microentities are eliminated from observational status. And the entire past and its contents are eliminated, since these are not now observable by us, and backward time travel, unlike space travel, is impossible.

As Schlagel has pointed out,[9] Van Fraassen's criterion for observability is arbitrary and has little relation to how the term "observable" is actually employed in science. Scientists use a wide array of detector instruments to enhance what our senses can record, and few would accept Van Fraassen's claim that such observations are different in kind from those our unaided senses report.[10] Moreover, Van Fraassen would have to accept as a limitation of human beings the fact that we can observe nothing beyond the temporal span of our own lives. This would reduce history to utter nonsense.

The empirically observable phenomena of history are artifacts—documents, tools, chairs, and what not. On Van Fraassen's view, the theory that postulates the existence and actions of George Washington is merely a device to connect descriptions of certain artifacts found at Valley Forge with descriptions of others found at Mount Vernon or the National Archives; Washington himself is not (and never was) real and no statement about Washington is (or ever was) true. Similar conclusions would hold for those scientists to whose work Van Fraassen refers (e.g., Newton, Darwin, and Einstein[11]) and those philosophers he discusses (e.g., Reichenbach, Acquinas, and Carnap[12]). How the theories created by these men might have come into being is, by Van Fraassen's approach, less than clear; one set of inscriptions is not usually regarded as the author of another set of inscriptions. Indeed, there would be no such thing as history in Van Fraassen's view; there would only be quite pointless sets of claims about relations among artifacts. There would also be no such thing as the past— at least the past beyond individual memory. Nor would it be open to Van Fraassen to reply that after all human beings did observe Washington and therefore he is observable. How does Van Fraassen know human beings observed Washington? Or that there were human beings in the eighteenth century? Or that there was an eighteenth century? These are not now observable. Their existence is a theoretical postulate, on the same epistemological footing as the electrons and photons whose reality Van Fraassen denies. The world of which Van Fraassen is willing to allow us knowledge is not that of science or of common sense.

Having limited the range of observables so drastically, Van Fraassen takes the further position that the aim of science is to describe observable regularities but not to explain them. An observable regularity is, Van Fraassen says, "merely a brute fact" that requires no explanation.[13] This view is defended on the ground that if all regularities must be explained, then we should be required to explain regularities in quantum mechanics by introducing hidden variables of a sort that quantum mechanics itself denies.[14] But this defense is hardly convincing. Because there may be certain areas of science where some regularities cannot be further accounted for, it does not follow that science should never seek to explain any regularities. As Peirce, both a professional scientist and a philosopher, wrote,

> Uniformities are precisely the sort of facts that need to be accounted for. That a pitched coin should sometimes turn up heads and sometimes tails calls for no particular explanation; but if it shows heads every time, we wish to know how this result has been brought about. Law is *par excellence* the thing that wants a reason.[15]

Peirce, of course, wrote before quantum mechanics appeared on the scientific scene, but his point is correct, as scientific practice shows. Scientists do seek to explain regularities wherever they can be explained.

The least convincing part of Van Fraassen's argument is his claim that portions of scientific theories that go beyond the description of appearances should be regarded as pleasant fictions not deserving of belief. It is not simply that the line Van Fraassen tries to draw between what is observable and what is not turns out to be very questionable; the deeper problem is that "without encountering these experimentally detected microphenomena, *there would be nothing to construct theories with*, and therefore no basis for drawing inferences predicting or explaining the behavior of *macro*phenomena."[16] Van Fraassen regards the theoretical portions of theories as devices for guiding experimental designs; to demonstrate his position, he analyzes the famous experiment of Robert Millikan to measure the charge of the electron.[17] But, as Schlagel points out,

> The experiment did consist of directly observing the movements of droplets of oil, but to design and execute it Millikan had to assume the existence, with precise magnitudes, of such unobservables as electrons, electric charges, electric fields, and gravity, otherwise he could not have performed the delicate calculations to determine the charge. Furthermore, Van Fraassen's claim that experiments are used to discover "regularities in the observable part of the world" is refuted by the fact that the intent of the experiment was not to observe the movement of the oil droplets, but to measure the electric charge on an *unobserved particle*. He therefore misses the crucial fact that the role of experimentation in theory construction consists of providing information *about microparticles*.[18]

Physicists believe that observable phenomena are caused by unobservable microphenomena and their investigations are directed to developing true theories about these microphenomena. Van Fraassen's interpretation of physical science would render the actual processes of scientific research unintelligible.

Van Fraassen also attacks the realist notion that scientific inquiry "converges" upon a true theory by offering an alternative explanation of scientific progress:

> I claim that the success of current scientific theories is no miracle. It is not even surprising to the scientific (Darwinist) mind. For any scientific theory is born into a life of fierce competition, a jungle red in tooth and claw. Only the successful theories survive—the ones which *in fact* latched on to actual regularities in nature.[19]

This argument assumes that the purpose of science is to describe regularities in appearances and thereby misconstrues what the competition among scientific theories is all about. But even if it were rephrased as a competition among theories to determine which most adequately explained the data, it would at best explain why one scientific theory might be preferred to another; it does nothing to explain why the scientific enterprise as a whole is successful. The increase in the power and adequacy of scientific theories over time is a fact (though not one that is available to Van Fraassen, since for him the past is unobservable and therefore unreal). That is not explained by saying we seek increasing power and adequacy. Science is no more competitive than theology: Theologians all seek to outdo each other in understanding God's will. There is no clear evidence that they have succeeded. Seeking is not enough. The real question is why the power and adequacy are achieved. That is a question that the realist argument for convergence does answer, but Van Fraassen's argument does not.

The second form of anti-realism that has particular relevance for historical knowledge is that of which Michael Dummett is the principal proponent. Dummett holds that, although there are many sorts of realism, all of them have the principle of bivalence as a fundamental premise.[20] Bivalence, according to Dummett, commits us to holding that every statement is either true or false, even in cases where there is no possibility that we can ever know whether the statement is in fact true or false; therefore bivalence commits us to the existence of real states of affairs of which we can have no evidence. This is a rather different way of describing realism than philosophers have traditionally adopted, and its implications are far reaching.

If one adopts bivalence and a truth condition theory of meaning (which I do not), one is surely committed to saying that every statement is either true or false by virtue of some state of affairs, whether that state of affairs is accessible to human knowledge or not; where it is not we are required to claim the existence of states of affairs forever inaccessible to us. In Dummett's view, such claims are gratuitous and should be rejected. To avoid them, Dummett has sought to apply to empirical knowledge the ideas developed by intuitionists concerning mathematical knowledge.[21] The intuitionists demand that any claim that a mathematical statement is true or false must be supported by a constructive proof either of the statement or of its negation becomes in the domain of empirical knowledge the requirement that any empirical statement of which either truth or falsity is to be claimed must be effectively decidable. As Dummett puts it,

> We are entitled to say that a statement P must be either true or false, that there must be something in virtue of which either it is true or it is false, only when P is a statement of such a kind that we could in a finite time bring ourselves into a position in which we were justified either in asserting or in denying P; that is, when P is an effectively decidable statement.[22]

Of the many kinds of realism with which Dummett is concerned, there are two which bear directly on the arguments given above: the reality of mental states, and the reality of past events and entities. I will take these in order. The task is not an easy one because it is not always clear just what Dummett's position really is. Part of the problem has to do with what Dummett means by "manifestable." Thus, speaking of an explanation of a speaker's grasp of the sense of an expression, he writes,

> The more specific general principle here proposed has been that the explanation, while given in terms of what the speaker knows, must be filled out by an explicit account of that in which such knowledge consists. Such an account must be given in terms of how that knowledge is delivered to him, and hence how it is manifested in his observable linguistic and non-linguistic behavior. This amounts to an interpretation of one component in Wittgenstein's slogan 'Meaning is use.'[23]

It is apparently Dummett's view that ascription of a concept to an individual must be warranted by observable behavior. Exactly what this means, however, is not perfectly clear.

Dummett has often attacked holism.[24] At the same time, he has lauded Quine's metaphorical description of scientific theory in "Two Dogmas" as a network connected to experience only at the periphery.[25] If I understand him correctly, Dummett regards the statements of scientific theories as fully meaningful and as effectively decidable, even though their confirmation is indirect. It would seem therefore that Dummett does not regard the entities postulated in scientific theories as fictional, as Van Fraassen does, but as fully real in a manner acceptable to his anti-realism. Entities whose existence is only indirectly confirmable are still "manifestable," as he employs that term. But as we have seen above, mental states, such as beliefs, concepts, meanings, desires, and so forth, are postulates within theories that are testable, and indeed confirmed, by empirical data—specifically by the behavior of people. I am not certain that Dummett views the matter in this way,[26] but it is difficult to see how he could accept scientific statements about microparticles and yet reject scientific statements about mental states. Then again, scientific statements seem not to be the focus of his interest.[27]

Dummett has also argued that statements about the past may be undecidable because there is no empirical basis for saying whether they are true or false:

> We are not therefore entitled to say, of any arbitrary statement about the past, that it must be either true or false independently of our present or future knowledge, or capacity for knowledge, of its truth-value. Of any statement about the past, we can never rule it out that we might subsequently come upon something which justified asserting or denying it, and therefore we are not entitled to say of any specific such statement that it is neither true nor false: but we are not entitled either to say in advance that it has to be either one or the other, since this would be to invoke notions of truth and falsity independent of our recognition of truth or falsity, and hence incapable of having been derived from the training we received in the use of these statements.[28]

When I first read this statement, I thought that Dummett was making the same point I have been laboring to make—namely, that we can only know what we have evidence for. But I am not sure now that such an interpretation was correct. In a later work, Dummett writes of past entities

> A verificationist must, rather, allow that a canonical verification may have been possible only under conditions that can never be recreated (since the belief in the general resurrection does not apply to animals, ships, cities, and so on). As our study of proof-theoretic justifications of logical laws makes clear, he has to admit as assertable statements for which we have an effective method of showing that they *could have* been verified, even if

they can no longer be; this is the role in our linguistic practice that he must assign to the conception of a canonical verification.[29]

Consider the following statement concerning Johanson's Lucy:

(1) Lucy was the first born of her mother's children.

Is this statement true, false, or undecidable? The answer for Dummett would evidently depend on how "could have been verified" is to be construed, and I am not sure what his answer would be. Nevertheless, it seems to me clear that this statement is either true or false even though undecidable. Lucy existed; her skeletal remains are proof of that. Lucy was a hominid. Unless our present theories of biology are wildly wrong, Lucy had a mother who had some finite number of children. Since female hominids have one child at a time,[30] Lucy was either the first-born of her mother's children or she wasn't. Therefore the statement must be true or false. But how could we ever know which? One would have had to observe the event and to have observed both Lucy and her mother over a considerable period of time to be able to decide the question. Certainly no evidence that we can ever hope to find now will enable us to decide the matter, so for us the statement is and will remain undecidable, but also for us it is either true or false, although we cannot tell which. Does Dummett's "could" stretch this far? "Could" cannot here mean that verification is physically possible. Backward travel in time is physically impossible. Nor can it mean that some human observer at that time in the past could have made the necessary observations. Lucy lived over three million years ago; there were no human observers at that time. Does "could" here mean possible in principle—logically possible? If so, then the statement of how (1) "could have been verified" would have to be:

(2) If a human observer had been present from the time that Lucy's mother became fertile until Lucy was born, he could have verified that Lucy was or was not the first born of her mother's children.

That (2) is counterfactual is obvious—and Dummett associates counterfactuals of this sort particularly with the realisms he rejects[31]—so it is not obvious what position he would take with respect to (1) and (2). Nevertheless, insofar as Dummett's anti-realism regarding the past is an assertion that knowledge about the past must rest on evidence available to us, it poses no problem for the view I have presented above. On the other hand, I see no evidence in Dummett's writing that he sees the past as itself a theoretical construct, which may well be the source of some of these problems.

More generally, when a reality is postulated as part of a theory that accounts for experience, then whether bivalence applies to statements about that reality is determined by the character of the reality postulated to exist. If the reality postulated is in certain respects indeterminate, bivalence will not apply; if it is postulated to be determinate, bivalence will apply. The past of which Lucy was a part is postulated to be determinate, at least at the macro level. This does not mean that every statement we can make about that past is decidable, as the Lucy example shows, but it does mean that such statements are nonetheless either true or false, although we may never know which.

This is not a gratuitous claim, since it follows from a theory confirmed by empirical data. Dummett has said that we cannot make decidable statements about events for which we have no evidence. I agree, but there is evidence for (1) derived from our theoretical knowledge (and the empirical evidence which supports it) although that evidence does not permit the assignment of a definite truth-value to the statement. Similarly, we are justified in making many statements about the past—for example, about the early history of the universe, or about the formation of the earth, or about human societies twenty thousand years ago—even though these statements are inferred from our present theories and we have no direct evidence for them. Of course we are not justified in making statements about past events or objects for which there is no basis at all. But whoever thought we were?

Relativism

The strongest relativist argument is the claim that truth itself is relative, so that different cultures or different conceptual schemes may involve different standards for judging what is true and what is false. Clearly, the existence of such variation in standards of truth is a fact.[32] Anthropologists have found different standards of truth (and other things as well) in other cultures, and even within a culture such as our own, people holding different conceptual schemes do hold different standards of truth—witness the conflict between Fundamentalists and scientists. Purely as a matter of fact, then, the relativists are right—such variation exists.

Does it follow, then, that there is no way to decide among these different views of truth? Have we, as it were, a babble of conceptual schemes among which no decision is possible? One may well wonder how such a decision could be reached. Obviously it cannot be reached by appeal to a further standard of truth without a regress. One might imagine various other standards that might be brought to bear. James believed truth was a species of the good: Perhaps one could argue that standards of goodness could be decisive. Or one might try to solve the problem by asking what it is rational to believe. But I think it fairly clear that such moves accomplish little. If we have no agreement on a best standard of truth, we are not likely to do better with a standard of goodness or of rationality. Any such approach seems certain to leave us where we were to begin with.

The fact that such an approach leads to a dead end suggests we are asking the wrong question. Standards of truth are part of conceptual schemes themselves parts of the world views of a group or a society. It seems more useful to ask why people come to hold one world view rather than another. Putting the question this way makes it an empirical question that could conceivably be answered—a question in the anthropology of knowledge. Of course, any answer so discovered would be a hypothesis or theory in a social science, and would therefore take for granted the scientific standard of what constitutes knowledge. But this is circular only if we then claim to *justify* the scientific standard by this approach. The intention here is not to answer the truth-relativist by justifying the scientific standard of truth, but the more modest one of asking how people might come to believe it. Since this is an empirical question, and one for which we have at present no accepted answer, the most that can be offered here is a modest hypothesis. But, as the issue is one of considerable interest and relevance to our inquiry, it may not be amiss to do so. How then do people decide on world views?

The term "world view" as used by anthropologists refers to the conceptualization a group or society has of the self and its environment—of the way the "world" is conceived by them. Self-awareness is "a generic human trait," wrote Hallowell in 1954,[33] and subsequent investigations have affirmed this judgement. So is awareness of a non-self or environment.[34] The way the self and its environment are conceived may vary radically from one group or society to another, as may the line distinguishing the two and the relations between them, but all cultures recognize these variables.

It must be emphasized that one is not interested here in what the self "really" is or in what the "real" environment is, but in how members of the society in question conceive these things. For this reason, Hallowell always distinguished the "behavioral environment," meaning the environment as conceived by members of the society, from the "real" environment, meaning the environment as conceived by the investigator,[35] and I will follow his lead. The world view, then, may be taken to be the conception of the self and its behavioral environment, and of the relations between these, held by members of a society or group. I believe it is now fully accepted by anthropologists that every culture has one or more world views as components.

Hallowell argued that the world view always provides to its adherents certain basic orientations essential for the functioning of any culture. He distinguished five of these. There is first a self-orientation that defines for members of that culture what the self is, and what its properties and powers are. Second, there is an object orientation that orients the self "to a diversified world of objects in its behavioral environment, discriminated, classified, and conceptualized with respect to attributes which are culturally constituted and symbolically mediated through language."[36] Among the objects of the behavioral environment are of course other "persons"—a category not necessarily coextensive with human beings. Third, there is a spatio-temporal orientation that defines for members of the culture the extent and nature of space and time and their own relations to these. These include the temporal duration of the self, the relation of the self to past and future persons and events, the possibilities of spatial movement, and so forth. Fourth, there is a motivational orientation "of the self toward the objects of its behavioral environment with reference to the satisfaction of its needs."[37] What is food and what is not, what can be used to make clothing, or scrapers, or atom bombs is defined by the particular world view in question, and these definitions tell members of the culture how their environment can be used to serve their requirements. Finally, there is a normative orientation that provides values, ideals, and standards that govern action and that provide the basis for evaluations of the self and others. A human social order is always a moral order.[38]

That these orientations are to be found in every world view is shown by both theoretical and empirical considerations. We have already seen that the concept of a physical object as continuous in time and space is part of our hardwired cognitive equipment, and it is therefore scarcely surprising to find an object orientation in all cultures. Similarly, motivational, spatio-temporal, and normative orientations appear to be functional necessities for any culture. But there are also numerous empirical studies of particular world views demonstrating that these orientations are indeed found.[39] Different anthropologists have proposed somewhat different ways of analyzing world views, but all of them are consistent with this model.

Anthropologists have shown in numerous studies that relatively isolated non-literate societies have often evolved world views that provide satisfactory adjustments to their environments. Clearly, this does not always happen, and a world view adequate for survival at one time may not be so at another. Many American Indian tribes had developed quite successful cultures for dealing with their environments, both behavioral and real, that were rendered hopelessly inadequate by the sudden arrival of Europeans. But the existence, even over relatively brief eras, of numerous different cultures with quite different world views shows clearly that cultural relativity is a fact. These world views often differ in their taxonomies, their concepts of the self, their views of experience, and many other characteristics. A culture in which dream experience is regarded as veridical experience of the world is going to have quite a different view of its behavioral environment than one in which dream experience is regarded as a type of fantasy.[40]

World views, like cultures, change as the nature of their environment changes, and one of the most striking changes that has happened in recent history is the end of isolation. The isolated villages of the anthropological literature are fast fading from the scene. As this happens, and clearly it will continue to happen until such isolation ceases to exist altogether, members of different cultures become aware of other cultures, other world views, other ways of conceptualizing themselves and their environments. One of the most striking results of this process has been the spread of science. Cultures as different from the West as Japan, China, India, and Iraq have adopted Western science and have become highly proficient at it.

This spread of science is an acknowledged fact. Some account for it on the basis of conquest. Western countries conquered other nations and imposed their world views upon subject peoples, indoctrinating them so thoroughly that they have come to believe the Western world view. By this account, we have here a clear-cut case of military and political power determining belief. Obviously, there is considerable truth to this account. But there are also problems with it. Why, if conquest is the answer, has not the whole of the Western world view been adopted wherever Western conquerors went? Certainly it was not for lack of trying! Religious missionaries have been among the most aggressive and didactic of conquerors, and in many cases they have succeeded—witness Latin America. But they have not always succeed. Islam is still unvanquished; devout Moslems fly F-16s and build chemical and biological weapons. Buddhism survives and still dominates large areas of the world; so does Hinduism. Not even three hundred years of English cruelty could weaken the hold of Catholicism on the Irish, and despite an unequalled record of subjugation and persecution lasting thousands of years, Judaism is today stronger than ever. One could go on. Yet historically Western conquerors have laid far more emphasis upon spreading their religious faiths than on spreading their scientific ideas. Then why has Western science spread so rapidly and relatively easily in comparison with its religion? There has never been a war over the truth of scientific beliefs, whereas the world's history is steeped in the blood of religious conflict.

If raw power does not provide an adequate explanation of the spread of science, can it be argued that science is somehow more compatible with the traditional values held by people in other cultures than are Western religions? I think not. No culture in history has ever created a picture of human nature and destiny so bleak, so utterly devoid of emotional comfort or solace, so contrary to human hopes and aspirations as that which modern science affords. That human beings are chance products of nature on a small planet orbiting a third-rate star, one among billions in an undistinguished galaxy that is itself one among billions of galaxies, that humans have existed for a brief instant of time and will soon become extinct—this is a picture that no culture, not even those like our own in which science is a major component of the world view, is prepared to accept completely. If congeniality to traditional values were the condition for the adoption of science, no society would permit it.

But science is not contrary to all human desires. The key to the success of science in winning converts appears to be its ability to provide what Hallowell called a "motivational orientation" superior to any other. It is the power and adequacy of science, in the senses already defined, that have made it irresistible. Science provides a higher degree of predictability of experience and a vastly greater control over nature in all its aspects than any other system of ideas ever devised by man. Basic needs such as curing disease, providing food, constructing shelter, and affording protection— these are more perfectly met by employing science than by any known alternative. The result has been the rapid adoption of both Western science and Western technology around the world, and since technology increasingly depends upon science as it becomes more sophisticated, both of them work to speed the adoption of science. This process, evident throughout the world, is already so far advanced that it is irreversible.

The result has been that many cultures have adopted science as a component of their motivational orientations (and of their self-, object, and spatio-temporal orientations) even though the scientific perspective ill accords with other aspects of their world views. This is even obvious in the case of Western cultures, including our own. Although most of our orientations are heavily influenced by science, our normative orientation clearly is much less so, and there are powerful groups within our society who reject many aspects of science—the Fundamentalists being only the most obvious example. Indeed, although well over a century has passed since Darwin published, there is still in the United States very limited movement toward the development of a naturalistic morality, as recent political campaigns have shown. The result has been a quite remarkable degree of inconsistency within Western world views. Yet we have good evidence that people find cognitive inconsistency unpleasant and strive to remove it.[41] Assuming that to be so, the steady penetration of science into more and more world views and cultures around the world is a dramatic demonstration of the adequacy and power of science and the degree to which these characteristics are valued in widely differing cultures.

It does not follow that science will displace all other components of world views. It is widely claimed that science and religion—at least some religions—are independent, and do not conflict. It is also claimed that statements about matters of fact are independent of statements about matters of value. These claims are issues on which there is presently lively debate, which we may gratefully leave to others. But however these issues are resolved, it seems clear that the role of science as arbiter of questions of empirical fact is now established in most Western cultures and is rapidly becoming established in culture after culture around the world.

What is the bearing of all this on the question of the relativity of truth? The rapidity with which science has spread through the various cultures of the world is apparently due to its demonstrable superiority to other ideational systems in providing a satisfactory motivational orientation. If that is so, one may predict with considerable confidence that the spread will continue until science becomes universal—that is, until it is everywhere adopted as providing a major part of the motivational orientation of every culture. That will mean that, at least with respect to the domain of empirical knowledge, the truth standard of science will be universally adopted. This truth standard may co-exist in harmony or in conflict with other truth standards asserted to hold over other domains, as is the case in our own culture and many others. But within the domain of empirical knowledge, it will become universally accepted because it is part of the scientific world view and science itself makes no sense without it.

Suppose science does become universally accepted in the manner described above; how does this affect the relativist's position? The point is not that relativism is proven false, for where there is no agreement on what constitutes truth, there will be no agreement on what constitutes falsity either. One cannot prove that one standard of truth is right and another wrong. The question is rather what persuades people to adopt one conceptual scheme, with its standard of truth, rather than another? What has made science convincing to people in other cultures is its power and adequacy—its ability to predict experience and to control many aspects of the environment. When antibiotics cure a disease, fertilizers produce more abundant crops, electricity brings light and refrigeration, people who have never known these things before are impressed and recognize the value to them of such added power. It is this ability of science to enable people to use their environment more effectively to satisfy their needs that makes it so attractive, and it is the ability of science to explain its own power and adequacy that makes it so persuasive. The answer to relativism—at least to relativism with respect to truth—is simply that it will cease to be a problem because the greater power and adequacy of science will lead to its universal adoption.

If this argument is correct, it is the fact that science has greater power and adequacy than any other system of ideas that is the reason for its steadily growing acceptance. But if science does bring greater power and adequacy than any other system of beliefs, how is that fact to be accounted for? The only explanation that seems adequate is that science does progressively reveal more and more features of the reality with which we all interact. The same considerations that explain the increasing success of science over time also explain its increasing success over space.

Even if this modest hypothesis is true, nothing follows from it with respect to questions of religion or morality or aesthetics. We do not at present know how to describe, in any adequate manner, how scientific thought interacts with conceptual schemes in these areas, and the fact that our own society, in which science is as highly developed as in any society in history, has in recent years undergone a religious revival should serve as a warning against hasty or unwarranted predictions. The day may come when we have an anthropology of knowledge adequate to explain and predict such matters, but that day is not yet.

Conclusion

In recent years, there has been a proliferation of specialties in philosophy, usually identified as "philosophy of _____." Thus we have the philosophy of law, of language, of what have you. Among these, the philosophy of history is certainly a senior partner, having been in existence longer than the others. But like them it is largely a matter of taking philosophic principles and concepts from other and more fundamental areas of philosophy and applying them to a particular subject. Although history as a subject does involve special problems of a philosophic nature, nevertheless it is based upon premises that are not unique to itself. I have argued in this work that of those premises underlying history, at least these eight are fundamental:

(1) There is a real world of which true knowledge is possible.

(2) There are other persons who have minds.

(3) It is possible for one person to know what another person thinks.

(4) A language spoken by one person can be correctly interpreted by someone from outside that linguistic community, and a text in one language can be translated into an approximately equivalent text in another language of comparable resources.

(5) There exists a past in which human beings lived and acted.

(6) We can have some accurate knowledge of the past.

(7) Members of one culture can understand members of other cultures, including members of antecedent states of their own culture.

(8) Human action is causally explainable.

None of these premises—not even (5) and (6)—are unique to history. But all of them are essential if the study of history is to yield results that satisfy the criteria historians themselves require of their subject. Thus our investigations in this book have roamed over subjects as diverse as cognitive psychology, philosophy of science, the theory of action, the problem of translation, the theory of reference, and many others. This has been necessary because history is no more an autonomous subject than is sociology or anthropology. All the human sciences share certain presuppositions; indeed, no field of knowledge is wholly autonomous—not even mathematics. To treat them as such is to suppress premises vital to the field.

For those of us who are historians, history is a subject of quite sufficient importance to justify the detailed study of its philosophic underpinnings. But there are further reasons for undertaking such a study. In the academic zoo, history occupies a peculiar status; it lies in a sort of no man's land between the humanities and the social sciences. Some of its practitioners claim it belongs in one of these categories, some, in the other, some, in both. This classificatory argument arises from genuine disagreements and a considerable amount of confusion on the part of historians as to just what these categories mean. Thus the long debate among historians (and philosophers of history) as to whether or not history is a science has been to a large extent confused by the image historians have had of science—an image due chiefly to Hempel and the positivists. Viewing science in these terms, it has been obvious to most historians that history cannot be made to fit that model.

This is one reason for the enormous popularity of Thomas Kuhn's writings—particularly of his book, *The Structure of Scientific Revolutions*. As many historians have interpreted Kuhn's work, he seemed to demolish the claim of science to lead to true knowledge, and so opened the way for relativistic, and indeed irrationalistic, versions. Kuhn, of course, has not been the only opponent of the positivist view of science, but historians recognize him as one of their own and have found his writings more accessible than those of Feyerabend and other philosophers. On the other side, the rise of so-called "literary theory" in recent years, with its debts to Heidegger, Gadamer, Ricoeur, and Derida, has created among humanists a passion for relativism and for a kind of linguistic view of the world which often approaches a semiotic idealism. Thus on the one hand the claims of science have seemed weakened, while on the other, various forms of "discourse analysis" have seemed to offer attractive alternatives.

The fascination of philosophers with language, so typical of recent decades, has contributed to this confusion. Of course language is important and has deserved the great emphasis it has received in philosophy, linguistics, psychology, anthropology, and other fields. But part of the attraction of language for some philosophers has been the belief that talk of language could be substituted for talk about mental states, such as concepts. It is not difficult to see how Kantian architectonics can be shifted from logic to language. Behaviorists found in language something observable that could be made proxy for thought. Too quick identification of languages and conceptual schemes, skeptical arguments about translation, talk of incommensurability, addiction to hermeneutics, neo-neo-Marxism, and a variety of other fads have contributed, often unintentionally, to a kind of politicized relativism that, in the hands of some, has helped to make of historical writing a form of propaganda.

Much of this nonsense can be avoided by a more careful examination of the premises underlying historical knowledge. While we all have a certain fascination with the sort of jaw-dropping skeptical arguments that claim to turn the world inside out, it is also the case that these skeptical arguments rarely stand the test of time and examination. Common sense is not always a reliable guide, but when common sense is violated, one does well to look very closely at the claims made against it. Doubtless some of my readers will consider some of the positions taken in this work to be contrary to common sense, but where they are so, I hope that the reasons given in support of them are sufficient to justify such deviations.

In the view taken here, language is not identical with or isomorphic with thought. From the fact that the Dani language contains no word for red, one would be wrong to conclude that the Dani have no concept of red. Language expresses thought, and certainly there is an important interaction between what we think and how we articulate what we think, but one cannot avoid dealing with concepts, beliefs, and similar mental states by talking about words. Different conceptual schemes can be formulated in a single language, and different languages may formulate the same conceptual scheme.

It is particularly important for the development of an understanding of history to drop the positivist model of science and of scientific explanation. Railton's theory, described in Chapter 3, has the great advantage of doing this without losing the valuable lessons of either the covering law model or the single causal statement view. Historians using Railton's model should have no trouble in reconciling what they do in practice with the notion of causal explanatory texts. It is a basic point about the actual practice of history that historians do seek truth and they do seek to provide causal explanations. That is simply a fact about what historians do. Railton's model shows how the causal explanations historians actually give relate to the broader scheme of scientific explanation in general. Further, the kinds of scientific theories used in explanations of actions, which are described in Chapters 4 and 5, are sophisticated versions of the sort of "folk psychology" explanations that historians have always used. Beliefs, desires, intentions, rules, plans, norms—these are the tools historians usually employ in describing and explaining the behavior of their subjects.

It is critical here to understand the explanatory role of culture. No feature of Hempel's model of explanation was less acceptable to historians than his insistence that all laws must be wholly general. Historians knew such a model could not be applied to historical subjects, and positivist polemics left them unmoved. But anthropologists had already solved that problem through the concept of culture. Once it is understood that following cultural rules provides an explanation for actions by members of the culture, the whole problem is transformed. There are, of course, universal laws governing human life and action—biological laws, the laws of learning, and so forth. But within a given society there exists a structure of rules and systems of belief and desire which, where members of the society are committed to this cultural system, can be used to explain the actions of those members, and to explain why actions of members of one culture differ from those of another. Hempel's model was unrealistic as a model of explanation in the social sciences because it ignored culture; once the explanatory function of culture is appropriately introduced into the situation, the problem of general laws in history becomes a non-problem.

Once it is accepted that concepts, desires, intentions, and so forth are legitimate scientific constructs in terms of which behavior can be explained, it becomes possible to approach problems such as meaning and reference in ways that do not warrant the skeptical results lately so popular. That there are other minds, that communication among people through language is a fact, that texts written in other tongues at other places and other times can be correctly interpreted—these are thoroughly defensible claims supported by empirical evidence. Claims of underdetermination, relativity of reference, and incommensurability among conceptual schemes turn out to be less disastrous than some have thought. It is possible for people to understand each other across cultural divides, even when each finds the other's beliefs bizarre.

History deals with the past. It has therefore been necessary to discuss at some length the basis for holding that there is a real past and what we can know about it. Clearly, questions of truth and reality are here involved, particularly in the light of anti-realist claims. The position argued here is a kind of realism, but one which I think cannot be called a metaphysical realism. I believe theories and hypotheses are confirmed or disconfirmed by our experience, and that they serve to explain that experience. To say that a theory is true, either in the ideal sense or in the sense of being the best confirmed theory we have, commits us to believing real what the theory says is real. If quantum theory is true, there really are wavicles. Similarly, if our theories about Alexander the Great or Hannibal or the battle of Bosworth are true, those people and events are (were) real. But to talk of realities of the existence of which we can have no evidence (if in fact anybody does so) seems to me silly. Thus I hope to have shown that the eight premises with which we began provide a solid support for historical knowledge.

Notes

1. John Heil, "Recent Work in Realism and Anti-Realism," *Philosophical Books* 30:65 (1989).

2. Michael Levin, "Realisms" *Synthese* 85:115–138 (1990).

3. Bas C. Van Fraassen, *The Scientific Image* (Oxford: Clarendon Press, 1980), 18. (Emphasis in original)

4. Ibid., 64. (Emphasis in original)

5. Ibid., 74. (Emphasis in original)

6. Ibid., 16.

7. Ibid., 17.

8. Ibid.

9. Richard H. Schlagel, "Experimental Realism: A Critique of Bas Van Fraassen's 'Constructive Empiricism'," *Review of Metaphysics* 41:789–814 (1987).

10. Ibid., 801.

11. Van Fraassen, *Scientific Image*, 40, 46, 105.

12. Ibid. 13, 25, 204.

13. Ibid., 24.

14. Ibid., 29, 53, 95.

15. Peirce, *The Collected Papers*, 6.12.

16. Schlagel, "Realism," 804. (Emphasis in original)

17. Van Fraassen, *Scientific Image*, 74-77.

18. Schlagel, "Experimental Realism," 806.

19. Van Fraassen, *Scientific Image*, 40. (Emphasis in original)

20. Michael Dummett, *The Logical Basis of Metaphysics* (Cambridge, Mass.: Harvard University Press, 1991), 322, 325.

21. Michael Dummett, *Truth and Other Enigmas* (Cambridge, Mass.: Harvard University Press, 1978), 17.

22. Ibid., 16–17.

23. Dummett, *Logical Basis*, 341.

24. Ibid., ch. 10.

25. Michael Dummett, "Reply to Loar" in Barry M. Taylor, ed., *Michael Dummett: Contributions to Philosophy* (Dordrecht: Martinus Nijhoff, 1987), 270–273.

26. Dummett, *Logical Basis*, 313–314. Dummett is here paraphrasing Wittgenstein, with apparent approval.

27. Michael Dummett, "Reply to Prawitz" in Taylor, *Michael Dummett*, 285.

28. Dummett, *Truth*, 364.

29. Dummett, *Logical Basis*, 309–310. (Emphasis in original)

30. It could I suppose be claimed that Lucy was a Siamese twin. This is I think clearly false. Siamese twins could not have been separated without fatal consequences at that time, and no bones of a twin were found with hers. But for those who wish to press the objection (1) can be rewritten as:

(1') Either Lucy was a Siamese twin or she was the first-born of her mother's children.

Given that Caesarian section is out of the question, there is no other way in which Lucy could have issued from her mother simultaneously with a sibling.

31. Dummett, *Logical Basis*, 181–183.

32. Clifford Geertz, "Anti Anti-Relativism" in Michael Krausz, ed., *Relativism: Interpretation and Confrontation* (Notre Dame, Ind.: University of Notre Dame, 1989), 12–34.

33. Hallowell, *Culture and Experience,* 75.

34. Michael Kearney, *World View* (Navato: Chandler and Sharp, 1984), ch. 3.

35. Hallowell, *Culture and Experience*, 86.

36. Ibid., 91.

37. Ibid., 100.

38. Ibid., 89–110.

39. Kearney, *World View*, chs. 4, 5, 6, 7. Michael Kearney, "World View Theory and Study," *Annual Review of Anthropology* 4:247–270 (1975).

40. Hallowell, *Culture and Experience*, 172–182.

41. Leon Festinger, *A Theory of Cognitive Dissonance* (Stanford, Calif.: Stanford University Press, 1962).

Name Index

Subject Index